Women and Reason

Women and Reason

Edited by
Elizabeth D. Harvey and
Kathleen Okruhlik

Ann Arbor

THE UNIVERSITY OF MICHIGAN PRESS

1995   1994   1993   1992   4   3   2   1

Library of Congress Cataloging-in-Publication Data

Women and reason / edited by Elizabeth D. Harvey and Kathleen
  Okruhlik.
      p.   cm.
   Includes bibliographical references.
   ISBN 0-472-10220-6 (alk. paper)
   1. Feminist theory. 2. Rationalism. 3. Reason. 4. Women—
History.   I. Harvey, Elizabeth D. II. Okruhlik, Kathleen, 1951-

HQ1190.W67   1992
305.42'01—dc20   91-42974
                                                       CIP

For Mark and Nicholas
Jim, Elizabeth, and Stephen

Acknowledgments

The idea for this volume of essays had its inception in a conference on women and reason that was sponsored by the Centre for Women's Studies and Feminist Research at the University of Western Ontario in February, 1989. Some of the essays in this collection were originally delivered at that conference, and the revisions to the papers reflect in part the exchange and critiques generated there. This volume would not have been possible without the support of the Centre for Women's Studies and Feminist Research, which has provided a crucial context for the flourishing of feminist research at Western. Julie Ashford's unstinting efforts and meticulous organizational skills were essential both for the conference and also for the preparation of the volume. Carole Farber generously provided assistance, the resources of the Centre, and moral support throughout the long process. We would also like to thank the Department of Philosophy, the Centre for the Study of Theory and Criticism, the Faculties of Arts and Social Science at the University of Western Ontario, and the Social Sciences and Humanities Research Council of Canada. Finally, we are grateful for the thoughtful comments from two anonymous readers for the University of Michigan Press.

Contents

Introduction
  Kathleen Okruhlik and Elizabeth D. Harvey   1

Intellectual Bases for Feminist Analyses: The Seventeenth and Eighteenth Centuries
  Hilda L. Smith   19

Lady Oracle: Changing Conceptions of Authority and Reason in Seventeenth-Century Philosophy
  Thomas M. Lennon   39

Birth of a New Physics or Death of Nature?
  Kathleen Okruhlik   63

From Species to Speculation: Naming the Animals with Calvin and Bacon
  Julie Robin Solomon   77

Love and Knowledge: Emotion in Feminist Epistemology
  Alison M. Jaggar   115

Feminist Skepticism and the "Maleness" of Philosophy
  Susan Bordo   143

The Gender of Creativity in the French Symbolist Period
  Patricia Mathews   163

Purity or Danger: Mondrian's Exclusion of the Feminine and the Gender of Abstract Painting
  Mark A. Cheetham   187

Physiology, Phrenology, and Patriarchy: The Construction of George Eliot
  Kristin Brady   201

Reasoning about Ourselves: Feminist Methodology in the Social
Sciences
  Alison Wylie   225

Women's Place in Communicative Reason
  Marie Fleming   245

The Unicorn in the Garden
  Lorraine Code   263

Contributors   283

Index   287

Introduction

KATHLEEN OKRUHLIK AND ELIZABETH D. HARVEY

Rationality and the hegemonic place it has occupied in Western thought have been scrutinized, examined, and criticized in the last decade or so by philosophers, scholars of the postmodern, historians of culture, and feminist theorists. This interest has manifested itself in diverse approaches and different disciplines, and the debate that is emerging is of particular importance to feminists because the legacy of rationality has shaped and continues to influence conceptions of society, subjectivity, and knowledge. According to some feminists, the concept of reason has been framed to exclude women; correlatively, femininity has been defined so as to exclude the rational. This claim has attracted much attention in recent literature, and, in some quarters, it has become feminist orthodoxy. What is generally seen to follow from such an analysis is the need to develop a new feminist epistemology, one that is independent of the old standards of rationality that systematically excluded women. Whether reason is ultimately seen as essentially and ineluctably exclusive of woman, relegating her to the position of irrational Other, or whether the rational faculty can be adapted to feminist methodologies is of central concern to considerations of reason in general and to many of the essays in this volume in particular.

One of the guiding principles informing the development of this collection of essays is the belief that global accounts of rationality must be supplemented with, tested against, and sometimes corrected by more closely focused, discipline-specific analyses. Some of the most compelling critiques of the relationship between women and reason come from individuals whose understanding of historical and disciplinary context is rich enough to take into account the multifarious ways in which sexism and androcentrism can manifest themselves in diverse settings. Although global critiques must continue to inspire and illuminate the search for alternative understanding, they cannot predict the specific shape and form such alternatives may take. Instead, these are likely to emerge piecemeal from various disciplines and may sometimes resist trans-historical and transdisciplinary analysis. A truly interdisciplinary under-standing of the problems at hand will have to arise from below, so to speak, rather than be imposed from above.

Rather than seeing reason as a monolithic entity that has remained unchanged from Plato forward, a number of the essays in this volume provide revisionary historical and disciplinary contexts, some of which demonstrate how reason was seen as a positive and even liberating force for some women. The volume includes both essays with predominantly historical orientations and essays that are philosophical or methodo-logical in approach, a blend that reflects the crucial imbrication of our evolving understanding of the past as a way of measuring and evaluating the present. The collection has three distinguishing characteristics. First, it is cross-disciplinary, drawing from a diverse range of specialities. It includes considerations of literature, art history, the history of medicine and science, and the theory of social science, political science, and his-tory. The resulting perspectives both represent and constitute a challenge to the bounded singularity of any individual disciplinary organization of knowledge. Second, the focus is on ways to advance the discussion about women and rationality through essays with relatively specific analyses of narrowly focused problems. Third, considerable historical material is provided, especially with respect to the seventeenth century, since many claims about women and rationality have been premised upon a particular way of looking at developments in science and phi-losophy at that time. What emerges from the collection is less a consensus about reason and feminism than an exploration of rationality's many different historical manifestations and their varied implications for fem-inists.

In order to frame the essays in this volume and to locate them in the context of recent debates, it may be helpful to recall some of the works that have set the agenda for present efforts to articulate the relationship between women and reason. One of the most important of these is *The Man of Reason: "Male" and "Female" in Western Philosophy* by Gene-vieve Lloyd.[1] Lloyd maintains that our trust in a Reason that has no sex has been largely self-deceiving and that Reason's traditional claims to universality do not stand up to historical or conceptual analysis. She argues that, from the very beginning of philosophical thought, "female-ness was symbolically associated with what Reason supposedly left behind—the dark powers of the earth goddesses, immersion in unknown forces associated with mysterious female powers." Maleness, on the other hand, was associated with clear determination. This association persisted and was encoded in articulations of the form-matter distinction in later Greek thought where active, determinate form was aligned with maleness and passive, indeterminate matter with femaleness.

Lloyd continues her historical analysis through Aristotle and Aquinas, the scientific revolution, and the Enlightenment, concluding with Simone de Beauvoir's analysis of woman as Other. Lloyd's claim is not that philosophers' conceptions of reason have been the same at all times and all places, but that, because philosophers have been (despite other differences among themselves) predominantly male, their conceptualizations of reason have reflected their sense of philosophy as a male activity. Whatever has been valued at different times and places has been identified with maleness "whether it be odd as against even numbers, 'aggressive' as against 'nurturing' skills and capacities, or Reason as against emotion."[2]

The remedy, in Lloyd's analysis, is not simply to "reclaim" and affirm the strengths of female "difference," however natural this response may be. For the very content of femininity, not just its subordinate status, has been formed within an intellectual tradition excluding women. Lloyd's is not a counsel of despair, however, nor a call for women to repudiate either reason or philosophy. "Fortunately," she says, "philosophy is not necessarily what it has in the past proudly claimed to be—a timeless rational representation of the real, free of the conditioning effects of history."[3] She sees within philosophy the resources for critical reflection on its own ideals and aspirations, resources likely to be utilized as women develop a presence in the discipline.

Many feminist theorists, including philosophers, have found additional resources for understanding the relation between women and reason in Carol Gilligan's empirical research on moral reasoning. In her influential work, *In a Different Voice*,[4] Gilligan investigates the hierarchy of moral development created by Lawrence Kohlberg and used extensively to assess the capacities of schoolchildren for ethical reasoning. According to Kohlberg's theory, human beings pass in an established and invariable order through several stages of moral growth, each cognitively superior to those preceding it. When the testing methods that were developed in conjunction with this theory were applied to girls and women, it turned out that they were typically at lower stages of moral development than boys and men of similar ages. These results provided a veneer of scientific respectability for the claim that females are less capable of moral reasoning than males. What Gilligan is able to point out is that Kohlberg's stages were originally based upon studies of males, establishing thereby a template that was consequently imposed upon females. Insofar as female moral reasoning diverged from the male model, it was judged to be not just different, but inferior.

In her empirical research, Gilligan found two different "voices" of moral reasoning. One of them spoke chiefly of abstract principles of justice; the other spoke of the importance of maintaining personal relationships when dealing with moral dilemmas. Although Gilligan found that the second voice, unrepresented in Kohlberg's analysis, was often the voice of girls and women, she is careful not to say that it is essentially female in character any more than the first is essentially male. The point is that an important dimension of ethical reasoning had been neglected by concentrating exclusively on one of these two voices—the one usually identified with male reasoning.

Other feminist theorists have argued that the notions of "autonomy" and "independence" that are entrenched in traditional accounts of moral reasoning are based on the experience and aspirations of a small minority of exceptionally privileged males; that social contract accounts of moral obligation are clearly inadequate in ways that reflect their neglect of female moral experience with respect to caring for the dependent individuals; and that the tendency to attach moral status to the public rather than the private domain is a product of male bias that systematically devalues female morality. In all these ways, our understanding of moral reasoning is said to be impoverished because it has been constructed to exclude female experience.

It is not ethics, however, but science that is usually taken as the paradigm of rational thought in the twentieth century. Consequently, many analyses of the gender of rationality focus on scientific method as the current embodiment of ideals of rationality. One of the most comprehensive and influential of these analyses is by Sandra Harding.[5] She imposes a typology on feminist critiques of science that seems not only to assign them to three different classes of analysis but also to reflect Harding's understanding of the developmental direction of feminist epistemology. In the first category are those critiques labeled "feminist empiricism." Here the aim is to show how, in certain cases, the application of scientific method has been subverted by the intrusion of such extrascientific factors as sexism and androcentrism, resulting in bad science. Neither scientific method nor the idea of objectivity is directly called into question by such analyses. Harding does not find these adequate because they cannot account for the pervasive androcentrism of science-as-usual (as opposed to "bad science"). She labels such accounts "feminist *empiricism*" because they are premised on the assumption that the standpoint of the knower is epistemologically irrelevant.

This assumption is denied by "standpoint epistemologists" who argue that the credentials of the knowledge claim depend, in part, on the situation of the knower. Just as Hegel's slave could know more than the master, so women may enjoy an epistemic advantage over men. A science based upon the standpoint of women would be an improvement over current science, according to standpoint epistemology. In this sense it is still a "successor science" project because its aim is to produce a *better* (epistemically superior) account of the world. A number of problems have been pointed out with this approach, but the most damaging is the existence of a multitude of epistemic viewpoints, no one of them essential to all women (or to all feminists). The epistemic perspective of a heterosexual African woman, for example, would likely be very different from that of a white lesbian in Brandon, Manitoba. On what grounds could one of these be privileged over the other as a standpoint from which to describe the world?

The recognition of this problem has led many theorists to embrace what Harding calls "feminist postmodernism" by giving up altogether the endeavor to become more and more objective and by accepting the existence of an irreducible plurality of alternative narratives about the way the world is. The notion of a scientific method that might allow us to transcend the constraints of culture, time, and place is repudiated once and for all by feminist postmodernists. They see that notion as just one of many illusions that permeate our inheritance from the scientific revolution, and it is partly in response to their critique that Harding calls for a complete rereading of "The Birth of Modern Science" as a text.

Other feminist critics, too, have looked to the seventeenth century for the source of the misogyny and androcentrism that characterize much of science 300 years later. For example, in her important 1980 book, Carolyn Merchant links the mechanization of the world-picture to the demise of an older, feminine-nurturant vision of the earth as a loving provider.[6] This older vision embodied, according to Merchant, a system of values that promoted harmonious cooperation with the environment and a holistic approach to understanding nature. She argues that the replacement of this view by the mechanical world-picture has had disastrous effects both for the environment and for women.

Evelyn Fox Keller,[7] too, has argued that the seventeenth century witnessed a contest between masculine and feminine principles: head versus heart, purified versus erotic stances toward knowledge, attitudes of domination of the object versus merging with the object of knowledge. The victory of masculine over feminine principles has meant, according to Keller, that even today a "masculine" cognitive stance is required of all working scientists: one that emphasizes autonomy, separation, and distance between subject and object. The defeat of feminine principles in the seventeenth century meant the banishment of "sympathetic understanding" from the methodology of science, in Keller's account.

Finally, Susan Bordo has built upon analyses such as those by Merchant and Keller to carry the thesis even further.[8] She distances herself from Genevieve Lloyd in arguing that it is a mistake to think of reason as timelessly masculine. Instead, she says, reason was "masculinized" at a particular point in our cultural development—in the seventeenth-century flight from the feminine. She argues that both the mechanistic reconstruction of the world and the objectivist reconstruction of knowledge embody a common psychological structure: "a fantasy of 'rebirthing' self and world, brought into play by the disintegration of the organic, female cosmos of the Middle Ages and Renaissance." She supports this view chiefly by applying the tools of psychoanalytic theory to a reading of Descartes's *Meditations*.

The essays in this volume both engage with and depart from this conception of the seventeenth century as a pivotal moment in the history of reason. Although much of the debate emerges from philosophy and the history of science, the repercussions of these theories, especially given the primacy of philosophic and scientific discourse, are profound. The recourse to reason and objectivity as neutral and valuable has influenced theories of social science and history, it has shaped the perceived relationship between what it means to be objective and what it means to be subjective, it has helped articulate conceptions of disease and pathology—both psychological and physiological, it has created a hierarchy among various disciplines and kinds of knowledge, and it has determined the languages that are used to articulate and communicate about knowledge.

The first four essays in the volume treat different aspects of the seventeenth-century context: the historical position of women, the language of prophecy, the history of science, and the relation of desire to knowledge. The opening essay in the volume, Hilda L. Smith's "Intellectual Bases for Feminist Analyses: The Seventeenth and Eighteenth Centuries," provides a perceptive corrective to transhistorical condemnations of reason as male. While Smith acknowledges the importance and validity of such philosophical analyses as Genevieve Lloyd's *Man of Reason*, she maintains that feminist critiques of reason are themselves formulated from a position of privilege by scholars who have been educated within the tradition of rational and scientific discourse. This empowering education was not available to the early feminists of the seventeenth and eighteenth centuries, who were excluded from the educational institutions that would have given them the tools to alter the limiting conception of their gender imposed upon them by a patriarchal society. The instrument that had the power to free women from their imprisoning female nature was reason, the very faculty they were supposed not to have. Yet it was only through rational argumentation—Mary Astell's application of Cartesian principles, for instance—that women were able to demonstrate their ability to think and, hence, their right to be included within the educational and legal systems that would enable them to play a social role outside the domestic sphere to which they had been confined.

The attractiveness of Cartesianism to women of the period was not unanticipated. The emerging norms for rational theory choice stood opposed to all forms of obscurantism and laid stress on the overarching importance of clarity and distinctness as hallmarks of scientific rationality. The claim of the new philosophy to have achieved these desiderata was sometimes summed up in the boast that "even women" could understand it. It is in this context that Thomas M. Lennon offers an account of the significance of the common seventeenth-century charge of oracularity. In "Lady Oracle: Changing Conceptions of Authority and Reason in Seventeenth-Century Philosophy," he argues that the charge of being an oracle is the charge of failing to fulfil the demands of the new conception of reason. Oracular discourse, in Lennon's analysis, has three chief characteristics: it is enigmatic; it is vehicular (in the sense that the speaker is an instrument who *conveys* rather than generates meaning); and it is typically spoken by a woman. Lennon does not argue, however, that it was the perceived gender of prophetic discourse (feminine) that made it seem so dangerous and the need to stamp it out so urgent. In this respect, his account differs significantly from Berg and Berry's 1981 analysis of female prophets in the seventeenth century.[9] He argues that oracular discourse was not condemned as objectionable because it was feminine; rather it was condemned as feminine because it was objectionable—objectionable on grounds involving the new conceptions of reason, truth, and appropriate grounds of belief.

Whereas Smith and Lennon stress the accessibility to women of Cartesian rationality, Julie Robin Solomon and Alison M. Jaggar emphasize the defects of the new rationality—especially as it affects women. Kathleen Okruhlik's essay "Birth of a New Physics or Death of Nature?" may be seen, in part, as an attempt to sort out these claims by disentangling some of the threads of our seventeenth-century inheritance. She pays special attention to the evolution of the doctrine of primary and secondary qualities, because that doctrine was central to the new epistemologies developed during the seventeenth century and because it seems to lie at the root of several feminist critiques of modern science. Okruhlik questions whether the notion of objectivity, premised upon the division of subject and object, is so narrowly masculine that it must be rejected by feminists. She argues that the danger lies not so much in the notions of objectivity and rationality *simpliciter,* but in the conjunction of an old-fashioned account of the relationship between the contexts of discovery and justification, on the one hand, and newer models of rational theory choice on the other. The older doctrine, which Jaggar discusses in her essay, considers that values and emotions may be important in the context of discovery but are insignificant in the context of justification. This doctrine made a certain amount of sense at the time that it was developed, but is no longer viable now that we recognize that theory choice is irreducibly comparative in nature. For if the most we can do is to choose the best alternative among the rival hypotheses that have actually been articulated and developed, there is no longer anything in the scientific method that will filter out those values that are shared by rival hypotheses. The social, political, and emotional commitments that were present in the context of theory generation will still inform the best justified theory if no rivals are present to challenge them.

Although feminists have often commented, in passing, on difficulties with the distinction between discovery and justification, Okruhlik argues that too little attention has been paid to the comparative nature of theory choice. It is this insight that allows us to see what was really wrong with Bacon's vision of science. The problem is not that there was no room for human bodies or human interests in his account, but that there was no provision for the diversity of human bodies and human interests. Bacon's theory of science was perfectly consonant with his political theory: just as an absolute monarch could be counted on to do what was best for his subjects, so a highly centralized, socially homogenous scientific elite could be counted on to develop science in such a way as to improve the lot of *all humanity*. The unexamined nature of this legacy is such that our accounts of scientific rationality in the last part of the twentieth century do not reflect any progress in the development of social and political theory since Bacon. One twentieth-century critic of this inheritance is Julie Robin Solomon, who finds new and powerful support for the interests of a centralized patriarchy in the seventeenth-century model of rationality. Her essay focuses not on Descartes, but on Francis Bacon, as a progenitor of the new rationality. John Calvin's work is seen by her as the source of an alternative conception—one that not only rejects the older (Scholastic) accounts of knowledge but also offers a preemptive challenge to those developed during the scientific revolution.

In "From Species to Speculation: Naming the Animals with Calvin and Bacon," Solomon reads two crucial commentaries on a centrally important passage from *Genesis,* Adam's naming of the animals. She argues that the text achieves the significance that it does because this account of man's origins stresses the faculty of reason, which allows him to distinguish among the animals and to understand his own essential difference from them. What commentators before Calvin tended to elide, however, was that Adam's calling the animals by name is intertwined and contiguous with his own search for a suitable mate. While Calvin's commentary recognizes Adam's intellectual sovereignty, he nevertheless acknowledges the extent to which rationality is bound up with desire. Knowledge for Calvin, then, can never be completely objective, as in the Baconian program, but, rather, is always informed by interest, for all human knowing is precipitated by desire.

In Solomon's interpretation, Bacon's scientific program lends a religious and cultural force to Adam's intellectual sovereignty over the animals, and scientific knowledge thus proffers the implicit promise of a recovery of the Edenic state. For Bacon, there is a progressive effacement of interest in cognition, so that knowledge entails a self-transcendence, particularly of the human body and the desire that it signifies. Bacon's model of knowledge, especially as it is figured in his utopian vision, *The New*

Atlantis, is dependent on the activities, images, and profit-seeking pursuits of the urban commercial classes, and yet these origins both of class and gender are effaced in favor of a rational, genderless system. Solomon's new historicist approach allows her to investigate the traces of class and gender present in the metaphoric structure of Bacon's discourse and to illuminate the process of commercial exploitation and subjugation of woman that Bacon's rhetoric elides but on which his program ultimately depends.

Whereas Solomon deals specifically with the possibility of rethinking the relationship between knowledge and desire, Alison Jaggar calls for the rehabilitation of emotion (generally) as an epistemic resource. Her essay, "Love and Knowledge: Emotion in Feminist Epistemology," is not chiefly historical in its orientation, but Jaggar does argue at some length that the view of emotion she wishes to oppose has its origins in the developments of the seventeenth century. Although there was already a strong tendency within the Western philosophical tradition to consider emotions as subversive of knowledge, Jaggar maintains that the contrast between reason and emotion was sharpened as the former came to be regarded as an instrumental faculty. The realms of nature and value were separated, with values being relocated in human beings. Thus, according to Jaggar, the reconceptualizations of reason and emotion during the seventeenth century went hand in hand: as reason came to be seen as a purely instrumental faculty incapable of determining ends, emotions came to be viewed as nonrational (often irrational) urges that an individual "suffered." Since values and emotions had been defined as variable, idiosyncratic, and subjective, trustworthy knowledge could be established only by methods that neutralized the values and emotions of the individual.

Jaggar argues that this understanding of the relationship between emotion and reason has gone unchallenged for too long—unchallenged even by recent epistemologists who reject many other aspects of our seventeenth-century heritage. She argues that emotion is vital to systematic knowledge and that we require a new epistemic model that is antifoundationalist and nonhierarchical—one in which emotions are neither more basic than nor subservient to reason or action in the process of theory building. Jaggar paraphrases Marx in claiming that the development of each of these faculties is a necessary condition for the development of all. Unless we manage to repudiate that aspect of our seventeenth-century heritage that opposes emotion to reason, we shall continue to deny ourselves an invaluable epistemic resource—one that may be especially useful in the development of feminist theory.

Yet to consider feminist theory as a monolithic endeavor is to misrepresent its diversity and its changing nature, for one of its defining characteristics has been the reflexivity that has continually been brought to bear on its aims and articulations. Recently, many feminists have begun to question what once seemed an unquestionable premise, that is, what it means to make gender the predominant category of analysis, since to do so privileges one perspective over the others that it excludes, such as race, class, or sexual orientation. Susan Bordo examines the consequences of this questioning in her essay, "Feminist Skepticism and the 'Maleness' of Philosophy," where she considers both the arguments of those who advocate a "theoretics of heterogeneity" as well as the claims of those who counsel making gender a crucial and privileged analytic category. To enshrine "difference" runs the risk of introducing a cultural relativism so radical that it obscures the way Western society and the organization of its institutions have tended to be bifurcated along lines of gender. The belief that one could somehow represent the heterogeneity of perspectives has become a fantasy as improbable (and as potentially incapacitating) as locating an Archimedean point. On the other hand, a vision that makes gender of primary importance has sometimes occluded the variations of historical context, and it has also promulgated a unitary definition of gender that erases differences within itself, such as class and race. In this way, early theories of gender ran the risk of imposing a structure as monolithic and rigid as the "male-normative" theories it sought to dismantle.

The issues that Bordo raises are central to this collection of essays, since the volume seeks to problematize the transhistorical view of reason that aligns women uncomplicatedly with the irrational at the same time that it acknowledges the pervasiveness of that paradigm. At stake is not only how we see history and its relationship to philosophy but also what the implications of a historical conception of reason are for feminist methodology. In other words, history—at least a type of history that recognizes both the importance of perspective and the place of the material—can be used as a way of denaturalizing philosophy's claims to universalism and objectivity by reintroducing what it has excluded: the material, the mundane, the corporeal. In a sense, feminists themselves are writing their critiques of reason from the margins, from the place of exclusion, and yet, to participate in the debate over reason is also to

participate in the very philosophic discourse that has marginalized them
in the first place. The challenges, then, are always double, since they
both engage in rational or philosophic discourse (a critique from within)
and also seek to dethrone philosophy as the hegemonic "master" discourse (a critique from without). To separate the "methodological" essays
from the historical essays in this volume, then, would be to segregate
philosophy from history and thus to imply a hierarchy of discourse. We
believe, however, that it is through our understanding of the historical
inheritance of reason's representation that its place and function within
a feminist methodology will become evident. In a similar way, the hegemony of reason is implicitly subverted through a variety of disciplinary
perspectives, some of which take not reason as their topic, but unreason.

Whereas reason has been enshrined within a post-Enlightenment
philosophic context, it is the principle of irrationality that is most closely
linked to artistic creativity in late nineteenth-century France. Patricia
Mathews analyzes the imbrication of medical and artistic terminology
in the late nineteenth-century French discourse of artistic creativity. In
"The Gender of Creativity in the French Symbolist Period," Mathews
argues persuasively that, according to the Symbolist model of creativity,
the artist had the capacity to perceive a system of correspondences
between spiritual and material worlds through an inspired revelation that
sometimes verged on madness. This state of inspired revelation was
thought to be heightened by pain and suffering, and, for some theorists,
insanity was seen as the ultimate paradigm of creativity, with madness
even possessing the capacity to transform a mediocre intelligence into
a brilliant one.

Yet as Mathews demonstrates, this model was coded according to
gender, so that whereas a male artist like van Gogh could cross the
boundary between insanity and artistic revelation without impugning
his genius, an analogous state of suffering and revelatory power in a
woman was compromised by her frail physiology. Because her feminine
nature was seen as inextricably linked to her unstable reproductive system, woman tended to be labeled as hysterical rather than creative.
Described by Freud as a "caricature of an artistic creation," hysteria
represented the "short-circuited" female version of the male creative
ecstasy that often resulted in great art. Yet despite the ravages of the
nineteenth-century cult of invalidism and the cultural invalidation that
the diagnosis of hysteria or madness carried with it for a woman, a

number of nineteenth-century women artists did evolve their own (sometimes unarticulated) models of creativity. Mathews examines the lives of two artists, Camille Claudel and Suzanne Valadon, and her conclusions reinforce Lorraine Code's observations on Claudel's life, for both agree that the powerfully shaping role that ideology plays ultimately constrains not only what women are able to accomplish but also the theoretical categories used to evaluate those achievements.

The issue of artistic creativity and its gendering is also the subject of Mark A. Cheetham's essay, "Purity or Danger: Mondrian's Exclusion of the Feminine and the Gender of Abstract Painting." He discusses the early twentieth-century writings of the Dutch painter, Piet Mondrian, in order to expose both the masculinist frame for abstract painting evident in these theoretical manifestoes and to demonstrate the longevity of the legacy that Mondrian bequeathed. Cheetham asserts that Neoplasticism is driven by "the radical exclusion" of what Mondrian deems the "feminine principle," and it is only by purifying art of that principle in a program of aesthetic eugenics that true art will be freed from its material roots. Cheetham examines two examples of artists working in the 1980s who have responded in different ways to Mondrian's vision, a German painter, Gerhard Merz, and a Canadian postmodern painter, Allyson Clay. Where Merz appears to endorse the tradition of pure Neoplasticism, alluding explicitly to Mondrian in his use of color and his inscription "to the men of the future," Clay provides a challenge to the tradition of abstraction that sought to erase all vestiges of the feminine. Clay's work, especially the installation piece that Cheetham analyzes, provides an excellent example of the postmodern feminist position that Bordo discusses. Clay's "Eye to Eye" is accompanied by a text offering "objective" instructions for making the painting that we see, a text that is framed by two other texts, one exposing the masculine bias of a painting manual and the other an erotic discourse. The texts provide, then, a multiple and complex challenge to the hegemony of the male, universal ideal of abstraction both by reinscribing what Mondrian had sought to exclude (text, body, desire, women) and also by furnishing a number of alternate perspectives, whose very presence subverts the unitary, dominant vision. The title of the painting, "Eye to Eye," incorporates a telling pun, invoking as it does the subjective *I* that speaks, an I that modifies and locates the eye, the scientific and objective instrument of vision.

Just as Patricia Mathews charts the progress of female artists within an ideological context hostile to their creative endeavors, so Kristin Brady anatomizes the position of a nineteenth-century woman writer. In "Physiology, Phrenology, and Patriarchy: The Construction of George Eliot," she examines not so much the way George Eliot represented women in her novels but rather the way she—as a female novelist—was constructed by her biographers and critics. Eliot tended to be perceived in terms of a nineteenth-century definition of gender, argues Brady, a conception that equated woman with her sexual organs. Yet Eliot defied these conventional categories by failing to conform to the cultural imperatives of Victorian womanhood; her critics tended either to insist on her essential womanhood (in spite of the evidence of her "masculine mind") or else to see her as a freak of nature, a kind of hermaphroditic being who combined within her body the features of both sexes. The alignment of woman with her uterus, far from according special creative powers to the female writer, tended to figure her as pathological because of the uterus's etymological and medical associations with hysteria. The threat represented by the woman writer was thus not only her femininity but the hysterical doubleness that signaled the erosion of the unitariness of literary truth. Further, feminine writing was judged as different from masculine writing, a difference that informed judgments of Eliot's work, whether as denigration of her inability to create male characters or as praise for the feminine multiplicity of observation (as opposed to the unitariness of masculine creativity).

Brady analyzes a text that formed the basis for many biographers' and critics' subsequent judgments of Eliot, a phrenological reading of her skull, taken from a cast allegedly made of her head in 1844. The reading of this evidence allows her biographer, Bray, to appropriate the language of scientific objectivity to underwrite sexual stereotypes, so that George Eliot's mind is reduced to a physical specimen, with the cast of her skull furnishing the traces and the definitive proof of her feminine weakness and impressionability. The phrenological reading that quickly became an implicit or explicit subtext of Eliot criticism provides a synecdoche for the reading of her mind and body by a patriarchal culture made anxious by the very literary powers she possessed in such abundance.

The treatment of George Eliot emphasizes again how scientific and supposedly objective evidence can be used as a way of marginalizing and silencing women, and it is only by denaturalizing that authoritative discourse that we can recognize the subjective biases that informed it.

It may seem paradoxical in the first instance, then, that much feminist theory should not only seek to reveal the often androcentric ideological assumptions that subtend the "objective" perspective, but that they should also align themselves with the revealed subjective position. Postmodern and feminist theory is often at pains to detail the speaker's position in history, and to locate that speaker in terms of class, race, and gender. Since any knowledge or speech is not only contingent on but is also enabled by these subjective factors, many feminist theorists overtly position themselves in relation to their objects of study, defining themselves as speakers and knowers. Yet this strategy is not without attendant difficulties; not all cultural biases are available for self-scrutiny in the first place, and many methodologies and disciplines have made objectivity a fundamental (and sometimes invisible) principle.

Although Okruhlik's essay deals with the division between subject and object, it concentrates on a period during which the objects of scientific study were mostly inanimate and unconscious. The rise of social science in the nineteenth and twentieth centuries complicated the situation immensely because, for the first time, the *objects* of scientific investigation included human beings—that is, objects who were themselves subjects, fully conscious centers of experience in their own right. The question then arose of how one might deal objectively with their experiences. Most feminist criticisms of science have focused on the social sciences, precisely because of the social scientific failure to deal adequately with female experience. In "Reasoning about Ourselves: Feminist Methodology in the Social Sciences," Alison Wylie asks what a feminist social science would look like: what status would it accord to the lived experiences of the women who are among its objects of study? Wylie distinguishes two models of feminist research that may be distilled from the large literature that has developed in response to this question. She calls one the "collectivist" model of inquiry and the other the "self-study" model. Although adherents to both will agree, in general terms, that feminist research must privilege the experiences of women, they diverge on the practical implications of making female experience central and ask whose experience is at issue, how this experience is to ground general explanatory accounts of women's situation, and whether the commitment to take women's experience seriously really entails that they can never "go beyond" it in the pursuit of these explanatory aims.

Wylie goes on to examine consciousness raising as a methodological tool for feminist researchers, stressing that the integrity and efficacy of personal experience must be a central topic for critical analysis, not a presupposition. Feminists must develop the analytical tools necessary for investigating the relationship between this experience and its context, a context structured by factors of race, class, age, ethnicity, nationality, and sexual orientation—as well as gender. They must provide an account of constructive feminist criticism that differentiates it clearly from the destructive forms common in dominant disciplinary traditions of research. The problems encountered by the two models examined earlier in the essay testify to the urgency of the need for such an account.

Marie Fleming's essay, "Women's Place in Communicative Reason," also addresses the methodological difficulties of trying to adapt an androcentric model to a feminist purpose by examining German philosopher Jürgen Habermas's concept of communicative reason. Feminists have resisted the tradition of autonomous reason as it is derived from Kant, since it tries to transcend bodies and other historical contingencies in its effort to achieve a position of disinterestedness. Communicative reason, on the other hand, is dialogic rather than monologic, demonstrates a predisposition toward integrating a historical perspective, and is grounded in human speech (anyone capable of speaking is entitled to participate). In fact, it displays affinities with the model presented in Carol Gilligan's more empirical research, which also stresses the narrative and contextual nature of women's moral reasoning. Yet despite the obvious possibilities the theory of communicative reason offers feminists, the issue of gender is strikingly absent from Habermas's own model and writings. His failure to theorize gender seriously compromises the usefulness of communicative reason for feminists, since Habermas never confronts the actual gendering of social roles. Yet some feminist critics, notably Seyla Benhabib, have argued that although communicative reason is fundamentally flawed, it contains within it the possibility of women's inclusion. Fleming examines Benhabib's feminist rehabilitation of Habermas, astutely pointing out the way in which Benhabib reinscribes a genderless society in which victory is implicitly accorded to the masculine. Fleming goes on to analyze the verbal contract that lies at the heart of communicative reason, maintaining that the rational argumentation that forms the basis for establishing rightness presupposes a set of invisible values that are already coded according to gender. Although her argument ultimately exposes the underlying similarities between autonomous and communicative reason rather than their differences, Fleming urges feminists both "to heighten the centrality of reason" in their critiques and also "to interrogate its manifestations in social and political life."

Further evidence of this urgency is to be found in Lorraine Code's essay, "The Unicorn in the Garden," for she demonstrates there how the refusal of scientific and other cultural institutions to acknowledge the experience of women quite literally drives them mad. She relates female madness and the treatment of it to the larger patterns of authority and expertise in a culture that venerates all things scientific. The crucial insight is the applicability to women's epistemic situation of Wittgenstein's dictum "Knowledge is in the end based on acknowledgement," for women can never function as fully rational agents in a culture that refuses to acknowledge their experiences. Instead they become convinced of their own madness and the madness of women generally. In even the simplest instances of "S knows that P," for example, "Sara knows that the cat is on the mat," Code shows how the systematic refusal of all others to acknowledge the evidence of Sara's senses could lead her to doubt her own epistemic adequacy—even her sanity. She concludes that "there is no more effective means of creating epistemic dependence than systematically withdrawing acknowledgment from a person's own cognitive utterances; no more effective way of maintaining structures of epistemic privilege and vulnerability than evincing a persistent distrust in a person's efforts to claim cognitive authority; no surer way of demonstrating a refusal to know a person *as* a person than observing her 'objectively' without taking seriously what her experiences meant to her."

The question of language, which figures so prominently in Habermas's theory of communicative reason, points to another connection with some of the essays in the volume. If people enter into the social contract only if they have access to speech, and if woman's putative irrationality has tended, in varying degrees throughout history, to condemn her to silence, then her more limited access to language, as Hilda Smith has convincingly argued, handicaps her from the start. Yet education and language are themselves complicated and multifaceted, erecting ideological barriers even as women are seemingly granted entrance into these privileged realms. We have only to think of Thomas Lennon's examination of prophetic language, where woman's relationship to discourse is primarily vehicular, or of Kristin Brady's discussion of the reception of George Eliot's writing, or of women's partial involvement in the visual languages of art as exemplified in the essays of Patricia Mathews and Mark Cheetham, to understand that participation in discourse does not necessarily constitute access to understanding or power. The essays that treat hysteria (Brady, Mathew, and Code) all display a recognition of the way hysteria, as the language the body uses when the tongue is silenced, becomes an alternate and marginalizing discourse. As Lorraine Code astutely points out, "experts" in psychiatric medicine such as Freud and Charcot were quick to impose their own interpretations on the "mute" gestures of their hysterical patients, thus engendering "epistemic dependence" by "systematically withholding acknowledgment." Language is just one aspect of the complex disciplinary structures within which and against which feminist theorists must struggle. What, then, must the feminist's relation to these privileged discourses be? To remain silent or to avoid complicity in furthering these patriarchal discourses is also implicitly to accept them, yet to participate in them is also to risk cooptation. It is in this arena of tension that critiques of rationality must be situated. That the best hope for women lies not in the rejection of "rational discourse" as an irredeemably masculine construct but in increased participation by feminists in the making of art and science and the discourses that interpret them is, we hope, evident from the essays in this volume.

NOTES

1. Genevieve Lloyd, *The Man of Reason: "Male" and "Female" in Western Philosophy* (Minneapolis: University of Minnesota Press, 1984).

2. Lloyd, *Man of Reason,* 104.

3. Lloyd, *Man of Reason,* 109.

4. Carol Gilligan, *In a Different Voice* (Cambridge, Mass.: Harvard University Press, 1982).

5. Sandra Harding, *The Science Question in Feminism* (Ithaca, N.Y.: Cornell University Press, 1986).

6. Carolyn Merchant, *The Death of Nature: Women, Ecology, and the Scientific Revolution* (San Francisco: Harper and Row, 1980).

7. Evelyn Fox Keller, *Reflections on Gender and Science* (New Haven: Yale University Press, 1985).

8. In this volume.

9. Christine Berg and Philippa Berry, "Spiritual Whoredom: An Essay on Female Prophets in the Seventeenth Century," in *1642: Literature and Power in the Seventeenth Century,* ed. Francis Barker, Jay Bernstein, John Coombs, Peter Hulme, Jennifer Stone, and Jon Stratton (Essex: University of Essex, 1981), 37–54.

Intellectual Bases for Feminist Analyses: The Seventeenth and Eighteenth Centuries

Hilda L. Smith

In tracing the development of rational thought in feminist writers of the seventeenth and eighteenth centuries, one is struck by their intense faith in the ability of reason to refute those who would define women's nature and restrict their lives through images of the "weaker vessel." Why this strong faith in reason permeates their writings and why they felt compelled to answer those who questioned women's rational abilities are essential questions to understanding the concerns of these early feminists. The term *weaker vessel*, utilized by Antonia Fraser in her compendium of attitudes and institutions comprising seventeenth-century stereotypes of feminine weakness, conjures up a physical image. The female being— body, mind, and soul—is inadequate to the tasks that confront it. As receptacles for thought and experience, women's mind and body lack the qualities and the range of skills to understand and then to act. Analyzing the nature and development of this image leads one in numerous directions. Yet these directions, while seemingly random and widely diverse, converge in a single view of women's capacities. That capacity—or better, incapacity—is embedded in women's perceived inadequate powers of reason.[1]

C. V. Wedgewood, in her classic treatment of the political downfall of Charles I in *The King's Peace, 1637-1641*, provides a useful parallel to aid in understanding how various authors could reach a single conclusion about the basis for male and female difference. Wedgewood, in constructing a narrative of Charles's alienation of his subjects, discusses diverse policies relating to personal monopolies; the alliance with France; the Queen's influence; ignoring Parliament; Scotland's position; the Anglican hierarchy; and royal and ecclesiastical courts. Each of these policies could have created problems for the monarch, but singly, and even taken as a whole, they might not have resulted in his execution. But they were not perceived independently, or even as a connected group; rather, they were each seen as evidence for the growing influence of Roman Catholics at the Stuart Court.[2]

In analyzing two discrete and unconnected policies of Charles I—one a reward to specific Catholics, the other a punishment to a group of Protestants—Wedgewood notes their broader significance: "The popular argument was ignorant, incorrect, but deadly: if the King, the head of the Anglican Church, persecuted honest Protestants and smiled upon Papists, it followed that the Church itself was being led back to Rome." The power of such a unified set of misconceptions grew clearer after 1640. According to Wedgewood, in five years the kingdom moved from being seen as "the most tranquil in Europe and their sovereign the happiest King in Christendom" to one with discord throughout the realm, and consequently "the King had pledged himself not to dissolve a Parliament which had destroyed his judicial powers, taken over the management of his finances, and awaited his return [to London] with an indictment such as had never before been presented to a reigning English sovereign." Whatever independent actions Charles pursued, a large number of his subjects interpreted them in a single context, his growing favoritism to a Roman Catholicism that represented a religious, social, and political threat to the realm and their position within it.[3]

In a parallel manner, a range of visions disparaging the nature of women—and the policies and attitudes they justified—were integrated to disparage women's intellect. Insistence on female rational deficiencies became the argumentative barrier to a variety of women's specific goals, such as a reformed legal structure, greater equality within marriage, access to a secondary and university education, the right to pursue interests outside the home, and the possibility of entering public debate on any question, including their own social role. Women's efforts to publish works on any topic, to marry according to their own will, to pursue an education or a professional calling, or to engage in any task beyond the domestic and decorative were always drawn up short by questions concerning their rational abilities.[4]

Seventeenth- and eighteenth-century feminists, when arguing for women's right and ability to pursue a life not constrained by this central, controlling set of "qualities" allegedly limiting women, situated their arguments in the arena of rational debate. They chose not to make primary attack on women's exclusion from the public institutions of their day or the intrinsically unequal nature of sexual relations within or outside the family. Rather, when speaking of institutional exclusion or relationships between the sexes, these early feminists returned again and again to the manner in which such exclusion and familial controls limited women's rational development. An ability to use their minds and to gain respect for their intellectual accomplishments was required to move beyond the constraints of custom. Indeed, there was no need to consider any feminist argument if, in fact, women were incapable of using reason to construct one.[5]

Two poems published near the turn of the eighteenth century suggest why reason had to be the first battleground. Anne Winchilsea's "The Emulation" presents a sharply expressed version of feminist anger against women's exclusion from serious learning.

> They let us learn to work, to dance, or sing,
>   Or any such like trivial thing,
> Which to their profit may Increase or Pleasure bring,
>   But they refuse to let us know
>   what sacred Sciences doth impart
> Or the mysteriousness of Art.
> In learning's pleasing Paths deny'd to go,
> From knowledge banish'd and their Schools;
> We seem design'd alone for useful Fools.[6]

Winchilsea knew that only if women were allowed to think, could they attack those who presumed to think and decide for them, a truth equally clear to Sara Fyge Egerton in "The Liberty."

> Shall I be one, of those obsequious Fools,
> That square there lives, by Customs scanty Rules;
> Condemn'd for ever, to the puny Curse,
> Of Precepts taught, at Boarding-school, or Nurse,
> That all the business of my Life must be,
> Foolish, dull Trifling, Formality.
> Confin'd to a strict Magick complaisance,
> And round a Circle, of nice visits Dance,
> Nor for my Life beyond the Chalk advance.[7]

Others would always chalk women's limits, unless women, in fact, were capable of raising questions and writing answers themselves. Partly because of their limited access to serious learning, early feminists glorified women's rational abilities. Surely, they would not have appreciated the irony that later scholars and feminists have fully sided with their male and conservative critics at the time in maintaining that reason and learning were traps, catching would-be feminists in the structures, principles, and practices that were, indeed, a male preserve.

Recently, philosophers, literary theorists, and, to a lesser extent, women's historians, have come to see such arguments by feminists, over the relative intellectual and rational abilities of the sexes, as futile. Yearning after the bitter fruit of the male intellectual system, such feminists, they argue, are buying into a set of values that places men's moral, intellectual, and personal development at the center of human experience and defines it as universal. These views have received widespread attention and appeared in works such as *Women's Ways of Knowing*, Carol Gilligan's *In a Different Voice*, and, in a philosophical construct, in Genevieve Lloyd's *Man of Reason: "Male" and "Female" in Western Philosophy.*[8] Lloyd insists on the maleness of reason and exploits the difficulties that the term's supposedly sex-specific characteristics pose for those developing a feminist perspective in philosophy. She outlines the nature of the problem in her introduction.

> Our trust in a Reason that knows no sex has, I will argue, been largely self-deceiving. To bring to the surface the implicit maleness of our ideals of Reason is not necessarily to adopt a sexual "relativism" about rational belief and truth; but it does have important implications for our contemporary understanding of gender difference. It means, for example, that there are not only practical reasons, but also conceptual ones, for the conflicts many women experience between Reason and femininity.[9]

Lloyd proceeds to trace the concept of reason as employed in classical philosophy from Plato to Augustine and Aquinas, through Descartes, Kant, Rousseau, and Hegel, and on to Sartre. Her analysis demonstrates that qualities of femininity do not operate in isolation from the masculinity of reason, but, rather, are constructed purposefully in contrast, and as complement, to the central human qualities that bind maleness to reason. Lloyd argues that although such a critique is at odds with the stated purposes of philosophical texts as they were written and as they have come to be studied, it is essential for feminist scholars.

Philosophers have defined their activity in terms of the pursuit of Reason, free of the conditioning effects of historical circumstance and social structures. But despite its professed transcendence of contingencies, Philosophy has been deeply affected by, as well as deeply affecting, the social organization of sexual difference.[10]

How then do current feminist scholarly critiques (which attack uses of equal reason in women's defense) relate to seventeenth- and eighteenth-century feminist writings? Perhaps one needs to begin with some recognition of the historical circumstances of the two feminist arguments if one is to avoid the professed transcendence of which Lloyd warns. Much more so than these early authors, today's feminist thinkers were trained in the language and scholarship of rationalist and scientific discourse. Sure training has produced both positive and negative results: if it has grounded their education too strongly in writings not cognizant of women's existence as a group, it has also given current feminists confidence and position to criticize such training. Feminist writers of the 1600s and 1700s were outside institutions of higher learning and were seldom systematically educated. They could attack, in strong language, the sexist bias of contemporary and past thinkers, but only from outside the age's institutionalized learning. They were outsiders denied the tools to raise such questions effectively, who faced a unified vision of women's less rational nature, on which foundation all restrictions against their aspirations rested.[11]

Those writing two and three centuries ago, while sometimes attacking scholasticism and the limited life and understanding of the scholar, could not question reason without supporting their opponents. It is today's feminists, comfortably within the academy and other institutions of learning and reason, who can question the worth of that training altogether.

It is also helpful to understand earlier feminists' stance in terms of the vision of women's supposed nonrational natures that they fought. Sermons, gynecological textbooks, educational treatises, household guides, political theory, and moral philosophy all tell, in part, the same story in explanation for any definitions of women's limited rational abilities. One is struck by the a priori nature that leads such references to be dropped, willy-nilly, supposedly without the need for proof or further explanation, in the course of works totally unrelated to questions of female rationality, or even rationality in general. For example, discussions of the Creation invariably centered on Eve's temptation of Adam, which somehow proved, not the man's innate stupidity or weakness, but the serpent's use of women's simple, weak nature and faulty rational powers. Centered in myriad contexts, this progression from the transgression of the first woman to the weaknesses of her descendants served as endless proof of women's failings.

In 1540, the humanist educator, Juan Vives, often noted for his progressive views concerning women's education, contended that a woman should not teach because she "is a frail thing, and of weak discretion, and that may lightly be deceived, which thing our first mother Eve sheweth, whom the Devil caught with a light argument," and, thus, he continued, a female teacher may "bring others into the same error."[12] Comparable discussions of women's limited rationality in the context of religion were tied to church discipline—the need for ministers to lead their flock (and some of their flock more than others)—the importance of family-based worship under the father's direction, all tied to Pauline restrictions on women's silence abroad and learning at home. Women's subordination regarding faith or proper behavior were, at heart, problems of a weak intellect that allowed the cleverness of the devil and his henchmen to draw them from the narrow path of righteousness.[13]

Two works that progressed through multiple printings during the seventeenth century, William Gouge's 1622 *Of Domesticall Duties* and Richard Brathwait's *English Gentlewoman* (first published in 1631), were supposedly general directions for household management and personal behavior, but were also discussions of women's intellectual inferiority emanating from biblical origins.[14] Above all, according to Gouge, women should be warned against the "overweening conceit of their own wisdom," while Brathwait warned them against any "dispute of high points of Divinity." A role model to avoid was "these *Shee-clarkes* [who] many times broach strange opinions, which, as they understand them not themselves, so they labour to intangle others of equal understanding."[15] While proper social behavior or religious belief (presumably tied more securely to issues of faith) would presumably be central here, women's problems with understanding and reason were again supreme.

If the centrality of reason in these social guides of a strongly religious bent is surprising, it is even stranger in gynecological textbooks of the age. Authors of seventeenth-century works on gynecology followed many of the errors of the ancients concerning conception and physiology, especially those mixed up with clear sexual bias. Works directed to women's health care during pregnancy accepted a view that men's and women's mental abilities were inherently different based on the level of moisture and degree of temperature of their bodies. Both health and reason were tied to the hot and dry, and those qualities were consistently male. Sperm from the right testicle produced these hot and dry qualities, and couples were admonished to engage in sexual intercourse in such a manner as to encourage the production of such seed.[16]

A typical work from 1652 advised:

> Those who seek the comfort of having wise children, must indeavor that they be born male; for the Female, through the cold and moist of their sex, cannot be indowed with so profound a judgement; we find indeed that they take with appearance of knowledge in sleight and easie matters, but seldom reach any farther than to a sleight superficial smattering in any deep Science.

The author claimed that female moisture "stifleth the operations of the rational soul, and also occasioneth sickness and short life . . . so that it appears that a good wit, and a sound body arise from one and the same quality, namely, drynesse."[17] Such, then, was the confounding of ill-informed physiological information with biased views of women's rational abilities. It is striking as well, omitting the physiological argument, how closely such statements conform to the current stereotype of women as students and intellectuals; they are skillful at superficial, facile knowledge but lack abstract analytical powers.

The denial of women's rational nature was also caught up in the habit of defining intellectual and educational experience without incorporating them. This was clear among educational theorists of the late seventeenth century in England and the authors of the *Encyclopédie* of the 1760s in France. Educational theorists consistently interchanged two sets of nouns. In discussing secondary education, the terms *scholar* and *boy* were used interchangeably, as were the terms *man* and *adult*. Such was not the case for *girls* and *women*, which were never allowed to stand for scholar or adult. These were not mere oversights, but intertwined a distinct male education with the process of a mature development in a system that excluded females. Not simply were girls excluded in reality from the grammar schools that prepared boys for university study, they were omitted from plans conceived as national educational programs. Put simply, to mature to adulthood based upon educational advancement, including the acquisition of a body of knowledge, was an experience appropriate only for males. In a general sense, this was because men

were the only true adults. Women indeed grew older, but did not develop
the independence based on a level of knowledge, economic independence,
and citizenship that was the mark of the true adult. Women's aging,
rather, was tied to sexual function and dependence within the family
circle.[18]

The confusion of general qualities of learning and aging with the
experience of males was especially clear in John Milton's "Tractate of
Education." Milton proposed a national educational program involving
schools that would house approximately 150 pupils in towns throughout
the country. Students would progress through a system of thorough
language training because if someone knew a smattering of "all the
tongues" of the earth but none thoroughly, he should "no more be
considered educated than a yeoman or tradesman competently wise in
his mother-dialect only."[19] Other than languages, his program called for
increasingly complex, abstract, and analytical training. Sex-linked, and
not simply educationally sound, qualities were at the heart of his system.
Its goal was to produce "brave men and worthy patriots," to teach
students "to delight in manly and liberal exercises" and to "scorn all
their childish and ill-taught qualities." Boys were to advance to manhood,
taking on as an integral part of their education the masculine qualities
associated with that status and the privileges and duties of citizenship.[20]
While supposedly distinct from those works directly attacking women's
minds, these seemingly thoughtless omissions of them were simply the
opposite side of the coin of women's lesser rationality and need for
knowledge.

During the following century, those Frenchmen compiling the
seventeen-volume *Encyclopédie* wanted to incorporate as complete a
picture of society as possible. According to Diderot, its principal editor
and author, its purpose was "knowing and expounding the whole system
of nature and the arts." Yet out of seventeen volumes, there were four
essays, equalling less than thirteen pages, devoted to women's experiences. In Diderot's "Necessity for an Encyclopedia and its Method of
Compiling One," he made clear that both the body of knowledge and
the process of gathering excluded women.[21] The process was exclusionary
because to complete such a massive task the work had to be shared, for
who can define "the verb to conjugate but a grammarian? Who is to
define azimuth but an astronomer, epic but a man of letters, exchange
but a financier, vice but a moralist, hypostasis but a theologian, meta-
phisics but a philosopher, chisel but an artisan." The *Encyclopédie*, whose

goal was inclusivity and which sought "eyewitness" accounts of each phase of life, could still ignore women. And this is especially significant since it was to be a new, secular, realistic knowledge, to replace older, less relevant approaches. As Diderot stated:

> People now dare to doubt Aristotle and Plato, and the time has come when works which still enjoy the highest reputation will soon loose part of it or fall entirely into oblivion. Some types of literature not modelled on real life and customs will be neglected. . . . Such is the effect of the progress of reason. . . . [22]

The central relevance of women as nonrational and nonlearned beings is clarified further by those prominent in seventeenth-century thought who recognize areas of female importance and even superiority. Much credence was given to women's sensitivity, natural delicacy, and preeminence due to motherhood. Thinkers such as Agrippa von Nettesheim, a sixteenth-century figure reprinted in the late seventeenth century, argued their premier status from being the last, and thus the zenith, of God's creations,[23] and Hobbes acknowledged their importance in his *Philosophical Rudiments Concerning Government and Society.*

> Thus in the state of nature, every woman that bears children, becomes both a mother and a lord. But what some say, that in this case the father, by reason of the pre-eminence of sex, and not the mother becomes lord, signifies nothing . . . at this day, in divers places women are invested with the principal authority . . . which in truth they have by the right of nature. . . . Add also, that in the state of nature it cannot be known who is the father, but by testimony of the mother; the child therefore is his whose the mother will have it, and therefore hers.[24]

Thus, Hobbes was willing to grant much to women on grounds of natural rights. Others argued women's minds were never seen as equal or superior. Seventeenth- and eighteenth-century feminists understood this and attacked such unified and debilitating judgments.

Seventeenth-century English feminists wrote fervently concerning the pleasures of pursuing rational, systematic thought and of its empowering quality. Shutting women up in the family circle, denying them access to works that required their full intellectual talents, and demeaning and discounting women's knowledge and writings were at the heart of everything wrong with women's lives during the 1600s. Their writings appeared from the 1650s through the first decade of the eighteenth century and addressed women's lack of serious education, the devaluing of their intellectual abilities, and the restrictions that the family placed on women's development as individuals. They were among the earliest writings to view women as a sociological group, not to stress, as had previous authors, the abilities of a few outstanding individuals or to view women as beings tied together primarily through biological or psychological natures. Written by individuals such as Margaret Cavendish, Duchess of Newcastle, Bathsua Makin, Hannah Wolley, Mary Astell, and the poets of the last decade of the seventeenth century, including Anne Winchilsea and Sarah Egerton (whose works were referred to earlier in this essay), they developed a systematic body of writings that pursued and elaborated common themes.[25]

The Duchess of Newcastle, who produced thirteen volumes in the areas of moral philosophy, natural and physical sciences, drama, poetry, and essays, began writing in the 1650s. In the introduction to her *Poems and Fancies*, she hoped for recognition of her work but expected little from men "for they hold Books as their crowne . . . by which they rule and governe."[26] Her analyses of women's rational abilities and their devaluation by men were mixed up with her doubts about her own abilities and those of her sex generally. Her concerns were clearly cast in the negative assessments of women common to her day: "It cannot be expected I should write so wisely or wittily as Men being of the Effeminate Sex, whose Brains nature hath mix'd with the coldest and softest Elements."[27] Yet the Duchess often argued strongly against what she called men's "Tyrannical Government," which had led to their "using us either like Children, Fools, or Subjects, that is, to flatter us to obey, and . . . not let us divide the World equally with them." Above all, this tyranny resulted both from and in women's denial of education: "If we were bred in Schools to mature our Brains, and to manure our Understandings, that we might bring forth the Fruits of knowledge," then women's intellectual output would be as great as men's. The theme of frustration of women's great intellectual potential ran through the Duchess's many topics. "They endeavour," she orated, "to bar us of all sorts of Liberty, and will fain bury us in their houses or Beds, as in a Grave."[28]

In another vein, she condemned the convention that decreed that sons only carry on the male line "whereas Daughters are but Branches which by Marraige are broken off from . . . whence they Sprang, & Ingrafted into the Stock of an other Family, so that Daughters are to bee accounted but as Moveable Goods or Furnitures that wear out." Seeking fame, which she believed was denied because of male intellectual monopolies, throughout her life, there is a charming blend in the Duchess's works of daily life, shrewd self-assessment, and sharp and fundamental criticism of society's destructive underevaluation of her sex. Perhaps this unsure blend is caught best in one of the numerous introductions to her writings. "I wish heartily my Braine had been Richer, to make you a fine Entertainment . . . and though I cannot serve you on Agget Tables, and Persian Carpets, with Golden Dishes or Chrystall Glasses, nor feast you with Ambrosia, and Nector, yet perchance my Rye Loafe and new Butter may taste more savoury, then those that are sweet, and delicious."[29] Even when most determined to pursue thought, women often argued in terms drawn from the kitchen and dining room, where society admitted their minds might properly dwell.

Hannah Wolley, an author of cookbooks and domestic guides for servants and women generally, and Bathsua Makin, a royal governess and teacher at a secondary school for girls, wrote less prolifically but were even more focused on women's forced ignorance. In introducing *The Gentlewoman's Companion,* Wolley's broader concerns are obvious. "The right Education of the Female Sex, as it is in a manner every where neglected, so it ought to be generally lamented." In the tart language she often employed, she offered one explanation: "Most in this depraved later Age think a Woman learned and wise enough if she can distinguish her Husbands Bed from another." Wolley, as each of these feminists, connected women's inadequate education to the unjust and self-interested power men exerted over them. "Vain man is apt to think we were meerly intended for the Worlds propagation, and to keep its humane inhabitants sweet and clean but, by their leaves, had we the same Literature, he would find our brains as fruitful as our bodies." Her desire, she claimed, was not "to infuse bitter rebellion into the sweet blood of Females," but her anger is clear against parents for "letting the fertile ground of their Daughters lie Fallow."[30] Bathsua Makin concurred, and saw custom at the heart of women's problems. "The Barbarous custom to breed Women low, is grown general amongst us, and hath prevailed so far, that it is verily believed (especially amongst a sort of debauched Sots) that Women are not endued with such Reason, as Men; nor capable of improvement by Education, as they [men] are." As much as any feminist writing during the 1600s, Makin saw learning as liberating and struck at those who would deny women education through jest or simple bias: "There is in all an innate desire of knowing, and the satisfying of this is the greatest pleasure. Men are very cruel that give them leave to look at a distance, only to know they do not know."[31]

Certainly the most well known of these authors was Mary Astell, who wrote from the 1690s through the early decades of the eighteenth century. Most influential was her *Serious Proposal to the Ladies*, which went through four editions by 1730. Originally published in 1694, it was followed in 1697 by the *Serious Proposal, Part II* and, in 1700, by *Some Reflections Upon Marriage*. She proposed that women should pursue a life of serious scholarship, and she suggested a women's college as being most conducive to that end. In the second part of her work, she outlined the curriculum to be pursued and the actual operations of the college in greater detail, while in her discussion of marriage she argued that contemporary marriage had made women men's "upper servants," and denied them control over their own lives.[32]

In the *Serious Proposal*, Astell presents the most systematic treatment of women's inferior education and its evil results during the seventeenth century. Strongly influenced by Descartes, she referred to his *Discourse on Method* in her marginalia throughout the *Serious Proposal*. A devout Anglican, she decried those who favored only simple faith for women, but urged her sisters to examine "the Doctrine and Precept of Christianity, the Reasons and Authority on which it is built." Such a process, which she saw emanating from Cartesian methods, should be applied to one's assessment of everything within the universe. Building upon arguments that have now become familiar, she implored women to become serious beings, "no longer to be Cheap and contemptible." The problem with her contemporaries, as she saw it, was that they were "like Tulips in a Garden, to make a fine show and be good for nothing." In her analysis, society basically denied women's humanity by insisting that they bloom without thinking.[33]

Her explanations for women's inadequacies were similar to the earlier feminists of her century. "Women are from their very infancy debar'd those advantages, with the want of which, they are afterwards reproached, and nursed up in those Vices which will hereafter be upbraided to them." Yet Astell's plans for women, more than her predecessors', emphasized systematic education. The present trouble with women's lives was that they provided "no opportunities for thoughtfulness and recollection" but, instead, forced "an unthinking mechanical way of living."[34]

In the second part of her proposal, she emphasized a mode of thinking that would stretch women's minds and allow them to live up to their intellectual potential. Her discussion emphasized the lengthy, critical, and constantly questioning route to truth. First she contended that

> Reason wills that we shou'd think again, and not form our Conclusions or fix our foot till we can honestly say, that we have without Prejudice or Prepossession view'd the matter in Debate on all sides, seen it in every light, have no bias to encline us either way, but are only determin'd by Truth itself, shining brightly in our eyes, and not permitting us to resist the force and Evidence it carries.

To enable this process to proceed, she wanted a curriculum that tested women's capacities and utilized readings "not loosly writ, but require an Attent and Awakened Mind to apprehend, and to take in the whole force of 'em." Only those works that were "writ with Order and Connexion, the Strength of whose Arguments can't be sufficiently felt unless we remember and compare the whole System," were acceptable. Much of this sounds like the falsely objective requirements under criticism by feminist philosophers, but from a woman living in an age that denied women the ability and opportunity to pursue systematic thought it was a liberating process.[35]

Without doubt, most of the religious and social literature available to women during the late seventeenth century did not fill this bill. And such a level of works were considered unnecessary or inappropriate for the female, because she was intended for a marriage that did not give her scope to employ them. Thus, Astell's reflections on marriage built upon her general demands for women's full use of their minds. Men sought land, property, a dowry, beauty, and a little wit in a wife. These expectations left little space for women to develop their true potential. In addition, men became disappointed in their partners when they lived according to the low expectations the system dictated, but Astell—ever the feminist—placed the opinions of one man into the context of all when she stated, "How can a Man respect his Wife when he has a Contemptible Opinion of her and her Sex?" Sadly for her, women thought "as humbly of themselves as their masters can wish," which led her to seek those "Millennium Days" when "a Tyrannous Dominion, which Nature never meant, shall no longer render useless, if not hurtful, the Industry and Understandings of half of Mankind."[36]

During the second half of the eighteenth century, feminists were still fighting many of the same intellectual battles. The most famous exchange was Mary Wollstonecraft's attack on Rousseau's vision of women as pleasers of men. Yet faith in reason, insistence on women's rational abilities, and a demand for their serious education also appeared in the works of Germaine de Staël, Catherine Macaulay, and Gabrielle-Emilie du Châtelet. Writing in the midst of the Enlightenment, they worked to claim a place for women in the changing intellectual vision of their day, where reason was peculiarly glorified. Seldom successful, they were forced to answer the same charges of women's lesser abilities, impertinent natures, and lowly interests.[37]

Wollstonecraft's *A Vindication of the Rights of Woman* emerged from English radical thought of the late eighteenth century. It is a complicated work that includes most of the possible arguments for women's equal position within society. However, Wollstonecraft notes the primacy of education and reason to her argument.

> Contending for the rights of woman, my main argument is built on this simple principle, that if she be not prepared by education to become the companion of man, she will stop the progress of knowledge and virtue; for truth must be common to all. . . .[38]

In contradicting men's unjustified power over women, she asks, "Who made man the exclusive judge, if woman partakes with him the gift of reason?" Certainly, Wollstonecraft spoke more readily about the political realm than did her seventeenth-century predecessors and tied more securely the use of reason to the pursuit of public virtue. Yet, it was reason that made women men's equals and was the tool that led them to develop a virtuous character, not the natural, instinctual qualities that Rousseau placed in their bosoms. Only through reason do we develop those qualities on which society depends because "from the exercise of reason, knowledge and virtue naturally flow."[39]

Thus, reason, for Wollstonecraft as well as for feminists of the late 1600s, operated as both a means and an end for women's existence. There was an inherent good in its exercise, and it provided the tool to seek the knowledge and virtue that led to a just and effective society.

On the continent, both Germaine de Staël and Madame du Châtelet were deeply interested in scholarly issues. De Staël was critical of much of the learning of her day and decried its lack of a rational and logical base. Her biographer, Christopher Herold, disagrees with those who would call her "a novelist and literary critic"; rather, she was "a political thinker, a moralist, and a philosopher of history." Beyond that, one needs to think of the origin of her intellectual interests. Again, according to Herold,

> She was a pure product of intellectualism and rationalism. Whatever could not be rationally apprehended and expressed—music, for instance—was mere entertainment or at best, stimulation to reverie.[40]

De Staël, echoing Mary Astell, told her sisters "if you do not breathe higher air, you are nothing but a well-taught doll." As convinced as others of the need for women to be educated as serious beings, de Staël saw the end of this education as not simply women's enhanced powers of reasoning. As with Mary Wollstonecraft, she, too, was concerned with virtue. Women were to be learned so that society would prosper. She strongly believed that "to enlighten, educate, improve women like men . . . that's the best secret for accomplishing all reasonable aims, for all social and political relations." Her contemporary, Madame du Châtelet was even more aware of the discouragement of women's intellect, given her interest in philosophy and science. In her translation of Isaac Newton's *Principia*—which was an essential tool for the empirically based social science of the Enlightenment—she explained in language geared to the interests of her audience the general applicability of his discoveries. Remembered now almost exclusively for her relationship with Voltaire, she was one of the most advanced and learned writers of the 1700s in France.[41] Yet, despite her knowledge of Newton's physics and her translation of Leibniz's works and Mandeville's *The Fable of the Bees*, she still felt ill educated and excluded from systematic training. In her introduction to Mandeville's moral treatise, she included an angry assault on women's limited learning.

> I feel the full weight of the prejudice which so universally excludes us from the sciences; it is one of the contradictions in life that has always amazed me, seeing that the law allows us to determine the fate of great nations, but that there is no place where we are trained to think.[42]

She informs her readers that, if she were king, "I would have women participate in all human rights, especially those of the mind." Thus, even given the greater attention to virtue and the differing intellectual interests of these eighteenth-century thinkers, they, too, felt compelled to emphasize the need for women's serious education and the utility of reason as strongly as did their seventeenth-century precursors.[43]

In analyzing feminist writings over a 150-year period, one is struck by the prominence of appeals to reason. In tracing the origins of modern feminism, most historians have turned to demographic trends—such as the late age at marriage or the growing numbers of single women moving to London during the late seventeenth century—as providing an impetus for feminist thought. Others have looked at institutions—such as the salon of eighteenth-century society—that brought together scholarly men and women with common interests. However, I think, if we listen to the women themselves, they will point to the motivating force inherent in their exclusion from institutions of higher education and a general demeaning of their minds. During the seventeenth century, Astell and others were strongly influenced by Descartes; later, eighteenth-century writers were in alliance with Enlightenment values. But it was not one set of ideas or a single intellectual influence that was key to their feminist arguments: it was, rather, a need to address the intellectual ill-treatment of their sex. Wherever they wrote, in poems, in introductions to scientific works, in response to sexist sermons, and even in introductions to cookbooks, they took occasion to remind the world that they, and other women, were working under a tremendous, but remediable, burden. That burden, in their minds, was never simply exclusion from formal education; it was, as well, always having their abilities questioned and their interests predetermined.

Today's feminists do not as easily view rational thought as a liberating process for women. They have come to be more concerned with the mode of learning—and with its sex-linked qualities—than male control over, and women's exclusion from, the fact or the place of learning. But, in raising serious and legitimate questions about how male-identified values are attached to discussions of reason, current scholars should remember that in the past and for many girls and women today the use of their minds—beyond the romances, the advertising, and the guidebooks on mothering, fashion, and household management—is as much a breath of fresh air, and a personally empowering act, as questioning reason itself may be for others. If control of our bodies is the current rallying cry, then the use of our minds was the feminist theme resonating throughout the 1600s and 1700s.

NOTES

1. Antonia Fraser, *The Weaker Vessel* (New York: Alfred A. Knopf, 1984). In her prologue, Fraser discusses the origins of the term *weaker vessel*; its widespread use during the seventeenth century makes clear the unified vision of women's physical and mental incapacities (1–6).

2. C. V. Wedgewood, *The King's Peace, 1637–1641* (New York: Macmillan, 1956), 441. Wedgewood builds the case for the public's attention being riveted on the Catholic faction, causing them to distrust Charles and link individual political, economic, and religious actions to the frightening specter of Catholicism.

3. Wedgewood, *King's Peace,* 116.

4. Although Charles's political downfall can be traced to a series of policies and events beginning with his personal rule in 1629, the manner in which many of his subjects tied these separate acts to an alliance with the Catholic faction reminds one of the continual return of authors of all stripes to women's intellectual deficiencies. Medical, religious, moral, and political essayists pointed to women's rational failings as reason for the devil's hold over them, as justification for their husbands' rule, as encouragement for desiring male children, and, generally, as an argument to circumscribe their physical, civic, sexual, religious, and moral choices.

5. For a more thorough discussion of this point, see Hilda L. Smith, *Reason's Disciples: Seventeenth-Century English Feminists* (Urbana: University of Illinois Press, 1982).

6. Anonymous, *Triumphs of Female Wit, in some Pindarick Odes; or, The Emulation* (London: Printed for T. Malthus, 1683), 2–3.

7. S[arah] E[gerton], *Poems on Several Occasions, together with a Pastoral* (London: Printed by J. Nutt, [1706]), 19.

8. Genevieve Lloyd, *The Man of Reason: "Male" and "Female" in Western Philosophy* (Minneapolis: University of Minnesota Press, 1984). Lloyd's view is not unique; it builds upon a large core of work by current feminist philosophers who criticize the development of Western philosophy and the study of Western philosophers as a masculinist activity. The distance between the known and the knower, the division between nature and reason and between thought and feeling, all take on sex-specific characteristics. Yet, this body of scholarship is problematic in at least two ways. While the reality of men's domination of Western thought is incontrovertible, to argue that reason is a sex-specific activity and that women are more easily identified with nature and feeling falls into the mother earth understanding of female nature, accepts the Cartesian mind-body split, and simply glorifies what philosophy has traditionally portrayed as subordinate emotions and natural functions. It can lead, as well, to an undervaluing of the intellectual products of women philosophers and scientists and to too great a concentration on reanalyzing male philosophers and thinkers from one more point of view.

9. Lloyd, *Man of Reason,* x.

10. Lloyd, *Man of Reason,* 108.

11. For a discussion of women's limited educational opportunities during the seventeenth century, see Smith, *Reason's Disciples,* 19–38; Josephine Kamm, *Hope Deferred: Girls' Education in English History* (London: Methuen, 1965); Margaret George, *Women in the First Capitalist Society: Experiences in Seventeenth-Century England* (Urbana: University of Illinois Press, 1988), 233–50.

12. Juan Vives, *The Instruction of a Christian Woman,* in *Vives and the Renaissance Education of Women,* ed. Foster Watson (New York: Longmans, Green, 1912), 56.

13. Much has been written concerning the limited role of women in organized religion during the seventeenth century and other periods. Two essays clarify structural changes in the family based on the religious leadership of the father that undercut equal access of women to God or to a position of authority or respect within established churches; see Christopher Hill, "The Spritualization of the Household," in *Society and Puritanism in Prerevolutionary England* (New York: Shocken Books, 1964), 443–81; Kathleen M. Davies, "'The Sacred Condition of Equality'—How Original Were Puritan Doctrines on Marriage?" *Social History* 5 (May, 1977): 563–80. More favorable analyses of women's role in the sectarian movement can be found in Keith Thomas, "Women and the Civil War Sects," *Past and Present* 13 (April, 1958): 42–62; Phyllis Mack, "Women as Prophets during the English Civil War," *Feminist Studies* 8 (Spring, 1982): 19–45.

14. William Gouge, *Of Domesticall Duties: Eight Treatises* (London: Printed by John Haviland for William Bladen, 1622); Richard Brathwait, *The English Gentlewoman, drawne out to the Body* (London: B. Alsop and T. Fawcet, 1631). Each of these works went through numerous editions throughout the seventeenth century, and there were many other domestic guides offering similar advice.

15. Gouge, *Domesticall Duties,* 303, 336–40; Brathwait, *English Gentlewoman,* 89.

16. A number of works based on misconceptions of women's health and physiological nature, deriving heavily from Greek sources, appeared during the 1600s. Discussions of these works can be found in Audrey Eccles, *Obstetrics and Gynaecology in Tudor and Stuart England* (Kent, Ohio: Kent State University Press, 1982); Hilda L. Smith, "Gynecology and Ideology in Seventeenth-Century England," in *Liberating Women's History,* ed. Berenice A. Carroll (Urbana: University of Illinois Press, 1976), 97–114.

17. *The Complete Midwifes Practice Enlarged,* 2d ed. (London: Printed for Nathaniel Brook, 1659), 288a, 290–91, 295.

18. For a discussion of educational reform in mid-seventeenth-century England and its omission of women, see Charles Webster, *Samuel Hartlib and the Advancement of Learning* (Cambridge: Cambridge University Press, 1970). For examples of works employing a falsely universal language in which boy and scholar and parent and man are synonomous, see Hezekiah Woodward, *A Childe's Patrimony Laid Out Upon The Good Culture of Tilling over his Whole Man* (London: J. Legatt, 1640); Christopher Wase, *Considerations Concerning Free Schools As Settled in England* (Oxford, 1678).

19. John Milton, *Milton on Education: The Tractate of Education,* ed. Oliver M. Ainsworth (New Haven: Yale University Press, 1928), 51–54.

20. Milton, *Milton on Education,* 57–62.

21. For a general discussion of the limited treatment of women in the *Encyclopédie,* see Sara Ellen Procious Malueq, "Women and the Encyclopédie," in *French Women and the Age of Enlightenment,* ed. Samia I. Spencer (Bloomington: Indiana University Press, 1984), 259–71.

22. *Denis Diderot's The Encyclopédie: Selections,* ed. and trans. Stephen J. Gendzier (New York: Harper Torchbooks, 1954), 92–97.

23. Agrippa von Netteshiem [Henricus Cornelius], *Female Preeminence; or The Dignity and Excellency of that Sex, above the Male* (London: Printed by T. R. and M. D. and are to be sold by Henry Million, 1670). In addition, two later, seventeenth-century popular

authors echoed Agrippa's views. See Nahum Tate, *A Present for the Ladies: Being an Historical Account of Several Illustrious Persons of the Female Sex*, 2d ed. (London: Printed for Francis Saunders, 1693); William Walsh, *A Dialogue Concerning Women, being a Defence of the Sex*, Written to Eugenia (Lady Mary Chudleigh) (London: Printed for R. Bentley and F. Tonson, 1691).

24. Thomas Hobbes, *The English Works of Thomas Hobbes of Malmesbury*, ed. Sir William Molesworth, vol. 2 of *Philosophical Rudiments Concerning Government and Society (1841)*, reprint ed. (Aalen: Scientia Verlag, 1962), 116–17.

25. See Smith, *Reason's Disciples*, 3–17.

26. Margaret Cavendish, Duchess of Newcastle, "To All Noble, and Worthy Ladies," in *Poems and Fancies* (1653) facs. (London: Scolar Press, 1972), n.p.

27. Margaret Cavendish, Duchess of Newcastle, "The Preface to the Reader," in *The Worlds Olio* (London: Printed for J. Martin and J. Allestree, 1655), n.p.

28. Margaret Cavendish, Duchess of Newcastle, "Female Orations," in *Orations of Divers Sorts*, 2d ed. (London: Printed by A. Maxwell, 1668), 238–40.

29. Margaret Cavendish, Duchess of Newcastle, "To Natural Philosophers," in *Poems and Fancies* (1653) facs. (London: Scolar Press, 1972), n.p.

30. Hannah Wolley, "Epistle Dedicatory" and "Introduction," in *The Gentlewoman's Companion; or A Guide to the Female Sex* (London: Printed by A. Maxwell for Dorman Newman, 1673), n.p.

31. Bathsua Makin, *An Essay to Revive the Antient Education of Gentlewomen, in Religion, Manners, Art and Tongues* (London: Printed by J. D. to be sold by Tho. Parkhurst, 1674), 3.

32. Mary Astell, *Some Reflections Upon Marriage*, 4th ed. (London: Printed for William Parker, 1730), 17–36. For a thorough discussion of Mary Astell's life and work, see Ruth Perry, *The Celebrated Mary Astell, An Early English Feminist* (Chicago: University of Chicago Press, 1986).

33. Mary Astell, *A Serious Proposal to the Ladies, for the Advancement of their True and Greatest Interest* (London, 1694), 2–3, 11–14.

34. Astell, *Serious Proposal*, 26.

35. Mary Astell, *A Serious Proposal to the Ladies, Part II* (London: Printed for Richard Wilkin, 1697), 44, 108–9.

36. Astell, *Some Reflections*, 37–38.

37. For two brief analyses of their lives and works in English, see Esther Ehrman, *Mme du Châtelet: Scientist, Philosopher, and Feminist of the Enlightenment* (Leamington Spa: Berg Publishers, 1986); Renee Winegarten, *Mme de Staël* (Leamington Spa: Berg Publishers, 1985). There are a number of general works, in particular J. Christopher Herold, *Mistress to an Age: A Life of Madame de Staël* (Indianapolis: Bobbs-Merrill, 1958), that devote little attention to her intellect, focus on her relationship with famous men, and concern themselves more with sexual relations than with her scholarship. One of the better treatments is *Madame de Staël on Politics, Literature, and National Character*, trans. and ed. with an introduction by Morroe Berger (Garden City, N.Y.: Doubleday, 1964). Perhaps most tragic are the sources of information about Mme du Châtelet that are embedded in the multivolume correspondence of Voltaire.

38. Mary Wollstonecraft, *A Vindication of the Rights of Woman* (New York: Norton, 1975), 4.

39. Wollstonecraft, *Vindication*, 5, 12.

40. Herold, *Mistress*, 193.

41. Winegarten, *de Staël*, 108–11; Ehrman, *du Châtelet*, 46–68.

42. Ehrman, *du Châtelet*, 61.

43. Ehrman, *du Châtelet*, 61.

Lady Oracle: Changing Conceptions of Authority and Reason in Seventeenth-Century Philosophy

Thomas M. Lennon

The research for my topic has coalesced from strands of research I have conducted in a variety of domains over a long time. Nearly two decades ago, while investigating the controversy between Malebranche and Arnauld over the nature of ideas, I became aware of a polemical metaphor whose use struck me as too obvious, extensive, and conscious to have been the mere *façon de parler* that it is for us. When Malebranche sought to ridicule Arnauld for failing properly to state and argue his views, for his biases, for his *ignoratio elenchi*, for his *petitiones principi*, for his obscurity, sophistry, and fallacy of every sort and description—in short, for portraying himself as an authority whose views need no justification—he called Arnauld an oracle. And when, in this most bitter of all philosophical debates, Arnauld sought to lay the very same charges, he riposted by calling Malebranche an oracle.[1] Once noted, this ironic metaphor began to appear all over the intellectual map of the late seventeenth century, to the point where I am now prepared to offer a hypothesis about its significance.[2]

The charge of being an oracle, it seems to me, is the charge of failing to fulfil the demands of the seventeenth century's new conception of reason. This is very obvious to me in the case of Malebranche and Arnauld, who, in exchanging the charge of oracularity, dispute the claim to the new way of clear and distinct ideas that Descartes held, or ought to have held, against the old, obscure way of ideas. But beyond this and many another intramural Cartesian dispute, the contest between the Cartesians and their many opponents, the Gassendists for example, was the same issue, writ large, about who could properly claim the new light of reason against the old oracular concept of truth.

The *crise pyrrhonienne* precipitated, for the seventeenth century, the issue of the criterion—the issue of the proper canons of acceptance. On the older canons, nothing could be accepted except on the basis of *something else*. This is the way of faith and of the oral tradition, according to which *scientia* is the interpretation of what is already propagated, having been established by the deity himself in some golden age and then conveyed from one generation to the next. Solomon provides its shibboleth of nothing new under the sun, heard in many contexts beyond philosophical, perhaps most notably in the *Quérelle*, the war between the ancients and moderns over the proper place of classical thought and expression in contemporary culture. As we shall later see in some detail, this is a conception of reason that is easily characterized, and thus easily rejected, in feminine terms. For the moment, one need only think of the Augustinian conception of philosophy as the *handmaiden* of theology.

On the new canons of acceptance, only what is ultimately *self-evident* is reasonable; indeed, reason may be defined as the faculty of the self-evident. This is a conception of reason shared by philosophers among whom there lay very deep disagreements concerning virtually everything else. For the paradigmatic empiricist Locke, knowledge is a matter of self-evident relations between empirically derived ideas. For the paradigmatic rationalist Descartes, knowledge is a matter of clarity and distinctness of innate ideas. The empirical derivation or innateness of ideas, I submit, is of less significance than the self-evidence of the ideas themselves.[3]

To make out this thesis I shall begin with a catalog of instances from a variety of contexts in which the charge of oracularity was laid in this period. The aim will be to provide not only evidence for the extensiveness and frequency of the metaphor but also the flavor of its use. I shall then attempt to show precisely what was meant by oracular discourse and how it was naturally described in disparagingly feminine terms. I shall conclude by examining the significance of this description and by indicating its surprising denouement in the period—surprising because, while the old oracular discourse was rejected as feminine, the new, transparent discourse was consciously extended to women.

The Malebranche-Arnauld polemic was not the first Cartesian context in which the charge of oracularity was laid. Nearly thirty years earlier, the Anglican apologist, Meric Casaubon, published *A Treatise Concerning Enthusiasm* (1655), in which he described Descartes as an enthusiast in the strict sense of the term and classified him with Teresa of Avila, among other mystics and alleged religious fanatics.[4] In a text from 1667 that has just been published under the title *On Learning,* Casaubon reported on Gassendi's *Disquisitio Metaphysica,* a ponderous rebuttal of Descartes's replies to his objections to the *Meditations:* "More need not be said by any man to show the vanitie, futilitie, nugacitie, of the confident, if not brainsick . . . undertaker."[5] He goes on to describe Descartes's "conceit, and presumption, to cast all philosophie into a new mould, and to proclaim himself the Oracle of the world. He doth not use these very words, and what he saith, he doth qualifie with a forte, but I think I doe not misreport his sense. . . . "[6]

The charge of oracularity was not confined to Cartesian debates or even to criticisms of Cartesianism. Jean-Baptiste de La Grange was perhaps the ablest defender of Aristotelianism in France during the latter half of the seventeenth century. (Surprisingly, La Grange was a member of the Oratory, which for the most part was a bastion of Cartesianism.) In *Les principes de la philosophie contre les nouveaux philosophes . . .* (1675), La Grange defended what he called the "ordinary" or "common philosophy taught in the academies of Europe for the previous 600 years." Descartes, of course, is subjected to systematic criticism (for espousing the creation of the eternal verities, thought as the essence of the mind, extension as the essence of body, etc.) but so is his chief rival, Gassendi, who is attacked for his views on the soul, on substantial form, on gravity, and so forth. According to La Grange, Gassendi would have done better to follow his own genius and give his own opinions rather than hanging on the doctrines of Epicurus as if interpreting an oracle.[7]

In *La philosophie divisée en toutes ses parties, établie sur les principes evidents & des nouveaux auteurs; et principalement des Peripateticiens et de Descartes* (1654), Jacques Du Roure, on the other hand, advanced what came to be called *la philosophie novantique.* The *novantique* thesis that there is really nothing new under the sun was here employed, however disingenuously, as a strategy to defend the new philosophy of Descartes as not substantively different from the old philosophy of Plato and Aristotle. If there is a difference, it is that "[Descartes] did not make a secret of his philosophy and taught clearly what the others perhaps said, but said obscurely in the oracular fashion of their time and country."[8]

Nor was it only in France that the charge of oracularity was being laid. As late as 1713, the English deist, Anthony Collins, for example, was still arguing the new universal, antiauthoritarian concept of reason by contrast with the old historical practice of the oracle. In his *Discourse of Free-thinking* of that year, he defended freethinking, which he defines in rather positivisitic terms as "the Use of the Understanding, in endeavoring to find out the Meaning of any Proposition whatsoever, in considering the nature of the Evidence for or against it, and in judging of it according to the seeming Force or Weakness of the Evidence."[9] Freethinking is like what he calls freeseeing, or looking and seeing something for ourselves. The alternative to this is to be told what we can all see for ourselves, eye-sight faith, which is determined by the fraudulent authority of others whose sight is no better than our own. Such a situation is preposterous with regard to sight; it ought to be with regard to reason but historically is not, and the first example he gives is that of the oracles. "The Whole Affair of *Oracles* . . . was nothing else but the Artifice of Priests to impose on the Senses of the People. The *Oracular Temples* or *Churches* were built in mountainous Countries, where of course there were abundance of Caverns and Holes, and where Ecchoes, Noises, and dismal Prospects struck those who visited them with a superstitious awe."[10]

Such an obvious deistic insinuation was not likely to go unchallenged by the defenders of orthodox revelation. Richard Bentley replied in his *Remarks* on Collins's book of the same year, drawing attention to Collins's pairing of *Churches* with *Oracular Temples* and to the substitutability of *Christian Creed* for *Confession of Eye-sight Faith*. According to Bentley, Collins thus employs the same hocus-pocus to accuse the Christians of the hocus-pocus they had attributed to the pagan oracles.[11] To undo Collins's argument, which however surreptitious is nonetheless consistent, Bentley lamely argues that the pagan superstitions with which Collins smears the Christians were not believed by anyone. That is, the preseventeenth-century rule of acceptance is still acceptable. Why? Because the argument for rejecting *its* predecessor, which would also undo it, was not needed in the first place. Oracularity has never had sway, and, a fortiori, never has had sway among orthodox Christians. Still later, in *The Procedure, Extent, and Limits of Human Understanding* (1728), Peter Browne attacked the source of Collins's and others' deism; he disparagingly referred to Locke as "The Standard and Oracle of Ideas in our Age."[12]

At this point we might profitably break off the catalog of instances of alleged oracularity to raise the question of why this rhetorical device should gain such currency in the period. One explanation might be that the oracles, themselves, had become an object of historical study and that this study provided and disseminated the rhetorical imagery. The most notable historical study of the oracles was undoubtedly Fontenelle's *Histoire des oracles* (1687). His aim there was "to attack the common view (1) that the oracles were attributable to demons and (2) that they ceased with the coming of Christ."[13] To achieve this aim, Fontenelle gives a history of the oracles: "their origin, their course, the different ways in which they were conveyed and finally their decline."[14] This history reveals that the seventeenth century attributes the oracles to demons because earlier Christian writers did so, and the latter did so basically for three reasons, all open to straightforward refutation: (1) the testimony of authors such as Eusebius;[15] (2) as an explanation of pagan miracles;[16] and (3) because the philosophy of Plato, itself congenial with Christianity, admitted demons, if not the evil ones elaborated by later Platonists.[17] In addition, "in the system of oracles as delivered by demons there is something of the marvellous [*il y a du merveilleux*] and from the least study of the human mind the effect on it of the marvellous is well known."[18] Having upset the basis for belief in demon-animated oracles, Fontenelle is thus able to argue that there was no special reason why the oracles would have ceased with the coming of Christ, that the overwhelming evidence is that they finally ceased only with the abolition of heathenism beginning with Constantine, and that their disappearance was inevitable on independent grounds, for the oracles relied on the deceits of the priests and the credulity of the people, both of which were undone by philosophy.[19]

How is it that the future secretary in perpetuity of the Royal Academy of Sciences came to write such a work as the *History of Oracles*? One thesis is that Fontenelle's attack on the oracles in fact represents an attack on Christianity. Such was certainly the view of Fontenelle's early, bitter critic, the Jesuit polemicist, Baltus. More recently, Lévy-Bruhl argued that, to reveal Fontenelle's hostility to Christianity, one has only to substitute the word *miracles* for *oracles* in his various arguments.[20] The thrust of this thesis seems to me undeniably cogent; Fontenelle is clearly intent on the extirpation of superstition and credulity, wherever they may occur, not excepting the Church—*il y a du merveilleux*. The only question concerns how far the thesis extends—a question that, in turn, mobilizes the whole issue of fideism that Popkin, for example, has debated with Pintard. To what extent are the claims of skepticism compatible with religious faith in people like Gassendi and Bayle? To what extent

might skeptical argument, in fact, be the ally of faith, as it was for La
Mothe Le Vayer for example, by weeding the mind of the pretences of
reason in order that it might fruitfully receive the seed of faith?[21] This
is not an implausible account of Fontenelle's position.[22] But even if we
reject it altogether and instead read Fontenelle's skepticism in Humean
or atheistic terms, there remains the problem of why so popular a writer
should fasten on so obscure an issue, at such length, merely as a vehicle
for such a politically dubious project.

Fontenelle himself tells us that he was motivated to his project by a
book published in 1683 by Van Dale, a Dutch Anabaptist physician,
who argued the same two theses concerning the demonic inhabitation
of oracles and their cessation with the advent of Christ. So impressed
was Fontenelle by *De oraculis ethnicorum* that he first thought of trans-
lating it into French for the benefit of women, and those gentlemen
whose Latin was insufficient. But he decided that the book was too
difficult and learned for women and most men, who are more interested
in style than scholarly substance. Of such attitudes in Fontenelle and
others I shall have more to say subsequently. In any case, Fontenelle
thus produced, instead, a thoroughly refurbished version of Van Dale's
book. Van Dale's book had been criticized the year after its appearance
in a work by George Moebius, dean of the faculty of theology at Leipzig,
whose scholarship was in turn questioned by Bayle, whose *Nouvelles
de la République des Lettres* also took polemical note previously of Van
Dale's book and subsequently of Fontenelle's.[23] While Fontenelle himself
sagaciously stood above this fracas, his cause against the Jesuit, Baltus,
was taken up by Leclerc, who was joined in it by Dumarsais.[24]

It is clear from this material that a deeper issue was involved than
the superficial concern about the ancient oracles. But if the deeper issue
was not anticlericalism, what was it? For one thing, it seems to me that
these apparently historical studies are not at all an explanation of the
frequency of the rhetorical image of the oracle; indeed, I have discussed
them here only as further evidence of the period's diverse preoccupation
with oracles. If anything, the causal connection is the other way around,
as is suggested by the relevant chronology. The charge of oracularity
exchanged between Malebranche and Arnauld precedes what would
be its likely source, namely, Fontenelle, and even Bayle's account of
Van Dale's book, which would not otherwise be known to them.[25]
Malebranche might conceivably have been acquainted with the historical question by the Oratorian Louis Thomassin, who raised it at

least in passing in his *Méthode d'étudier . . . chrétiennement . . . les lettres humaines . . .* (1681).[26] But even this work is too late to explain the involvement of La Grange, for example. The earliest, barely relevant historical study that I have been able to discover is Thomas Stanley's *History of Philosophy,* first published in five parts between 1655 and 1662 and thereafter enjoying an extensive, if now largely unappreciated, influence. He published, as an appendix to the last part, a translation of the *Oracles of Zoroaster* as collected by Patricius. This is essentially a Genesis, involving the production of mind, jinns, ideas, heaven, soul, time, body, man, demons, and so on. He also produced translations of the commentaries of Pletho and Psellus, which suggest certain connections that I am about to develop. Pletho makes clear, as Patricius's text perhaps does not, that the divinity is approached only through speech of the soul, a feminine principle. "The Paternal mind, (*viz.* The Second God and ready maker of the Soul) admits not her Will or Desire until she come out of her Oblivion, which she contracted by Connection with the Body; and until she speak a certain word, or conceive in her thoughts a certain Speech,"[27] thus interrupting what Patricius calls the paternal, "Divinely nourished Silence."[28] Psellus, in fact, conceives of the soul in linguistic terms. Commenting on the same text, he says, "The Paternal Mind doth not admit . . . the Soul, before she hath called back to her Memory the Sacred Watchwords which she received from him, and pronounce the good Speech. . . . For the Soul consists of Sacred Words. . . ."[29] However this material may be stretched, it comes too late to explain the charge of oracularity laid by Du Roure, for example, not to mention Casaubon's charge against Descartes, for which it would have been the most likely source.

The full story, it seems to me, must begin with the very nature of oracular discourse, which was universally perceived to exhibit three characteristics. It was thought, first, to be exceedingly *enigmatic,* often just ambiguous; second, it was *vehicular* in the sense that the speaker as an instrument merely conveys rather than generates meaning; and third, it was, almost without exception, *spoken only by a woman.* The model was, of course, the Delphic oracle, the description of which went as follows. The prophetess, or Pythia as she was called,[30] mounted a tripod and there, influenced by vapors from a chasm, fell into a frenzy and conveyed the obscure prophecies of the Apollonian deity. The historical development of this stereotypical description is a rather complex issue; suffice it to say that it derives from, among other elements, some fanciful etymologies in Plato, a confusion in Lucan of the Delphic oracle with Virgil's description of the Sybil of Cumae, and Chrysostom's proleptic Christian misogyny.[31] The description was in place early in the Christian era and continued intact into the seventeenth century. I cite the 1688 translation of Fontenelle to give the flavor: "The _Priestesses_ were those only who deliver'd the _Oracles viva voce_, and who with a thousand Antik motions and grimaces acted the Possess'd on the _Tripos_, and seemed to rage, with the inspirations of the God."[32]

In these terms, the language of the row between Malebranche and Arnauld, which first led me to this study, begins to lose some of its puzzle. The issue between them is what Malebranche calls "the most abstract of all metaphysical questions," namely, the nature of ideas. Exceedingly technical details aside, ideas for Arnauld are modifications of the individual mind; to this view, Malebranche objects that "man is [thus] unto himself his own illumination and reason."[33] For him, our ideas are the very ideas or archetypes in God's mind, with the result that men participate in the universal Reason of God Himself, "the Eternal Wisdom [to wit, Christ] who enlightens and nourishes minds with the intelligible substance of the truth He contains...." Such enthusiastic language did not charm the analytic Arnauld, for whom Malebranche was a visionary,[34] lost in an idiosyncratic theory of ideas,[35] whose style belongs only to a "prophet, sent extraordinarily from God,"[36] and who, most relevantly to our issue of canons of acceptance, ceaselessly _dogmatizes_ by committing the fallacies listed at the outset of this essay.[37] Arnauld repeatedly complains of Malebranche's failure to respond properly to his criticisms of his theory of ideas. His response is so short— "so enigmatic that apparently his only concern was to be incomprehensible.... [I]nstead of refuting the elucidation I had given to this business of ideas or else agreeing with it, he tried only to obscure it, with his bizarre and confused thoughts, repeating all that he has said about it in other books, as if they were oracles to which everyone was obliged to pay due."[38] According to Arnauld, Malebranche fears the astonishment people would feel if they closely examined his view and so he advances it only in "an obscure and enigmatic way."[39] In reply, Malebranche accuses Arnauld of dogmatizing by inventing _new_ dogmas and of calumnies obvious to all but those who read only his books.[40] "But those who do not believe in the Oracle" will be horrified.[41]

The one feature of oracular discourse so far missing or not obvious in the rhetoric of this dispute is its characterization as feminine. There is a connection, however, both structural and historical, that also ties seventeenth-century concerns with canons of acceptance to the historical stereotype of the oracle. The charge of oracularity as enigmatic, vehicular, feminine discourse, I submit, is a historical continuation of the charge of diabolical possession. Mention of the tripod aside, Fontenelle's description of the Pythia could be substituted verbatim in any of the antiwitchcraft tracts of the previous two centuries. It is no surprise, therefore, when Malebranche effectively accuses Arnauld of witchcraft: "To have impious views and to insinuate them into others is a crime of the Demon."[42]

The interesting Cartesian background to this may, in fact, have been the witch trial at London in 1634, where Grandier, accused of insinuating diabolical possession into a convent of Ursuline nuns, responded by raising the possibility that, not he or the nuns, but everyone else participating in the trial was an instrument of the devil without knowing it. This trial was closely followed and drew an enormous number of curious spectators, including perhaps Descartes, who may have formed there his hypothesis of deception by the *malin génie*, a generalization of the possibility suggested by Grandier. In these terms, the epistemological project of Cartesianism is an effort at exorcising universal diabolical possession. But beyond this speculation,[43] two centuries of witchcraft texts connect the historical stereotype of the oracle with diabolical possession and, thus, with the issue of canons of acceptance.

The best known of these texts is, of course, the *Malleus Maleficarum*, the "Hammer of Witches," of 1486–87. The *Malleus* does not explicitly associate witchcraft with the oracle, but it does elaborate the concepts that later make the association possible. The *Malleus* correctly perceived that most of those convicted of witchcraft were women and then, "without in any way detracting from a sex in which God has always taken great glory that His might should be spread abroad," gave a long explanation of why that should be so, thus in no small way helping to establish the gender of witches convicted over the next two centuries.[44] The chapter in which this question arises is entitled "Concerning witches who copulate with Devils," and so in it we find all manner of sexual projection and phobia that would be hilarious had it not been so deadly.[45] Thus, the authors argue, distorting Proverbs 30:15–16, that "all witchcraft comes from carnal lust, which is in women insatiable. . . . There are three things that are never satisfied, yea, a fourth thing which says not, It is enough; that is, the mouth of the womb, wherefore for the sake of

fulfilling their lusts they consort even with devils."[46] But the proclivity
of women to witchcraft is also attributed to their speech.

> There are three things in nature, the Tongue, an Ecclesiastic and a Woman,
> which know no moderation in goodness or vice. . . . [Women] have slippery
> tongues, and are unable to conceal from their fellow-women those things
> which by evil arts they know; and since they are weak, they find an easy
> and secret manner of vindicating themselves by witchcraft. . . . [Woman] is a
> liar by nature, so in her speech she stings while she delights us. Wherefore
> her voice is like the song of the Sirens, who with their sweet melody entice
> the passers-by and kill them. . . . [And again distorting Proverbs 5:3–4,] Her
> mouth is smoother than oil. But her end is bitter as wormwood.[47]

While obviously preparing the way for doing so, the *Malleus* itself
does not explicitly associate witchcraft with oracles. The connection is
made explicit in Reginald Scot's tract of 1584, *The Discoverie of Witchcraft*. Scot produces an interesting etymology for the Hebrew word *Ob*,
which is translated at various places as *Pytho* or *Pythonicus spiritus*.[48]
Literally, the word means "bottle" and is so used in these texts "because
the *Pythonists* spake hollow; as in the bottome of their bellies, whereby
they are aptlie in Latine called *Ventriloqui*." Scot then relates many
instances of witchcraft in just this sense.[49] Since Scot's purpose is to
debunk witchcraft and put an end to its persecution, he exploits its
connection with oracles to expose it as fraudulent. "With this kind of
witchcraft, *Apollo* and his oracles abused and cousened the whole
world"[50]—principally through ambiguous predictions, through predictions when fulfilment depended on conditions bound to be satisfied, and
through foreknowledge of the questions to be asked. Despite what he
takes to be their patently fraudulent operation, Scot attributes their
disappearance to the coming of the Christ.

> Whatsoever hath affinitie with such miraculous actions, as witchcraft, con-
> juration, &c: is knocked on the head, and nailed on the crosse with Christ,
> who hath broken the power of the divels, and satisfied Gods justice. . . . [Scot
> quotes Zechariah 13:2 to the same effect and then continues:] It is also written;
> I will cut off thine inchanters out of thine hand, and then shalt have no more
> soothsaiers. And indeed the gospell of Christ hath so laid open their knaverie,
> &c: that since the preaching thereof, their combes are cut, and few that are
> wise regard them.[51]

The connection between witchcraft and the oracles remained intact over the next century. In a remarkable text of 1690, *Pandaemonium, or The Devil's Cloyster*, Richard Bovet explicitly identifies the oracle, specifically that at Delphi, with devil worship, which is to say, witchcraft. He cites an oracle delivered to Augustus that, although reported as early as Eusebius, is now regarded as not genuine.[52] Questioned by Augustus concerning his successor, the oracle was at first silent and then replied: "A Hebrew boy, a god who rules among the blessed, bids me leave this house and go back to Hades. So go in silence from my altars."[53] Bovet finds this announcement of Christ no more commendable than any other pagan prophecy. Citing Johan Weyer's antiwitchcraft text *De prestigiis daemonum* (1563), which classified the Pythia with the Sybils, he condemns the oracle along with the Sybils.

> Although some extraordinary Prophecies relating to the Birth of the Glorious Messiah, are to be found in some of their Writings, yet will not those excuse the gross *Daemonaltry* of the rest, any more than that Praediction of the *Delphick* Oracle before cited can be supposed to Atone for the wretched Derelictions of the *True* and *Holy God*, occasioned by the libidinous quest of the Nations after that Idol.[54]

Bovet's concern was not just with witchcraft, for by 1690 the fury of its persecution was largely spent, but with another instance of demonaltry, namely, papism. To emphasize the continuity of the Popes with pre-Christian "confederacies with the Devil,"[55] Bovet is generally inclined to emphasize the role of the Delphic priests. Even so, citing Heywood's *History of Women*,[56] he relates Iamblicus's account of Delphic inspiration as produced by exhalations and vapors (or fire) from a chasm (or cave) while the Pythia was seated in her brass tripod.[57] The gender of the Sybils, including the Pythia, and the connection of the Sybils with devil worship, are made abundantly clear by Bovet.[58]

In summary, then, regardless of the attitude taken toward witchcraft, the tendency was to associate it both exclusively with women and with the oracles. Whether witchcraft was regarded from a pre-Reformation perspective as the worst of crimes (Kramer and Sprenger) or as an aberration of orthodox dogma (Scot) or as a particularly heinous instance of popery (Bovet), it was clear that the witch was a woman and her speech oracular. Less clear is the connection with the issue of seventeenth-century canons of acceptance to which we may now profitably return.

My own is not the first investigation of prophetic discourse in the seventeenth century. Christina Berg and Philippa Berry have studied the English revolutionary period. Their thesis is that Lady Eleanor Davies, Anna Trapnel, and Mary Cary typified some dozen or so female prophets of the period in providing an expression of political resistance against the acceptance of sexually based social differences. Such expression was initially of political use to Cromwell, but its usefulness naturally declined as the revolution was entrenched, until finally it was restricted as an outright threat. According to Berry and Berg, these women posed a greater threat than any male prophet of the period, not only because their utterances tended to be more chaotic, but also because they raised the question of the gender of the possessors of *logos* or meaning. In the extreme version of this question one finds a number of women in the period announcing themselves literally pregnant with Christ.[59] The full explanation offered by Berry and Berg tends to be rather speculative, suggesting that these women impugned the accepted gender of political and theological discourse and raised "the awful, scarcely conceivable possibility that God might actually be a woman."[60] The shorter version of their thesis is:

> In what respect exactly did this kind of discourse constitute a threat? We believe that its threat lay precisely in its feminine character. By the sustaining of a multiplicity of various levels of speech and meaning, as well as by relinquishing the *I* as the subjective center of speech, the extremist forms of prophetic discourse constitutes an extremely dangerous challenge to conventional modes of expression and control within seventeenth-century patriarchal society.[61]

This thesis cannot be correct, however; certainly the perceived gender of prophetic discourse cannot have been a necessary condition for silencing it. For the most obvious prophetic movements, suppressed far more vigorously than anything discussed by Berry and Berg, were not identified as feminine. On the contrary, the Anabaptists, the Quakers, and the Camisards, or French Prophets, were most noticeably men. The Anabaptist movement (fl. 1520–35) integrally involved prophecy, was led by men, and was condemned no less by official Protestantism (Luther, Calvin, Zwingli, and Knox) than by Catholics. "The real issue [between Luther and the Anabaptists] was not infant versus adult baptism, but something that cut much deeper. It was the question whether there should or should not be 'liberty of prophesying.'"[62] That there should not be liberty of prophesying was correctly perceived by Luther to be a condition for reinstitutionalizing religion.[63] For the Anabaptists espoused theocratic resistance to all secular power and objected to tithes, institutions of property, oaths, and so forth. The Anabaptists, at least those whose names come down to us, were mostly men: the Zwickau prophets Munzer and Storch, Melchior Hofman, the notorious Jack of Leyden, and the pathetic Thomas Schuggar. An exception is Joan Bochner, burned by Cranmer for holding the view that Christ was not born of the Virgin's flesh.[64]

In the period discussed by Berg and Berry, the Quakers reproduced "some of the more disconcerting characteristics of Anabaptist prophesying."[65] Their prophecies involved denunciations delivered with an air of catastrophe in such unsettled times. "Their most startling, and not their most edifying method of foretelling judgments was to run through the streets completely naked; which was . . . an Anabaptist trick. [No less than Fox himself] is already defending this practice in 1652."[66] It was pointed out that sometimes these prophesying streakers were women; but what this means is that sometimes, and probably typically, they were men. Needless to say, such behavior did nothing to alleviate the persecutions being suffered by the Quakers.

Later in the century the Camisards engaged in similar activities, earning themselves the more generic designation of French Prophets. These were the Huguenots, primarily from the Cévennes, who, in response to the Revocation of the Edict of Nantes (1685), advocated the armed rebellion that eventuated in one of the grizzliest chapters in the history of French wars of religion. The rebellion was initially a matter of guerilla warfare in remote areas, but then came to assume a larger scale, more organized aspect beginning with the War of Spanish Succession (1701). A feature of both aspects was the role of prophets who decided questions of military strategy, usually without success, as well as the fate of prisoners, usually without mercy. Prophecy figured in the movement from the outset. Du Serre, a Dauphinois glass manufacturer, early on took it upon himself to initiate some fifteen children into the four grades of prophecy. These children went about the countryside exhibiting their enthusiasm with rather sensational results. They were of both sexes, as were the later prophets, both during the rebellion and, after its defeat, during their exile in Germany and England, where they may have been connected with the development of the Moravian brethren and Methodism.[67]

Prophetic or oracular discourse, therefore, was not perceived as a threat and suppressed because it was perceived as feminine. If anything, I submit, the connection is the other way around—discourse was described as oracular, thus feminine, because it was objectionable on much wider grounds involving the seventeenth century's new conception of reason, truth, and the appropriate grounds of belief. To describe discourse as feminine was certainly not necessary for condemning it, but it may well have been close to sufficient, given the connections I have tried to make between oracularity and the old canons of acceptance.

To conclude, I would like briefly to depict the denouement of this issue, which raises the obvious issue of the gender of the new canons of acceptance. Hilda Smith has examined, in detail, the case of seventeenth-century English feminists, that is, women writing about women in a way critical of their intellectual restriction (e.g., 89 percent female illiteracy versus 20 percent male) and their domestic subordination (e.g., men invariably controlled family finances). Her examination argues that the vast majority of these feminists were royalists and later Tories, on whom the impact of the Revolution was entirely negative.[68] This provides further evidence that the analysis offered by Berry and Berg is wrongheaded or that the cases they analyze are very atypical of the feminist literature.[69] Even more interesting, however, is the sociophilosophical basis that Smith finds for this literature.

> Seventeenth-century rationalism, particularly René Descartes's writings, provided the crucial ingredient for these feminists' proof of women's essential equality and gave incentive to work for a society where women could employ their powers to the fullest to understand truth, both godly and secular. By coming to the realization that women were thinking individuals and not a historical, unchanging species whose sexuality defined them as more emotional, weaker, and less intellectual than men, they rejected inherent sexual differences.[70]

English feminists tended toward rationalism because they did not have access to the scientific societies,[71] or to the equipment and experimental training that empiricism recommended.[72] In addition, empirical science was not of direct relevance to their problems qua women. Rationalism, however, emphasized the fixed and universal character of the human species and generally attributed to mere custom the inequality between the sexes.[73] A good example is Mary Astell, who, in *A Serious Proposal to the Ladies, For the Advancement of their time and greatest Interest*

(1694) and *Some Reflections upon Marriage, Occasion'd by the Duke and Duchess of Mazarine's Case* (1700), consciously argued on more or less Cartesian grounds that women's inferiority was largely attributable to a lack of education and proposed the founding of a women's college to remedy the defect.[74]

The situation in France was very similar to the one described by Smith for England. Because of its availability in the vernacular and its non-scholastic, relatively informal literary quality, Cartesianism was the philosophy of choice among women, especially in the salons. The salon of Mme. De Grignan was a principal bastion of Cartesianism, as a result of which her mother, Mme. de Sevigné, was led to study Descartes. Mme. de Sablé hosted another center for the study of Cartesianism, and Mmes. de Bonnevant, de Gendreville, d'Outresale, and d'Hommecour were all similarly disposed. Mlle. de la Vigne, another admirer of Descartes, was invited by his niece, Catharine, to write an account of her uncle's doctrine, and Mlle. Marie Dupré was so identified with the doctrine as to be called *la Cartésienne*.[75]

The attractiveness of Cartesianism to women in the period was not unnoticed or even unforeseen. Complaining in an ironic vein against obscurantism, Malebranche at one point claimed that Descartes's philosophy was rejected by some people because its principles are far too simple and easy. "There are no obscure, mysterious terms in this philosophy; women and people who know neither Greek nor Latin can learn it; therefore, it must be something insignificant, and [it must be] inappropriate for great geniuses to apply themselves to it."[76] As Descartes had explained to Vatier, he wrote in French precisely in order that "even women should be able to understand something."[77] Attesting to Descartes's success is the work of F. G. Poullain de la Barre, who argued *The Equality of the Sexes* (1673) on Cartesian principles. Two years earlier, *Education of Ladies* emphasized the philosophy of Descartes as the best means to exploit the reason and common sense had by everyone; his recommended reading is a textbook course in Cartesianism: the *Port-Royal Logic*, Descartes's *Discourse on Method* and *Meditations*, Cordemoy's *Distinction*, the fourth part of Rohault's *Physics*, and Descartes's *Treatise on Man* with LaForge's notes.[78] Nothing like this was conceivable under the old canons of acceptance, replaced in the seventeenth century. One looks in vain for earlier counterparts to Anne Conway, Princess Elizabeth, Christina of Sweden, or even Damaris Cudworth Masham.

The patronizing attitude of Descartes and Malebranche is, of course, only too apparent. We have already seen such condescension in Fontenelle's explanation of why he chose to make Van Dale's book available in French.[79] Despite these attitudes, however, Cartesianism introduced a conception of reason to which women could lay full claim in theory and did lay claim to an unprecedented and increasing extent in practice.[80] The charge of oracularity was used to argue against a conception of reason and truth that was thus characterized as feminine but from which women were excluded, and in favor of one to which they at least began to be admitted.

NOTES

1. There were frequent accusations of calumnious ridicule and insult, unfairness and violation of Christian charity, plain bad faith, dissimulation, deliberate equivocation, and so forth. It was also one of the longest of philosophical polemics. Arnauld's opening salvo, *Des vrayes et des fauses idées*, which criticized Malebranche's *De la recherche de la vérité* of 1674-75, came in 1683. Malebranche was still replying in 1709, fifteen years after the death of Arnauld. For more on the details of the polemic, see Malebranche, *Oeuvres complètes* (hereafter: *OC*), vols. 6-7, introduction.

2. Not all references to oracles were pejoratively ironic. In the *Epistre* of his *Discours*, for example, the Cartesian, François Bayle, said of the abbé Bourdelot that he is "like an oracle to whom the most learned of the most distant countries rush." And Bourdelot himself referred to Condé as an oracle in his *Conversations de l'Académie*. That there should have been ironic uses of the metaphor, in fact, required that there also have been honorific uses. I am grateful to Erica Harth for making me realize this.

3. The difference between the old and new canons of acceptance is also reflected by a changed conception of the deity. Before the seventeenth century, God is typically, if not invariably, conceived as the uncaused cause of everything else. With the seventeenth century, He is conceived as *causa sui*, cause of Himself, independently of everything else. It is no accident, then, that the ontological argument, moribund since Aquinas, is suddenly resurrected in the seventeenth century. Nor is it a peculiarly rationalist aberration. While Locke was not impressed by it, Robert Boyle certainly was.

4. See Spiller, *Casaubon*, esp. 66-75. Cartesian enthusiasm was criticized by a variety of opponents for the rest of the century and beyond: most notably by Locke and Berkeley, but also by the Aristotelian John Sergeant, by Swift, by the anti-Erasmian Thomas Baker, by the antideist Peter Browne, by the eclectic Richard Burthogge, and by Molyneux, among others. For the details of this criticism, which to a large extent parallels the charge of oracularity, see Lennon, *Battle of the Gods*.

5. Spiller, *Casaubon*, 204.

6. Spiller, *Casaubon*, 204-5.

7. La Grange, *Les principes*, 31ff. He also castigated the Cartesians in these terms. "In my view, Descartes and Rohault imagined that they were oracles; and, as the character

of oracles is to say things without proving them, they thought that they would debase their quality as oracles if they were to stoop to proving what they wanted to say" (402).

8. Du Roure, *La philosophie*, preface.

9. Collins, *Discourse*, 5.

10. Collins, *Discourse*, 19.

11. Bentley, *Remarks*, 24–26.

12. For more on Browne, see John Yolton, *John Locke*, esp. 197.

13. Fontenelle, *Histoire*, 1.

14. Fontenelle, *Histoire*, 1.

15. A celebrated oracle was delivered to Augustus in response to his question about a successor: "A Hebrew boy, a god who rules among the blessed, bids me leave this house and go back to Hades. So go in silence from my altars." Following Van Dale, Fontenelle subjects the alleged oracular consultation by Augustus to various kinds of criticism. For one thing, the story is not to be found in Eusebius, but is attributed to him by Cedrenus, whose scholarship and intelligence are open to question. It was Cedrenus who reported the story of the talking dog that relayed messages between Saint Peter and Simon Magus. Saint Peter astonishingly instructed this watchdog to tell Simon Magus of his presence, who no less astonishingly instructed the dog to tell Peter to enter. "This is what is called writing history among the Greeks," says Fontenelle. Also, Eusebius himself is and was known to have made mistakes. Furthermore, such a favorable oracle, if credible, would have been exploited, as it was not, by Christian writers such as Justin Martyr or Tertullian (Fontenelle, *Histoire*, 16; Fontenrose, *Delphic Oracle*, 349).

16. Against oracular demons as an explanation of pagan "miracles," Fontenelle questions the facts they were called upon to explain: "I am not so much convinced of our ignorance about things that are whose cause is unknown to me as of our ignorance of those that are not whose cause we [nonetheless] discover" (Fontenelle, *Histoire*, 33). To illustrate the point, Fontenelle describes the case of the seven-year-old Silesian child who, in 1593, grew a golden tooth, thus eliciting the most extraordinary explanations until someone finally thought to question (successfully, need it be said) whether such a dental prodigy had, in fact, occurred.

17. Fontenelle argues that such Platonic texts that are cited are not to be taken literally, that Plato's account of demons may be of a piece with the rest of his "stories."

18. Fontenelle, *Histoire*, 17. In an ethnographically interesting account, Fontenelle supposes that, while men continued to consult oracles, they may have done so without believing in them; it was the custom. "Among the pagans religion was a practice in which speculation was of no great importance. . . . [It] required only ceremonies and no heartfelt conviction" (69–70). Oracles were rejected by Cynics, Peripatetics, and Epicureans, although the Stoics believed in them. "The great Chrysippus accepted beliefs acceptable by the least woman [*femmelette*]" (80). Furthermore, not all early Christians really believed that the oracles were animated by demons but agreed that they were only for the sake of an argument against pagans; and some pagans, e.g., Porphyry, feigned belief to expose credulity (chap. 9). Finally, the oracles were open to bribery, e.g., by Cleomenes in his deposition of Demaratus, and to pressure, as before Alexander, Augustus, and Lysander.

19. Fontenelle, *Histoire*, discours 2.

20. See Marsak, *Achievement*, cii. Still later, Carré followed his mentor Lévy-Bruhl in taking Fontenelle's attack to be directed against all miracles, which Fontenelle refutes with

two sorts of procedure: (1) a physiopsychological explanation of what happened, based on laws that we know to be universal; and (2) a historicocritical effort to get the facts straight (Carré, *La philosophie*, 429 ff.). Carré supposes that Fontenelle was able to publish his book with impunity because it was part of the effort to distinguish witchcraft from other crimes. The 1670s were the heyday of Guibourg, La Voisin, Brinvilliers et al., and it was important to distinguish their superstitious behavior from their criminal activities, such as poisoning. Thus, the royal decree of 1682 that indicted the prosecution of witchcraft absent some other crime (Carré, *La philosophie*, 447ff.).

21. According to La Mothe Le Vayer, once the mind has been exposed to the skeptical juxtaposition of contradictory views and must thus suspend its rational assent, it is like "a well-prepared field, worthy to receive the seeds of heaven, i.e., its infused graces and supernatural gifts, which then cannot fail to take proper root and produce in it fruits worthy of so noble a tillage" (La Mothe Le Vayer, *La vertu des payens*, in *Oeuvres*, 5:307).

22. Marsak, for example, proposes it (*Achievement*, civ), although Popkin as far as I know has not asserted it himself anywhere.

23. It was not likely that such a topic would go unnoticed by Bayle. The first article of the first issue of the *Nouvelles de la République des Lettres* was devoted to Van Dale's book, on which Bayle claims to report only as a historian, without disclosing his own views. It is obvious, however, that Bayle takes the thrust of Van Dale's argument to be entirely successful (*Nouvelles de la République des Lettres*, March, 1884; Bayle, *Oeuvres*, 1:7). This becomes even more obvious two years later in Bayle's defense of Van Dale against the criticisms of Moebius (*Nouvelles*, June, 1886; Bayle, *Oeuvres*, 1:578–79). The only question concerns the significance of Bayle's claims that error is not improved by age, that his philosophical century requires solid proof for its beliefs, that obdurate adherence to error would portray Christians as merely credulous, and that, thus, "Religion is better served than might be thought by refuting falsehoods that seem to favor it" (Bayle, *Oeuvres*, 1:4). At least part of the answer to this question was indicated three years later when, at the end of a long and laudatory review of Fontenelle's *Histoire des oracles*, Bayle reports that Van Dale is supposed to have been asked to write a treatise showing how religious devotions associated with miraculous events at certain chapels and monasteries were nothing more than self-serving ruses. Were he to do so, says Bayle, Fontenelle would be unable to touch it. The other part of the answer involves the significance of Bayle's iconoclasm; this is, itself, the vexed question of whether, overall, Bayle should be read as a religious skeptic (Julien Eymard d'Angers), a fideist (Richard Popkin), or as the deist hero of the Enlightenment. Bayle was also a source for Moréri, whose *Dictionnaire* article on the topic further disseminated concern with the oracle. Moréri attributes the oracle's responses to the *impostures* of its priests, who manipulated the mouth of the Pythia—a matter for him of obvious *tromperie* and *fourberie* exploiting the credulousness of simple people. The coming of Christ, moreover, made no difference; those oracles, for example, whose disappearance Plutarch discussed so famously had disappeared 400 years before Christ, and those that were in operation at the time of Christ continued to operate. Furthermore, the alleged oracles that foretold the coming of Christ to their own dismay, most notably the prediction of Augustus's successor, were patent fabrications. Moréri goes even farther than Fontenelle by giving a sociological account of oracular demise, suggesting that the oracles largely disappeared due to the effects of the Persian wars. Only in a single

sentence, as if by afterthought, does Moréri attribute the disappearance of those oracles after Christ to the preaching of the Gospel.

24. See Carré, *La philosophie*, 454ff.

25. Malebranche had finished his *Réponse* to Arnauld by December, 1683. See Malebranche, *OC*, 6–7:viii.

26. Fontenelle drew attention to this work in the preface to his *Histoire*. For the relation between Thomassin and Fontenelle, see Carré, *La philosophie*, 427ff. Thomassin's thesis was that most if not all oracles were deceptions of men by men.

27. Stanley, *History of Philosophy*, pt. 19, 52.

28. Stanley, *History of Philosophy*, pt. 19, 48.

29. Stanley, *History of Philosophy*, pt. 19, 61. Before Stanley, Milton, for example, in his "On the Morning of Christ's Nativity," only repeated the received view that the oracles ceased with the coming of Christ.

> The Oracles are dumb,
> No voice or hideous hum
> Runs through the arched roof in words deceiving.
> *Apollo* from his shrine
> can no more divine,
> With hollow shriek the steep of *Delphos* leaving.
> No nightly trance, or breathed spell,
> Inspires the pale-ey'd Priest from the prophetic cell.
>   (Milton, 173–80, see also "Paradise Regained," 1.434–41)

Keith Thomas points out that part of the reform in the Church of England had been the abolition of auricular confession. This left a void in several ecclesiastical domains. For one thing, it was subsequently perceived that moral standards were thereby regrettably relaxed, as evidenced, for example, by higher rates of illegitimacy and prenuptial pregnancy—a perception corroborated by modern population studies of the period. In addition, an important vehicle for ensuring doctrinal orthodoxy was relinquished, for part of medieval confession had involved examination in the articles of faith. Finally, an important source of guidance and counsel of various psychotherapeutic sorts was no longer available; the lives of penitents were affected in more than strictly religious ways by their confessors. To fill these voids, at least partially, certain often charismatic figures among monists and preachers came to be regarded as appropriate psychotherapists. One such was the Bible translator, John Rainolds, who, because he was able to resolve doubt, was called an oracle—according to Thomas, a term applied to many of his colleagues (Thomas, *Religion*, 182–88).

30. First mentioned by Theognis 807–8; see Fontenrose, *Delphic Oracle*, 204.

31. See Fontenrose, *Delphic Oracle*, chap. 7.

32. Fontenelle, of course, continues: "But in all probability the Priests had a Warehouse of Written *Prophecies*, of which they were the Masters, the Dispensers, and the Interpreters" (Marsak, *Achievement*, 92).

33. Malebranche, *Réponse*, 50.

34. Despite the etymology, an oracle is one who speaks. Yet the etymology helps associate it with visionaries and seers.

35. Arnauld, *Des vrayes*, 182.

36. Arnauld, *Défense*, 372.

37. Arnauld, *Défense*, 373.

38. Arnauld, *Défense*, 379.

39. Arnauld, *Défense*, 355.

40. Malebranche, *Réponse*, 31.

41. Malebranche, *Trois lettres*, 256.

42. Malebranche, *Réponse*, 198.

43. First proposed by Popkin, *History of Scepticism*, 180–81.

44. Kramer and Sprenger, *Malleus Maleficarum*, question 6, pt. 1.

45. As elsewhere in the text, which also raises such questions as whether witches can "obstruct the Venereal Act," or "work some Prestidigatory Illusion so that the Male Organ appears to be entirely removed and separate from the Body."

46. Kramer and Sprenger, *Malleus Maleficarum*, 47.

47. Kramer and Sprenger, *Malleus Maleficarum*, 42, 44, 46.

48. See Deut. 18; Isaiah 19; Samuel 28.

49. Scot, *Discoverie*, 101. As to the etymology of *Pytho*, Scot relates that Apollo slew a serpent at Delphos so called, whence the Pythonists took their name (109).

50. Scot, *Discoverie*, 107.

51. Scot, *Discoverie*, 129.

52. See Fontenelle, *Histoire*, 1.

53. Fontenrose, *Delphic Oracle*, Q250, 349. Bovet's translation reads: "A Boy / Of Hebrew Offspring, whom the Gods Adore, / Commands one hence, to Hell, my proper shore; / Henceforth forebear Our Altars to implore" (Bovet, *Pandaemonium*, 40).

54. Bovet, *Pandaemonium*, 62.

55. The cults of Roman Catholicism "are the old delusions continued; whereby they drew the Ancient Pagans after their Oracles, Groves, and Pythons, &c, and the Papists now a days into an Adoration of Images, Altars, and Relicks. Still the *old Confederacy* is kept up, tho under new Forms, and Notions" (Bovet, *Pandaemonium*, 97).

56. Bovet, *Pandaemonium*, 78. I take this work to be Thomas Heywood (d. 1641), Γυναικεῖον: *or, Nine Books of Various History, Concerning Women* (London, 1640).

57. An account repeated by Plutarch, Strabo, the Pseudo-Longinus, and others, but now regarded as false. See Fontenrose, *Delphic Oracle*, 198ff.

58. Bovet, *Pandaemonium*, 63ff.

59. See the case of Mary Adams in Berg and Berry, "Spiritual Whoredom," 50–51.

60. Berg and Berry, "Spiritual Whoredom," 52. I have found no evidence of anyone in this or any other context from the period who actually said that God might be a woman. Certainly, Berg and Berry provide none.

61. Berg and Berry, "Spiritual Whoredom," 40–41.

62. Knox, *Enthusiasm*, 134.

63. An exception to this attitude was Melancthon: "I have given [the Anabaptists] a hearing, and it is astonishing what they tell of themselves; namely that they are positively sent by God to teach; that they have familiar conferences with God, that they can foretell

events, and to be brief, that they are on a footing with prophets and apostles. . . . I see strong reasons for not despising these men" (quoted in Knox, *Enthusiasm*, 128).

64. Knox, *Enthusiasm*, 126, 135.

65. Knox, *Enthusiasm*, 150.

66. Knox, *Enthusiasm*, 151.

67. Knox, *Enthusiasm*, chap. 15.

68. Smith, *Reason's Disciples*, x–xi.

69. Smith recognizes that the Quakers, Katherine Evans and Margaret Fell Fox, were exceptions to her general claim.

70. What this means is that historically women were advantaged by just the philosophy, the extirpation of whose historical influence is being called for by one line of contemporary feminist argument. Following Hilary Rose, Sandra Harding argues that feminist successor epistemology unifies the manual, mental, and emotional activity that she thinks uniquely characterize women's work. "This epistemology . . . stands in opposition to the Cartesian dualisms—intellect vs. body, and both vs. feeling and emotion—that underlie Enlightenment and even Marxist visions of science . . ." (Harding, *Science Question*, 142).

71. The Royal Society admitted 551 members in the seventeenth century; none was a woman. See Hunter, *Royal Society*.

72. Smith, *Reason's Disciples*, 62–63.

73. Thus women tended to be among the moderns in the *Quérelle*. Thus, too, does Bracken take Locke's rejection of all but nominal essences to be a support for racism. He is wrong about racism, but may be right about sexism. There is no necessary connection between nominalism/realism and toleration/intolerance—the fixed, real essence of man may include or exclude women and nonwhites; nominal essences may do likewise. Historically, however, intolerance fed on realism; if one claims there are fixed essences, one usually claims also to know them. Thus, Popper's closed society.

74. See Smith, *Reason's Disciples*, 167ff. Significantly, Astell had an important correspondence with John Norris, the English Malebranche.

75. Reynier, *La femme*, 166.

76. Malebranche, *Search after Truth*, 454.

77. February 22, 1638; AT I.560.

78. Poullain de la Barre, *De l'education*, 306–9.

79. He displayed the same attitude as the *vulgarisateur* of Cartesian vortex theory. In his *Conversations on the Plurality of Worlds*, Fontenelle explains that he

> introduced a woman [into the *Conversations*] to be instructed in things of which she never heard; and . . . made use of this Fiction, to render the book more acceptable, and to give encouragement to Ladies, by the Example of one of their own Sex, who without any supernatural parts, or tincture of Learning, understands what is said to her. . . . I shall desire no more of the fair Ladies, than that they will read this System of Philosophy, with the same application that they do a Romance or a Novel. 'Tis true, that the Ideas of this Book are less familiar to most Ladies, than those of Romances are, but they are not more obscure. (Preface)

The English translator of this work, Aphra Behn, objected to Fontenelle's condescension, admitting that while he allows the Marchioness "some very learned observations, she also says many silly things" (Smith, *Reason's Disciples*, 63).

80. This was true of the Cartesians despite their generally authoritarian position relative to that of their empiricist opponents, particularly the Gassendists, in the latter half of the century. Hilda Smith argues that, in England, Hobbes and Locke effectively worsened the status of women. Hobbes argued egalitarianism but only in the state of nature where, in fact, women are superior given their control over childrearing and the assignment of paternity; but in society men band together to exclude women even from the family as it came to be defined. Locke, in the *First Treatise*, argued egalitarianism against Filmer's misinterpretation of the Fifth Commandment, but then, in the *Second Treatise*, based society in the creation and control of property conceived so as to exclude women. Both, thus, based status on an exclusionary concept of citizenship as opposed to the medieval concept of position that was open to women even if only through the absence or death of a husband (Smith, *Reason's Disciples*, 57–59). The Cartesians, like Plato, were authoritarian and antihistorical, yet sexually egalitarian.

REFERENCES

Arnauld, A. *Défense . . . contre la réponse au livre des vraies et des fausses idées* (1684). In *Oeuvres de . . . Arnauld*, vol. 38. Paris, 1790.

Arnauld, A. *Des vrayes et des fausses idées, contre ce qu'enseigne l'auteur de la recherche de la vérité* (1683). In *Oeuvres de . . . Arnauld*, vol. 38. Paris, 1790.

Bayle, François. *Discours sur l'experience et la raison dans lequel on montre la necessité de les joindre dans la physique, dans la medecine, et dans la chirurgie.* Paris, 1675.

Bayle, Pierre. *Oeuvres diverses.* Hildesheim: Georg Olms, 1964.

Bentley, Richard. *Remarks Upon a Late Discourse of Free-thinking* (1713). New York: Garland Publishing, 1978.

Berg, Christine, and Philippa Berry. "Spiritual Whoredom: An Essay on Female Prophets in the Seventeenth Century." In *1642: Literature and Power in the Seventeenth Century,* ed. Francis Barker, Jay Bernstein, John Combes, Peter Hulme, Jennifer Stone, and John Stratton. Colchester: University of Essex Press, 1981.

Bovet, Richard. *Pandaemonium,* ed. M. Summers. Wakefield, England: E.P. Publishing Ltd., 1975.

Bourdelot, Abbé. *Conversations de l'Académie de M. l'abbé Bourdelot.* Paris, 1672.

Bracken, Harry M. *Mind and Language: Essays on Descartes and Chomsky.* Dordrecht: Forris, 1984.

Carré, J.-R. *La philosophie de Fontenelle, ou le sourire de la raison.* Paris: F. Alcan, 1932.

Collins, Anthony. *A Discourse of Free-thinking, Occasion'd by the Rise and Growth of a Sect called Free-thinkers* (1713). New York: Garland Publishing, 1978.

Du Roure, Jacques. *La philosophie divisée en toutes ses parties, établies sur les principes évidents et des nouveaux auteurs; et principalement des Peripatetiens, et de Descartes.* Paris, 1654.

Fontenelle, B. *Histoire des Oracles,* ed. Louis Maigron. Paris, 1908.

Fontenrose, Joseph. *The Delphic Oracle: Its Responses and Operations with a Catalogue of Responses.* Berkeley: University of California Press, 1978.

Harding, Sandra. *The Science Question in Feminism*. Ithaca, N.Y.: Cornell University Press, 1986.

Hunter, Michael. *The Royal Society and Its Fellows, 1660–1700: The Morphology of an Early Scientific Institution*. Bucks, England: The British Society for the History of Science, 1982.

Knox, R. A. *Enthusiasm: A Chapter in the History of Religion, with Special Reference to the XVII and XVIII Centuries*. Oxford: Clarendon Press, 1950.

Kramer, H., and J. Sprenger. *The Malleus Maleficarum of Heinrich Kramer and James Sprenger*, ed. and trans. Montague Summers. New York: Dover, 1971.

La Grange, Jean-Baptiste de. *Les principes de la philosophie, contre les nouveaux philosophes Descartes, Rohault, Regius, Gassendi, le P. Maignan, & C.* Paris, 1675.

La Mothe Le Vayer. *Oeuvres*. Dresden, 1757–59.

Lennon, Thomas M. *The Battle of the Gods and Giants: The Legacies of Descartes and Gassendi, 1655–1715*. Princeton, N.J.: Princeton University Press, forthcoming.

Malebranche, Nicholas. *Oeuvres complètes*, gen. ed. A. Robinet. Paris: J. Vrin, 1958–70.

Malebranche, Nicholas. *Réponse de l'auteur de la Recherche de la Verité au Livre de Mr. Arnauld, des vrayes et des fausses Idées* (1684). In *OC*, vols. 6–7.

Malebranche, Nicholas. *The Search After Truth*, trans. T. M. Lennon and P. J. Olscamp. Columbus: Ohio State University Press, 1980.

Malebranche, Nicholas. *Trois lettres de l'auteur de la Recherche de la Verité, touchant La Défénse de Mr. Arnauld contre La Réponse au Livre des vrayes & fausses Idées* (1685). In *OC*, vols. 6–7.

Marsak, Leonard M. *The Achievement of Bernard le Bouvier de Fontenelle*. New York: Johnson Reprint, 1970.

Milton, John. *Paradise Regained, The Minor Poems, and Samson Agonistes*, ed. M. Y. Hughes. New York: Odyssey Press, 1937.

Moréri, Louis. "Oracle." In *Le Grand Dictionnaire historique*. Paris, 1712.

Popkin, Richard H. *The History of Scepticism from Erasmus to Spinoza*. Berkeley: University of California Press, 1979.

Popper, Karl. *The Open Society and Its Enemies*. 4th ed. New York: Harper Torchbooks, 1962.

Poullain de la Barre, F. *De l'education des dames pour la conduite de l'esprit dans les sciences et dans les moeurs*. Paris, 1671.

Reynier, Gustave. *La femme au XVIIe siècle*. Paris: J. Tallandier, 1929.

Scot, Reginald. *The Discoverie of Witchcraft* (1584), ed. Brinsley Nicholson. Totowa, N.J.: Rowman and Littlefield, 1973.

Smith, Hilda. *Reason's Disciples: Seventeenth-Century English Feminists*. Urbana, Ill.: University of Illinois Press, 1982.

Spiller, Michael R. G. *"Concerning Natural Experimental Philosophie": Meric Casaubon and the Royal Society*. The Hague: Martinnus Nijhoff, 1980.

Stanley, Thomas. *The History of Philosophy: Containing the Lives, Opinions, Actions, and Discourse of the Philosophers of Every Sect*. 3d ed. London, 1701.

Thomas, Keith. *Religion and the Decline of Magic*. Harmondsworth: Penguin, 1973.

Yolton, John W. *John Locke and the Way of Ideas*. Oxford: Oxford University Press, 1956.

Birth of a New Physics or Death of Nature?

KATHLEEN OKRUHLIK

The title of this essay is derived from the names of two books that describe those events of the sixteenth and seventeenth centuries known collectively as the scientific revolution. The first, *The Birth of a New Physics* by I.B. Cohen, represents a point of view that is familiar, at least in its broad outlines, to all of us. The period in question is portrayed as a time of unparalleled genius, a time when the human intellect triumphed against the forces of superstition and liberated itself from the chains of ignorance through heroic exercise of the imagination. Cohen encapsulates this point of view in the book's final sentence, where he asks, "Who, after studying Newton's magnificent contribution to thought, could deny that pure science exemplifies the creative accomplishment of the human spirit at its pinnacle?" (Cohen 1985, 184).

Some feminist theorists writing about the events of the scientific revolution have been rather less enthralled. Carolyn Merchant's 1980 book, *The Death of Nature: Women, Ecology, and the Scientific Revolution,* is an important example. She describes the period in question as profoundly gynophobic and argues that the mechanistic worldview developed at that time has led to ecological disaster and to a socioeconomic order that subordinates women. The damage done to the environment and the injury to women are linked through the identification of nature as feminine and of woman as natural. A dualism of nature and culture is said by Merchant to be a key factor in Western civilization's advance at the expense of nature. She argues that, since the seventeenth century, European culture has increasingly set itself above and apart from all that is symbolized by nature, with disastrous results for the environment and for women.

Merchant pursues this theme by tracing the demise of the Aristotelian and neo-Platonic worldviews and their replacement during the seventeenth century by mechanism. The world that was lost at that time was organic in its conception: for sixteenth-century Europeans, the root metaphor binding together the self, society, and the cosmos was that of an *organism*. This metaphor was a flexible one that could function simultaneously at several levels. So, for example, nature in a generalized sense was seen as female; but also the earth or geocosm was universally viewed as a nurturing mother—a living human body with breath, blood, sweat, and elimination systems. The mother earth was able to give birth to stones and metals within her womb through marriage to the sun (Merchant 1980, 24–25).

The important thing here is not the metaphorical description per se but the normative structure associated with it. Merchant argues that the view of earth as a nurturing mother brought with it moral constraints against exploitation—as, for example, in mining, which was often identified as a sort of rape of mother earth. She cites George Agricola's 1556 work, *De Re Metallica.*

> The earth does not conceal and remove from our eyes those things which are useful and necessary to mankind, but, on the contrary, like a beneficent and kindly mother she yields in large abundance from her bounty and brings into light of day the herbs, vegetables, grains, and fruits, and trees. The minerals, on the other hand, she buries far beneath in the depth of the ground, therefore they should not be sought. (Merchant 1980, 34)

Merchant traces the changes in the metaphorical representation of nature as woman as these develop in the sixteenth and seventeenth centuries. Nature ceases to be represented so much as a loving, nurturing mother and reemerges as a lewd and lusty whore who must be exploited and dominated by the new science and technology. Some of the more notorious and most often cited metaphors are those employed by Francis Bacon, as in the following example from *De Dignitate et Augmentis Scientiarum.*

> For you have but to follow and as it were hound nature in her wanderings, and you will be able when you like to lead and drive her afterward to the same place again. . . . Neither ought a man to make scruple of entering and penetrating into these holes and corners, when the inquisition of truth is his whole object. . . . (Bacon [1623] 1870, 4:296)

A similar theme had been introduced by Bacon in his early essay "The Masculine Birth of Time," where he proclaimed: "I am come in very truth leading to you Nature with all her children to bind her to your service and make her your slave" (Farrington 1964, 62). And in "The Refutation of Philosophers," he advised that "Nature must be taken by the forelock, being bald behind. All this tardy subtlety and meticulous care after the time for observation is gone permits one only to clutch at Nature, never to lay hold of her and capture her" (Farrington 1964, 130). Merchant argues that passages like these reveal that the new philosophy implicitly embodies the view of a male knower who manipulates, dominates, and exploits the object of his knowledge.

Although Evelyn Fox Keller reaches slightly different conclusions from Merchant regarding the role of gender metaphors during the scientific revolution, she too argues that attention to these is crucial to a proper understanding of modern science. In particular, she maintains that the scientific revolution provided crucial support for the polarization of gender required by industrial capitalism. Concepts of rationality, objectivity, and the will to dominate nature supported *both* the new science and the institutionalization of a new definition of manhood.

> The scientific mind is set apart from what is known, that is, from nature, and its autonomy is guaranteed . . . by setting apart its modes of knowing from those in which that dichotomy is threatened. In this process, the characterization of both the scientific mind and its modes of access to knowledge as masculine is indeed significant. Masculine here connotes, as it so often does, autonomy, separation, and distance . . . a radical rejection of any commingling of subject and object. (Keller 1985, 79)

In a similar vein, Susan Bordo argues that Cartesian rationalism and objectivism are best understood not simply as the articulation of a new epistemological ideal, but as a defensive intellectual "flight from the feminine," resulting from anxiety over separation from the organic female universe. "The result," she says, "was a 'super-masculinized' model of knowledge in which detachment, clarity, and transcendence of the body are all key requirements" (Bordo 1987, 8).

The suggestion that sometimes emerges from this line of thought is that our concepts of rationality and objectivity are so deeply masculinist in their seventeenth-century origins that any truly feminist account of science must be premised upon their rejection. The dangers of this response, however, are very great. We surely do not wish to accept the patriarchal identification of women with nature, thereby supporting the inference that if the mechanical philosophy was bad for nature then it must have been bad for women too. Nor do we want to accede too hastily to the attribution of certain (subjective, personal, empathetic, intuitive, interactive, relational, or holistic) "ways of knowing" to women when these attributions, too, are the products of a deeply sexist culture. Finally and most importantly, we want to be able to argue that feminist theories are *better* than their androcentric or sexist rivals, in the sense of being more rational and more objective; but this hope is lost to us if we surrender, as masculinist, the very concepts of rationality and objectivity.

Therefore, I should like to look a little more closely at our seventeenth-century heritage with an eye to disentangling the various threads of that inheritance. In particular, I shall focus on the distinction between primary and secondary qualities as the site at which several of those threads intersect and an important site for the development of our notion of objectivity. My hope is to show that we can jettison the physical ontology that underlay that distinction as well as certain metaphysical and epistemological positions associated with it while retaining a fairly robust notion of objectivity. I shall then go on to examine the scope and limits of that notion, arguing that we shall do better to look for the roots of sexist science in the limits placed on rationality by irreducibly comparative theory choice, rather than in the simple exclusion of certain psychological and epistemological attitudes alleged to be characteristic of women. The first step in this procedure is to set the stage for the primary/ secondary qualities distinction.

When the Aristotelian and neo-Platonic worldviews gave way to the mechanistic worldview, it was not simply the case that the dominant scientific metaphor switched from that of a living body to that of a great clockwork. Instead, several distinct intellectual trends came together and formed a new constellation of ideas. In addition to the mechanization of the worldview, there are two developments to bear in mind here. The first is the notion of human beings (men?) as more than just passive observers of nature, but as interveners and manipulators. We have already seen Francis Bacon advocating experiment over mere observation; it is, indeed, this active interventionism that signifies the "masculine birth of time" for him. Although this contrasts sharply with the Aristotelian view, which promoted passive observation of the living organism, there are strong continuities here with the neo-Platonic or Hermetic view of the magus as one who could manipulate and operate upon nature. Conjoined with the new view of the universe as a machine, this interventionist view makes the scientist a sort of mechanic who comes to understand the great clockwork of the universe by taking it apart and breaking it down to its smallest machine parts. Organisms are perhaps best understood in terms of overall function, but machines are best understood in terms of their component parts.

In addition to the machine metaphor and the emphasis on the interventionist role of the scientist, we must consider (perhaps most important of all) the role of mathematization in the making of the scientific revolution. In some ways, the whole point of banishing the organic view of nature was to make matter amenable to mathematical treatment. Organisms are self-moving and indeterminate. Therefore, so long as nature was seen as permeated by living forces, so long as there was an *anima mundi* (or world soul), mathematical treatment of moving bodies could not succeed. The death of nature was brought about (nature was killed) in order to make possible the mathematical treatment of physical phenomena. It is true that the ontology that replaced the living ontology of Aristotle was likened to a giant machine clockwork at the macrolevel, but this clockwork also had a corpuscular microstructure that guaranteed the smooth, regular, determinate functioning of the universal clockwork.

It was believed that the smallest elements of bodies possessed a number of nonrelational, purely intrinsic, and fundamental properties that were amenable to mathematical treatment. These properties were called *primary* properties; and they included extension, mass, impenetrability, and mobility. These primary properties (and perhaps a few others) were thought to account for the real structure of the external world. Other properties, those not possessed by single corpuscles in isolation, were called *secondary* properties, and they included colors, tastes, sounds, and smells. The ultimate inventory of the universe's furniture would not require reference to any but primary properties. Reference to secondary properties could be reduced to a description in terms of primary properties, and this reduction had explanatory primacy.

This was one way of drawing the primary/secondary distinction; but it is probably not the one familiar to most twentieth-century readers. While the distinction sketched here is tied very closely to a particular physical ontology, the familiar distinction is generally couched in somewhat more epistemological terms. So, for example, one is asked to consider what happens if one hand is immersed in cold water and another in hot before placing both in a sink of tepid water. The tepid water will feel warm to the hand previously immersed in cold water and cool to the one previously immersed in hot water. The same water feels different to the two hands; and so it is concluded that the properties of being warm or cool are not properties of the object (i.e., the water) but of the perceiving subject. Those properties or qualities that are located in the independently existing external object are called primary; those that are in the perceiving subject are called secondary.

These two ways of drawing the primary/secondary distinction were made to yield the same lists of properties, but it is important to remember that their conceptual foundations are distinct. The drive to separate appearance from reality already had a long and varied history by the seventeenth century. What was new at the time of the scientific revolution was the identification of the real with the mathematizable properties of corpuscles. Representational realism was the epistemology that developed to go along with this corpuscular ontology. According to representational realism, there is an external world that exists entirely independently of us and to which we have epistemic access through ideas. In particular, our ideas of primary properties reflect real features of this independently existing world, whereas our ideas of secondary properties do not. From these metaphysical and epistemological commitments, certain methodological desiderata flow.

If science is to develop an accurate picture of reality, within this account, then it must rely upon methods that privilege primary properties and systematically screen out the secondary; only those ideas that mirror elements of external reality have a place in science. This means that not only sensory qualities must be systematically eliminated, but also any trace of emotion, value, or personal interest; for, in addition to being colorless, tasteless, odorless, and so on, external reality is devoid of emotion and value-neutral. Insofar as the methods of scientific inquiry could successfully screen out subjective elements of all kinds, they guaranteed theoretical objectivity. Originally, this meant that they ensured that the theory had an objective referent; but gradually, another sense of theoretical objectivity evolved alongside this one. An objective theory was not just one with an objective referent, but one that had been arrived at using the methods of science. These methods were meant to exclude bias, partiality, arbitrariness, and idiosyncrasy as a means of guaranteeing reference to an independently existing object; but later the two considerations (ontological and methodological) became separable. So a theory could be objective either in the sense that it successfully referred to what is metaphysically real or in the sense that it was arrived at through the employment of objective methods.

We could even go so far as to distinguish three senses in which the ascription of a property might be said to be objective: (1) the property in question is primary rather than secondary; (2) the ascription succeeds in picking out a referent in the external world; and (3) methods of inquiry designed to yield impartial and nonarbitrary claims led to the ascription.

The first sense of objectivity is tied to a particular physical ontology, that of seventeenth-century mechanism. The second is tied to metaphysical realism, the doctrine that the external world exists independently of us and our epistemic activities. The third is committed to no particular physical or metaphysical ontology. My claim is that feminist critics should have no qualms about discarding the first two senses of objectivity (which have outlived their usefulness anyway), but that the third (methodological) sense is indispensable to feminist theory and practice. Let me now try to unpack these claims.

The particular physical ontology posited by seventeenth-century mechanism is the one deplored by Carolyn Merchant as marking the death of nature and the beginning of ecological disaster. The chief source of difficulty would seem to lie in the type of part-whole relationship prescribed by corpuscularianism whereby ultimate reality is said to lie in the smallest parts of matter. This gives rise to a quite literal, physical sense of reduction. Generally, when we say that one theory *reduces* to another, we mean simply that the objects and properties of the first can be fully explained in terms of the second; but, in the mechanical philosophy, this sort of reduction goes in tandem with a sort of decomposition, a *physical* reduction to smallest parts, the properties of which are (in the ideal case) mathematizable and purely intrinsic. This particular bit of ontology has been outgrown by modern science, although the general view that some sort of physicalism is an aim of science remains. Advocating a role for holism in the ecological sciences (and, thereby, rejecting a specific brand of reductionism) does not, therefore, entail the rejection of scientific objectivity in all its senses.

A related question that remains to be confronted is whether reductionism in this broader sense (understood as a commitment to physicalism) is intrinsically dangerous to feminist theorizing. As a matter of fact, the rhetoric of debates in biology, in the social sciences, and, most notoriously, in sociobiology sometimes seems to suggest that this must be the case. When feminists argue for the importance of history and current culture in accounting for the subordinate status of women (or the subordinate status of some racial groups), they are often accused of substituting a political for a scientific agenda. Philip Kitcher (1985, 201) has expressed the problem nicely: "To deny that biology is the key to understanding human behavior and human society is allegedly to take refuge in a nonphysical 'mind' or 'will' or to appeal to a fictitious entity 'culture' with peculiar and ill-defined characteristics." In other words, introducing historical and cultural considerations into the understanding of human behavior is portrayed as analogous to reintroducing vital forces or the *anima mundi*—the very undoing of the achievements of the scientific revolution.

But this is nonsense. To say that human behavior must be understood largely in terms of history and present culture is not to say that we must introduce a new, nonphysical entity called "Culture" that has to be added to our inventory of forces. It does not require us to abandon physicalism at all but only to insist that group characteristics cannot be treated as the mere summation of the characteristics of individuals. It is true that we have left behind a particular view of the part-whole relationship that was embedded in the mechanical philosophy; but that is true generally. We have *not* abandoned, I want to argue, the search for a unified and objective account of human experience. We have simply pointed out that such an account cannot be achieved unless we abandon a particularly crude form of reductionism, already discredited in other areas.

Giving up the physical ontology of the seventeenth century does not force us to abandon metaphysical realism, however. We could remain committed to the view that there is an external reality, the structure of which is independent of all human epistemic activity, while admitting that our earlier attempt to characterize that reality failed. In this case, the second sense of objectivity would still be relevant. We might, on the other hand, maintain that Kant discredited the notion that it is possible to make meaningful reference to reality as it exists independent of rational activity. Nothing we can say about any object describes the object as it is "in itself," independently of its effect on us; all knowledge depends upon a contribution from the knowing subject. And so the clean distinction between purely objective and purely subjective properties is no longer tenable.

The important point, however, is that, in giving up "the subject-object split," Kant did not surrender the notion of objectivity; he certainly believed that we have objective knowledge. The truth of our objective knowledge claims, however, did not depend, for Kant, upon a definition of "truth" as correspondence to some noumenal reality. Instead, "truth" itself was defined in terms of the *methodological* requirement to seek systematic unity in nature (Okruhlik 1986). Thus, the objectivity that Kant embraced fits nicely under the third of the three senses in the preceding discussion.

Contemporary philosophers of science who are sympathetic to Kant's rejection of metaphysical realism do not usually follow him in trying to establish an ahistorical and universal framework for objective knowledge claims, but they do seek a methodological (rather than ontological) basis for objectivity. Generally, they find it in the rigorous application of the prevailing canons of scientific theory acceptance, maintaining that the search for objective accounts of human experience can continue so long as it is recognized that the objectivity being sought is modest, in the sense that it is only objectivity-for-human-beings.

Feminist critics, however, may scoff at this claim and argue that even the ideal of objectivity-for-human-beings is a masculine illusion, which has contributed to the subordination of women as well as the poor and a variety of racial groups. Even this allegedly modest conception of objectivity is far too pretentious because it has allowed scientists to deny their own biases and to ignore the centrality of lived experience.

This last phrase, "the centrality of lived experience," is bound to cause trouble for those who pride themselves on being hard-headed and analytic. But it can be understood in two ways: as referring to the lived experience of the human subject who is being studied by the social scientist, for example (i.e., the lived experience of the known, the object of the knowledge), or to the lived experience of the knower, the subject of the knowledge. It is the first sense that Elizabeth Fee has in mind in the following passage.

> The relationship of scientific authority to the population, or expert to nonexpert, is one of an immense and protected distance. It parallels the privileged relationship of the producer of knowledge, the subject, to the object of knowledge: the knowing mind is active, the object of knowledge entirely passive. This relationship of domination has been immensely productive in allowing the manipulation and transformation of natural processes to serve particular human ends; when transferred to the social sciences, it also serves as a justification for the attempted manipulation of human beings as the passive objects of social engineering. Women, who have already been defined

as natural objects in relation to man, and who have been viewed traditionally as passive, have special reason to question the political power relation expressed in this epistemological distancing. The subject/object split legitimizes the logic of domination of nature; it can also legitimate the domination of man by man, and woman by man. (Fee 1981, 386)

Here the problem is that methods appropriate for an impartial and complete understanding of inanimate objects are not appropriate for an impartial and complete understanding of conscious objects. To treat centers of consciousness as if they were objects is to fail to be objective in the methodologically defined sense, to ignore the lived experience of research subjects is to fail epistemically as well as morally. Objectivity, in this case, demands that we take subjectivity into account. The problem here stems not so much from the seventeenth-century distinction between subject and object as from later problems introduced by the rise of positivism and the growth of the social sciences in the nineteenth and twentieth centuries.

Let me turn my attention, therefore, to the second question: whether the lived experience of the knower, the epistemological agent, influences the content of science. The traditional story is that the scientific method, rigorously applied, allows the content of science to transcend biases of time, place, gender, race, politics, and so on. I have argued at length elsewhere (Okruhlik 1984) that this notion must be modified in the light of feminist and other critiques; because I think the point is an important one and relevant to the current discussion, I shall summarize it here briefly.

Traditionally, philosophy of science has been quite willing to grant that social and psychological factors (including, perhaps, gender) play a role in science; but that role has been a strictly delimited one, contained entirely within the so-called context of discovery or, alternatively, within those episodes called "bad science" in which the canons of rationality were clearly violated in favor of other interests (the Lysenko Affair is a standard example here).

In the context of discovery or theory generation, says the traditional story, anything goes: the source of one's hypotheses is epistemically irrelevant; all that matters is the context of justification. If you arrived at your hypothesis by reading tea leaves, it does not matter so long as the hypothesis is confirmed or corroborated in the context of justification. You test the hypothesis in the tribunal of nature and, if it holds up, then you are justified in holding on to it—whatever its origins. The idea here is that the canons of scientific theory choice supply a sort of filter that removes social, psychological, and political contaminants as a hypothesis passes from one context to the next. This view made a certain amount of sense in the first half of this century, when models of theory evaluation held that hypotheses were compared directly to nature.

But this view, which shears the context of discovery or theory generation of all epistemic significance, makes no sense at all given current models of scientific rationality that view theory choice as irreducibly comparative. That is, we now recognize that one does not actually compare the test hypothesis to nature directly in the hope of getting a yes or no (true or false) answer; nor does one compare it to all possible rival hypotheses. We can only compare a hypothesis to its extant rivals— that is, to other hypotheses that have actually been articulated to account for phenomena in the same domain and developed to the point of being testable. So the picture underlying current debates regarding theory choice looks something like figure 1.

Each of the nodes is meant to represent a decision point at which the scientist must choose among alternative rivals. Methodological objectivists argue that as long as the proper machinery of theory assessment is brought to bear at each of the nodes, the rationality of science is preserved. How the nodes were generated in the first place is irrelevant, as long as the right decisions are made at each juncture. There may be interesting sociological stories to tell about the generation of the various alternative hypotheses, but sociological influences are effectively screened from affecting the content of science by the decision procedure operating at the nodes. This procedure will tell us which theory is preferable to its extant rivals on purely objective grounds.

My point, however, is that this procedure, even if it operates perfectly, will not insulate the content of science from sociological influences once we grant that these influences do affect theory generation. If our choice among rivals is irreducibly comparative, as it is in this model, then scientific methodology cannot guarantee (even in the most optimistic scenario) that the preferred theory is true—only that it is epistemically superior to the other actually available contenders. But if all these contenders have been affected by sociological factors, nothing in the appraisal machinery will completely "purify" the successful theory.

Suppose, for the sake of example, that figure 1 represents the history of theories about female behavior. These theories may, in many respects,

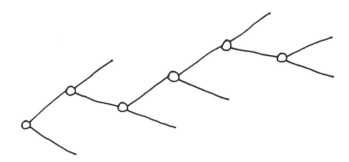

Fig. 1. Diagram representing comparative models of rational theory choice. Each of the nodes represents a point at which a decision must be made among rival theories.

be quite different from one another; but if they have all been generated by males operating in a deeply sexist culture, all will be contaminated by sexism. Nonsexist rivals will never even be generated. Hence, the theory that is selected by the canons of scientific appraisal will simply be the best of the sexist rivals; the very *content* of science will be sexist, no matter how rigorously we apply objective standards of assessment in the context of justification. It is the conjunction of the old-fashioned view of the relationship between discovery and justification with new-fangled models of irreducibly comparative theory evaluation that is untenable.

So, if my account is right, it does not necessarily follow that the presence of androcentrism and sexism in science makes rational theory choice impossible, but it *does* follow that the scientific method, by itself as currently understood, cannot be counted upon to eliminate sexist or androcentric bias from science. In light of this, we can either content ourselves with much more modest claims for rationality, understood in this narrow sense (i.e., scientific method in the context of justification), or we can enlarge our concept of rationality by reclaiming the epistemic significance of the social and political factors that inform the context of theory generation by trying to take into account the ways in which the situation of knowers may influence the range of hypotheses from among which we make our rational choices. Bacon's theory of scientific rationality, whatever its failings, was consonant with his social and political theories: just as he believed that the monarch could represent the political interests of all members of the kingdom, so he assumed that a privileged male elite could represent the needs and interests of all humanity in the advancement of science. Our theories of scientific rationality, however, reflect no progress in social or political thought since Bacon.

Bearing this in mind, let me make a few final remarks about whether the seventeenth century marked the birth of a new physics or the death of nature. Clearly it did both; but neither description will allow us to deal adequately with the relationship of feminist theory to our seventeenth-century heritage. The traditional, very optimistic account of the origins of science does little to help us understand how so much sexist theory has been able to hide behind the mantle of science. Merchant's very important account, too, fails to satisfy completely—although it raises many provocative questions. Some of my dissatisfaction stems from a failure to understand how tightly Merchant wants to link her analyses of nature and women. Her thesis about nature, that the view of nature as a machine to be exploited legitimated the destruction of the natural environment, is supported by a clear and sustained argument. One can see very well how ecological concerns might have been better served had nature continued to be viewed metaphorically as an organism rather than a machine.

The situation, however, is not so clear with respect to women. We do not want to say that whatever is bad for nature is bad for women because that is to buy into the very identification of women and nature that feminist theory *ought* to be resisting. This is not meant to denigrate in any way the importance of metaphor in the shaping of thought; it just seems that the ontology of the mechanical worldview and the new methodology of science should have opened a window of opportunity for women. At least the *literal* ontology of the mechanistic worldview was sexless and genderless (as well as colorless, odorless, etc.); and at least the *rhetoric* of the new methodology was egalitarian in opposition to the older rhetorics of privileged access. What happened to women as a result of the scientific revolution, then, cannot be understood simply in terms of changing ontologies or transformations of dominant metaphors.

We must consider, also, what happened to the relationship between women and *reason* as a result of developments in the seventeenth century. Reason became increasingly identified with the employment of the scientific method to the exclusion of a variety of earlier faculties including, for example, practical reasoning. Although, in principle, the methods of science were to have been as accessible to women as to men, in practice they were not. Women were not allowed the education, the leisure, or the laboratory space necessary to participate fully in this new form of rationality, which, as Genevieve Lloyd points out (1984, 39), became a sort of cultural attainment rather than a natural faculty. The incredible success of the new science further concentrated power in the hands of a small class of men, not because it was intrinsically more sexist or more androcentric than the earlier science, but because it was more successful. That the virtual exclusion of women from the making of modern science has been harmful to women goes, I should think, without saying; that it has also been harmful to science and to our conceptions of rationality and objectivity is one of the things I hope to have demonstrated.

NOTE

Work on this essay was supported by a grant from the Social Sciences and Humanities Research Council of Canada.

REFERENCES

Bacon, F. [1623] 1870. *De Dignitate et Augmentis Scientiarum.* In *The Works of Francis Bacon,* ed. James Spedding, Robert Leslie Ellis, and Douglas Devon Heath, 14 vols. London: Longmans Green.

Bordo, S. 1987. *The Flight to Objectivity: Essays on Cartesianism and Culture.* Albany: SUNY Press.

Cohen, I. B. 1985. *The Birth of a New Physics.* 2d ed. New York: Norton.

Farrington, Benjamin 1964. *The Philosophy of Francis Bacon.* Liverpool: Liverpool University Press.

Fee, E. 1981. "Is Feminism a Threat to Scientific Objectivity?" *International Journal of Women's Studies* 4:387–93.

Keller, E. F. 1985. *Reflections on Gender and Science.* New Haven: Yale University Press.

Kitcher, P. 1985. *Vaulting Ambition: Sociobiology and the Quest for Human Nature.* Cambridge, Mass.: MIT Press.

Lloyd, G. 1984. *The Man of Reason: "Male" and "Female" in Western Philosophy.* Minneapolis: University of Minnesota Press.

Merchant, C. 1980. *The Death of Nature: Women, Ecology, and the Scientific Revolution.* San Francisco: Harper and Row.

Okruhlik, K. 1984. "A Locus of Values in Science." University of Western Ontario. Typescript.

Okruhlik, K. 1986. "Kant on Realism and Methodology." In *Kant's Philosophy of Physical Science,* ed. R. E. Butts, 307–32. Dordrecht: Reidel.

From Species to Speculation: Naming the Animals with Calvin and Bacon

JULIE ROBIN SOLOMON

And the Lord God said, It is not good that the man should be alone; I will make him an help meet for him. And out of the ground the Lord God formed every beast of the field, and every fowl of the air; and brought them unto Adam to see what he would call them: and whatsoever Adam called every living creature, that was the name thereof. And Adam gave names to all cattle, and to the fowl of the air, and to every beast of the field; but for Adam there was not found an help meet for him. And the Lord God caused a deep sleep to fall upon Adam, and he slept: and He took one of his ribs, and closed up the flesh instead thereof; And the rib, which the Lord God had taken from man, made He a woman, and brought her unto the man.

Genesis 2:18–22

They seemed far closer than when their names had stood between myself and them like a clear barrier.... And the attraction that many of us felt, the desire to smell one another's smells, feel or rub or caress one another's scales or skin or feathers or fur, taste one another's blood or flesh, keep one another warm ... and the hunter could not be told from the hunted, nor the eater from the food.

Ursula K. Le Guin, "She Unnames Them"

The biblical narrative of Adam's naming of the animals in the garden of Eden, a prelude to the creation of Eve, is one of the pivotal documents of Western patriarchy. For when the Archpatriarch and his human subaltern come together in Eden it is to accomplish nothing less than the patriarchal definition of human being. In the epigraph from Genesis, human specificity is founded on two activities attributed to the male of the species: a species-specific sexual desire and knowing. Under divine impetus, the first man's search for a mate constitutes human being as biologically unique, as a species distinct from all others. In turn, Adam's naming does not simply discriminate among the kinds of animals, nor

merely mark them off from human nature; it crucially distinguishes
Adam as the animal that knows and names, whose species distinctiveness
is metacritical—predicated on an ability to distinguish the species of
others. While Adam's naming and desiring are distinct within the narrative, Adam's two species-defining behaviors are, nonetheless, intimately
bound. Adam is the only animal whose speciation is defined through
speculation; his acts of knowing and desiring shape one another. Adam
names the animals when seeking a suitable sexual partner; thus, his
knowing is a particular response to desire. The *Genesis Rabba*, a fifth-
century midrash, brings out the formative sexual context here, reading
Adam's naming as a euphemism for Adam's unsatisfactory sexual coupling with the animals.[1] Conversely, Adam's act of naming objectifies
what his desire had led him to learn.

To define human being in terms of masculine desire and masculine
knowledge is extraordinarily empowering for patriarchy. And it is perhaps because both are fundamental acts of patriarchal empowerment
that desiring and knowing become mutually imbricated within Western
culture. *The Epic of Gilgamesh* tells of Enkidu's acquisition of human
consciousness through sexual union, the bible speaks of Adam "knowing"
Eve, and our contemporary usage of the words *conceive* and *conception*
continues to subliminally reinforce this connection.[2] If the connection
between the two acts appears firmly grounded in the West, the character
of that connection stands forth as conflict-ridden for the patriarchal
culture that frames it. The yoking of desire with knowing raises disturbing questions over which member of the pair deserves precedence
and the consequences of that precedence. And (as I will subsequently
discuss) although the privileging of masculine desire empowers patriarchy, desire also signals a vulnerability that jeopardizes the authority
of the subject thus empowered. The difficulty of the relation between
desiring and knowing seems to burst forth in the disjointed, fractured
narrative of Adam, the animals, and Eve that Genesis offers us; the
episode consists of awkward breaks and shifts back and forth between
the search for Adam's mate and the naming of the animals. The indecisive
narrative alternately connects and separates patriarchy's defining acts of
human being. The passage seems to call out for commentary, to inspire
the sensitive reader to verbal suturing.

In "She Unnames Them," Ursula Le Guin responds as a radical feminist, undoing the defining patriarchal dictates of the biblical passage.

In place of Adam's naming, Le Guin's Eve advocates feminine "un-naming," an act that defines postmasculine humanness as the choosing-not-to-know. This Eve erases categorical distinctions between man and the animals so that the animals "seemed far closer than when their names had stood between myself and them like a clear barrier."[3] And in lieu of Adam's species-specific sexual desire, Le Guin introduces a female polymorphous perversity, an expansive sexuality that embraces scales, skin, feathers, or fur with equal ardor. There is something deeply wild, Amazonian, Utopian, and liberating about Le Guin's separatist fantasy that ends with Eve leaving Adam in the garden awaiting a perpetually deferred supper, while she freely embarks with her new, unnamed friends. But while Le Guin's separatism of 1985 provides a liberation, it also represents a loss—that of the opportunity to investigate desire's intricate interlacings with reason. Her feminist anti-intellectualism, her radical know-nothingism, effectively collapses the troubled, fissured relation between male knowing and male desire into a celebration of antirationalist female desire. The fissure is gone but not interrogated; the ability to explore its historical and ideological significance is precluded.

That opportunity vanishes, as well, in the work of contemporary feminist literary critics and theologians who do not study the interwoven narratives of Adam's search for a mate and his naming of the animals as a unit, but attend primarily to the important problems presented by the secondariness of Eve's creation.[4] This focus on Eve has been an important and necessary one for the fine scholarship of Mary Nyquist and Patricia Parker. Nevertheless, some problems do emerge from it. First, the failure to make the connection between Adam's search and Adam's naming puts feminists in the same conceptual boat as Francis Bacon, who, in *The Advancement of Learning* (1605), also fails to account for the complicated character of the connection between Eve and the animals.[5] Bacon's discursive maneuver divorces reason from desire and, thus, narratively encodes the "objectivity" of scientific method. The formal congruence between the readings of Bacon and later feminists underlines how difficult a task it is to rethink a fruitful relation between reason and desire within the intellectual discourse of Western culture. Such a reconception would involve reassessing the entrenched value of "disinterested inquiry," a value that many (though by no means all) feminist scholars have assimilated.[6]

Second, the neglect of this narrative's doubleness has prevented some particularly rich explorations. The exclusive focus on Eve's creation drains some of the episode's textual polyvalence and impedes investigation into the ways in which interested readers have ideologically exploited this narrative's complexity in the service of their own historically unique conceptions of patriarchy. The documents of Western culture that figure and trace the relation between reason and desire, between man and woman, trace, in large measure, a patriarchal history. But the history of patriarchy is, in fact, the history of patriarchies, of specific settlements and distributions of power among genders, classes, races, and numerous other social divisions. A reading of the biblical episode of Adam's naming of the animals that hopes to provide access to that varied history must attend to the ways in which particular commentators have interpreted the passage in light of their socioeconomic circumstances, political adherences, and historically framed notions about the nature of knowing.

It is to that end that I examine how two influential male figures, John Calvin and Francis Bacon, read the biblical episode of Adam's naming of the animals. Study of their opposed renderings of the passage reveals how the ideological intertwining of class and gender assumptions shape each writer's schematization of knowing. Both men embed visions of an ideal type of domestic emotional economy within their writings. For Calvin, that ideal type is father-centered, bourgeois, and focused on the proper objectification of legitimate male desire. This affective substructure undergirds Calvin's notion of proper human knowledge as interested and embodied. While some readers may initially deem my study of Calvin's advocacy of embodied knowing antithetical to more traditional readings of Calvin's "loathing" of the flesh, I hope to show that these two moments are, in fact, merely two aspects of the same sensibility.

For Bacon, the ideal family is, while father-centered, ultimately state-controlled, and focused on the proper political channeling, rather than realization, of individual male desire. Such an interpretation may conflict with other readings of Baconian science that stress the seemingly progressive and productive elements of the Baconian program.[7] I do not intend to dismiss such assessments, but rather to reframe them to reveal how Bacon goes about discursively incorporating new productive possibilities into the repertory of the Absolutist regime within which he operated. That act of incorporation comes most clearly into view in Bacon's metaphorical vision of the parasitic intervention of the Absolutist state into the family life of its most productive citizens. The articulation of Bacon's parastitic schema in its relation to Calvin's permits me to dissect the two-tiered social structure that makes up Francis Bacon's ideological regime of "objectivity." For Baconian "objectivity" is by necessity a hybrid creature, bred through the subordination of the activities of one class or gender to the desires of another.[8]

John Calvin's exegesis will be the prime mover here. For while the sixteenth-century theologian is a defender of patriarchy, his version of it remains outside the Baconian constitution of legitimate scientific knowledge. Calvin's commentary on Adam's naming of the animals is a touchstone for assessing Bacon's later reading of the episode and provides the conceptual tools for a materialist rereading of the passage that confronts the difficult relation between knowing and desire head-on.

The history of the construal of Genesis 2:18–20 is an ideological chronicle and by no means a clear-cut one. If Calvin's privileging of desire represents, as we shall see, one salient position and Bacon its opposite, most other commentators fall somewhere between. It is a history filled with implicit assumptions rather than explicit explanations, of discursive evasions rather than emphatic discourses. Nonetheless, two trends can be noted. First, construals of Genesis 2:18–20 before Calvin tend to emphasize Adam's demonstration of rationality as the essential meaning of the passage and as the distinguishing mark of human being, irrespective of his search for a mate. And second, those commentators who do discuss the search for a mate do not explicitly or suitably explain the character of the connection between the search and the naming. An example of the first type of commentary is that of the first-century Hellenistic Jew, Philo of Alexandria, who virtually eliminates Eve from his discussion of the passage, claiming that God brought the animals to Adam to kindle an "innate capacity" for knowing within him: "Quite excellently does Moses ascribe the bestowal of names also to the first man: for this is the business of wisdom and royalty, and the first man was wise with a wisdom learned from and taught by wisdom's own lips. . . ."[9]

Following Philo, St. Augustine applauds man's ability "to dominate these creatures by the power of reason and not just by physical force." But woman is more prominent in Augustine; he spends pages musing on how she is a help to the man. And he boldly claims he will make a connection between the search and the naming when he states:

> Now we must try to understand why all the beasts of the field and all the birds of the air were brought to Adam to be named by him, and why thereafter

there seemed to be a need to create for him a woman made from his side
since no helper had been found for him like himself among the animals.[10]

Yet Augustine disappoints us, thus falling within the second exegetical
category, when he provides no better explanation than that the passage
must contain a "figurative" and "prophetic" meaning.

Later commentators are equally evasive or silent on the question of
the relation between the two passages. St. Thomas Aquinas treats Adam's
naming and the search for Eve as if they were totally separate narratives.[11]
Pico della Mirandola merely mentions man's dominating reason.[12] And,
even with the Reformation, woman and Adam's search are not connected
to the naming; Luther merely lauds Adam's "great intelligence and wisdom" for "as soon as he saw an animal, he knew its nature and purpose."[13]

Calvin's sixteenth-century interpretation of the episode differs from
previous, contemporaneous, and immediately subsequent construals of
the passage not so much in content as in explicitness and emphasis. For,
while recognizing the importance of Adam's intellectual sovereignty,
Calvin does not value reason over species-specific desire as the preeminent and distinctive attribute of human being.[14] In fact, he levels the
two attributes rhetorically and thus makes explicit what is missing or only
implicit in other commentators—the disjointed connection between
Adam's search for a mate (Gen. 2:18) and the naming of the animals
(Gen. 2:19). For verse nineteen

> is a more large exposition of the former sentence. . . . For he saith that none
> of all those creatures which God had made, when a muster or viewe of them
> was taken, was founde to be a meet mate and yokefellowe for Adam: neither
> was there that affinitie of nature, that Adam might choose him a mate and
> companion of his life from out of any one kind. Neither happened this through
> ignorance. For creatures of every kinde came foorth before the presence of
> Adam: and he named them not at a venture, but of knowledge he gave to
> every one his owne and proper name: yet notwithstanding there was no equall
> proportion betweene him and them. So that unless a wife of his owne kinde
> had beene given unto him, he had been left destitute of a convenient and
> meete helpe.[15]

Calvin's smoothing over of the fissure, the abrupt narrative leap
between the two verses, conforms to his overall exegetical intent: that of
proving the unified integrity of Scripture. And to achieve this unity he
often had recourse to the rhetorical trope of amplification.[16] But Calvin's

interpretation here does much more than achieve unity. At the very least, it conflates the physical with the rational. Beyond that, however, this exegesis inverts the privileging of reason over desire implicit in earlier commentaries. By arguing that Adam's naming of the animals is but an extension of his search for a mate, Calvin suggests that human knowing is precipitated by human desire—and thus that human specificity is more a consequence of Adam's desire for Eve than of his rationality.

The free expression and pursuit of desire, while empowering, connects the self to a world of others and, in so doing, subordinates aspects of the self to that world. Calvin's reading thus exposes the profound instability of precedence and power within the activity of desiring.[17] It exposes the ways in which the desiring self is enamored of, made vulnerable to, and, thus, reformulated by the object of desire. Adam's naming of the animals in searching for a mate then signals as much the first man's submission to desire as his subordination of the animals. This dialectic of desire is suppressed in other biblical commentaries, where woman is cast as a biological afterthought—a being who emerges "after thought." Calvin, however, resurrects the dialectic by making the search for a mate the precondition and goal of Adam's knowing. The Genevan reveals Adam's desire, whose objectification appears subsequent to knowledge, as actually, though unrepresentably, prior to it. Eve or the desire for her defines Adam's speculative project from the first.[18]

Calvin's commentary on Genesis, which exposes Adam's determination by desire, topples the preeminent place accorded to reason in previous commentaries, and thus the rationalist underpinnings of the traditional patriarchal constitution of human being.[19] Reformation scholars have long noted Calvin's attack on Scholastic rationalism and his belief in the insufficiency of reason for the attaining of theological "certainty."[20] Repeatedly, Calvin reminds his readers that man "comprehendeth not God" after the fall (2.2.19) and that "we cannot comprehende so great largeness of matters," for we only have a "small taste" according to our capacity, of God's infinite "goodness, power, and wisdome" (*Commentarie upon Genesis*, 17). In his *Commentarie*, Calvin claims that the rational supports to Adam's "proper" naming are now "worn away" (75). And in contradistinction to God and the angels, human understanding is limited by a gross and dull fleshiness. Calvin lambastes the pride and vanity of men who "measure him [God] according to the preposition of their owne fleshly dullnesse" (1.4.1) and he displays a keen sense of the limited capacity of embodied knowing.

> We beholde the worlde with our eyes, we tread upon the earth with our feet,
> we feele with our hands . . . but there is such an infinite reach of the power . . .
> of God as amazeth and astonisheth all our senses. (*Commentarie*, 17).[21]

Calvin's denigration of human reason works to elevate the transcendent wisdom of God, making the Almighty the only sure and absolute measure of the universe.[22] But the denigration of human reason has more potent, paradoxical, and, for Calvin, perhaps counterintuitive effects. For the paltry insignificance of human understanding has important consequences for the behavior of Calvin's God and for the practical workings of the human world. For although Calvin reminds his reader that he is but formed from clay and should not "be delighted beyonde measure in his fleshe" (*Commentarie*, 57), it is the "flesh" that comes to "measure" and determine both God's pedagogy and the everyday reality of human understanding. It is because men are fleshly beings that human knowing must proceed from the body and in terms of material human interest. It is because humanity cannot comprehend God as he is, that God must "accommodate" himself to the understanding of men.[23]

Stated simply, the exegetical theory of accommodation maintains that, owing to the insurmountable differences between divine and human understanding, God must stoop to the level of human comprehension in Scripture to provide human beings with saving knowledge. As with other commentators, Calvin's recourse to the scriptural principle of accommodation emphasizes the enormous intellectual distance between man and God. Calvin claims that God approaches us "after the proportion of our capacity" (1.14.11).

> For what man yea though he be sclenderly witted doth not understand that God doth so with us speake as it wet [sic] childishly as nurses do with their babes. Therefore such maners of speech doo not so plainly expresse what God is, as they do apply the understanding of him to our sclender capacitie which to do, it behooved of necessitie that he descended a great way beneath his owne height. (1.13.1)

Yet, simultaneously, Calvin's metaphorical description of the mechanism of scriptural accommodation makes human knowing, in all its embodied mediocrity, the effective measure for all communication between the human and the divine. Divine accommodation to human capacity manifests itself bodily and most vividly through Christ's earthly incarnation.[24] However, the corporeal dimension of divine accommodation takes on cognitive significance in Calvin's description of the Scriptures as a particular kind of intellectual help that God offers man for his salvation. In the *Institutes* and the *Commentarie on Genesis*, Calvin pictures Scripture as a pair of "spectacles," an intellectual tool for the focusing of the human mind on God's truth.

> For as olde men, or poore blinde, or they whose eyes are dimme sighted, if you lay a faire booke before them, though they perceive that there is some what written therein, yet can they not read two wordes together: but being holpen with spectacles sett betweene them and it, they begin to read distinctlie: so the Scripture gathering up together in our mindes the knowledge of God, which otherwise is but confused, doth remove the mist, and plainly shew us the true God. (1.6.1)

While the concept of scriptural "spectacles" underlines the inherent defects of knowing through the human body, the figurative shape of the corrective visual tool—"spectacles"—conforms to the outline of the body, and its extending virtues depend upon the body's capacity to be extended and enhanced. Here, Calvin's metaphor does double service, both pointing to the insufficiencies of embodied knowing and making the body the standard of measure for what can be accomplished conceptually. Elsewhere, Calvin gives embodied human understanding more weight. For the embodied human mind becomes not only the measure for tools used to extend its capacities, but the gauge for the content of practical knowledge and, ultimately, the effective measure of theological truth.[25]

References to the bodily nature of human knowing are rife in Calvin's writings. He refers to the "heart" as "the intellectual part of the soul" and notes that the "flesh" includes "our mind and reason because they are carnal." Knowing appears as a kind of bodily "seeing" in his work,[26] and the knowledge of faith in God is preeminently a knowledge from the body.

> The seat of faith is not in the head, but in the heart. Yet I would not contend about the part of the body in which faith is located: but as the word *heart* is often taken for a serious and sincere feeling, I would say that faith is a firm and effectual confidence, and not a bare notion only.[27]

The bodily character of Calvin's notion of understanding appears again in his claim that "the knowledge of faith standeth rather in certaintie

than in comprehending" (3.2.14). Rejecting the idea that the knowledge
of faith involves a grasping, a "comprehension" beyond the bodily self,
Calvin instead figures knowledge as "certainty"—what H. Jackson
Forstman assimilates to an inner convincing.[28] Derived from the Latin
cernere, meaning 'to sift' and akin to the Greek *krinein* and *keirein*,
meaning 'to separate' and 'to cut,' Calvin's "certainty" etymologically
encodes that physical, indeed, bodily measuring that constitutes Calvin's
theological epistemology.[29]

It is in his commentary on *Genesis* that Calvin most effectively constructs the bodily nature of human knowing. For, in the commentary,
Adam knows and names the animals as other than his bodily self. The
first man arrives at knowledge through measuring these others against
the integral needs of his body and finds them unfit mates. There is no
"affinitie of nature" (*Commentarie*, 74) between Adam and the animals.

> . . . he gave to every one his owne and proper name: yet notwithstanding
> there was no equall proportion between him and them. So that unlesse a
> wife of his owne kinde had been given unto him, he had been left destitute
> of a convenient & meet helpe. (*Commentarie*, 75–75)

Adam's knowing, elsewhere presented as an incorporeal, intellective
essence, is now decidedly a knowing circumscribed by the body, its
needs, interests, and desires. Eve and Adam's desire for her come to
objectify those constraints and the capabilities of the desiring body that
both delimit and produce human knowing. Calvin rewrites Adam's
"proper" naming, the mere disclosing of true and proper essences, as
desirous human social activity. It is desire for a mate, a companion, that
brings Adam to apply his knowledge (*Commentarie*, 71–72). It is the
desire for Eve that leads Adam to acknowledge his difference from and
intellectual superiority over the beasts of the field. It is the desire for
Eve that brings Adam to self-consciousness: "whereby Adam was taught
to knowe himself, as by looking in a glasse" (*Commentarie*, 75). And,
it is the desire for Eve that leads Adam to name in accordance with his
own interests, giving the animals the "affection of subjection that they
might willingly offer themselves unto man" (*Commentarie*, 75).

Calvin's biblical commentary brings to the fore what is focal to his
conception of human understanding: that all useful knowledge, whether
of God or the natural world, is subjective, interested knowledge. It is
our subjective experience, according to Calvin, that leads us to the

knowledge of God: "Therefore every man is by the knowledge of himselfe, not only prycked forward to seke God, but also lead as it were
by the hand to finde him" (1.1.1).[30] The opening words of the *Institutes*
make the conflation of desire and reason, self and object, primary:
"Knowledge of God and of our selves, are thinges conjoyned"; it is hard
to "discern" which kind of knowledge "engendereth the other" (1.1.1).
Calvin goes on to say that "we can not plainly and perfectly know God,
unlesse we have withal, a mutual knowledge of our selves" (1.15.1).[31]
Disinterested knowledge of God is a contradiction in terms, for "what
profiteth it to know such a God with whome we may have nothing to
do" (1.11.1)?[32] Edward A. Dowey calls Calvin's brand of theological
understanding "Correlative Knowledge" and cites H. R. Mackintosh to
characterize Calvin's epistemology as

> a mode of thought which concerns not the intellect merely, but the whole
> personality of the man who awakens to it and adopts it. To think existentially,
> therefore, is to think not as a spectator of the ultimate issues of life and death,
> but as one who is committed to a decision upon them.[33]

Reading Calvin's notion of proper theological understanding as exis-
tentially derived from the body seemingly contradicts more traditional
assessments of Calvin's puritanical "loathing" of the flesh as the seat of
lustful desire. In *Calvin against Himself*, Suzanne Selinger has argued
that Calvin's notion of sin was "so extreme" that human nature itself
was equated with sinfulness.

> the unifying theme running through Calvin's censoriousness at every level of
> communal life is an obsession with sin, with the pervasive corruption of
> human nature by its carnality, with the constant presence of a bodily life
> pitted against the spirit and threatening contamination and contagion.[34]

Even human emotions are "contrary" to Calvin's notion of "faith," according to Selinger, "because they impinge upon, interfere with, try to take
control of [the intellectual's] mind."[35] Elsewhere, Robin May Schott
observes that, for Calvin, the

> corruption of the flesh . . . derives . . . from the raging of lustful desire that is
> inherent in the mortal body. Therefore, to strive against sin requires that one
> constantly discipline desires that are a natural and inevitable component of
> physical existence.[36]

Yet, the apparent contradiction between Calvin's version of embodied knowing and his disciplining of sinful desire, as Selinger and Schott describe it, is lessened, if not eliminated, by *not* equating the disciplining of human desire with its total eradication. After all, as Schott herself points out, it is a "lust . . . which overflows without measure," a "desire . . . against the law of God," an "inordinate desire," not desire *tout court* that Calvin seeks to eliminate.[37] And Selinger herself acknowledges that intimate experience and personal interest stand behind Calvin's notion of "saving knowledge." First, such knowledge is predicated on "personalism"—that is, on an immediate, "relational," and thus personal sense of living in God's presence. And second, the acquisition of "saving knowledge" is ultimately an "existential concern" inextricably bound to the character of human being.[38] For Calvin, the one true and overarching human interest is that of salvation, and it is upon that abiding existential desire that Calvin founds the intimate relation between the Christian and God as well as the discipline of faith. I would venture to add that it is because Calvin bases so much of his theology on the power of man's intimate interest in saving knowledge that he is so wary of those untoward physical interests and desires that may come to contaminate the very foundation of his vision of faith.

Calvin's existential, multidimensional mode of understanding, which William Bouwsma has labeled holistic, takes into account the complex fabric of human being.[39] Calvin's bodily mode of knowing is perhaps best considered a theological materialism. For it is his thoroughgoing materialism that permits him to explore and validate certain aspects of the relationship between reason and desire—a relationship effaced by previous theologians and evaded by the twentieth-century feminist Ursula Le Guin. And it is Calvin's materialism that finds an echo in the writing of the twentieth-century literary Marxist Terry Eagleton. For, like Calvin before him, Eagleton argues that human knowledge is necessarily a function of human interests.

> It is not just as though we have something called factual knowledge which may then be distorted by particular interests and judgements, although this is certainly possible; it is also that without particular interests we would have no knowledge at all, because we would not see the point of bothering to get to know anything. Interests are *constitutive* of our knowledge, not merely prejudices which imperil it.[40]

While in some ways materialist, Calvin was certainly no feminist.

Although he denigrated those centralized patriarchal institutions and discourses that privileged human reason, Calvin recouped patriarchy through his elevation of the patriarchal Godhead and through setting up the holistic (male) individual as a patriarchal arbiter of knowledge. Nonetheless, Calvin's reweighting of the relationship between reason and desire represented a challenge to the way in which previous patriarchal discourses—notably Scholasticism—legitimated human knowledge. Further, I would argue that Calvin's materialist epistemology, unbeknown to him, also provided an important conceptual backdrop against which Francis Bacon, whose mother was a Calvinist, would argue in his scientific writings. For while both men were intellectual reformers, Calvin's reformation of knowledge reinvests the individual knower with authority, while Bacon's scientific stricture of disinterestedness harnesses the activity of knowing to the interests of a centralized monarchical power.

English readings of Adam's naming of the animals show the effects of Calvin's influence. Many exegetes add to the traditional lauding of Adam's wisdom extended discussions of Eve's suitability as a mate, the sacrament of marriage, and thus, implicitly, Adam's desire. Bishop Gervase Babington (1596) acknowledges the importance of Adam's superior intellect, which provides Eve with "direction and abilitie."[41] But he also waxes eloquent on the institution of "mariage" and figures God as He who furnishes the means to satisfy human desire—as the provider par excellence. The Brownist Henoch Clapham (1597) speaks of how "Man / with the wisdom of his spirit / giveth names," but also describes Adam's yearning for a mate after seeing "every [other] creature mated and denominated / Ye man yet wanteth his yoke fellow."[42] For the Separatist Henry Ainsworth (1616), the "giving of names is a signe of soveraigntie" and "manifesteth also Adams wisedome." But he also acknowledges Adam's desire in describing Eve's creation as "meet and commodious for him."[43] Calvin's exegetical legacy displays itself fully in John Milton, whose Adam reveals how desire fueled his naming.

> I nam'd them, as they pass'd, and understood
> Thir Nature, with such knowledge God endu'd
> My Sudden apprehension: but in these
> I found not what methought I *wanted still*.[44]

While Calvin's authority is evident in many English accounts of the biblical passage, there appears to be an interesting exception to his influence: interpreters near to the Stuart monarchy tend to revert back to a pre-Calvinist exegesis, one that distances Adam's sovereign reason from desire. For example, Andrew Willet, friend of James I, defends Adam's "great knowledge and wisdome" and explains the presentation of the animals as a "trial of Adam's wisdom" and the founding of the Hebrew language. But, although he acknowledges that the survey of the animals was part and parcel of Adam's search for a mate, he emphatically rejects the erotic rabbinic interpretation of the passage that Calvin's exegesis reactivates.

> . . . it must be understood of the nature of man, that an helpe could not be found answerable to him . . . but impious is the conceit of R. Sel. that man companied with every sort of beast, and so could finde none apt and meet for him.[45]

This occlusion of Adam's bodily desire continues with William Guild, Scottish Chaplain to Charles I, who merely mentions that "Adam had perfect wisedome and knowledge, as may be seene in naming of all the creatures."[46]

It is likely that Francis Bacon, James I's eventual Lord Chancellor, knew of Calvin's reading of Adam's naming of the animals both because his mother, Ann Bacon, was a well-read Calvinist, and because conceptual convergences and even verbal echoes between the writings of the two men indicate that Bacon was familiar with Calvin's thought.[47] Thus, Bacon's rendering of the passage is perhaps the most telling of all the English divergences from Calvin's exegesis. Bacon first alludes to the passage in his essay *Valerius Terminus; or The Interpretation of Nature* (ca. 1603). In discussing his program for science, Bacon refers to Adam's sovereignty attained through the proper naming of the animals: ". . . (for whensoever he [man] shall be able to call the creatures by their true names he shall again command them) which he had in his first state of creation" (3:222). But it is in his narration of the passage in *The Advancement of Learning* (1605) that the full measure of his distance from Calvin can be taken. For Bacon's minute sketch of Adam's life in the garden of Eden invariably reminds us of what he has left out: the search for a mate that precedes Adam's naming. In Bacon's account, knowing, not desiring, is the first act of man in Paradise.

> After the creation was finished, it is set down unto us that man was placed in the garden to work therein; which work so appointed to him could be no

other than work of contemplation; that is, when the end of work is but for exercise and experiment, not for necessity; for there being then no reluctation of the creature, nor sweat of the brow, man's employment must of consequence have been matter of delight in the experiment, and not matter of labour for the use. Again, the first acts which man performed in Paradise consisted of the two summary parts of knowledge; the view of creatures, and the imposition of names. (6:137–38)

Adam's intellectual activity in Eden is central to Bacon's scientific program, giving cultural and religious force to his secular scientific goals. The fostering of scientific knowledge held out the saving opportunity of an approximate return to Eden, to prelapsarian perfect understanding of God's glorious works, and to human domination of the natural world. And Bacon's particular reading of Adam's intellectual activity reveals the specific character of the knowledge that Bacon was interested in advancing. While Calvin reads the narrative of Adam's naming of the animals as an amplification of the previous verse, which mentions Adam's search for bodily and social satisfaction, Bacon totally ignores the bodily impetus of verse 18 in *The Advancement of Learning* and concentrates solely on Adam's act of naming the animals.

For Bacon, man's knowledge does not proceed out of his sexual or social needs. Neither Eve nor Adam's desire for a mate figures in Bacon's version of the passage. Bacon's reading, in fact, divorces the conditions of the body from the pursuits of the mind. Ultimately, Bacon's effacement of Eve and Adam's desire for her narratively encodes the emergence of Baconian objectivity—a knowing beyond the immediate physical, psychological, and social interests of any individual.

Bacon's epistemology differs from that of Calvin's in two interrelated ways: first, in his alienation of the human body, and second, in his negative attitude toward the role of interest in cognition. Alienation of the human body is evident throughout Bacon's scientific discourse. While Calvin achieves cognitive "certainty" through an inward turning, Bacon seeks understanding through an outward grasping, a comprehension, beyond the embodied self—an appropriative discovery of the world.[48] According to Bacon, man's embodiedness necessitates the effort of self-transcendence: for man, as a "spirit newly enclosed within a body" is "allured with appetite of light and liberty of knowledge" (3:217). Alienation of the human body recurs in Bacon's use of Pico della Mirandola's myth of human origins. As Pico explains in "On the Dignity of Man," when God came to create man at the last, he found that he had nothing unique to bestow upon his new creature, having distributed all available attributes already. Therefore, the deity gives to man "in composite fashion, whatsoever had belonged individually to each and every thing."[49] Pico views man as the being who is literally not himself, whose body is essentially other. In *The Wisdom of the Ancients*, Bacon seconds Pico in viewing man as self-alienated—a being "most mixt and compounded." Yet he takes his inference further; for it is that self-alienating complexity that makes possible, in Bacon's mind, the "most admirable vertues and faculties"—rationality being the most "admirable" of all.[50]

The intrinsic otherness of Pico's man, which predisposes him to contemplation of and connection with that which is other, enables Bacon to account for the human tendency to probe and penetrate the outer world without having to introduce the more dangerous concept of material human interest. What one soon discovers is that Bacon dearly wants to conserve the more generalized and abstracted act of appropriation, the human grasping of the world that is fueled by human interest, but minus the specific interests themselves. Bacon works hard to eliminate any aspect of interested human being, bodily or otherwise, that compromises what, to him, is the pure outwardness of the search for knowledge. Thus, in *The Advancement of Learning*, Bacon rejects the neo-Platonic gesture of "making of man" into a *"communis mensura"* (6:277). And, in the *New Organon*, Bacon justifies that rejection.

> For it is a false assertion that the sense of man is the measure of things. On the contrary, all perceptions as well of the sense as of the mind are according to the measure of the individual and not according to the measure of the universe. (8:77)

The New Organon's doctrine of the "Idols of the Mind" owes much to Bacon's concerted repression of the inward, self-interested aspects of human knowing. The repression of the "Idols" is a rejection of what is intrinsic to human being—the limitations of nature ("tribe"), the idiosyncrasies of birth ("cave"), the effects of education ("theater"), and the specific character of social life ("marketplace"), both "adventitious and innate."[51] Bacon's "Idols" are partly derived from medieval and Renaissance optical theory, which maintained that all entities in the universe emitted "species," that is, incorporeal "rays," "idols," or "likenesses" of themselves that enabled vision.[52] Natural philosophers, from the Arab Al-Kindī to the English Robert Grosseteste and Roger Bacon, also maintained that emitted "species" or "idols" were the means by which all things in the world affected all other things. Francis Bacon transforms this theory of "species" effect into an epistemological concept that he then works to contain, erode, and eliminate. The "species," or "idols," those "likenesses" of the human mind, become, for Bacon, not the instrument of necessary human effectiveness—the stuff of the self that enables human beings to alter the world for their own benefit—but, rather, a distorting impediment to the achievement of useful outer knowledge.

> . . . this is certain: that as an uneven mirror distorts the rays of objects according to its own figure and section, so the mind, when it receives impressions of objections through the sense, cannot be trusted to report them truly, but in forming its notions mixes up its own nature with the nature of things. (8:45)

Thus, curiously, the very same facilities of the human mind hold out starkly opposed significance for Calvin and Bacon. Calvin maintains that interest spurs human beings on to knowledge, while Bacon believes interest stalls human thinking. With Bacon, we are a long way from Calvin's holistic, dialectical sense of human understanding. Further examination of their disparate cognitive systems is warranted if we are to understand the social and ideological significance of their representations of knowing.

One would expect enormous disparities between the epistemologies of two such different men: one, a sixteenth-century cleric's son, a French reformer, who effectively set up a theocratic state in a smallish Swiss city; the other, a seventeenth-century English statesman, resident of the large metropolis of London and Lord Chancellor of a Stuart monarchy. It is beyond the scope of this essay to account for the complicated character of those differences fully. Instead, I would like to account for the ways in which differences in their class perspectives and political allegiances, as these appear in their attitudes towards domestic desire, shape their accounts of knowing. The sensibility that I attend to here emerges in both Calvin's theological writings and Bacon's scientific texts by means of implicit and explicit assumptions about relations between husband and wife, the meeting of intimate human needs, and the management of the household.

Calvin's socioeconomic roots were urban and clerical. He was born in 1509 in the episcopal city of Noyon, France, the son of a canon lawyer who had achieved the status of city burgher on the basis of his administrative skill.[53] While intimate with the Hangest family, the leading nobles of the city, Calvin recognized his own middling status, describing himself as "a man of the people."[54] Later, Calvin's religious reformism led him into conflict with the anti-Protestant policy of the Absolutist Francis I. And by 1535, Calvin felt the need to go into exile.[55] Repressed by French Absolutism, Calvin owed his chance at practical theological administration to the citizens of the commercial city of Geneva, who had successfully struggled against the domination of the aristocratic House of Savoy. Although his relationships with these citizens were often fraught with tension, Calvin's eventual success at Geneva—at once political and theological—led the city council to offer him the status of city burgher, which he accepted.[56] Firm on questions of public order and the necessity of obedience to princes, Calvin nevertheless detested tyranny and made provisions for passive disobedience to the ungodly commands of sovereigns (he reserved active resistance to tyranny to governmental "lesser magistrates"). In keeping with the governing civic structure of Geneva, Calvin seems to have preferred a theocratic republicanism to Absolutist rule.[57]

A glance at Calvin's defense of marriage and his own happy home life recaptures the domestic expectations of a sixteenth-century Protestant bourgeois.[58] Calvin, like so many other exegetes, took the occasion of the biblical description of the creation of Eve to defend the holy sacrament of marriage, an institution "ordeined of God" (_Commentarie_, 76): "for he [God] appointed man to a matrimoniall life, not to his destruction, but to his salvation" (_Commentarie_, 72).[59] Calvin was extremely content in his own marriage, and his emotional view of his wife, Idelette de Bure, as an extraordinarily suitable helpmate, certainly resonates with his own biblical commentary. At her death he lamented:

> I have been bereaved of the best companion of my life, who, if any severe hardship had occurred, would have been my willing partner, not only in exile and poverty, but even in death. As long as she lived she was the faithful helper of my ministry. From her I never felt even the lightest hindrance.[60]

Calvin's heartfelt reminiscence resumes his domestic expectations: a wife is to be both a companion and a selfless helper, one who subordinates her interests to those of her husband. Marriage is the place within which the male expresses desire and the female satisfies. Calvin's patriarchalism is patent here, but the structure of marriage described here represents much more. The dominant position of the desirous male is evident, but the significance of female accommodation perhaps more profound. I conjecture that Calvin's compliant female harbors a good deal of subterranean material concerning the desire and capacity of the city burgher to transform the world to suit his needs through a process of objectification—of object making. The artisanal character of the vocabulary that Calvin uses to describe Eve is revealing. In the following passage, Calvin virtually accords her the title of first humanly inspired object.

> ... when in the person of the man, mankinde was created, the common worthines of the whole nature, was with one title generally adorned, where it is said, Let us make man: and that it was not needfull to be repeated in the creating of the woman, which was nothing else but the addition and furniture of the man. (*Commentarie*, 72)

Like a newly created chair or table, Eve is the "furniture" of man—a physical embodiment of his inner desires.[61] And the object-producing power accorded to the male through his possession of a compliant female is heightened when Calvin declares that the created world is God's "furniture" (*Commentarie*, 19).

Clearly patriarchal, Calvin's sympathies embrace a form of patriarchy suited to the values and expectations of a city burgher—one who viewed his world as eminently transformable, whether that transformation took the form of producing and transporting new objects, building new buildings, overthrowing an oppressive aristocratic regime (as the Genevans had), or reforming religion. Such expectations, though suitably modeled by them, can clearly transcend the polarities of gender. For, as Calvin indicates in his exegesis, Eve has not cornered the entire market on accommodation. In fact, for Calvin, transcendental bourgeois that he is, God takes the cake when it comes to accommodating Adam's needs: God is a "provident Householder" who has "furnished" the earth for Adam's use and "stored" it with all necessities (1.14.2), even to the point of commercial opulence.

> So hath he marvellously garnished the heaven and the earth with so absolutely perfect plentie, varietie and beautie of all things as possibly might be, as it were a large and gorgeous house furnished and stored with aboundance of most finely chosen stuffe. (1.14.20)[62]

The bourgeois structuring of male marital desire elaborated here informs and frames Calvin's religious thinking. For female marital adaptation models accommodation to the capacity of the embodied male intellect so prevalent in Calvin's theological epistemology. Further, this marital dynamic of suiting to the capacity and desires of the (male) individual replicates, at the affective level, a practice significant to Calvin's religious Reformism itself. Calvin eschews those forms of established church practice—confession, penance, religious "works"—that strive to adapt the Christian to the Divine, externally. Instead, he favors porous forms of worship that enable God to penetrate, by means of accommodation, to the innermost (desirous) reaches of the human understanding.[63] Ultimately, Calvinist epistemology represents one of the most important systems of early modern Western thought that recognizes and utilizes individual human desire as its motive force. This, I think, is the salient fact about Calvin's thought, irrespective of whether or not one ties that thought to bourgeois modes of managing desire. And it is this salient fact that contrasts so markedly with Bacon's self-conscious containment of individual desire within his scientific master plan for the English Absolutist state.

Bacon's courtly allegiances are unquestionable. Son of Elizabeth's Lord Keeper, Nicholas Bacon, Francis Bacon was born in 1561 within, as Fulton Anderson describes it, "the shadow of the court." Under Elizabeth, he endured slow advancement, rising only to the level of Queen's Counsel. But under James, Bacon's political career took off and he advanced beyond the political position of his father when he became Lord Chancellor in 1618.[64] Bacon's scientific ideas were shaped by his own political interests as a court official. And once James came to the throne, he cast his scientific program in a form that he hoped would gain intellectual acceptance and financial support from the reigning monarch. Assuring James that his scientific method is nothing more than the product of "your Majesty's times" (8:24) and that the whole "business" can be "done as if by machinery" (8:61), Bacon figured science in the *New Atlantis* as a mechanized process of observation and collection that would serve as a centralized tool for monarchal governance.

Bacon's principal biographer, James Spedding, assures us that Bacon's marriage to Alice Barnham, an alderman's daughter, was "peaceable and quiet," indeed, a "very suitable match."[65] However, there is evidence that suggests that the marriage was not a happy one. Alice may have been unfaithful, and Bacon left her a cool "nothing beyond her legal 'right'" in his will.[66] In his essay "Of Marriage and Single Life," Bacon dissuades those who would attain public stature from wedlock: "He that hath *Wife* and *Children*, hath given Hostages to Fortune; For they are impediments, to great Enterprises, either of Vertue, or Mischiefe. Certainly, the best workes, and of greatest Merit for the Publike, have proceeded from the *unmarried*, or *Childlesse Men*; which, both in Affection, and Meanes, have married and dowed the Publike."[67] In contrast to this negative evaluation of marriage, Bacon's description of male friendship is warm and laudatory, for though "*Princes* . . . had Wives, Sonnes, Nephews . . . yet all these could not supply the Comfort of *Friendship*." Additionally, it is only the male friend who can proffer disinterested, context-sensitive, and necessary advice: "A Man cannot speake to his Sonne, but as a Father; To his Wife, but as a Husband; To his Enemy, but upon Termes: whereas a *Frend* may speake as the Case requires, and not as it sorteth with the Person."[68]

It is difficult to read these passages without reflecting upon Bacon's own situation as a married man in search of "great Enterprises" within a male-dominated royal court, where the king doted upon male favorites, where masculine power politics was indistinguishable from male intimacy.[69] There is, thus, good reason to consider Bacon's own affective imbrication in the homosocial, if not homosexual, world of the Jacobean court. Although not discussed by the Victorian biographer, Spedding, there is evidence to suggest that Bacon engaged in homosexuality, what he elsewhere refers to in the *New Atlantis* as "masculine love." In a letter of 1593 written by his mother to his brother Anthony, Ann Bacon complains of Francis's close, apparently sexual, relationship with his servant, Henry Percy, that "bloody Percy," whom Francis "keepeth . . . yea as a coach companion and a bed companion,—a proud profane costly fellow, whose being about him I verily fear the Lord God doth mislike and doth less bless your brother in credit and otherwise in health."[70] And, Bacon ultimately left Percy "one hundred pounds" in his will.[71] The contemporary diarist Simonds D'Ewes recounts Bacon's vices, stressing his fiscal irresponsibility, but concluding with hostile sexual innuendo.

> His most abominable and darling sin, I should rather bury in silence than mention it, were it not a most admirable instance how men are inflamed by wickedness, and held captive by the devil.[72]

And finally, in his late seventeenth-century *Brief Lives*, John Aubrey openly proclaimed Bacon a "[pederast]," asserting that "His ganimeds and favourites tooke bribes. . . .''[73]

Arguably, Bacon's homosexual predilections underwrite the affective structure of his scientific vision—a vision that associates scientific error and erroneous technical production with heterosexual desire and female reproduction, and that imagines the scientific community as a closed society of powerful autonomous "Fathers" and male workers. The Lord Chancellor's chaplain, William Rawley, who comments on Bacon's child-lessness to stress the parthenogenetic capacity of the male mind, seems to confirm a reading of Bacon's scientific project as a fantasy of homo-sexual autonomous production.

> Children he had none; which though they be the means to perpetuate our Names after our Deths, yet he had other Issues to perpetuate his Name, the Issues of his Brain; in which he was ever happy and admir'd, as *Jupiter* was in the production of *Pallas*.[74]

While Bacon's scientific project may, indeed, be partially generated out of a homosexual psychosocial matrix, that overdetermination is not enough to account for all that divides the emotional economy of Bacon's scientific program from that which undergirds Calvin's epistemology. For it is not Bacon's occasional indulgence in visions of male mental par-thenogenesis that decisively separates Bacon's schema from that of Cal-vin. Rather it is Bacon's frequent repression of any act that would realize or objectify individual interest or desire that distinguishes Bacon's emble-matic emotional economy (both homosexual and heterosexual) from that of Calvin. In effect, Calvin's commodious marital felicity, so suited and immediately responsive to male need, is thoroughly revamped by the Lord Chancellor, who implicitly rejects the validity of suiting the world to individual, private desire. At times, it is desire itself that must be contained; at other times, it is only desire's capacity to realize its aims through world or object making that must be curtailed. So, for instance, while activating the language of reproductive desire in his essay "Thoughts and Conclusions," Bacon simultaneously tempers its capacity to realize by transposing its meaning into bureaucratic efficiency. Although, in the essay, he describes his new scientific idea as a "masculine birth," that bodily metaphor does not connote even a fantasy of homo-sexual objectification. For "Masculine birth" (biologically appropriately) is no birth, no creation at all, but rather, as Bacon tells us, the "better use and management of the human mind."[75] Indeed, Bacon provides his own personal, male version of uncreative creation or unborn "masculine births" in his dedicatory epistle to James I in *The Great Instauration*, where he denies his own creative input into his scientific program: "And to say truth, I am wont for my own part to regard this work as a child of time rather than wit . . ." (8:23).

As Genevieve Lloyd has pointed out, Bacon makes ample use of matrimonial metaphors in his scientific essays to describe both the proper commerce between mind and nature, and the hoped-for inventions that their conjunction will enable.[76] In "The Refutation of Philosophies," Bacon hopes to "establish a chaste and lawful marriage between Mind and Nature. . . ."[77] And, in *The Great Instauration*, he compares "the true relation between the nature of things, and the nature of the mind" to

> the strewing and decoration of the bridal chamber of the Mind and Universe . . . out of which marriage let us hope . . . there may spring helpes to man, and a line and race of inventions that may in some degree subdue and overcome the necessities and miseries of humanity. (8:46)

Yet, while Bacon seems easily to employ the marriage trope to figure those "inventions" that proper scientific practice will "produce," we must pay close attention to the multivalent meanings of the words Bacon uses. For invariably the connotations of the words used work against the idea that this "marriage" *produces* products. First of all, the fruits of this marriage are inventions, not creations. Thus, they are as much, if not more, things come upon or discovered as things made. The verb *to spring* accentuates this sense of "invention" as an unproduced, unmotivated appearance or discovery. A parallel passage in Bacon's essay "The Masculine Birth of Time" further etiolates the productive or creative aspects of this marriage. Bacon here avers that "what I purpose is to unite you with *things themselves* in a chaste, holy, and legal wedlock; and from this association you will secure an increase beyond all the hopes and prayers of ordinary marriages. . . ."[78] In using the word *secure* to underline the appropriative rather than productive character of scientific "increase," and in focusing on the "chaste" quality of the union, Bacon undercuts our sense that the coupling of mind and nature itself leads to cognitive production.

Indeed, it is at the beginning of this essay that Bacon clearly reveals the paradoxical, nonproductive productivity of this marriage and thereby

who or what is the producer of the "inventions" of the new science.
What we find is that this marriage has little (if anything) to do with the
actual production of scientific findings. For the marriage proposed is not
to be between a potent, and thus productive, human male mind and a
nubile, fertile, and nurturing female nature. Rather, this marriage is more
accurately the enslavement of an always-already fecund mother nature
to a ruling and appropriative (but nonproductive) male mind: "I am
come in very truth leading to you Nature with all her children to bind
her to your service and make her your slave" ("Masculine Birth," 62).

Yes, Bacon is interested in scientific products or "inventions," but his
political agenda often obfuscates his representation of the process by
which they are produced, and even more, precludes the imagining of
individual human beings as makers. Consequently, if at times the trope
of heterosexual marital fruition enables Bacon to articulate his notion
of new scientific practice, it is nonetheless heterosexual desire that takes
the brunt of Bacon's repression of desirous human mental production—
presumably because it is heterosexual, rather than homosexual, desire
that leads to reproduction, to the objectification of personal desire in
the world. Bacon's official circumvention of domestic desire in the rules
for courtship in the *New Atlantis* marks an early stage in this repression.
In Thomas More's *Utopia*, prospective spouses were permitted glimpses
of the bodies of their future partners before agreeing to the marriage
contract. Bacon's Bensalemites abhor such a practice as beyond the
bounds of decency. Thus they

> have a much more civil way; for they have near every town a couple of pools
> (which they call *Adam and Eve's pools*) where it is permitted to one of the
> friends of the man, and another of the friends of the woman, to see them
> severally bathe naked. (5:394–95)

Presented as a decorous solution for an indelicate moral problem, the
observing intercessors of Bensalemite courtship, presumably dispassionate in their reportage of the assets and defects of the nuptial partners,
short-circuit the flow of premarital desire.[79] Set in the "Adam and Eve"
pools of a postlapsarian polity, Bacon once again has deftly rewritten
the story of Adam's search for a mate. Once again he denies the virtue
of bodily knowledge and separates all Adams from their Eves, distancing
the domain of knowledge from that of desire.

But the bureaucratic transfiguration of domestic activity and heterosexual reproductive desire in Bacon's scientific writing perhaps reaches

its apogee in the Bensalemite "Feast of the Family," where female bodily reproduction is excised from the fraternity of scientific practitioners, much as Eve is physically alienated from Adam's male body. In the *New Atlantis*, the "Feast of the Family" is a ritual enactment of masculine social power that serves Bacon as an emblem of his "masculine" restructuring of scientific knowing. Performed when a man lives to see thirty descendants, the ceremony involves the patriarch's judicious ordering of family business, the public chartering of his authority within the family, and the festive celebration of paternal power. Notably, the mother of the family, as Carolyn Merchant points out, is conspicuously hidden away.

> . . . and if there be a mother from whose body the whole lineage is descended, there is a traverse placed in a loft above on the right hand of the chair with a privy door and a carved window of glass, leaded with gold and blue, where she sitteth but is not seen. (5:387)[80]

Bacon's festive parable, which involves repression of the maternal body, signifies one of the major presuppositions of Baconian science: scientific activity that is susceptible to rational control and standardization is to be publicly recognized and applauded, whereas activity that is not capable of procedural control is, while noted, to be repressed and systematically excluded from representation. Such activity is not to form part of the public discourse on the nature of scientific knowing. Thus, the mother, whose bodily procreation represents those aspects of mental creativity indebted to the rationally incalculable constitution of human bodily being, is exiled to the margins of scientific activity.

While the loving wife faces ritualistic exile, the bourgeois householder of the "Feast of the Family," the Tirsan, undergoes a metamorphosis from loving husband to a petty state bureaucrat. Marital satisfaction and help, represented by the body of his wife, is obscured from view and out of reach. His personal rewards must now come not through the immediate gratification of desire, but through the bureaucratic effort of rightly ordering and administering the affairs of his family. The final outcome is public celebration and the family's receipt of an official state "charter" that represents state penetration and control over the intimate bounds and bondings of human desire (5:385–90).

Bacon's curiously fractured domestic emotional economy, enabled by the intervention of the Absolutist state into the families of its citizens, forms the affective substructure of his discourse on knowledge. What is less apparent, however, is the extent to which this substructure (along with the entire scientific project that it undergirds) is overdetermined by Bacon's understanding of the right relation between the commercial classes and the Absolutist state. In fact, what enables Bacon to conceive of his program of scientific objectivity is his ability to think beyond the boundaries of his class. His scientific program hinges on his bifurcated vision that, like a conceptual palimpsest, overlays the activities of one class with the interests of another.

Bacon's family myths in the *New Atlantis* concern the relationship between the activities of productive citizens and the interests of the Absolutist state that governs them. Bacon sustains this social focus throughout his writings. Travelers, craftsmen, and merchants loom large in Bacon's figurative pantheon of scientific actors, particularly in the *New Atlantis*.[81] But while the external activities of artisanal makers and commercial profit seekers are preserved within Bacon's fable, their motives for action are gutted. That local human interest, which propels individual pursuit of new objects and the transformation of known ones, Bacon separates from the minds and bodies of his scientific investigators. The Baconian scientist grasps without intention. Individual desire is displaced onto the generalized notion of social betterment, a good determined by the organs of a centralized monarchical authority. Thus the motive of profit, materially evident in commerce, and spiritually apparent in Calvin's discourse on knowledge, vanishes in Bacon's new oxymoronic men of science, those selfless "Merchants of Light" who travel to collect new knowledge for the general betterment of the monarchical state of Bensalem.

That Bacon insists on "Merchants of Light" not "Courtiers" or "Political Agents of Light" is significant here; it suggests that Bacon's scientific program, while geared to the interests of monarchy, is nonetheless modeled on the profit-seeking pursuits and activities of another class entirely: that of the urban commercial classes. Bacon's two-tiered vision couples the interests of monarchy with the activities of merchants. Most important, his texts reveal the socially constructed nature of the concept of "objectivity." For Bacon's early seventeenth-century formation of scientific "objectivity" depends upon the monarchical state's recognition, appropriation, and selective suppression of the interests and activities of other classes.

And vanishing alongside commercial class desire are those gendered others, women, whose very presence seems to elicit and represent those individual interests, desires, and makings that Bacon hopes to contain. In the early essay, "The Masculine Birth of Time," Bacon masculinizes the proverbial myth of Truth as the "daughter" of Time. Attacking the methods of the schools, Bacon portrays the errors of the human mind as a kind of female procreation: "The fact is, my son, that the human mind in studying forth nature becomes big under the impact of things and brings forth a teeming brood of errors." In contrast, Bacon assures his reader that scientific truth proceeds through a kind of nonhuman informational parthenogenesis: "Genuine truth is uniform and self-reproducing."[82]

Ultimately, however, Bacon requires those troubling others—those merchants and citizens, mothers and daughters, whose interests and ambitions he works so assiduously to reconceive and quiet. Not just because he needs their mindless set of hands to observe, note, and appropriate the knowledge embedded in nature. But because his concrete consciousness of their gendered, socioeconomic, and cultural difference provides the material stuff through which he produces a clear notion of human interest. It is their difference from him that enables him to think, not "objectively" but of "objectivity." It is Bacon's appreciation of the material power achieved through the pursuit of commercial class interest that leads him to manufacture that political strategy of scientific self-distancing and repression, a form of scientific objectivity.

To anatomize what I take to be Bacon's production of scientific disinterestedness is not to treat Bacon anachronistically or to ascribe to him an epistemology akin to twentieth-century positivism. Nor is it to ignore the fact that Bacon saw his scientific project as promoting important interests—the public interest in ameliorating the human condition, which, in the hands of a Lord Chancellor, was inextricably connected to the king's interest in stabilizing and augmenting the power of the Crown. Rather, this analysis strives, first, to make clear Bacon's contribution to an early modern notion of individual scientific "disinterestedness"—one that would form a component of later configurations of objectivity. And second, it aims to show that Bacon's articulations of "disinterestedness" were conceived dialectically—as a political response to his perception of the existence of divergent class interests.

Ultimately, those troublesome others heighten Bacon's ideological self-consciousness. They play Eve to his Adam. And so, by extension, does Calvin. For Bacon's epistemology depends crucially upon a model of knowledge akin to Calvin's, one that is tied to the workings of human gratification. He needs that schema in order to sever it, to harness its pursuing power, while detaching that force from the embodied interests of the class that produced it.

NOTES

1. See Robert Graves and Raphael Patai, *Hebrew Myths* (New York: Doubleday, 1964), 65, 67; J. A. Phillips, *The History of an Idea: Eve* (New York: Harper and Row, 1984), 32.

2. For the story of Enkidu, see the second millennial B.C. *Epic of Gilgamesh* (Harmondsworth: Penguin Books, 1960), 60–67. Robert J. Bauer discusses the Renaissance history of the dual meaning of the word *conceit* in "A Phenomenon of Renaissance Epistemology," *Journal of the History of Ideas* 31 (1970): 281–88.

3. Ursula Le Guin, "She Unnames Them," *New Yorker*, January 21, 1985, 27.

4. See Mary Nyquist, "Gynesis, Genesis, Exegesis, and the Formation of Milton's Eve," in *Cannibals, Witches, and Divorce: Estranging the Renaissance*, ed. Marjorie Garber (Baltimore: Johns Hopkins University Press, 1987), 147–208; Patricia Parker, "Coming Second: Women's Place," in *Literary Fat Ladies: Rhetoric, Gender, Property* (London: Methuen, 1987), 178–233; and Phyllis Trible, *God and the Rhetoric of Sexuality* (Philadelphia: Fortress Press, 1978). Nor has this complex episode been a critical rallying point for feminist historians of science interested in the intersections between gender and knowing. See, for example, Evelyn Fox Keller, *Reflections on Gender and Science* (New Haven: Yale University Press, 1985); Carolyn Merchant, *The Death of Nature: Women, Ecology, and the Scientific Revolution* (San Francisco: Harper and Row, 1980).

5. Francis Bacon, *The Advancement of Learning* (London, 1605), rpt. in *The Works of Francis Bacon*, vol. 6, ed. James Spedding, Robert Leslie Ellis, and Douglas Devon Heath (New York: Hurd and Houghton, 1872), 138. All subsequent references to the works of Francis Bacon, unless otherwise specified, will be to this edition with volume number and page number cited in the text.

6. Feminists have wrestled with the political and patriarchal meanings of objectivity for a long time. See Virginia Woolf's grappling with the interested notion of feminist "anger" in *A Room of One's Own* (New York: Harcourt, Brace and World, 1929), 32–35. Woolf ends up on the side of objectivity in criticizing Charlotte Brontë's prose as "deformed and twisted" by feminist interest (72–73). The contemporary feminist critic Myra Jehlen finds room for objective measures of literary "quality" in "Archimedes and the Paradox of Feminist Criticism," *Signs* 6 (Summer, 1981): 575–601. In contrast, Evelyn Fox Keller explodes the patriarchal myth of objectivity in *Reflections on Gender and Science* (see particularly chap. 4) and Catherine A. Mackinnon provides a skillful analysis of "objectivity" as the norm for the "male state" in "Feminism, Marxism, Method, and the State: Toward Feminist Jurisprudence," *Signs* 8 (Summer, 1983): 635–58.

7. See, for example, Paolo Rossi, *Francis Bacon: From Magic to Science* (London: Routledge and Kegan Paul, 1968); Benjamin Farrington, *Francis Bacon: Pioneer of Planned Science* (London: Weidenfeld and Nicholson, 1963).

8. It is my contention that "objectivity" is always a function of the relationship between

two human beings or two classes of human beings and the world in which they find themselves. Although the forgers of "objectivity" tend to describe it as an attribute of an individual, such ascriptions are part and parcel of the effort to suppress and efface the interests of one class or being in favor of another and to inscribe that pervasive effacement within the psyches of individuals.

9. Philo of Alexandria, "On the Account of the World's Creation Given by Moses," in *Philo*, trans. F. H. Colson and Rev. G. H. Whitaker (Cambridge, Mass.: Harvard University Press, 1971), 1:119, 117. Woman only appears in Philo's "Allegorical Interpretation" of the passage, where she represents those helps to the masculine soul offered by sense perception (227–33).

10. St. Augustine, *The Literal Meaning of Genesis*, trans. John Hammond Taylor, S.J. (New York: Newman Press, 1982), 2:87–88, 75, 83.

11. St. Thomas Aquinas, *Summa Theologiae* (New York: McGraw-Hill, 1963), 13:97, 155. Aquinas acknowledges that "Adam understood the natures of all the animals, and by the same token understood everything else" (97).

12. Pico della Mirandola, *Heptaplus*, trans. Douglas Carmichael (New York: Bobbs-Merrill, 1965), 125.

13. Martin Luther, *Luther's Commentary on Genesis*, trans. J. Theodore Mueller (Grand Rapids, Mich.: Zondervan, 1958), 1:57. See also the emphasis on the importance of reason in the interpretation of this passage in Arnold Williams, *The Common Expositor: An Account of the Commentaries on Genesis, 1527–1633* (Chapel Hill: University of North Carolina Press, 1948), 80–85.

14. Calvin acknowledges reason as a distinguishing attribute of human being: "Reason is propre to our nature, which maketh us to differ from brute beastes" (*The Institution of the Christian Religion Written in Latine By Maister John Calvine and translated into English accordyng to the author's last edition*, trans. T. N. [London, 1562], 2.2.17). All future references to Calvin's *Institutes* will be to this edition with book, chapter, and paragraph number in the text.

15. John Calvin, *Commentarie Upon Genesis*, trans. Thomas Tymme (London, 1578), 74–75. All future references to this work will be to this edition and abbreviated in the text as *Commentarie* with page number.

16. See Nyquist, "Gynesis, Genesis," 168–69. H. Jackson Forstman discusses Calvin's associated use of synecdoche in *Word and Spirit: Calvin's Doctrine of Biblical Authority* (Stanford: Stanford University Press, 1962), 108.

17. Patricia Parker discusses the involuted dynamics of Eve's secondariness in *Literary Fat Ladies*, 178–201, where what comes last comes to precede what came first. In his commentary, Calvin also redefines secondariness by claiming that Eve's creation "perfected" mankind, which was before not finished: "Mankind was perfected, which before was like unto a building begonne but not finished" (*Commentarie*, 76). On secondariness see also Nyquist, "Gynesis, Genesis," 158–60. Forstman discusses Calvin's use of the trope of inversion "hysteron proteron"—where the "first is put last," *Word and Spirit*, 108. Interestingly, in book 8 of *Paradise Lost* (in *John Milton: Complete Poems and Prose*, ed. Merritt Y. Hughes [Indianapolis: Bobbs-Merrill, 1957]), John Milton subordinates rationality to Eve.

All higher knowledge in her presence falls
Degraded, Wisdom in discourse with her

Loses discount'nanc't, and like folly shows;
Authority and Reason on her wait,
As one intended first, not after made
Occasionally. . . .

(ll. 551–56)

18. Curiously, the biblical narrative itself seems to work to contain Calvin's unsettling exegesis; in verse 23, Adam names his mate "Woman," figuring a rational ordering of that desire that precipitated naming in the first place. We see this same exposing and containing of male susceptibility to desire in the Sumerian *Epic of Gilgamesh*, where the wild man Enkidu, companion of the forest creatures, achieves his species-specific human identity (including civility and wisdom) by being seduced by a courtesan. The courtesan has been put up to the trick, however, and desire thus contained, by the patriarch, Gilgamesh, King of Uruk (*Epic of Gilgamesh*, 61–63). See also Richard Bernheimer, *Wild Men in the Middle Ages* (Cambridge, Mass.: Harvard University Press, 1952), 3, 71, 135. Conjecturally, the telling of stories about the relationship between reason and desire within patriarchal culture is spurred on by desire's troubling dynamic.

19. In so doing, Calvin sets the stage for Protestant rethinking of this passage and, ultimately, for a Protestant reformulation of patriarchy. Calvin's Protestant successors were quick to take up the task of reformulation. For example, writing after (and arguably through) Calvin, the sixteenth-century French Protestant Guillaume Dubartas, in *His Divine Weekes and Workes* (trans. Josuah Sylvester [London, 1611]), explores much the same territory with Calvin's exegetical twist. In his praises for the beauteous woman who tempts man into civility and rationality, Dubartas blurs the distinction between the powerful effects of desire and the containments of reason; in fact, Dubartas's verses reevoke the sensibility of Calvin's biblical exegesis, where desire precipitates reason.

Com, com and see the woman's rapting features
Without whom (heer) man were But half a man,
But a wilde wolf, but a Barbarian,
Brute, ragefull fierce, moody, melancholike
Hating the Light, whome nought but nought could like.

(17)

In the same vein, the Genevan divine Giovanni Diodati infuses Adam's rational naming with Adam's desire in his discussion of the passage. For Adam's naming is not simply a show of rational authority, but a display of willfulness. God gives Adam "the authority to give and change his subjects names as he pleaseth" (*Pious and Learned Annotations Upon the Holy Bible* [London, 1651], sig. D1b).

20. For Calvin's attacks on Scholasticism and his dethronement of reason, see William Bouwsma, *John Calvin: A Sixteenth Century Portrait* (Oxford: Oxford University Press, 1988), 54, 133, 156; Charles Partee, *Calvin and Classical Philosophy* (Leiden: Brill, 1977), 34.

21. In the *Institutes*, Calvin urges his readers to acquiesce in his understanding of the bodily limits of human cognition.

Let us therefore willingly abide enclosed within these boundes wherewith it pleased

God to envyron us, and as it were to pen up our mindes that they should not stray abrode with libertie of wandring. (1.14.1)

Calvin's attack on vain human reasoning takes a comic turn in his *Commentarie*, where he answers the vain question of what God was doing before creating the world by quipping: "He was not then idle, bicause he had made and ordeined hell for curious persons" (19).

22. Thus, if patriarchy suffers blows at Calvin's hands, it is powerfully recouped in his displacement of the supreme virtue of rationality onto the mind of the Heavenly Father.

23. The exegetical theory of "accommodation" has a history almost as old as that of Christian exegesis itself. Clement (150?–213?) and Origen (185–254?) borrowed the concept from Philo of Alexandria and it reappears in the work of John Chrysostom (347?–407) and St. Augustine. According to Forstman, Calvin made frequent use of this exegetical tool in his biblical commentaries (*Word and Spirit*, 100). Calvin's attraction to the theory may owe something to his Christian humanist training, which cultivated an appreciation for persuasion, the important and powerful effect of rhetoric within human culture. As William Bouwsma has pointed out, accommodation has an affinity to the Renaissance humanist concept of decorum—the rhetorical suiting of words and speeches to the capacity and interests of one's audience. See Bouwsma, *John Calvin*, 113–27.

24. Accommodation also appears in God's objectification of his glory in the world itself. For although his "substance in deed is incomprehensible so that his divine Majestie far surmounteth all mennes senses: but he hath in all his works graven certaine markes of his glorie" (1.5.1).

25. References to the sanctity of the human body abound in Calvin's writings. For Calvin, the chief seat of the divine image in man is dually located in the mind and the bodily heart (*Commentarie*, 44). And in the *Institutes*, he talks of the body as God's "temple" (3.25.7) and claims that there is "no part of man, not so much as the body, wherein did not some sparks [of God's image] appeare" (1.4.3). See also Bouwsma, *John Calvin*, 134.

26. Cited by Bouwsma, *John Calvin*, 132–33, 72.

27. Calvin, *Commentary on Romans*, quoted in Forstman, *Word and Spirit*, 101. For Calvin, it is embodied human experience that leads us to the knowledge of God: "Therefore every man is by the knowledge of himselfe [the experienced misery of the human condition], not only prycked forward to seke God, but also lead as it were by the hand to finde him" (1.1.1).

28. On Calvin's notion of "certainty," see Forstman, *Word and Spirit*, 9, 101, 125.

29. In the *Institutes*, Calvin alludes to the neo-Platonic concept of man as a functional measure of the world around him: "a little world," that is, "a rare representation of the power, goodnesse and wisedome of God" (1.5.3). For related discussions of man as a measure of the world, see Nicholas of Cusa, *The Layman on Wisdom and the Mind*, trans. M. L. Fuhrer (Ottawa: Dovehouse Editions, 1989), 57; also see Elaine Scarry's discussion of this same theme in the work of Nicholas of Cusa, Da Vinci, and Donne in "Donne: 'But Yet the Body is his booke,'" in *Literature and the Body: Essays on Populations and Persons*, ed. Elaine Scarry (Baltimore: Johns Hopkins University Press, 1988), 70–105.

30. For the importance of experience to the epistemology of Calvin and Puritanism as a whole see Bouwsma, *John Calvin*, 158; Partee, *Calvin*, 37; John Morgan, *Godly Learning* (Cambridge: Cambridge University Press, 1986), 4, 25, 58–61. See also Robert K. Merton,

Science, Technology, and Society in Seventeenth-Century England (New York: Harper and Row, 1970), 92–95, on the confluence of rationalism and empiricism in Puritan thought. For an opposing view that stresses the rational character of Puritan theology, see Perry Miller, *The New England Mind* (Cambridge, Mass.: Harvard University Press, 1954).

31. Conversely, Calvin argues that man "never commeth unto the true knowledge of himself unlesse he have first beholde the face of God" (1.1.2).

32. It is interesting to note that, in the *Institutes,* Calvin veritably collapses the distinction between appetite and human understanding in his taxonomic discussion of the faculties of the human mind.

[T]he office of Understanding, [is] to discerne betweene objects, or things set before it, as eche of them shal seme worthy to be liked or misliked. . . . (1.15.7)

According whereto, Aristotle himself hath truely sayd that fleeing or folowing is in appetite such a like thing, as in the understanding minde is affirming and denying. (1.15.7)

33. Edward A. Dowey, Jr., *The Knowledge of God in Calvin's Theology* (New York: Columbia University Press, 1952), 26, but see also 18–25, 27–28 for Dowey's definition of Calvin's "correlative" understanding. Forstman characterizes Calvin's theological epistemology as "knowledge for me" (*Word and Spirit,* 73).

34. Suzanne Selinger, *Calvin against Himself* (Hamden, Conn.: Archon Books, 1984), 42, 2; see also 60, 62, 83.

35. Selinger, *Calvin,* 81.

36. Robin May Schott, *Cognition and Eros: A Critique of the Kantian Paradigm* (Boston: Beacon Press, 1988), 80.

37. Calvin, *Institutes,* 3.10.3, quoted in Schott, *Cognition,* 76–77.

38. Selinger, *Calvin,* 27, 43.

39. See Bouwsma, *John Calvin,* 133, 134, 150, 160 for descriptions of Calvin's "holistic" understanding.

40. Terry Eagleton, *Literary Theory: An Introduction* (Minneapolis: University of Minnesota Press, 1983), 14.

41. Gervase Babington, *Certaine Plaine, Briefe, and Comfortable Notes, upon every Chapter of Genesis* (London, 1596), 22–24.

42. Henoch Clapham, *Bibliotheca Theologica; or, A Librarye Theological* (Amsterdam, 1597), 6b.

43. Henry Ainsworth, *Annotations upon the First Book of Moses Called Genesis* (London, 1616), C1b. William Hunnis, Protestant and conspirator against the Catholic Queen Mary, versified the book of Genesis in *A Hyve Full of Honye: Contayning the First Book of Moses, Called Genesis* (London, 1579). His rhymes formally smooth over, but do not explain, the narrative break in Adam's search for a mate.

It is not good (said God) that man
should be alone I see
I wyll an helper make to him,
companion for to bee.

Out of the ground, did God then make,
Ech beast upon the Earth,
and every Foul in th'ayre that flyes,
and all that draweth breathe.
And God did bringe all beastes and souls,
to view of Adam's Eye
which was to see, what kynde of name,
he then would call them by.
And Adam, called every Beast,
and every Foule by name,
As we do use at this same day,
to nominate the same.
In slomber then was Adam cast,
and God a ribbe did take,
Out from his side and of the same
a woman he did make.

44. Milton, *Paradise Lost*, ll. 352–55 (italics added). Mary Nyquist points out that Milton's conflation of reason and desire amounts to a kind of "rational burning"—where rational companionship becomes a necessary component of satisfactory human sexuality ("Gynesis, Genesis," 190).

45. Andrew Willet, *Hexapla in Genesin; that is, A Sixfold Commentarie upon Genesis* (London, 1632), 29–30.

46. William Guild, *Moses Unvailed* (London, 1620), 5.

47. There are important shared theological and epistemological assumptions in the thought of Calvin and Bacon. Biographers of Bacon, noting the strong Calvinism of Francis Bacon's mother, Ann Bacon (to whom Theodore Beza, Calvin's successor at Geneva, dedicated his *Meditations*), have presumed (to my mind inaccurately) the same religious predilections on the part of her son (see Fulton Anderson, *Francis Bacon: His Career and His Thought* [Westport, Conn.: Greenwood Press, 1962], 24–25). Bruce Deason, in "The Philosophy of a Lord Chancellor" (M.A. thesis, Princeton Theological Seminary, 1978), discusses the moderate reformism of the Bacon household. Deason notes the similarities in the thought of the two men, including a belief in the vanity of human reason and in the need to develop external helps to guide the human mind. Perhaps most notably, both thinkers develop a doctrine concerning the "Idols of the Mind" (279–94). According to Calvin, "there hath been scarcely at any time any one man found, that did not forge to himselfe an idole or fansie in stede of God. . . . For eche mannes witt is to himself as a maze, so that it is no mervaile that every severall nation was diversely drawen into severall devises, and not that onely, but also that eche severall man had his severall Gods by himself" (1.5.11). For Bacon's doctrine of the "Idols of the Mind," see the *New Organon* (8:76–99). Hiram Haydn has argued for the epistemological conjunctions between sixteenth-century religious reformers and early seventeenth-century scientists in his notion of a "Counter-Renaissance"—a joint revolt against the primacy of rationalist argument and a turn to experiential theology and empiricism, respectively (*The Counter-Renaissance* [New York: Charles Scribner's Sons, 1950]). If Bacon did not study the works of the Genevan directly, at the very least he assimilated his notions from conversations with those who evidently had.

48. In his preface to the *Great Instauration*, Bacon speaks approvingly of royal appropriation: "It is the glory of God to conceal a thing, but it is the glory of the King to find a thing out" (7:36). And in the same text, Bacon characterizes scientific discovery in the language of martial appropriation: "For I do not propose merely to survey these regions in my mind, like an augur taking auspices, but to enter them like a general who means to take possession" (8:40). In the final analysis, while Calvin rejects "comprehension" for "certainty," Bacon is willing to go beyond the bounds of certainty, to remain among "incertainties" (8:33) in order to comprehend a knowledge beyond the self.

49. Pico della Mirandola, *On the Dignity of Man*, trans. Charles Glenn Wallis (New York: Bobbs-Merrill, 1965), 4.

50. Francis Bacon, *The Wisdom of the Ancients*, trans. Arthur Gorges (New York: Garland, 1976), 126–27.

51. For Bacon's complete discussion of the "Idols of the Mind," see *New Organon* (8:76–99). Bacon was not alone in his repression of human desire. His contemporary, Thomas Hill, also stresses the intellect over the desirous body in his *Arte of Vulgar Arithmeticke* (1600).

> For the sacred scriptures testifie that God created Adam to his owne image and similitude, which cannot be understood of body and bodily shape (sith God is a spirit, but in the minde or soule, wherein if *Adam* lackt humaine knowledge, how could he comprehend the knowledge of the divine maiestie, or in anything be more unlike to his creator, who knoweth all things. (Biii)

52. For discussions of the medieval optical theory of "species," see three works by David Lindberg, "The Genesis of Kepler's Theory of Light: Light Metaphysics from Plotinus to Kepler," *Osiris*, 2d ser., 2 (1986): 5–42; *Theories of Vision from Al-kindi to Kepler* (Chicago: University of Chicago Press, 1976); *Roger Bacon's Philosophy of Nature* (Oxford: Clarendon Press, 1983). Wayne Schumaker has translated John Dee's work on "species," the *Propaedeumata*, in *John Dee on Astronomy* (Berkeley: University of California Press, 1978). For Francis Bacon's familiarity with the idea that "species" emanate from all beings, see *The Wisdom of the Ancients*, where he reads the hirsute Greek god Pan as a symbol of nature.

> [The] body of *Nature* is elegantly and with deepe judgement depainted hairy, representing the beames or operations of creatures: for beames are as it were the haires and bristles of *Nature*, and every creature is either more or lesse beamie, which is most apparent in the facultie of seeing, and no lesse in every vertue and operation that effectuals upon a distant object: for whatsoever workes up any thing afarre off; that may rightly bee saide to darte forth rayes or beames. (26)

53. Williston Walker, *John Calvin* (New York: Schocken Books, 1969), 18–24. See also *The Catholic Encyclopedia* (New York: The Encyclopedia Press, 1913), 3:195.

54. Quoted in Walker, *John Calvin*, 28.

55. Francis's strenuous repression of French Protestants in 1534 induced Calvin to write him an open letter in the *Institutes* (1536). Courteous as Calvin's address to the King was, the letter was civicly forthright in its defense of the French reformers (sig. Aiii–Aviii).

56. See Walker, *John Calvin*, particularly chaps. 7–13.

57. Bouwsma, *John Calvin*, 207–10.

58. In *The Family Sex and Marriage in England, 1500–1800* (New York: Harper and Row, 1979), Lawrence Stone argues that a dramatic shift in fundamental attitudes toward marriage and the family took place between 1560 and 1640, fueled, in large part, by the decay in traditional kinship structures, the Reformation, the growth of common law abstraction, and the rise of "possessive market individualism," among other things (100). Stone notes the cool remoteness of family relations within the early sixteenth-century aristocratic "open lineage family." In contrast to it, he traces the late seventeenth-century growth of "affective individualism"—marital love and commitment—that emerged in large part out of shifts in socioeconomic relations. See particularly chaps. 4–6.

59. Gervase Babington (*Certaine Notes*) reads Genesis 2:18 as justifying the holiness of marriage (22–23), while in *Questions and Disputations Concerning the Holy Scripture* (London, 1601), the English divine, Nicholas Gibbens, also characterizes marriage as a "holy ordinance of God" (94).

60. Quoted in Bouwsma, *John Calvin*, 23.

61. The "prevailing sense" of the word *furniture* in the sixteenth century was our modern one: "movable articles, whether useful or ornamental in a dwelling house" (*OED*). The word also signified the "condition of being equipped whether in body or mind" and "that with which one is provided." For a sophisticated treatment of the objectification of desire in the everyday world, see Elaine Scarry, *The Body in Pain: The Making and Unmaking of the World* (Oxford: Oxford University Press, 1985).

62. This emphasis on God as "meet" provider appears in the work of English Protestants. Gervase Babington rejoices: "O how we may cleave and cling to the providence of this God in all comfort of our mindes, that thus thinketh of what may bee good for us before ever we thinke of it our selves, and not onlie thinketh of it, but provideth it, and prepareth it for us" (*Certaine Notes*, 24). Henry Ainsworth celebrates God's creation of Eve as "meet and commodious for him [Adam]" (*Annotations*, C1b). In *Tetrachordon* (in *The Works of John Milton* [New York: Columbia University Press, 1931]), Milton assures us of the "true fitnes of that consort which God provided him [Adam]" (4:92). And in *Prototypes, or, the Primarie Precedent. Presidents out of Genesis* (London, 1640), William Whately evokes another fantasy of commercial grandeur when he declares that man was not created

till the sixth day when a fit place for him to dwell in, and all necessary furniture for the place, and all needful servants and attendents were before provided for his use. God saw it not fit to bring man into the world, before it was garnished and stored with all contents usefull for him. (3)

63. For a concise description of Calvin's rejection of "works" and his doctrine of regeneration through the Holy Spirit, see *The Encyclopedia of Religion and Ethics*, ed. James Hastings (New York: Charles Scribner's Sons, 1911), 3:148–52.

64. Anderson, *Francis Bacon*, 20–21.

65. *The Letters and Life of Francis Bacon*, ed. James Spedding (London: Longmans, Green, Reader and Dyer, 1868–74), 3:291–92.

66. Anderson, *Francis Bacon*, 232.

67. Francis Bacon, *The Essayes or Counsels, Civill and Morall* (London, 1625), 36.
Bacon's conflicting feelings about marriage and family also emerge in these verses, which
John Aubrey purports were written by him.

> Domestic cares afflict the husband's bed
> Or paines his hed;
> Those that live single take it for a curse,
> Or doe things worse;
> Some would have children; those that have them mone,
> Or wish them gone.
> What is it then to have, or have no wife,
> But single thraldome or a double strife?

> Our owne affections still at home to please
> Is a disease. . . .
> (Quoted in John Aubrey, *Brief Lives,* ed. Andrew Clark [Oxford: Clarendon Press,
> 1898], 1:73)

68. Bacon, *Essayes or Counsels,* 155, 163.

69. According to Joseph Cady, Bacon was also exposed to royal homosexuality at the
French Court of Henry III when he was a member of Sir Amias Paulet's embassy to the
French crown from September, 1576, to February, 1579. For this and Cady's discussion of
"masculine love" in Bacon's *New Atlantis,* see "Masculine Love, Renaissance Writing, and
the New Invention of Homosexuality," forthcoming in the *Journal of Homosexuality.* For
a different account of homosexuality in the Renaissance, see Alan Bray, *Homosexuality
in Renaissance England* (London: Gay Men's Press, 1982).

70. *Letters of Francis Bacon,* ed. James Spedding, 1:244.

71. *Letters of Francis Bacon,* ed. James Spedding, 7:542.

72. Sir Simonds D'Ewes, *Autobiography and Correspondence of Sir Simonds D'Ewes,*
ed. James Orchard Halliwell-Phillips (London: Richard Bentley, 1845), 1:192. The editor
of D'Ewes's autobiography, James Orchard Halliwell-Phillipps, apparently excised a portion
of D'Ewes's manuscript, although in a note he claims that D'Ewes also charged that Bacon
was

> so notorious while he was at York House, in the Strand, and at his lodgings in Gray's
> Inn, Holborn, that the following verses were cast into his rooms:

> "Within this sty a *hog* doth lie,
> That must be hang'd for villany."

> (192)

73. Aubrey, *Brief Lives,* 1:71. Bacon's own family circle was involved in homosexual
practice. His brother Anthony was arrested in 1586 for sodomy in Montauban, France,
where he was apparently accused of the "abuse" of his pages (see Daphne Du Maurier,
Golden Lads [London: Victor Gollancz, Ltd., 1975], 66–67). Bacon's brother-in-law, Mervyn

Touchet, second earl of Castlehaven, was executed as a pederast on May 14, 1631 (see Aubrey, *Brief Lives*, 1:71).

74. William Rawley, *The Life of the Right Honorable Francis Bacon* (London, 1657), 7.

75. Francis Bacon, "Thoughts and Conclusion," in *The Philosophy of Francis Bacon*, trans. Benjamin Farrington (Liverpool: Manchester University Press, 1964), 92.

76. Genevieve Lloyd, *The Man of Reason: "Male" and "Female" in Western Philosophy* (Minneapolis: University of Minnesota Press, 1984); see particularly 10–17.

77. Francis Bacon, "The Refutation of Philosophies," in *The Philosophy of Francis Bacon*, trans. Benjamin Farrington, 131.

78. Francis Bacon, "The Masculine Birth of Time," in *The Philosophy of Francis Bacon*, trans. Benjamin Farrington, 72.

79. For an astute reading of the passage that complements mine, see J. Weinberger, "Science and Rule in Bacon's Utopia: An Introduction to the Reading of the *New Atlantis*," *American Political Science Review* 70 (September, 1976): 865–85.

80. See the account of the episode in Merchant, *Death of Nature*, 174.

81. See particularly Bacon's discussion of the work of the "Merchants of Light" and the "Pioners or Miners," as well as his description of the mechanical and other experiments of the scientific community of the House of Salomon (5:398–413). See also Bacon's use of travel metaphor in "Thoughts and Conclusions," 92, and the *New Organon*, 8:129. Paolo Rossi has written the ground-breaking work on Bacon's debt to the culture of craftsmen and mechanicians in *Francis Bacon: From Magic to Science* (London: Routledge and Kegan Paul, 1968). See also Edgar Zilsel, "The Sociological Roots of Science," *American Journal of Sociology* 47 (1941–42): 544–62.

82. Francis Bacon, "Masculine Birth of Time," 70–71. See also Evelyn Fox Keller's treatment of this essay and her analysis of Bacon's "feminization" of the scientific mind in *Reflections*, 34–40.

Love and Knowledge: Emotion in Feminist Epistemology

Alison M. Jaggar

Within the Western philosophical tradition, emotions have usually been considered potentially or actually subversive of knowledge.[1] From Plato until the present, with a few notable exceptions, reason rather than emotion has been regarded as the indispensable faculty for acquiring knowledge.[2]

Typically, although again not invariably, the rational has been contrasted with the emotional, and this contrasted pair then often linked with other dichotomies. Not only has reason been contrasted with emotion, but it has also been associated with the mental, the cultural, the universal, the public, and the male, whereas emotion has been associated with the irrational, the physical, the natural, the particular, the private, and, of course, the female.

Although Western epistemology has tended to give pride of place to reason rather than emotion, it has not always excluded emotion completely from the realm of reason. In the *Phaedrus*, Plato portrayed emotions, such as anger or curiosity, as irrational urges (horses) that must always be controlled by reason (the charioteer). In this model, the emotions were not seen as needing to be totally suppressed, but rather as needing direction by reason: for example, in a genuinely threatening situation, it was thought not only irrational but foolhardy not to be afraid.[3] The split between reason and emotion was not absolute, therefore, for the Greeks. Instead, the emotions were thought of as providing indispensable motive power that needed to be channeled appropriately. Without horses, after all, the skill of the charioteer would be worthless.

The contrast between reason and emotion was sharpened in the seventeenth century by redefining reason as a purely instrumental faculty. For both the Greeks and the medieval philosophers, reason had been linked with value in so far as reason provided access to the objective structure or order of reality, seen as simultaneously natural and morally justified. With the rise of modern science, however, the realms of nature and value were separated: nature was stripped of value and reconceptualized as an inanimate mechanism of no intrinsic worth. Values were relocated in human beings, rooted in their preferences and emotional responses. The separation of supposedly natural fact from human value meant that reason, if it were to provide trustworthy insight into reality, had to be uncontaminated by or abstracted from value. Increasingly, therefore, though never universally,[4] reason was reconceptualized as the ability to make valid inferences from premises established elsewhere, the ability to calculate means but not to determine ends. The validity of logical inferences was thought independent of human attitudes and preferences; this was now the sense in which reason was taken to be objective and universal.[5]

The modern redefinition of rationality required a corresponding reconceptualization of emotion. This was achieved by portraying emotions as nonrational and often irrational urges that regularly swept the body, rather as a storm sweeps over the land. The common way of referring to the emotions as the "passions" emphasized that emotions happened to or were imposed upon an individual, something she suffered rather than something she did.

The epistemology associated with this new ontology rehabilitated sensory perception that, like emotion, typically had been suspected or even discounted by the Western tradition as a reliable source of knowledge. British empiricism, succeeded in the nineteenth century by positivism, took its epistemological task to be the formulation of rules of inference that would guarantee the derivation of certain knowledge from the "raw data" supposedly given directly to the senses. Empirical testability became accepted as the hallmark of natural science; this, in turn, was viewed as the paradigm of genuine knowledge. Often epistemology was equated with the philosophy of science, and the dominant methodology of positivism prescribed that truly scientific knowledge must be capable of intersubjective verification. Because values and emotions had been defined as variable and idiosyncratic, positivism stipulated that trustworthy knowledge could be established only by methods that neutralized the values and emotions of individual scientists.

Recent approaches to epistemology have challenged some fundamental assumptions of the positivist epistemological model. Contemporary theorists of knowledge have undermined once rigid distinctions between analytic and synthetic statements, between theories and observations, and even between facts and values. However, few challenges have thus far been raised to the purported gap between emotion and knowledge. In this essay, I wish to begin bridging this gap through the suggestion that emotions may be helpful and even necessary, rather than inimical, to the construction of knowledge. My account is exploratory in nature and leaves many questions unanswered. It is not supported by irrefutable arguments or conclusive proofs; instead, it should be viewed as a preliminary sketch for an epistemological model that will require much further development before its workability can be established.

Emotion

What Are Emotions?
The philosophical question, "What are emotions?" requires both explicating the ways in which people ordinarily speak about emotion and evaluating the adequacy of those ways for expressing and illuminating experience and activity. Several problems confront someone trying to answer this deceptively simple question. One set of difficulties results from the variety, complexity, and even inconsistency of the ways in which emotions are viewed, both in daily life and in scientific contexts. It is, in part, this variety that makes emotions into a "question" at the same time that it precludes answering that question by simple appeal to ordinary usage. A second difficulty is the wide range of phenomena covered by the term *emotion:* these extend from apparently instantaneous, knee-jerk responses of fright to lifelong dedication to an individual or a cause; from highly civilized aesthetic responses to undifferentiated feelings of hunger and thirst;[6] from background moods such as contentment or depression to intense and focused involvement in an immediate situation. It may well be impossible to construct a manageable account of emotion to cover such apparently diverse phenomena.

A further problem concerns the criteria for preferring one account of emotion to another. The more one learns about the ways in which other cultures conceptualize human faculties, the less plausible it becomes that emotions constitute what philosophers call a "natural kind." Not only do some cultures identify emotions unrecognized in the West, but there is reason to believe that the concept of emotion itself is a historical invention, like the concept of intelligence (Lewontin 1982) or even the concept of mind (Rorty 1979). For instance, anthropologist Catherine

Lutz argues that the "dichotomous categories of 'cognition' and 'affect' are themselves Euroamerican cultural constructions, master symbols that participate in the fundamental organization of our ways of looking at ourselves and others [1985, 1986], both in and outside of social science" (1987, 308). If this is true, then we have even more reason to wonder about the adequacy of ordinary Western ways of talking about emotion. Yet we have no access either to our own emotions or to those of others independent of or unmediated by the discourse of our culture.

In the face of these difficulties, I shall sketch an account of emotion with the following limitations. First, it will operate within the context of Western discussions of emotion: I shall not question, for instance, whether it would be possible or desirable to dispense entirely with any-thing resembling our concept of emotion. Second, although this account attempts to be consistent with as much as possible of Western under-standings of emotion, it is intended to cover only a limited domain, not every phenomenon that may be called an emotion. On the contrary, it excludes as genuine emotions both automatic physical responses and nonintentional sensations, such as hunger pangs. Third, I do not pretend to offer a complete theory of emotion; instead, I focus on a few specific aspects of emotion that I take to have been neglected or misrepresented, especially in positivist and neopositivist accounts. Finally, I would defend my approach not only on the ground that it illuminates aspects of our experience and activity that are obscured by positivist and neopositivist construals, but also on the ground that it is less open than these to ideological abuse. In particular, I believe that recognizing certain neglected aspects of emotion makes possible a better and less ideologically biased account of how knowledge is, and so ought to be, constructed.

Emotions as Intentional

Early positivist approaches to understanding emotions assumed that an adequate account required analytically separating emotion from other human faculties. Just as positivist accounts of sense perception attempted to distinguish the supposedly raw data of sensation from their cognitive interpretations, so positivist accounts of emotion tried to separate emo-tion conceptually from both reason and sense perception. As part of their sharpening of these distinctions, positivist construals of emotion tended to identify emotions with the physical feelings or involuntary bodily movements that typically accompany them, such as pangs or qualms, flushes or tremors; emotions were also assimilated to the sub-duing of physiological function or movement, as in the case of sadness, depression, or boredom. The continuing influence of such supposedly scientific conceptions of emotion can be seen in the fact that "feeling" is often used colloquially as a synonym for emotion, even though the more central meaning of "feeling" is physiological sensation. In such accounts, emotions were not seen as being *about* anything: instead, they were contrasted with and seen as potential disruptions of other phenomena that *are* about some thing, phenomena such as rational judgments, thoughts, and observations. The positivist approach to understanding emotion has been called the Dumb View (Spelman 1982).

The Dumb View of emotion is quite untenable. For one thing, the same feeling or physiological response is likely to be interpreted as various emotions, depending on the context of experience. This point often is illustrated by reference to a famous experiment; excited feelings were induced in research subjects by the injection of adrenalin, and the subjects then attributed to themselves appropriate emotions depending on their context (Schachter and Singer 1969). Another problem with the Dumb View is that identifying emotions with feelings would make it impossible to postulate that a person might not be aware of her emotional state, because feelings, by definition, are a matter of conscious awareness. Finally, emotions differ from feelings, sensations, or physiological responses in that they are dispositional rather than episodic. For instance, we may truthfully assert that we are outraged by, proud of, or saddened by certain events, even if at that moment we are neither agitated nor tearful.

In recent years, contemporary philosophers have tended to reject the Dumb View of emotion and have substituted more intentional or cognitivist understandings. These newer conceptions emphasize that intentional judgments as well as physiological disturbances are integral elements in emotion.[7] They define or identify emotions not by the quality or character of the physiological sensation that may be associated with them, but rather by their intentional aspect, the associated judgment. Thus, it is the content of my associated thought or judgment that determines whether my physical agitation and restlessness are defined as "anxiety about my daughter's lateness" rather than as "anticipation of tonight's performance."

Cognitivist accounts of emotion have been criticized as overly rationalist, inapplicable to allegedly spontaneous, automatic, or global emotions, such as general feelings of nervousness, contentedness, angst, ecstasy, or terror. Certainly, these accounts entail that infants and animals experience emotions, if at all, in only a primitive, rudimentary form. Far from being unacceptable, however, this entailment is desirable because it suggests that humans develop and mature in emotions as well as in other dimensions, increasing the range, variety, and subtlety of their emotional responses in accordance with their life experiences and their reflections on these.

Cognitivist accounts of emotion are not without their own problems. A serious difficulty with many is that they end up replicating within the structure of emotion the very problem they are trying to solve—namely, that of an artificial split between emotion and thought—because most cognitivist accounts explain emotion as having two "components": an affective or feeling component and a cognition that supposedly interprets or identifies the feelings. Such accounts, therefore, unwittingly perpetuate the positivist distinction between the shared, public, objective world of verifiable calculations, observations, and facts and the individual, private, subjective world of idiosyncratic feelings and sensations. This sharp distinction breaks any conceptual links between our feelings and the "external" world: if feelings are still conceived as blind or raw or undifferentiated, then we can give no sense to the notion of feelings fitting or failing to fit our perceptual judgments, that is, being appropriate or inappropriate. When intentionality is viewed as intellectual cognition and moved to the center of our picture of emotion, the affective elements are pushed to the periphery and become shadowy conceptual danglers whose relevance to emotion is obscure or even negligible. An adequate cognitive account of emotion must overcome this problem.

Most cognitivist accounts of emotion thus remain problematic in so far as they fail to explain the relationship between the cognitive and the affective aspects of emotion. Moreover, in so far as they prioritize the intellectual over the feeling aspects, they reinforce the traditional Western preference for mind over body.[8] Nevertheless, they do identify a vital feature of emotion overlooked by the Dumb View, namely, its intentionality.

Emotions as Social Constructs

We tend to experience our emotions as involuntary individual responses to situations, responses that are often (though, significantly, not always) private in the sense that they are not perceived as directly and immediately by other people as they are by the subject of the experience. The apparently individual and involuntary character of our emotional experience is often taken as evidence that emotions are presocial, instinctive responses, determined by our biological constitution. This inference, however, is quite mistaken. Although it is probably true that the physiological disturbances characterizing emotions (facial grimaces, changes in the metabolic rate, sweating, trembling, tears, and so on) are continuous with the instinctive responses of our prehuman ancestors and also that the ontogeny of emotions to some extent recapitulates their phylogeny, mature human emotions can be seen neither as instinctive nor as biologically determined. Instead, they are socially constructed on several levels.

The most obvious way in which emotions are socially constucted is that children are taught deliberately what their culture defines as appropriate responses to certain situations: to fear strangers, to enjoy spicy food, or to like swimming in cold water. On a less conscious level, children also learn what their culture defines as the appropriate ways to express the emotions that it recognizes. Although there may be cross-cultural similarities in the expression of some apparently universal emotions, there are also wide divergences in what are recognized as expressions of grief, respect, contempt, or anger. On an even deeper level, cultures construct divergent understandings of what emotions are. For instance, English metaphors and metonymies are said to reveal a "folk" theory of anger as a hot fluid contained in a private space within an individual and liable to dangerous public explosion (Lakoff and Kovecses 1987). By contrast, the Ilongot, a people of the Philippines, apparently do not understand the self in terms of a public/private distinction and consequently do not experience anger as an explosive internal force: for them, rather, it is an interpersonal phenomenon for which an individual may, for instance, be paid (Rosaldo 1984).

Further aspects of the social construction of emotion are revealed through reflection on emotion's intentional structure. If emotions necessarily involve judgments, then obviously they require concepts, which may be seen as socially constructed ways of organizing and making sense of the world. For this reason, emotions are simultaneously made possible and limited by the conceptual and linguistic resources of a society. This philosophical claim is borne out by empirical observation of the cultural variability of emotion. Although there is considerable overlap in the emotions identified by many cultures (Wierzbicka 1986), at least some emotions are historically or culturally specific, including perhaps *ennui, angst,* the Japanese *amai* (in which one clings to another, affiliative love), and the response of "being a wild pig," which occurs among the Gururumba, a horticultural people living in the New Guinea Highlands (Averell 1980, 158). Even apparently universal emotions, such as anger or love, may vary cross-culturally. We have just seen that the Ilongot experience of anger is apparently quite different from the contemporary Western experience. Romantic love was invented in the Middle Ages in Europe and has been modified considerably since that time; for instance, it is no longer confined to the nobility, and it no longer needs to be extramarital or unconsummated. In some cultures, romantic love does not exist at all.[9]

Thus there are complex linguistic and other social preconditions for the experience, that is, for the existence of human emotions. The emotions that we experience reflect prevailing forms of social life. For instance, one could not feel or even be betrayed in the absence of social norms about fidelity: it is inconceivable that betrayal or, indeed, any distinctively human emotion could be experienced by a solitary individual in some hypothetical presocial state of nature. There is a sense in which any individual's guilt or anger, joy or triumph presupposes the existence of a social group capable of feeling guilt, anger, joy, or triumph. This is not to say that group emotions historically precede or are logically prior to the emotions of individuals; it is to say that individual experience is simultaneously social experience.[10] In later sections, I shall explore the epistemological and political implications of this social rather than individual understanding of emotion.

Emotions as Active Engagements
We often interpret our emotions as experiences that overwhelm us rather than as responses we consciously choose: that emotions are to some extent involuntary is part of the ordinary meaning of the term *emotion*. Even in daily life, however, we recognize that emotions are not entirely involuntary and we try to gain control over them in various ways ranging from mechanistic behavior-modification techniques designed to sensitize or desensitize our feeling responses to various situations to cognitive techniques designed to help us to think differently about situations. For instance, we might try to change our response to an upsetting situation by thinking about it in a way that will either divert our attention from its more painful aspects or present it as necessary for some larger good.

Some psychological theories interpret emotions as chosen on an even deeper level, interpreting them as actions for which the agent disclaims responsibility. For instance, the psychologist Averell likens the experience of emotion to playing a culturally recognized role we ordinarily perform so smoothly and automatically that we do not realize we are giving a performance. He provides many examples demonstrating that even extreme and apparently totally involving displays of emotion are, in fact, functional for the individual and/or the society.[11] For example, students requested to record their experiences of anger or annoyance over a two-week period came to realize that their anger was not as uncontrollable and irrational as they had assumed previously, and they noted the usefulness and effectiveness of anger in achieving various social goods. Averell notes, however, that emotions often are useful in attaining their goals only if they are interpreted as passions rather than as actions, and he cites the case of one subject led to reflect on her anger who later wrote that it was less useful as a defense mechanism when she became conscious of its function.

The action/passion dichotomy is too simple for understanding emotion, as it is for other aspects of our lives. Perhaps it is more helpful to think of emotions as habitual responses that we may have more or less difficulty in breaking. We claim or disclaim responsibility for these responses depending on our purposes in a particular context. We could never experience our emotions entirely as deliberate actions, for then they would appear nongenuine and inauthentic, but neither should emotions be seen as nonintentional, primal, or physical forces with which our rational selves are forever at war. As they have been socially constructed, so may they be reconstructed, although describing how this might happen would have to be a long and complicated story.

Emotions, then, are wrongly seen as necessarily passive or involuntary responses to the world. Rather, they are ways in which we actively engage and even construct the world. They have both "mental" and "physical" aspects, each of which conditions the other; in some respects they are chosen but in others they are involuntary; they presuppose language and a social order. Thus, they can be attributed only to what are sometimes called "whole persons," engaged in the ongoing activity of social life.

Emotion, Evaluation, and Observation
Emotions and values are closely related. The relationship is so close, indeed, that some philosophical accounts of what it is to hold or express

certain values reduce these phenomena to nothing more than holding or expressing certain emotional attitudes. When the relevant concept of emotion is the Dumb View, then simple emotivism is certainly too crude an account of what it is to hold a value; in this account, the intentionality of value judgments vanishes and value judgments become nothing more than sophisticated grunts and groans. Nevertheless, the grain of important truth in emotivism is its recognition that values presuppose emotions to the extent that emotions provide the experiential basis for values. If we had no emotional responses to the world, it is inconceivable that we should ever come to value one state of affairs more highly than another.

Just as values presuppose emotions, so emotions presuppose values. The object of an emotion—that is, the object of fear, grief, pride, and so on—is a complex state of affairs that is appraised or evaluated by the individual. For instance, my pride in a friend's achievement necessarily incorporates the value judgment that my friend has done something worthy of admiration.

Emotions and evaluations, then, are logically or conceptually connected. Indeed, many evaluative terms derive directly from words for emotions: desirable, admirable, contemptible, despicable, respectable, and so on. Certainly it is true (pace J. S. Mill) that the evaluation of a situation as desirable or dangerous does not entail that it is universally desired or feared, but it does entail that desire or fear is viewed generally as an appropriate response to the situation. If someone is unafraid in a situation perceived generally as dangerous, her lack of fear requires further explanation; conversely, if someone is afraid without evident danger, then her fear demands explanation; and, if no danger can be identified, her fear is denounced as irrational or pathological. Thus, every emotion presupposes an evaluation of some aspect of the environment while, conversely, every evaluation or appraisal of the situation implies that those who share that evalution will share, ceteris paribus, a predictable emotional response to the situation.

The rejection of the Dumb View and the recognition of intentional elements in emotion already incorporate a realization that observation influences and, indeed, partially constitutes emotion. We have already seen that distinctively human emotions are not simple instinctive responses to situations or events; instead, they depend essentially on the ways that we perceive those situations and events as well on the ways that we have learned or decided to respond to them. Without characteristically human perceptions of and engagements in the world, there would be no characteristically human emotions.

Just as observation directs, shapes, and partially defines emotion, so too emotion directs, shapes, and even partially defines observation. Observation is not simply a passive process of absorbing impressions or recording stimuli; instead, it is an activity of selection and interpretation. What is selected and how it is interpreted are influenced by emotional attitudes. On the level of individual observation, this influence has always been apparent to common sense, which notes that we remark very different features of the world when we are happy, depressed, fearful, or confident. This influence of emotion on perception is now being explored by social scientists. One example is the so-called Honi phenomenon, named after a subject called Honi who, under identical experimental conditions, perceived strangers' heads as changing in size but saw her husband's head as remaining the same.[12]

The most obvious significance of this sort of example is in illustrating how the individual experience of emotion focuses our attention selectively, directing, shaping, and even partially defining our observations, just as our observations direct, shape, and partially define our emotions. In addition, the example has been taken further in an argument for the social construction of what are taken in any situation to be undisputed facts, showing how these rest on intersubjective agreements that consist partly in shared assumptions about "normal" or appropriate emotional responses to situations (McLaughlin 1985). Thus these examples suggest that certain emotional attitudes are involved on a deep level in all observation, in the intersubjectively verified and so supposedly dispassionate observations of science as well as in the common perceptions of daily life. In the next section, I shall elaborate this claim.

Epistemology

The Myth of Dispassionate Investigation
As we have already seen, Western epistemology has tended to view emotion with suspicion and even hostility.[13] This derogatory Western attitude toward emotion, like the earlier Western contempt for sensory observation, fails to recognize that emotion, like sensory perception, is necessary to human survival. Emotions prompt us to act appropriately, to approach some people and situations and to avoid others, to caress or cuddle, fight or flee. Without emotion, human life would be unthinkable. Moreover, emotions have an intrinsic as well as an instrumental value. Although not all emotions are enjoyable or even justifiable, as we shall see, life without any emotion would be life without any meaning.

Within the context of Western culture, however, people have often been encouraged to control or even suppress their emotions. Consequently, it is not unusual for people to be unaware of their emotional state or to deny it to themselves and others. This lack of awareness, especially combined with a neopositivist understanding of emotion that construes it as just a feeling of which one is aware, lends plausibility to the myth of dispassionate investigation. But lack of awareness of emotions certainly does not mean that emotions are not present subconsciously or unconsciously, or that subterranean emotions do not exert a continuing influence on people's articulated values and observations, thoughts, and actions.[14]

Within the positivist tradition, the influence of emotion is usually seen only as distorting or impeding observation or knowledge. Certainly it is true that contempt, disgust, shame, revulsion, or fear may inhibit investigation of certain situations or phenomena. Furiously angry or extremely sad people often seem quite unaware of their surroundings or even of their own conditions; they may fail to hear or may systematically misinterpret what other people say. People in love are notoriously oblivious to many aspects of the situation around them.

In spite of these examples, however, positivist epistemology recognizes that the role of emotion in the construction of knowledge is not invariably deleterious and that emotions may make a valuable contribution to knowledge. But the positivist tradition will allow emotion to play only the role of suggesting hypotheses for investigation. Emotions are allowed this because the so-called logic of discovery sets no limits on the idiosyncratic methods that investigators may use for generating hypotheses.

When hypotheses are to be tested, however, positivist epistemology imposes the much stricter logic of justification. The core of this logic is replicability, a criterion believed capable of eliminating or canceling out what are conceptualized as emotional as well as evaluative biases on the part of individual investigators. The conclusions of Western science, thus, are presumed to be objective, precisely in the sense that they are uncontaminated by the supposedly subjective values and emotions that might bias individual investigators (Nagel 1968, 33–34).

But if, as has been argued, the positivist distinction between discovery and justification is not viable, then such a distinction is incapable of filtering out values in science. For example, although such a split, when built into the Western scientific method, is generally successful in neutralizing the idiosyncratic or unconventional values of individual investigators, it has been argued that it does not, indeed, cannot, eliminate

generally accepted social values. These values are implicit in the identification of the problems that are considered worthy of investigation,
in the selection of the hypotheses that are considered worthy of testing,
and in the solutions to the problems that are considered worthy of
acceptance. The science of past centuries provides ample evidence of the
influence of prevailing social values, whether seventeenth-century atom-
istic physics (Merchant 1980) or nineteenth-century competitive interpretations of natural selection (Young 1985).

Of course, only hindsight allows us to identify clearly the values that
shaped the science of the past and, thus, to reveal the formative influence
on science of pervasive emotional attitudes, attitudes that typically went
unremarked at the time because they were shared so generally. For
instance, it is now glaringly evident that contempt for (and perhaps fear
of) people of color is implicit in nineteenth-century anthropology's interpretations and even constructions of anthropological facts. Because we
are closer to them, however, it is harder for us to see how certain
emotions, such as sexual possessiveness or the need to dominate others,
are currently accepted as guiding principles in twentieth-century sociobiology or even defined as part of reason within political theory and
economics (Quinby 1986).

Values and emotions enter into the science of the past and the present
not only at the level of scientific practice but also at the metascientific
level, as answers to various questions: What is science? How should it
be practiced? And what is the status of scientific investigation versus
nonscientific modes of inquiry? For instance, it is claimed with increasing
frequency that the modern Western conception of science, which identifies
knowledge with power and views it as a weapon for dominating nature,
reflects the imperialism, racism, and misogyny of the societies that created it. Several feminist theorists have argued that modern epistemology
itself may be viewed as an expression of certain emotions alleged to be
especially characteristic of males in certain periods, such as separation
anxiety and paranoia (Flax 1983; Bordo 1987) or an obsession with
control and fear of contamination (Scheman 1985; Schott 1988).

Positivism views values and emotions as alien invaders that must be
repelled by a stricter application of the scientific method. If the foregoing
claims are correct, however, the scientific method and even its positivist
construals themselves incorporate values and emotions. Moreover, such
an incorporation seems a necessary feature of all knowledge and conceptions of knowledge. Therefore, rather than repressing emotion in

epistemology, it is necessary to rethink the relationship between knowledge and emotion and construct conceptual models that demonstrate the mutually constitutive rather than oppositional relationship between reason and emotion. Far from precluding the possibility of reliable knowledge, emotion as well as value must be shown as necessary to such knowledge. Despite its classical antecedents and as in the ideal of disinterested inquiry, the ideal of dispassionate inquiry is an impossible dream, but a dream none the less or perhaps a myth that has exerted enormous influence on Western epistemology. Like all myths, it is a form of ideology that fulfills certain social and political functions.

The Ideological Function of the Myth

So far, I have spoken very generally of people and their emotions, as though everyone experienced similar emotions and dealt with them in similar ways. It is an axiom of feminist theory, however, that all generalizations about "people" are suspect. The divisions in our society are so deep, particularly the divisions of race, class, and gender, that many feminist theorists would claim that talk about people in general is ideologically dangerous because such talk obscures the fact that no one is simply a person but instead is constituted fundamentally by race, class, and gender. Race, class, and gender shape every aspect of our lives, and our emotional constitution is not excluded. Recognizing this helps us to see more clearly the political functions of the myth of the dispassionate investigator.

Feminist theorists have pointed out that the Western tradition has not seen everyone as equally emotional. Instead, reason has been associated with members of dominant political, social, and cultural groups and emotion with members of subordinate groups. Prominent among those subordinate groups in our society are people of color, except for supposedly "inscrutable orientals," and women.[15]

Although the emotionality of women is a familiar cultural stereotype, its grounding is quite shaky. Women appear to be more emotional than men because they, along with some groups of people of color, are permitted and even required to express emotion more openly. In contemporary Western culture, emotionally inexpressive women are suspect as not being real women, whereas men who express their emotions freely are suspected of being homosexual or in some other way deviant from the masculine ideal.[16] Modern Western men, in contrast with Shakespeare's heroes, for instance, are required to present a facade of coolness, lack of excitement, even boredom, to express emotion only rarely and then for relatively trivial events, such as sporting occasions, where the emotions expressed are acknowledged to be dramatized and so are not taken entirely seriously. Thus, women in our society form the main group allowed or even expected to express emotion. A woman may cry in the face of disaster, and a man of color may gesticulate, but a white man merely sets his jaw.[17]

White men's control of their emotional expression may go to the extremes of repressing their emotions, failing to develop emotionally or even losing the capacity to experience many emotions. Not uncommonly, these men are unable to identify what they are feeling, and even they may be surprised, on occasion, by their own apparent lack of emotional response to a situation, such as a death, where emotional reaction is perceived to be appropriate. In some married couples, the wife is implicitly assigned the job of feeling emotion for both of them. White, college-educated men increasingly enter therapy in order to learn how to "get in touch with" their emotions, a project other men may ridicule as weakness. In therapeutic situations, men may learn that they are just as emotional as women but less adept at identifying their own or others' emotions. In consequence, their emotional development may be relatively rudimentary; this may lead to moral rigidity or insensitivity. Paradoxically, men's lacking awareness of their own emotional responses frequently results in their being more influenced by emotion rather than less.

Although there is no reason to suppose that the thoughts and actions of women are any more influenced by emotion than the thoughts and actions of men, the stereotypes of cool men and emotional women continue to flourish because they are confirmed by an uncritical daily experience. In these circumstances, where there is a differential assignment of reason and emotion, it is easy to see the ideological function of the myth of the dispassionate investigator. It functions, obviously, to bolster the epistemic authority of the currently dominant groups, composed largely of white men, and to discredit the observations and claims of the currently subordinate groups, including, of course, the observations and claims of many people of color and women. The more forcefully and vehemently the latter groups express their observations and claims, the more emotional they appear and so the more easily they are discredited. The alleged epistemic authority of the dominant groups then justifies their political authority.

The preceding section of this paper argued that dispassionate inquiry was a myth. This section has shown that the myth promotes a conception of epistemological justification vindicating the silencing of those, especially women, who are defined culturally as the bearers of emotion and so are perceived as more "subjective," biased, and irrational. In our present social context, therefore, the ideal of the dispassionate investigator is a classist, racist, and especially masculinist myth.[18]

Emotional Hegemony and Emotional Subversion

As we have already seen, mature human emotions are neither instinctive nor biologically determined, although they may have developed out of presocial, instinctive responses. Like everything else that is human, emotions, in part, are socially constructed; like all social constructs, they are historical products, bearing the marks of the society that constructed them. Within the very language of emotion, in our basic definitions and explanations of what it is to feel pride or embarrassment, resentment or contempt, cultural norms and expectations are embedded. Simply describing ourselves as angry, for instance, presupposes that we view ourselves as having been wronged, victimized by the violation of some social norm. Thus, we absorb the standards and values of our society in the very process of learning the language of emotion, and those standards and values are built into the foundation of our emotional constitution.

Within a hierarchical society, the norms and values that predominate tend to serve the interests of the dominant groups. Within a capitalist, white suprematist, and male-dominant society, the predominant values will tend to be those that serve the interests of rich, white men. Consequently, we are all likely to develop an emotional constitution that is quite inappropriate for feminism. Whatever our color, we are likely to feel what Irving Thalberg has called "visceral racism"; whatever our sexual orientation, we are likely to be homophobic; whatever our class, we are likely to be at least somewhat ambitious and competitive; whatever our sex, we are likely to feel contempt for women. Such emotional responses may be rooted in us so deeply that they are relatively impervious to intellectual argument and may recur even when we pay lip service to changed intellectual convictions.[19]

By forming our emotional constitution in particular ways, our society helps to ensure its own perpetuation. The dominant values are implicit in responses taken to be precultural or acultural, our so-called gut responses. Not only do these conservative responses hamper and disrupt our attempts to live in or prefigure alternative social forms but also, and in so far as we take them to be natural responses, they blinker us theoretically. For instance, they limit our capacity for outrage; they either prevent us from despising or encourage us to despise; they lend plausibility to the belief that greed and domination are inevitable human motivations; in sum, they blind us to the possibility of alternative ways of living.

At first, this picture may seem to support the positivist claim that the intrusion of emotion only disrupts the process of seeking knowledge and distorts the results of that process. The picture, however, is not complete; it ignores the fact that people do not always experience the conventionally acceptable emotions. They may feel satisfaction rather than embarrassment when their leaders make fools of themselves. They may feel resentment rather than gratitude for welfare payments and hand-me-downs. They may be attracted to forbidden modes of sexual expression. They may feel revulsion for socially sanctioned ways of treating children or animals. In other words, the hegemony that our society exercises over people's emotional constitution is not total.

People who experience conventionally unacceptable, or what I call "outlaw" emotions are often subordinated individuals who pay a disproportionately high price for maintaining the status quo. The social situation of such people makes them unable to experience the conventionally prescribed emotions: for instance, people of color are more likely to experience anger than amusement when a racist joke is recounted, and women subjected to male sexual banter are less likely to be flattered than uncomfortable or even afraid.

When unconventional emotional responses are experienced by isolated individuals, those concerned may be confused, unable to name their experience; they may even doubt their own sanity. Women may come to believe that they are "emotionally disturbed" and that the embarrassment or fear aroused in them by male sexual innuendo is prudery or paranoia. When certain emotions are shared or validated by others, however, the basis exists for forming a subculture defined by perceptions, norms, and values that systematically oppose the prevailing perceptions, norms, and values. By constituting the basis for such a subculture, outlaw emotions may be politically (because epistemologically) subversive.

Outlaw emotions are distinguished by their incompatibility with the dominant perceptions and values, and some, though certainly not all, of these outlaw emotions are potentially or actually feminist emotions.

Emotions become feminist when they incorporate feminist perceptions and values, just as emotions are sexist or racist when they incorporate sexist or racist perceptions and values. For example, anger becomes feminist anger when it involves the perception that the persistent importuning endured by one woman is a single instance of a widespread pattern of sexual harassment, and pride becomes feminist pride when it is evoked by realizing that a certain person's achievement was possible only because that individual overcame specifically gendered obstacles to success.[20]

Outlaw emotions stand in a dialectical relation to critical social theory: at least some are necessary for developing a critical perspective on the world, but they also presuppose at least the beginnings of such a perspective. Feminists need to be aware of how we can draw on some of our outlaw emotions in constructing feminist theory, and also of how the increasing sophistication of feminist theory can contribute to the reeducation, refinement, and eventual reconstruction of our emotional constitution.

Outlaw Emotions and Feminist Theory

The most obvious way in which feminist and other outlaw emotions can help in developing alternatives to prevailing conceptions of reality is by motivating new investigations. This is possible because, as we saw earlier, emotions may be long term as well as momentary; it makes sense to say that someone continues to be shocked or saddened by a situation, even if she is, at the moment, laughing heartily. As we have seen already, theoretical investigation is always purposeful, and observation always selective. Feminist emotions provide a political motivation for investigation and so help to determine the selection of problems as well as the method by which they are investigated. Susan Griffin makes the same point when she characterizes feminist theory as following "a direction determined by pain, and trauma, and compassion and outrage" (Griffin 1979, 31).

As well as motivating critical research, outlaw emotions may also enable us to perceive the world differently from its portrayal in conventional descriptions. They may provide the first indications that something is wrong with the way alleged facts have been constructed, with accepted understandings of how things are. Conventionally unexpected or inappropriate emotions may precede our conscious recognition that accepted descriptions and justifications often conceal as much as reveal the prevailing state of affairs. Only when we reflect on our initially puzzling irritability, revulsion, anger, or fear may we bring to consciousness our gut-level awareness that we are in a situation of coercion, cruelty, injustice, or danger. Thus, conventionally inexplicable emotions, particularly though not exclusively those experienced by women, may lead us to make subversive observations that challenge dominant conceptions of the status quo. They may help us to realize that what are taken generally to be facts have been constructed in a way that obscures the reality of subordinated people, especially women's reality.

But why should we trust the emotional responses of women and other subordinated groups? How can we determine which outlaw emotions are to be endorsed or encouraged and which rejected? In what sense can we say that some emotional responses are more appropriate than others? What reason is there for supposing that certain alternative perceptions of the world, perceptions informed by outlaw emotions, are to be preferred to perceptions informed by conventional emotions? Here I can indicate only the general direction of an answer, one whose full elaboration must await another occasion.[21]

I suggest that emotions are appropriate if they are characteristic of a society in which all humans (and perhaps some nonhuman life too) thrive, or if they are conducive to establishing such a society. For instance, it is appropriate to feel joy when we are developing or exercising our creative powers, and it is appropriate to feel anger and perhaps disgust in those situations where humans are denied their full creativity or freedom. Similarly, it is appropriate to feel fear if those capacities are threatened in us.

This suggestion, obviously, is extremely vague and may even verge on the tautologous. How can we apply it in situations where there is disagreement over what is or is not disgusting or exhilarating or unjust? Here I appeal to a claim for which I have argued elsewhere: the perspective on reality that is available from the standpoint of the subordinated, which in part at least is the standpoint of women, is a perspective that offers a less partial and distorted and, therefore, more reliable view (Jaggar 1983, chap. 11). Subordinated people have a kind of epistemological privilege in so far as they have easier access to this standpoint and, therefore, a better chance of ascertaining the possible beginnings of a society in which all could thrive. For this reason, I would claim that the emotional responses of subordinated people in general, and often of women in particular, are more likely to be appropriate than the emotional responses of the dominant class. That is, they are more likely to incorporate reliable appraisals of situations.

Even in contemporary science, where the ideology of dispassionate inquiry is almost overwhelming, it is possible to discover a few examples that seem to support the claim that certain emotions are more appropriate than others in both a moral and epistemological sense. For instance, Hilary Rose claims that women's practice of caring, even though warped by its containment in the alienated context of a coercive sexual division of labor, has nevertheless generated more accurate and less oppressive understandings of women's bodily functions, such as menstruation (Rose 1983). Certain emotions may be both morally appropriate and epistemologically advantageous in approaching the nonhuman and even the inanimate world. Jane Goodall's scientific contribution to our understanding of chimpanzee behavior seems to have been made possible only by her amazing empathy with or even love for these animals (Goodall 1986). In her study of Barbara McClintock, Evelyn Fox Keller describes McClintock's relation to the objects of her research—grains of maize and their genetic properties—as a relation of affection, empathy, and "the highest form of love: love that allows for intimacy without the annihilation of difference." She notes that McClintock's "vocabulary is consistently a vocabulary of affection, of kinship, of empathy" (Keller 1984, 164). Examples like these prompt Hilary Rose to assert that a feminist science of nature needs to draw on heart as well as hand and brain.

Some Implications of Recognizing the
Epistemic Potential of Emotion

Accepting that appropriate emotions are indispensable to reliable knowledge does not mean, of course, that uncritical feeling may be substituted for supposedly dispassionate investigation. Nor does it mean that the emotional responses of women and other members of the underclass are to be trusted without question. Although our emotions are epistemologically indispensable, they are not epistemologically indisputable. Like all our faculties, they may be misleading, and their data, like all data, are always subject to reinterpretation and revision. Because emotions are not presocial, physiological responses to unequivocal situations, they are open to challenge on various grounds. They may be dishonest or self-deceptive, they may incorporate inaccurate or partial perceptions, or they may be constituted by oppressive values. Accepting the indispensability of appropriate emotions to knowledge means no more (and no less) than that discordant emotions should be attended to seriously and respectfully rather than condemned, ignored, discounted, or suppressed.

Just as appropriate emotions may contribute to the development of knowledge, so the growth of knowledge may contribute to the development of appropriate emotions. For instance, the powerful insights of feminist theory often stimulate new emotional responses to past and present situations. Inevitably, our emotions are affected by the knowledge that the women on our faculty are paid systematically less than the men, that one girl in four is subjected to sexual abuse from heterosexual men in her own family, and that few women reach orgasm in heterosexual intercourse. We are likely to feel different emotions toward older women or people of color as we reevaluate our standards of sexual attractiveness or acknowledge that black is beautiful. The new emotions evoked by feminist insights are likely, in turn, to stimulate further feminist observations and insights, and these may generate new directions in both theory and political practice. There is a continuous feedback loop between our emotional constitution and our theorizing such that each continually modifies the other and is, in principle, inseparable from it.

The ease and speed with which we can reeducate our emotions is unfortunately not great. Emotions are only partially within our control as individuals. Although affected by new information, they are habitual responses not quickly unlearned. Even when we come to believe consciously that our fear or shame or revulsion is unwarranted, we may still continue to experience emotions inconsistent with our conscious politics. We may still continue to be anxious for male approval, competitive with our comrades and sisters, and possessive with our lovers. These unwelcome, because apparently inappropriate, emotions should not be suppressed or denied; instead, they should be acknowledged and subjected to critical scrutiny. The persistence of such recalcitrant emotions probably demonstrates how fundamentally we have been constituted by the dominant worldview, but it may also indicate superficiality or other inadequacy in our emerging theory and politics.[22] We can only start from where we are—beings who have been created in a cruelly racist, capitalist, and male-dominated society that has shaped our bodies and our minds, our perceptions, our values and our emotions, our language, and our systems of knowledge.

The alternative epistemological models that I suggest would display the continuous interaction between how we understand the world and who we are as people. They would show how our emotional responses to the world change as we conceptualize it differently and how our changing emotional responses then stimulate us to new insights. They would demonstrate the need for theory to be self-reflexive, to focus not only on the outer world but also on ourselves and our relation to that world, to examine critically our social location, our actions, our values, our perceptions, and our emotions. The models would also show how feminist and other critical social theories are indispensable psychotherapeutic tools because they provide some insights necessary to a full understanding of our emotional constitution. Thus, the models would explain how the reconstruction of knowledge is inseparable from the reconstruction of ourselves.

A corollary of the reflexivity of feminist and other critical theory is that it requires a much broader construal of the process of theoretical investigation than positivism accepts. In particular, it requires acknowledging that a necessary part of the theoretical process is critical self-examination. Time spent in analyzing emotions and uncovering their sources should be viewed, therefore, neither as irrelevant to theoretical investigation nor even as a prerequisite for it; it is not a kind of clearing of the emotional decks, "dealing with" our emotions so that they will not influence our thinking. Instead, we must recognize that our efforts to reinterpret and refine our emotions are necessary to our theoretical investigation, just as our efforts to reeducate our emotions are necessary to our political activity. Critical reflection on emotion is not a self-indulgent substitute for political analysis and political action. It is, itself, a kind of political theory and political practice, indispensable for an adequate social theory and social transformation.

Finally, the recognition that emotions play a vital part in developing knowledge enlarges our understanding of women's claimed epistemic advantage. We can now see that women's subversive insights owe much to women's outlaw emotions, themselves appropriate responses to the situations of women's subordination. In addition to their propensity to experience outlaw emotions, at least on some level, women are relatively adept at identifying such emotions, in themselves and others, in part because of their social responsibility for caretaking, including emotional nurturance. It is true that women, like all subordinated peoples, especially those who must live in close proximity with their masters, often engage in emotional deception (and even self-deception) as the price of their survival. Even so, women may be less likely than other subordinated groups to engage in denial or suppression of outlaw emotions. Women's work of emotional nurturance has required them to develop a special acuity in recognizing hidden emotions and in understanding the genesis of those emotions. This emotional acumen can now be recognized as a skill in political analysis and validated as giving women a special advantage both in understanding the mechanisms of domination and in envisioning freer ways to live.

Conclusion

The claim that emotion is vital to systematic knowledge is only the most obvious contrast between the conception of theoretical investigation that I have sketched here and the conception provided by positivism. For instance, the alternative approach emphasizes that what we identify as emotion is a conceptual abstraction from a complex process of human activity that also involves acting, sensing, and evaluating. This proposed account of theoretical construction demonstrates the simultaneous necessity for, and interdependence of, faculties that our culture has abstracted and separated from each other: emotion and reason, evaluation and perception, observation and action. The model of knowing suggested here is nonhierarchical and antifoundationalist; instead, it is appropriately symbolized by the radical feminist metaphor of the upward spiral. Emotions are neither more basic than observation, reason, or action in building theory, nor secondary to them. Each of these human faculties reflects an aspect of human knowing inseparable from the other aspects. Thus, to borrow a famous phrase from a Marxist context, the development of each of these faculties is a necessary condition for the development of all.

In conclusion, it is interesting to note that acknowledging the importance of emotion for knowledge is not an entirely novel suggestion within the Western epistemological tradition. That archrationalist, Plato himself, came to accept in the end that knowledge required a (very purified form of) love. It may be no accident that, in the *Symposium*, Socrates learns this lesson from Diotima, the wise woman.

NOTES

This essay originally appeared in *Inquiry* 32 (1989): 151–76. It is used here with permission of the publisher. A similar version appeared in Alison M. Jaggar and Susan R. Bordo, eds., *Gender/Body/Knowledge: Feminist Reconstructions of Being and Knowing* (New Brunswick, N.J.: Rutgers University Press, 1989).

I wish to thank the following individuals who commented helpfully on earlier drafts of this essay or made me aware of further resources: Lynne Arnault, Susan Bordo, Martha Bolton, Cheshire Calhoun, Randy Cornelius, Shelagh Crooks, Ronald De Sousa, Tim Diamond, Dick Foley, Ann Garry, Judy Gerson, Mary Gibson, Sherry Gorelick, Marcia Lind, Helen Longino, Catherine Lutz, Andy McLaughlin, Uma Narayan, Linda Nicholson, Bob Richardson, Sally Ruddick, Laurie Shrage, Alan Soble, Vicky Spelman, Karsten Struhl, Joan Tronto, Daisy Quarm, Naomi Quinn, and Alison Wylie. I am also grateful to my colleagues in the Fall, 1985, Women's Studies Chair Seminar at Douglass College, Rutgers University and to audiences at Duke University, Georgia University Center, Hobart and William Smith Colleges, Northeastern University, the University of North Carolina at Chapel Hill, and Princeton University for their responses to earlier versions of this essay. In addition, I received many helpful comments from members of the Canadian Society for Women in Philosophy and from students in Lisa Heldke's classes in feminist epistemology at Carleton College and Northwestern University. Thanks, too, to Delia Cushway, who provided a comfortable environment in which I wrote the first draft.

1. Philosophers who do not conform to this generalization and constitute part of what Susan Bordo calls a "recessive" tradition in Western philosophy include Hume and Nietzsche, Dewey and James (Bordo 1987, 114–18).

2. The Western tradition as a whole has been profoundly rationalist, and much of its history may be viewed as a continuous redrawing of the boundaries of the rational. For a survey of this history from a feminist perspective, see Lloyd 1984.

3. Thus, fear or other emotions were seen as rational in some circumstances. To illustrate this point, Vicky Spelman quotes Aristotle as saying (in the *Nicomachean Ethics*, bk. 4, chap. 5): "[Anyone] who does not get angry when there is reason to be angry, or who does not get angry in the right way at the right time and with the right people, is a dolt" (Spelman 1982, 1).

4. Descartes, Leibniz, and Kant are among the prominent philosophers who did not endorse a wholly stripped-down, instrumentalist conception of reason.

5. The relocation of values in human attitudes and preferences in itself was not grounds for denying their universality, because they could have been conceived as grounded in a common or universal human nature. In fact, however, the variability, rather than the commonality, of human preferences and responses was emphasized; values gradually came to be viewed as individual, particular, and even idiosyncratic rather than as universal and objective. The only exception to the variability of human desires was the supposedly universal urge to egoism and the motive to maximize one's own utility, whatever that consisted in. The value of autonomy and liberty, consequently, was seen as perhaps the only value capable of being justified objectively because it was a precondition for satisfying other desires.

6. For instance, Julius Moravcsik has characterized as emotions what I would call "plain" hunger and thirst, appetites that are not desires for any particular food or drink (Moravcsik 1982, 207–24). I myself think that such states, which Moravcsik also calls instincts or appetites, are understood better as sensations than emotions. In other words, I would view so-called instinctive, nonintentional feelings as the biological raw material from which full-fledged human emotions develop.

7. Even adherents of the Dumb View recognize, of course, that emotions are not

entirely random or unrelated to an individual's judgments and beliefs; in other words, they note that people are angry or excited *about* something, afraid or proud *of* something. In the Dumb View, however, the judgments or beliefs associated with an emotion are seen as its causes and, thus, as related to it only externally.

8. Cheshire Calhoun pointed this out to me in private correspondence.

9. Recognition of the many levels on which emotions are socially constructed raises the question of whether it makes sense even to speak of the possibility of universal emotions. Although a full answer to this question is methodologically problematic, one might speculate that many of what we Westerners identify as emotions have functional analogues in other cultures. In other words, it may be that people in every culture behave in ways that fulfil at least some social functions of our angry or fearful behavior.

10. The relationship between the emotional experience of an individual and the emotional experience of the group to which the individual belongs may perhaps be clarified by analogy with the relationship between a word and the language of which it is a part. That a word has meaning presupposes that it is part of a linguistic system without which it has no meaning; yet the language itself has no meaning over and above the meaning of the words of which it is composed together with their grammatical ordering. Words and language presuppose and mutually constitute each other. Similarly, both individual and group emotion presuppose and mutually constitute each other.

11. Averell cites dissociative reactions by military personnel at Wright Patterson Air Force Base and shows how these were effective in mustering help to deal with difficult situations while simultaneously relieving the individual of responsibility or blame (Averell 1980, 157).

12. These and similar experiments are described in Kilpatrick 1961, chap. 10, cited in McLaughlin 1985, 296.

13. The positivist attitude toward emotion, which requires that ideal investigators be both disinterested and dispassionate, may be a modern variant of older traditions in Western philosophy that recommended people seek to minimize their emotional responses to the world and develop instead their powers of rationality and pure contemplation.

14. It is now widely accepted that the suppression and repression of emotion has damaging if not explosive consequences. There is general acknowledgement that no one can avoid at some time experiencing emotions she or he finds unpleasant, and there is also increasing recognition that the denial of such emotions is likely to result in hysterical disorders of thought and behavior, in projecting one's own emotions on others, in displacing them to inappropriate situations, or in psychosomatic ailments. Psychotherapy, which purports to help individuals recognize and "deal with" their emotions, has become an enormous industry, especially in the United States. In much conventional psychotherapy, however, emotions are still conceived as feelings or passions, "subjective" disturbances that afflict individuals or interfere with their capacity for rational thought and action. Different therapies, therefore, have developed a wide variety of techniques for encouraging people to "discharge" or "vent" their emotions, just as they would drain an abscess. Once emotions have been discharged or vented, they are supposed to be experienced less intensely, or even to vanish entirely, and consequently to exert less influence on individuals' thoughts and actions. This approach to psychotherapy clearly demonstrates its kinship with the "folk" theory of anger mentioned earlier, and it equally clearly retains the traditional Western assumption that emotion is inimical to rational thought and action. Thus, such

approaches fail to challenge and, indeed, provide covert support for the view that "objective" knowers are not only disinterested but also dispassionate.

15. E. V. Spelman (1982) illustrates this point with a quotation from the well-known contemporary philosopher R. S. Peters, who wrote, "We speak of emotional outbursts, reactions, upheavals, and women" (*Proceedings of the Aristotelian Society*, n.s. 62).

16. It seems likely that the conspicuous absence of emotion shown by Mrs. Thatcher is a deliberate strategy she finds necessary to counter the public perception of women as too emotional for political leadership. The strategy results in her being perceived as a formidable leader, but as an Iron Lady rather than a real woman. Ironically, Neil Kinnock, leader of the British Labour Party and Thatcher's main opponent in the 1987 general election, was able to muster considerable public support through television commercials portraying him in the stereotypically feminine role of caring about the unfortunate victims of Thatcher economics. Ultimately, however, this support was not sufficient to destroy public confidence in Mrs. Thatcher's "masculine" competence and gain Kinnock the election.

17. On the rare occasions when a white man cries, he is embarrassed and feels constrained to apologize. The one exception to the rule that men should be emotionless is that they are allowed and often even expected to experience anger. Spelman (1982) points out that men's cultural permission to be angry bolsters their claim to authority.

18. Someone might argue that the viciousness of this myth was not a logical necessity. In an egalitarian society, where the concepts of reason and emotion were not gender bound in the way they still are today, it might be argued that the ideal of the dispassionate investigator could be epistemologically beneficial. Is it possible that, in such socially and conceptually egalitarian circumstances, the myth of the dispassionate investigator could serve as a heuristic device, an ideal never to be realized in practice but nevertheless helping to minimize "subjectivity" and bias? My own view is that counterfactual myths rarely bring the benefits advertised and that this one is no exception. This myth fosters an equally mythical conception of pure truth and objectivity, quite independent of human interests or desires, and in this way it functions to disguise the inseparability of theory and practice, science and politics. Thus, it is part of an antidemocratic worldview that mystifies the political dimensions of knowledge and unwarrantedly circumscribes the arena of political debate.

19. Of course, the similarities in our emotional constitutions should not blind us to systematic differences. For instance, girls rather than boys are taught fear and disgust for spiders and snakes, affection for fluffy animals, and shame for their naked bodies. It is primarily, though not exclusively, men rather than women whose sexual responses are shaped by exposure to visual and sometimes violent pornography. Girls and women are taught to cultivate sympathy for others; boys and men are taught to separate themselves emotionally from others. As I have noted already, more emotional expression is permitted for lower-class and some nonwhite men than for ruling-class men, perhaps because the expression of emotion is thought to expose vulnerability. Men of the upper classes learn to cultivate an attitude of condescension, boredom, or detached amusement. As we shall see shortly, differences in the emotional constitution of various groups may be epistemologically significant in so far as they both presuppose and facilitate different ways of perceiving the world.

20. A necessary condition for experiencing feminist emotions is that one already be a feminist in some sense, even if one does not consciously wear that label. But many women

and some men, even those who would deny that they are feminist, still experience emotions compatible with feminist values. For instance, they may be angered by the perception that someone is being mistreated just because she is a woman, or they may take special pride in the achievement of a woman. If those who experience such emotions are unwilling to recognize them as feminist, their emotions are probably described better as potentially feminist or prefeminist emotions.

21. I owe this suggestion to Marcia Lind.

22. Within a feminist context, Berenice Fisher suggests that we focus particular attention on our emotions of guilt and shame as part of a critical reevaluation of our political ideals and our political practice (Fisher 1984).

REFERENCES

Averell, James R. 1980. "The Emotions." In *Personality: Basic Aspects and Current Research*, ed. Ervin Staub. Englewood Cliffs, N.J.: Prentice Hall.

Bordo, S. R. 1987. *The Flight to Objectivity: Essays on Cartesianism and Culture.* Albany, N.Y.: SUNY Press.

Fisher, Berenice. 1984. "Guilt and Shame in the Women's Movement: The Radical Ideal of Action and Its Meaning for Feminist Intellectuals." *Feminist Studies* 10:185–212.

Flax, Jane. 1983. "Political Philosophy and the Patriarchal Unconscious: A Psychoanalytic Perspective on Epistemology and Metaphysics." In *Discovering Reality: Feminist Perspectives on Epistemology, Metaphysics, Methodology and Philosophy of Science*, ed. Sandra Harding and Merrill Hintikka. Dordrecht: Reidel.

Goodall, Jane. 1986. *The Chimpanzees of Bombe: Patterns of Behavior.* Cambridge, Mass.: Harvard University Press.

Griffin, Susan. 1979. *Rape: The Power of Consciousness.* San Francisco: Harper and Row.

Hinman, Lawrence. 1986. "Emotion, Morality, and Understanding." Paper presented at the annual meeting of the Central Division of the American Philosophical Association, St. Louis.

Jaggar, Alison M. 1983. *Feminist Politics and Human Nature.* Totowa, N.J.: Rowman and Allanheld.

Keller, E. F. 1984. *Gender and Science.* New Haven: Yale University Pres.

Kilpatrick, Franklin P., ed. 1961. *Explorations in Transactional Psychology.* New York: New York University Press.

Lakoff, George, and Zoltan Kovecses. 1987. "The Cognitive Model of Anger Inherent in American English." In *Cultural Models in Language and Thought*, ed. N. Quinn and D. Holland. New York: Cambridge University Press.

Lewontin, R. C. 1982. "Letter to the Editor." *New York Review of Books*, February 4, 40–41.

Lloyd, Genevieve. 1984. *The Man of Reason: "Male" and "Female" in Western Philosophy.* Minneapolis: University of Minnesota Press.

Lutz, Catherine. 1985. "Depression and the Translation of Emotional Worlds." In *Culture and Depression: Studies in the Anthropology and Cross-cultural Psychiatry of Affect and Disorder*, ed. A. Kleinman and B. Good. Berkeley: University of California Press.

Lutz, Catherine. 1986. "Emotion, Thought, and Estrangement: Emotion as a Cultural Category." *Cultural Anthropology* 1:287–309.

Lutz, Catherine. 1987. "Goals, Events, and Understanding in Ifaluck and Emotion Theory." In *Cultural Models in Language and Thought*, ed. N. Quinn and D. Holland. New York: Cambridge University Press.

McLaughlin, Andrew. 1985. "Images and Ethics of Nature." *Environmental Ethics* 7: 293–319.

Merchant, Carolyn M. 1980. *The Death of Nature: Women, Ecology, and the Scientific Revolution*. New York: Harper and Row.

Moravcsik, J. M. E. 1982. "Understanding and the Emotions." *Dialectica* 36, nos. 2–3: 207–24.

Nagel, E. 1968. "The Subjective Nature of Social Subject Matter." In *Readings in the Philosophy of the Social Sciences*, ed. May Brodbeck. New York: Macmillan.

Quinby, Lee. 1986. Discussion following talk at Hobart and William Smith Colleges.

Rorty, Richard. 1979. *Philosophy and the Mirror of Nature*. Princeton, N.J.: Princeton University Press.

Rosaldo, Michelle Z. 1984. "Towards an Anthropology of Self and Feeling." In *Culture Theory*, ed. Richard A. Shweder and Robert A. LeVine. Cambridge: Cambridge University Press.

Rose, Hilary. 1983. "Hand, Brain, and Heart: A Feminist Epistemology for the Natural Sciences." *Signs: Journal of Women in Culture and Society* 9, no. 1: 73–90.

Schachter, Stanley, and Jerome B. Singer. 1969. "Cognitive, Social, and Psychologial Determinants of Emotional State." *Psychological Review* 69:379–99.

Scheman, Naomi. 1985. "Women in the Philosophy Curriculum." Paper presented at the annual meeting of the Central Division of the American Philosophical Association, Chicago.

Schott, Robin M. 1988. *Cognition and Eros: A Critique of the Kantian Paradigm*. Boston: Beacon.

Spelman, E. V. 1982. "Anger and Insubordination." Typescript.

Wierzbicka, Anna. 1986. "Human Emotions: Universal or Culture-Specific?" *American Anthropologist* 88:584–94.

Young, R. M. 1985. *Darwin's Metaphor: Nature's Place in Victorian Culture*. Cambridge: Cambridge University Press.

Feminist Skepticism and the "Maleness" of Philosophy

Susan Bordo

In the late 1970s in the United States, contemporary American feminism took an important turn. From an initial emphasis on legal, economic, and social discrimination against women, feminists began to consider the deep effects of the gender organization of human life on Western culture—on the literary, scientific, and philosophical canon that we call "the Western intellectual tradition." Earlier feminist works had criticized that tradition for its explicit gender biases: objectionable images of women, misogynist theory, the lack of representation of women's concerns and voices, and so forth. In the late 1970s, however, a deeper "hermeneutics of suspicion" emerged among feminists. We began to realize that gender bias may be revealed in one's *perspective* on the nature of reality, in one's style of thinking, in one's approach to problems—quite apart from any explicit gender content or attitudes toward the sexes.

Recently, some contemporary feminists have taken yet another critical turn. Criticizing what they see as the historical oversimplifications and unconscious ethnocentrisms of earlier feminist readings of culture, more recent perspectives urge a new caution, a new skepticism about the use of gender as an analytical category. These perspectives, like much contemporary thought, are informed by what might be called a "theoretics of heterogeneity"—an attunement to multiple interpretive possibilities, to the plurality of interpenetrating factors that comprise any object of analysis, and to the "differences" that fragment all general claims about culture. According to such perspectives, to theorize culture or history along gender lines—to speak of "male" and "female" realities or perspectives—is to homogenize diversity and obscure particularity.

Although most commonly associated with postmodern continental perspectives,[1] such a theoretics of heterogeneity, particularly with respect to its implications for a cultural understanding of philosophy, is strikingly and articulately exemplified by the Anglo-American analyst Jean Grimshaw. In *Philosophy and Feminist Thinking*, emphasizing what she describes as the "extremely variegated nature" of human experience,[2] Grimshaw presents two major skeptical challenges to the notion that the history of philosophy can meaningfully and nonreductively be characterized as "male." One such challenge concerns the assumption that the historical traditions of Western philosophy, culturally heterogeneous as they are, can be said to exhibit characteristic enough features to permit *any* generalizations about content or style, gender based or otherwise. At stake here is the question of how one "reads" the history of *philosophy*. Her other challenge concerns the legitimacy, however one resolves this first issue, of characterizing philosophical perspectives (or, indeed, *any* perspectives) as "male." At stake here is the question of whether philosophy's historical concerns reflect, in some meaningful way, the historical fact of male dominance within the discipline.

Grimshaw does not deny, it should be emphasized, the explicit misogyny of many philosophers, or the persistent exclusion of women from their conceptions of human nature and human excellence. Indeed, she devotes many pages to examining the *sexism* of philosophy. What she questions, rather, is the notion that there is anything distinctively "male" about the *perspective* (or perspectives) that philosophy brings to problems, quite apart from beliefs and attitudes about women and men. In her book, she presents many interesting substantive criticisms of particular accounts of the "maleness" of philosophy. These will not be dealt with here. Rather, my goal is to describe a context of legitimacy for a certain *kind* of enterprise. There are complexities and cautions that must be taken into account in approaching the question of philosophy's "maleness." But, I argue, the question is neither ill founded nor unanswerable. In defending such a notion, I will also indicate a context in which the insights of Grimshaw's skepticism may be profitably employed. Finally, I briefly discuss some of my own concerns about gender skepticism as a potential theoretical turn within feminism, and advocate a more practical, contextual approach to problems of heterogeneity and generality.

Before I do any of these, however, it is necessary to present some theoretical background to the issue. In the United States, two works—Dorothy Dinnerstein's *Mermaid and the Minotaur*[3] and Nancy Chodorow's *Reproduction of Mothering*[4]—were especially influential in charting two important directions that feminist conceptions of the "maleness" of philosophy were to take.

Dinnerstein's central focus was on destructive cultural attitudes toward nature, the human body, mortality, and sexuality. These attitudes are gender biased, Dinnerstein argued, not in the sense that they are exclusively or even distinctively held by men, but, rather, in the sense that they ultimately derive from a gynophobia to which both men and women are vulnerable, insofar as they have been raised within a system of female-dominated infant care. Within such a system, everything pleasurable *and* everything terrifying about bodily needs, desires, and vulnerabilities are first experienced in the arms of a woman—the mother. As a consequence, the entire arena of spontaneous bodily experience becomes associated with "woman" in general and remains split off from the cultural psyche—now identified with all that is "mind," and coded as male. Split off in this way, our ambivalence toward the body remains culturally unintegrated and destructive, particularly for those on whom it is "projected": woman and nature.

Dinnerstein's cultural emphasis has affinities with developments in French feminism. Inspired by Lacanian psychoanalysis, the key category here is that of phallocentrism, the reign of the phallus operating as a metaphor for the cultural privileging of unity, stability, identity, and self-mastery over the "maternally connoted" values of body, spontaneity, multiplicity, loss of self, and so on.[5] Both men and women, Julia Kristeva argues, find reality constructed for them through the template of this symbolic system; for her (although not for other French feminists), there is no specifically feminine form of discourse. Women, insofar as they participate fully in the dominant symbolic order, are just as "phallic" as men; some men, on the other hand (e.g., iconoclastic artists and philosophers), have often been inspired disrupters of that order.

Nancy Chodorow's emphasis, in contrast, was on *differences* in the psychology and "cognitive style" of men and women, differences stemming from constrasting patterns in the development of male and female infants. Because a more rigorous individuation from the mother is demanded of boys, they grow up, Chodorow argued, insisting on clear and distinct boundaries between self and others, self and world, and defining achievement in terms of emotional detachment and autonomy.

Possibilities for the application of Chodorow's ideas to the analysis of our male-dominated intellectual traditions immediately presented

themselves to feminists from many disciplines. Adopting her emphasis
on gender difference, many U.S. feminists began to see the individualist
and objectivist biases of dominant traditions in the disciplines and professions as "masculine"—that is, as connected to characteristic features
of the construction of male psychology and personality. Carol Gilligan's
influential *In a Different Voice* emerged from this stream of feminist
thought.[6] In it, she elaborated the consequences of the privileging of
detachment and individual autonomy in developmental theory and in
our dominant ideals of moral reasoning. Created by men, such theories
and ideals establish, as normative, a view of social relations and a
hierarchy of ethical values that, Gilligan argued, do not reflect the more
relational picture of reality underlying the ethical reasoning of women.
(It should be noted, however, that Gilligan does not view the different
"voices" she describes as essentially or only related to gender. She discovers them in her clinical work exploring gender difference, but the
chief aim of her book, as she describes it, is to "highlight a distinction
between two modes of thought and to focus a problem of interpretation
rather than to represent a generalization about either sex.")[7]

The feminist critique of the Western philosophical tradition has been
nourished by insights from what I have here characterized in terms of
"Dinnersteinian/Kristevan" (on the one hand) and "Chodorovian" (on
the other hand) approaches. Writing from a variety of perspectives,
feminist philosophers have by now produced a formidable body of gender
analysis directed at the traditions of Western philosophy and specific
authors within it.[8] Many argue that philosophy has been "masculine" in
a psychological sense; others have focused on the persistence of gynophobic themes and/or phallocentric structurings of reality.

Feminist controversy surrounds the historical generalizations involved in
such characterizations of philosophy. What I will call the skeptical position on the history of philosophy has been articulated in a number of
different (and sometimes contradictory) ways. Grimshaw, pointing to
the many conceptual transformations that have marked the history of
Western metaphysics and epistemology, has argued that attempts to spec-
ify dominant continuing themes in Western thought necessarily involve
a homogenizing and distorting ahistoricism. The so-called mind/body
problem, for example, so central to modern epistemology, has no equivalent in classical Greek culture—for the concept of mind in the modern
sense of consciousness was philosophically developed only in the modern
era. To speak of a "mind/body problem" in Plato or Aristotle, thus, is

to ahistorically map the categories of the present onto those of the past.[9] Other feminists, pointing to the contradictions and debates *within* historical periods, have argued that it is illegitimate to identify distinct historical periods. Rosalind Petchesky, tracing continuing organicist images and metaphors into the seventeenth century, has argued that any marking of a "transformation" from an organic to a mechanistic worldview, which some feminists have seen as a decisive historical moment in a modern "masculinization" of thought,[10] is a distorting construction. The existence of multiple and competing voices, discoverable at every historical juncture, renders suspect any reading of history that claims to mark the end of one worldview and the triumph of another.[11]

I share the historicist and pluralist sensibilities of such critics. It should be noted, however, that one cannot hold both Grimshaw's and Petchesky's pluralisms at the same time. If history is read, as Petchesky advocates, as absolute heterogeneity, then the deep conceptual transformations that Grimshaw points to become *her* distortingly univocal rendering of the multiple voices of history. A more consistent pluralism would acknowledge that philosophy is marked both by important historical ruptures— such as the birth of modern science—*and* by constant contestation and debate within the philosophical conversation of particular periods. What is difficult to see, however, is how acknowledging such heterogeneity entails denying that there have been continuing dominant perspectives, both within historical eras and across them. Grimshaw's and Petchesky's conceptions of history and philosophy appear to assume an unsupportable "either/or" conception of change/continuity and dominance/multiplicity. Let me elaborate this criticism.

First, as Michel Foucault's very different conception of history suggests, in "reading" particular periods, one need not *choose* between a reading that reveals heterogeneity and one that acknowledges the hegemony of a particular historical discourse. Within the history of philosophy, resistant and alternative voices frequently have spoken against a dominant discourse; indeed, often within the work of a single thinker, it is possible to discern both a dominant and a "recessive" strain, the latter speaking for the excluded and the devalued.[12] Grimshaw and Petchesky both present such examples as counterevidence against various feminist attempts to describe general coherencies in the history of philosophy. In their frameworks, apparently, hegemony must be seamless or it cannot be counted as hegemony. A more Foucauldian approach, on the other hand, emphasizes that cultural dominance is never *total.*

In fact, precisely by virtue of its dominance, a reigning discourse creates its own sites of resistance and contestation. First, in the very process of establishing its norms, it constructs and defines all those who are deviant *as* resistant, "outside," as the constant shadow (to use Jung's term) of the cultural norm. Moreover, intellectual dominance does not take the form of univocal, magisterial decree, but exercises itself through perpetual local "battles" (Foucault's metaphor) organized around "innumerable points of confrontation (and) focuses of instability."[13] Dominance emerges *through*, not in the absence of, contestation. At certain points, dominant categories, precisely because they are so ubiquitously present in culture, may even spawn "reverse discourses" that employ those categories on behalf of the marginalized. The movements for women's and homosexual rights, for example, drew their initial rhetoric from the categories of liberal humanism and possessive individualism. Today, we are beginning to recognize the losses as well as the gains from that strategy. But, in fact, in the early stages of these movements, no other political rhetoric was as culturally available to as many people: the language of individual rights seemed as natural as the air we breathed. The appearance of naturalness, of course, is a chief mode through which discourses establish and maintain their dominance.

Second, when reading *across* particular periods, a reading that reveals continuity and one that reveals discontinuity are not, as Grimshaw appears to believe, mutually exclusive interpretive strategies. Examples of conceptual change (e.g., of concepts of Mind, Reason, and so forth) do not constitute evidence that there are no transhistorical elements in Western philosophy. For example, although the "mind/body problem" as such may have been invented in the seventeenth century, there is no denying that the body is constituted as a problem for many philosophers. Certainly, the connotations and images have changed with historical circumstances from era to era. For Plato, for example, living in a culture whose imperialist conquests had opened the doors to an influx of diverse peoples, customs, and morals, raising the spectre of cultural relativism in the face of a once-stable system of values, "the body" is imagined as the site of epistemological and moral confusion, its unreliable senses and volatile passions continually deceiving us into mistaking the transient and illusory for the permanent and the real. For the ruling philosophy of the Middle Ages, on the other hand, "the body" is imagined quite differently. Scientific and moral knowledge is stable and in order, as yet unperturbed by the geographical discoveries, religious upheavals, and technological innovations that were to so upset the prevailing picture of the world in the sixteenth and seventeenth centuries. Within this closed universe, whose contours were shaped by the narratives, images, and values of Christianity, the quest for spiritual purity rather than epistemological certainty was the constant struggle. The body now becomes dominantly imagined as the site of unwanted desire—"the slimy desires of the flesh," as Augustine called sexual passion—threat to spiritual progress and ultimate union with God, and symbolized, for him, in the spontaneously and rebelliously tumescent penis, insisting on its "law of lust" against the attempts of the spiritual will to gain control. We thus see considerable conceptual versatility in the construction of "the body." What remains ubiquitous, however, is the casting of the body as the enemy of purity and control, whether spiritual (as for Augustine) or epistemological (as for Plato and Descartes).

The construction of body-as-enemy is one variant of a more general motif that French feminism has helped us to discern. Hélène Cixous and Luce Irigaray work with categories derived from both de Beauvoir and Derrida and argue that, despite major conceptual shifts, a distinctive *form* and a characteristic *logic* runs throughout the history of Western philosophy.[14] The form is that of hierarchical opposition: the bifurcation of reality into mutually opposed elements, one of which is privileged and identified with Self, the other of which is disdained and designated as Other. To Anglo-American philosophers, the term *dualism* may be more familiar. But it must be stressed that the dualism discussed here is not a self-conscious philosophical "position" to be contrasted to materialism, monism, and so forth. It is, rather, the implicit and sometimes unconscious structuring that underlies virtually all such "positions"—a structuring that Derrida has called *"the* metaphysical exigency."[15] Although the specific content of this structuring is not fixed, indeed it varies culturally, what remains constant is its binary logic, which posits a ground, a center, a positivity—and then, defined against that positivity, that which is inferior, derivative, negative, a "fall" from the higher term. For example, we see a frequent philosophical identification of Self with mind, and body with threatening Other. Western philosophy's historical obsessions with "pure" thought, certainty, clear and distinct perception, its search for ultimate categories with which to order the world—these projects, too, assume a hierarchical, oppositional construction of reality. For the hope that they may succeed depends upon the conceptualization and circumscription of a privileged human faculty—whether "reason" or observation—whose *essential* relation to objects is transparent and pure (Rorty's "mirror of nature" is one historical variant) and that is capable of transcending that which threatens to mire it in obscurity and chaos: emotion, perspective, human interest, and so forth. The agonistic struggle implied in this description derives from the precariousness of the dualist construction itself: on some level, the Other is felt to be the part of the self that it actually is; hence, the necessity for constant vigilance against it.[16]

Even if Grimshaw were to concede that such a reading of the history of philosophy does provide at least some partial illumination of that history, the question would rightfully remain: in what sense, if any, is a binary structuring of reality "male"? Clearly, dualism is not "male" in any innate sense—for many male philosophers have protested strongly against philosophy's implicit dualisms and have eloquently presented perspectives that are critical of the philosopher's quest for purity, ultimacy, grounding, and authority. Nietzsche, Dewey, and Derrida come immediately to mind. Some insight on the "maleness" of binary thinking might seem to be provided by the fact, pointed out by French and American feminists alike, that the hierarchical oppositions of Western thought have consistently been gender coded. Reason, for example (and, after the seventeenth century, science), is frequently conceptualized as a distinctively male capacity. In contrast, those faculties against which reason variously has been defined, and which it must transcend—the instincts, the emotions, sense perception, materiality, the body—typically have been coded as female.[17]

If Dinnerstein and Kristeva are right, however, such coding is a consequence of "maternal connotations" and associations that both men *and* women develop through the infantile experience of body care by a woman. In that case, responsibility for such a symbolic system is appropriately attributed to the patriarchal division of labor, which has designated the woman as chief infant caretaker. This is not the same, however, as connecting hierarchical dualisms to a distinctively "masculine" perspective of reality. To establish that, one needs to show that there are significant differences in the perspectives of men and women, differences that dispose men, at least more so than women, to see the world dualistically.

One way of approaching this, as noted earlier, is through an examination of differences in the psychological development of males and females—for example, the work of Nancy Chodorow. This approach, in its focus on patterns of child rearing specific to the bourgeois, nuclear family, has obvious limitations. The developmental scenarios Chodorow describes—requiring an unprecedented emphasis on infant nurturing and on the socialization of children into "masculine" and "feminine" roles—are clearly historically specific. Arising alongside industrialization and the rigid designation of "public" and "private" spheres, such developmental patterns cannot provide an illumination of the construction of male personality during the classical period of Greek philosophy or in the Middle Ages (when it is not even clear that childhood existed, let alone a gendered childhood). For this reason, analyses such as Chodorow's can have only a limited historical application to the interpretation of philosophical themes and concerns. Thus circumscribed, however, they may be tremendously useful—for example, in exploring the Enlightenment emphasis on objectivity, autonomy, and individual rights. It is striking that such an emphasis emerges historically alongside the development of the modern bourgeois family and its ideologies of autonomous, public "masculinity" and nurturant, other-oriented "femininity."

The fact that one cannot provide an account of philosophy's "maleness" in terms of some transhistorical male personality development does not entail, however, that there are no transhistorical practices that have conditioned Western men's and women's perspectives in significantly different ways. Although the rigidly dualistic sexual division of labor that we inherited (and its highly developed ideologies of "masculinity" and "femininity") is the product of industrial culture, the organization of human labor into male and female spheres goes back as far as the ancient Greeks. If Foucault and Bourdieu are right (as I believe they are) about the primacy of the habits of everyday life, the concrete practices that organize the time, space, and activity of the body, then we would expect such an organization (which exhibits a good deal of historical variation, but presents significant continuities as well) to have some important consequences for the construction of male and female experience.

For Grimshaw, of course, the "lack of consensus" (as she calls it) in the interpretation and conceptualization of such practices precludes the possibility of legitimate generalizations along such lines. Women have perceived childbearing, for example, "as both the source of their greatest joy and as the root of their worst suffering";[18] thus, she concludes, the practices of reproduction cannot be used as a source of insight into the difference gender makes. I do not dispute the obvious existence of multiple valuations and cultural constructions of events such as giving birth. But one does not require an "essentialist" view of reproduction in order to make the sorts of arguments that Grimshaw dismisses a priori. In Iris Young's essay on "Pregnant Embodiment,"[19] for example, one does not find a statement of one, invariant experience of pregnancy, but an exploration of pregnancy (experienced within certain cultural conditions) as *one* source of nondualistic perspective on mind and body. Philosophy has historically been deprived of such sources of alternative insight by its lack of inclusion of women's perspectives. Grimshaw, however, appears to take the White Rabbit's more Cartesian view of such matters. "What does it matter," he asks Alice, "where my body happens to be? My mind goes on working all the same!"

The thorny question of whether there exist significant transcultural patterns and coherencies in the gender organization of human life is a major source of feminist debate. But even if Grimshaw were to allow that such elements exist, she would insist that we are methodologically prohibited from isolating and describing them.

> The experience of gender, of being, a man or a woman, inflects much if not all of people's lives. . . . But even if one is always a man or a woman, one is never *just* a man or a woman. One is young or old, sick or healthy, married or unmarried, a parent or not a parent, employed or unemployed, middle class or working class, rich or poor, black or white, and so forth. Gender of course inflects one's experience of these things, so the experience of any one of them may well be radically different according to whether one is a man or a woman. But it may also be radically different according to whether one is, say, black or white or working class or middle class. The relationship between male and female experience is a very complex one. Thus there may in some respects be more similarities between the experience of factory labor for example, or of poverty and unemployment—than between a working-class woman and a middle-class woman—experiences of domestic labor and childcare, of the constraints and requirements that one be "attractive," or "feminine," for example.
>
> Experience does not come neatly in segments, such that it is always impossible to abstract what in one's experience is due to "being a woman" from that which is due to "being married," "being middle class," and so forth.[20]

Grimshaw emphasizes, absolutely on target, that gender never exhibits itself in "pure" form, but in the context of lives that are shaped by a multiplicity of influences that cannot be "neatly" sorted out. This does not mean, however (as Grimshaw goes on to suggest), that abstractions about gender are methodologically illicit or perniciously homogenizing of differences among people. Certainly, we shall never find the kind of theoretical "neatness" that Grimshaw, nostalgic for a Cartesian universe of clear and distinct "segments," requires of such abstraction.[21] But as anyone who has taught courses in gender knows, there are many junctures at which, for example, women of color and white women discover profound commonalities in their experience (as well as profound differences). One can, of course, adjust one's methodological tools so that these commonalities become indiscernible under the finely meshed grid of various "inflections" (or the numerous counterexamples that can always be produced). But what then becomes of social criticism? Theoretical criteria such as Grimshaw's, which measure the adequacy of generalizations in terms of their "justice" to the "extremely variegated nature of human life" (102), must find nearly *all* social criticism guilty of distorting abstraction. Her "inflection" argument, although designed to display the fragmented nature of gender, in fact deconstructs race, class, and historical coherencies as well. For the "inflections" that modify experience are endless, and *some* item of difference can always be produced that will shatter any proposed generalizations. If generalization is only permitted in the absence of multiple inflections or interpretive possibilities, then cultural generalizations of any sort—about race, about class, about historical eras—are ruled out. What remains is a universe composed entirely of counterexamples, in which the way men and women "see" the world is purely as particular individuals, shaped by the unique configurations that form that particularity.[22]

Grimshaw presents her skeptical methodological point as an argument against the legitimacy of specifying "male" and "female" points of view. In the context of the history of philosophy, however, her point may be employed differently—to illuminate rather than dispute the "maleness" of philosophy. For a *particular* intersection of gender, race, and class has been typical of Western philosophy, and only in terms of such an intersection can we get a handle on the particular constructions of masculinity that have informed the history of the discipline.

The authors of our classical philosophical traditions have predominantly been white, economically and socially privileged males. (The "Western intellectual tradition" is thus, as Lucius Outlaw once remarked, properly speaking, a minority tradition.) We have no way of imagining what their work would look like if they had written "only" as white, or "only" as males. Nor can we isolate the "maleness" of philosophy from the contexts of dominance and subordination that have constructed gender, class, and race in our culture. The fact that philosophy has been dominated by white, privileged men has meant that it has developed from the center of power rather than the margins of culture. This has surely had as significant an effect on its development as the fact that it has been authored by men. But given the particular conjunction of gender and power characteristic of Western history, we have no way of separating these elements. The "phallic-ness" of Western metaphysics is inseparable from its "centrism" (or its whiteness).[23]

It should be no surprise when we find, then, that dominant historical dualisms are overdetermined with respect to race, gender, and class. So, for example, the hierarchical, oppositional construction of reason/unreason may be coded in a variety of ways, including (but not exclusively) as male/female. We also find unreason coded as African (e.g., in Hegel), and class linked and associated with practical, manual activity (a continual subtheme, as Dewey has pointed out, in Greek philosophy). But despite this flexibility with regard to the content of the duality, its hierarchical form is constant; it posits a revered identity (reason, mind, spirit, the white race, the male sex, and so forth), and then defines what is different, Other, and inferior to it (body, matter, practical activity, woman, African).

This structuring has served a multitude of philosophical and ideological purposes; it is overdetermined, after all, by the intersection of at least three separate axes of privilege and power. As regards gender, it can be seen that, through the consistent philosophical identification of women with the bodily arena of unreason, a powerful ideological support is created for keeping women in their "material" place, excluded from those activities seen as requiring rationality and objectivity. Instead, we are relegated to the corruptible, practical realm of which the "man of reason" wishes to have no part: the mundane care of the body, food preparation, the management of everyday dirt and disorder, and so forth.[24] Along the same lines, Lucius Outlaw has described the mind-body distinction as essentially a master-slave distinction, establishing for the "man of reason" that "the other folks have the bodies ... I am the mind."[25] (Thus, it is justified to treat those other folks the way one would soulless matter: to be owned, sold, traded.)

It is not women alone, then, who have been relegated to the "material" arena. But being overdetermined by gender, race, and class is not equivalent to being undetermined by gender. The hierarchical dualisms of

Western culture did not descend from an androgynous heaven; they are the product of a historical conversation that has been almost exclusively male and reflect the material privileges that male dominance has entailed. It is difficult to conceive of any marginalized or subordinated group dreaming up such a metaphysics—although, of course, we often reproduce and perpetuate it, living within a culture that is organized, though not seamlessly, along such lines. Examples of women who "think like men" (especially as we attain position and authority) do not invalidate correlations of gender and perspective; rather, they reveal the sedimented and entrenched power of our male-created institutions and symbolic systems. At the same time, the position of marginality, as Kristeva argues, confers a certain potential for disruption of those systems. It is no accident, surely, that the beginnings of the current philosophical reassessment of objectivism and foundationalism followed close on the heels of the public emergence, in the 1960s and 1970s, of those groups marginalized by the dominant metaphysics.

Feminist skepticism has operated as a necessary corrective to the sometimes unitary and universalizing notions of identity, perspective, and voice that emerged from early gender theory. That theory, usually based on the experiences of white, middle-class men and women, has often been guilty, as Grimshaw and others have rightly pointed out, of perpetuating the exclusion of difference that has been characteristic of "male-normative" theories. From another, equally valid perspective, the universalizations of gender theory—along with the work of those who attempted to speak for "black experience" and "black culture"—performed a crucial cultural work on the shoulders of which we all stand. This work, understood in the context of historical process, played an essential role in demystifying the Enlightenment ideology of abstract, universal "man," the featureless bearer of "human" rights and responsibilities, the disembodied mirrorer of nature. For this conception, the particularities of human locatedness—race, class, gender, religion, geography, ethnicity, historical place, personal autobiography—are so much obscuring (and ultimately irrelevant) detritus that must be shaken loose from the mirror of mind if it is to attain impartial moral judgment or clear and distinct insight into the nature of things. Such unclouded and disinterested insight is possible for all persons (as Descartes most clearly articulated), given the right method—a method that will allow reason (or our powers of observation) to rise above the limitations of located, embodied, partial perspective, to achieve what Thomas Nagel has called "the view from nowhere."[26]

Although Nietzsche was the first to mount a direct assault on the notion of perspectiveless thought, it was Marx who initially discerned the first fault lines in the mythology of Enlightenment humanism and forged the tools of political and social analysis to reveal them: Man, he insisted, is fragmented by history, and by class. The liberation movements of the 1960s and 1970s added race and gender to class, completing the powerful modernist triumvirate of demystifying and "locating" categories, shattering the myth of unity assumed by the "universal voice" of the "Western intellectual tradition" and exposing its pretensions to neutral perspective. The official stories of that tradition—of its philosophy, religion, literature, material history—now required radical reconstruction. Not only were vast areas of human experience unrepresented, but what *had* been privileged in the dominant traditions of Western culture now had to be seen as the products of historically situated individuals with very particular class, race, and gender interests. The imperial categories that had provided justification for those stories— Reason, Truth, Human Nature, and Tradition—now were displaced by the (historical, social) questions: *Whose* Truth? *Whose* Nature? *Whose* Tradition?

For many contemporary critics, the difficulty of specifying adequate answers to such questions has become a central theoretical issue. Gender, as Grimshaw and others have emphasized, is only one axis of a complex, heterogeneous construct, constantly interpenetrating, in historically specific ways, with race, class, age, ethnicity, sexual orientation, and so forth. This, I believe, is a crucial and sobering insight that ought to keep us on guard against facile and homogenizing generalizations about gender (or any aspect of social identity). However, the corollary notion that is often covert in these critiques, that it is somehow possible (given the right method or the correct politics) to do "justice" (as Grimshaw puts it) to the heterogeneity of things, is another matter. Here, the modernist epistemological fantasy of adequate representations returns— in the new, postmodern form of what I have elsewhere called a "dream of everywhere":[27] no longer allied with the quest for unity or fixity, but configured around the adequate representation of "difference."

Such a fantasy is no less grandiose than the Cartesian dream of Archimedean detachment or any other ambition to achieve representational mastery. No matter how attentive the scholar is to the axes that constitute social identity, some of these axes will be ignored or marginalized and others selected. (Attending to the "intersection of race, class, and gender" does not overcome this.) This is an inescapable fact of human embodiment, as Nietzsche was the first to point out: "The eye . . . in which the active and interpreting forces, through which alone seeing becomes seeing *something* are supposed to be lacking" is "an absurdity and a nonsense."[28] This selectivity, moreover, is never innocent. We always "see" from points of view that are invested with our social, political, and personal interests, inescapably "centric" in one way or another, even in the desire to do justice to heterogeneity.

Nor does attentiveness to difference assure the adequate representation of difference. Certainly, we often err on the side of exclusion and, thus, submerge and ignore large areas of human history and experience. But attending *too* vigilantly to difference can just as problematically construct an Other who is an exotic alien, a breed apart. As Foucault has reminded us, "everything is dangerous"—and every new context demands that we reassess the "main danger."[29] This requires a hyper- and pessimistic activism, not an alliance with "correct" theory. For no theory—not even one that measures its adequacy in terms of justice to heterogeneity, locality, nuance—can place itself beyond danger.

In practical terms, this means that we can never be reassured that our ideas will be "politically correct"; they will be forever haunted by a voice from the "margins," already speaking (or perhaps presently muted but awaiting the conditions for speech), awakening us to what we have excluded, effaced, damaged. This is how we learn, as Minnie Bruce Pratt recognizes.

> When I am trying to understand myself in relation to folks different from me, when there are discussions, conflicts about antisemitism and racism among women, criticisms, criticisms of me, and I get afraid when, for instance, in a group discussion about race and class, I say I feel we have talked too much about race, not enough about class, and a woman of color asks me in anger and pain if I don't think her skin has something to do with class, and I get afraid; when, for instance, I say carelessly to my Jewish lover that there were no Jews where I grew up, and she begins to ask me: how do I know? do I hear what I'm saying? and I get afraid: when I feel my racing heart, breath, the tightening of my skin around me, literally defenses to protect my narrow circle, I try to say to myself: . . . Yes, that fear is there, but I will try to be at the edge between my fear and outside, on the edge at my skin,

listening, asking what new things will I hear, will I see, will I let myself, feel, beyond the fear.[30]

Pratt does not imagine that the "correct" methodological approach could ever enable the self to transcend ethnocentrism. Rather, she realizes that confrontation with what she calls the "narrow circle of the self" and what it has excluded is a constant risk/inevitability. She dares to speak anyway, to interact with concrete others and allow their actual differences to put her in *her* place (reveal her locatedness to her) rather than put "difference" in its place, through "theorizing" it "adequately."

The best strategies for "doing justice" to heterogeneity, I believe, are institutional, not epistemological. Here, the requirement is shifted from the methodological dictum that we forswear talk of "male" and "female" realities, to the messier, practical struggle to create institutions, communities, conversations that will not permit *some* groups of people to make determinations about "reality" for *all*. For academics, this means not only struggling against explicit racism and sexism and seeking cultural diversity in the recruitment of faculty and students, but attention to the practical arenas (hiring, tenure, promotion, publication criteria, etc.) that privilege certain styles, language, and orientations over others. It means recognition that sexism, racism, and heterosexism are deep psychocultural currents that cannot be cured merely by better theory. And it requires suspicion of and resistance to the hegemony of intellectual discourses and professional practices whose very language requires "membership" to understand and that remain fundamentally closed to difference (regarding it as "politically incorrect," "theoretically unsophisticated," "unrigorous," and so forth). We deceive ourselves if we believe that theory is attending to the inclusion of "difference" so long as so many actual differences—individual and cultural—are excluded from the conversation.

For the remainder of this essay, I would like to displace the discourse of adequation, acknowledge that generalizations about gender can obscure and exclude as well as reveal and illuminate (determinations, I believe, that must be made from context to context, not by methodological fiat), and raise some concerns about what may be obscured by too relentless an emphasis on heterogeneity. I want to advocate a more practical, contextual approach to problems of heterogeneity and generality. From such a standpoint, general categories of identity—race, class, gender, and so forth—remain vital, in certain contexts, for social criticism. Let me mention just some of those.

Identity politics, for example, require such totalizations (e.g., the "black women" of the Combahee River Collective) at particular moments in their development; they are useful, "life-enhancing fictions" (as Nietzsche might say) that lift veils of personal mystification and enable the recognition of solidarity with others. General categories of social identity continue to be essential, too, to the ongoing exposure and analysis of the biases of Western culture. One of my arguments in this essay has been that too wholesale a commitment to the representation of historical heterogeneity can obscure the transhistorical hierarchical patterns that inform our traditions. The biases of philosophy reflect not only the particular historical situations of various authors but also configurations of race, class, and gender that have been characteristic of the social situations of the authors of our classical canon. What has been called the phallogocentrism of Western metaphysics is the product of the overdetermined privilege—racial, class, and gender privileges— that has allowed imaginations of the pure, the transparent, the one, the true, the clean, the clear, the authoritative, to form such a central motif in the historical conversation of those for whom the messy, the bodily, the "vicissitudes of (everyday, practical) existence" (as Dewey described it) can always be constructed as Other, because they are *taken care of* by others.

More generally, I worry that the intellectual dominance of a "theoretics of heterogeneity" will (once again) obscure the dualistic nature of the actualities of power in Western culture. Contemporary feminism, like many social movements arising in the 1960s, developed out of the recognition that to live in our culture is not (despite powerful social mythology to the contrary) to participate equally in some free play of individual diversity. Rather, one always finds oneself located within structures of dominance and subordination—not least important of which have been those organized around gender. Certainly, the duality of male/female is a "discursive formation," a "social construct." So, too, is the racial duality of black/white. But as such, each of these constructed dualities has had profound consequences for the experiences of those who "live" them.

Feminism, in exposing the *gendered* nature of Western thought, has contributed significantly to intellectually dismantling the Enlightenment mythology of abstract, universal man and its epistemological corollary of an abstract, universal reason. There is no "view from nowhere," feminists have insisted; all thought is socially located. Disquietingly, skeptical feminism may be in the process of installing a *new* version of the "view from nowhere" by deconstructing gender right out of operation as a tool for relocating reason from the Cartesian heavens of disembodied rationality and into the bodies of actual human beings. Without such general categories of identity, the notions of social interest, location, and perspective—notions that give content and force to the critique of abstract humanism and the "view from nowhere"—are no longer usable. They remain theoretically in force, while we are hobbled in making the general claims that drive them home in practice.

This is a practical, not a theoretical, worry. Past feminist efforts have begun to produce visible results in the philosophy curriculum, as more and more philosophers are acknowledging the patterns of exclusion and bias in our discipline and are attempting to reconceive their courses accordingly. But there are others, we should remember, who would reinstate the "great works," undisturbed by gender, race, class, or cultural analysis, to the center of our curriculum, and recrown the future Philosopher-King as the only student worth teaching. Within this institutional struggle, feminists would do well to hold fast to the analytical category of gender and not allow it to become lost in a Sargasso Sea of counterexamples and endlessly multiple meanings. This is not to say that a cultural understanding of philosophy requires univocal, fixed conceptions of social identity and location. Rather, we need to reserve *practical* spaces for both old-fashioned generalist criticism (which still provides, as I have argued, crucial kinds of insights into history and culture) and attention to complexity and nuance as well. At this particular juncture, we may pay a very high institutional and political price for our intellectual deconstructions.

NOTES

This essay was first presented at a symposium at the American Philosophical Association Eastern Division meeting, Washington, D.C., December, 1988. An abbreviated version appeared in *Journal of Philosophy*, 75, no. 11 (November, 1988): 619–29 in connection with that presentation. Parts of one section have also appeared in the *Feminism and Philosophy Newsletter* 88, no. 2 (March, 1989): 19–25. Thanks to Lynne Arnault, Ted Koditscheck, Mario Moussa, Linda Nicholson, Jean O'Barr, Jonathan Shonscheck, Lynne Tirrell, Jane Tompkins, and Lee Ann Whites for helpful suggestions.

1. See Susan Bordo, "Feminism, Postmodernism, and Gender Skepticism," in *Feminism/Postmodernism*, ed. Linda Nicholson (New York: Routledge, 1989), for discussion of these perspectives.

2. Jean Grimshaw, *Philosophy and Feminist Thinking* (Minneapolis: University of Minnesota Press, 1986), 102.

3. Dorothy Dinnerstein, *The Mermaid and the Minotaur* (New York: Harper and Row, 1977).

4. Nancy Chodorow, *The Reproduction of Mothering* (Berkeley: University of California Press, 1978).

5. See Julia Kristeva, *About Chinese Women* (New York: Urizen, 1977).

6. Carol Gilligan, *In a Different Voice* (Cambridge, Mass.: Harvard University Press, 1982).

7. Gilligan, *Different Voice*, 2.

8. See the March, 1989, issue of the *Newsletter on Feminism and Philosophy* for a representative bibliography.

9. Grimshaw, *Philosophy*, 66.

10. See Susan Bordo, *The Flight to Objectivity: Essays on Cartesianism and Culture* (Albany, N.Y.: SUNY Press, 1987); Brian Easlea, *Witch Hunting, Magic, and the New Philosophy* (Atlantic Highlands, N.J.: Humanities Press, 1980); Sandra Harding, "Is Gender a Variable in Conceptions of Rationality?" *Dialectica* 36 (1982): 225–42; James Hillman, *The Myth of Analysis* (New York: Harper and Row, 1972).

11. Rosalind Petchesky, "Body Politics in the Seventeenth Century," colloquium on Women, Science, and the Body, Cornell University, May, 1987.

12. Bordo, *Flight to Objectivity*, 114–18.

13. Michel Foucault, *Discipline and Punish* (New York: Vintage, 1979), 27.

14. Hélène Cixous, "The Laugh of the Medusa," *Signs* 1 (Summer, 1976): 875–93; Hélène Cixous with Catherine Clément, *The Newly Born Woman* (Minneapolis: University of Minnesota Press, 1986); Luce Irigaray, *Speculum of the Other Woman* (Ithaca, N.Y.: Cornell University Press, 1985).

15. Jacques Derrida, "Limited Inc.," *Glyph* 2 (1988): 66.

16. Some specific examples of such hierarchical, binary oppositions are: intelligible / sensible, transcendental / empirical, literal / metaphorical, objective / subjective, reality / appearance, rigorous / soft, and (in ethics) duty / compassion.

17. Cixous, "Laugh"; Cixous with Clément, *Newly Born Woman*; Irigaray, *Speculum*; Genevieve Lloyd, *The Man of Reason: "Male" and "Female" in Western Philosophy* (Minneapolis: University of Minnesota Press, 1984).

18. Grimshaw, *Philosophy*, 73.

19. Iris Young, "Pregnant Embodiment: Subjectivity and Alienation," *Journal of Medicine and Philosophy* 9 (1984): 45–62.

20. Grimshaw, *Philosophy*, 84–85.

21. Grimshaw consistently creates a "straw woman" out of feminist gender theory by suggesting (incorrectly) that it typically argues for "a radical, total disjunction between male and female realities," a "distinctively female point of view that is in all respects inaccessible to men," or "uniquely female" perspectives on reality. This reified, rigidly dichotomous understanding of gender difference is Grimshaw's projection and rarely to be found, in my opinion, in the works she criticizes.

22. Lynne Arnault makes a similar point in "The Uncertain Future of Feminist Standpoint Epistemology" (LeMoyne College-Philosophy, typescript).

23. The authors of our classical philosophical canon have also overwhelmingly been Christian. I thank Bat-Ami Bar On for reminding me of this crucial fact, which bears not only on the "structural" motifs discussed in this essay, but on the dominance of particular categories and themes in the nature of philosophy.

24. Here, it is particularly and bitingly ironic when conceptions of philosophy employ images of "cleaning the litter with which the world is filled" (as James called it) in describing the task of the philosopher: Danto's "conceptual housekeeping," Raphael's "mental clearance." Raphael even reminds us, in the style of a *Good Housekeeping* article, that mental clearance, like cleaning the house, "is not a job that can be done once and for all. You have to do it every week. The mere business of living continues to produce more rubbish, which has to be cleared regularly." Raphael here picks up on Locke's famous description of the philosopher as an "under-labourer . . . removing some of the rubbish that lies in the way of knowledge." Such metaphors evoke the realm of the material, practical, and everyday precisely to offer a vision of their transcendence. The conceptual "housekeeper," it turns out, "executes" his tasks in a hierarchical, dualistic neighborhood within which it is the Other that makes all the mess. For Danto, this messy side of town is inhabited by the other disciplines, constantly generating conceptual confusion, but too "robustly busy," as he says, to tend to the cleaning of their own houses. Quine's use of the cleaning metaphor is even more suggestive of class associations: he speaks, in *Word and Object*, of the philosopher's task as "clearing the ontological slums." See D. Raphael, *Problems of Political Philosophy* (London: Macmillan, 1976), 16; Arthur Danto, *What Philosophy Is* (New York: Harper and Row, 1968), 10; W. V. O. Quine, *Word and Object* (Cambridge: Cambridge University Press, 1960), 275.

25. Workshop on racism and the history of philosophy, Le Moyne College, June, 1987.

26. Thomas Nagel, *The View from Nowhere* (Oxford University Press, 1986).

27. Susan Bordo, "The View from Nowhere and the Dream of Everywhere: Heterogeneity, Adequation, and Feminist Theory," *Feminism and Philosophy Newsletter*, March, 1989, 19–25. See also Bordo, "Feminism, Postmodernism."

28. Friedrich Nietzsche, *On the Genealogy of Morals* (New York: Vintage, 1969), 119.

29. Michel Foucault, "On the Genealogy of Ethics," in *Beyond Structuralism and Hermeneutics*, ed. Hubert Dreyfus and Paul Rabinow (Chicago: University of Chicago Press, 1983), 232.

30. Minnie Bruce Pratt, "Identity: Skin, Blood, Heart," in *Yours in Struggle*, ed. Elly Bolkin, Minnie Bruce Pratt, and Barbara Smith (New York: Long Haul Press, 1984), 18.

The Gender of Creativity in the French Symbolist Period

PATRICIA MATHEWS

During the late nineteenth-century Symbolist period in France, preoccupation with an agitated emotional state of heightened awareness and
passionate discontent was central to discourses ranging from creativity
to pathology. However, the significance of this emotional state differed
dramatically according to one's gender. For males, ecstatic, passionate
suffering was the avenue to the sublime revelation of ultimate truth and
creativity, whereas, for women, such states were seen as feeble-minded
manifestations of mental illness. This essay represents an initial attempt
to outline the nature of creativity as it was understood during this period,
based on an interdisciplinary model of mystical revelation through a
suffering that was close to madness; and, equally, to describe the ways
in which such suffering by women was considered to result from their
inherent tendency to debilitating madness, in which creativity had no
place. I will conclude with a brief sketch of two women artists of the
period, as they are contained within or negotiate this model.[1]

During the Symbolist period in France, dating from about 1885 to
1895, the model on which meaning was structured shifted from the Realist
investigation of natural appearances and reflection of the social framework to a search for the symbolic, transcendent absolute inherent in
all things.[2] Artists who adhered to this mystical, idealist view of the
world sought the hidden relations between the spiritual and material
worlds, described as either neo-Platonic ideas, essences, and absolutes,
or Baudelairean correspondences. In his homage to the teachings of the
eighteenth-century Swedish mystic Emmanuel Swedenborg, Baudelaire
succinctly characterizes this worldview: "Everything, form, movement,
number, color, perfume, in the spiritual as in the natural world, is
significant, reciprocal, conversely related, and corresponding."[3]

The visionary artist, or *poet-voyant*, had the exceptional ability to perceive this langauge of correspondences lost to most of us. The artist looks into his own soul, the eyes of his "interior self" open, and the correspondences between the natural and the spiritual world are revealed to him.[4] He has become a seer, a *voyant*, a visionary. As Baudelaire notes, the artist's creativity lies as much in his perceptual faculties as in his ability to create.

The experience of inspired revelation was thought to be characterized by an overwhelming emotional state that verged on madness. The French Symbolist critic Albert Aurier describes the emotion felt in the presence of the essential inner truth of any artistic motif as "transcendental emotivity." He defines this emotion as equivalent to "ecstasy," an emotion that moves one "body and soul," and one that only the true artist is capable of experiencing. The soul will "vibrate" and "shiver" before the "drama of the undulating abstractions" (that is, the ideas behind appearances) revealed to him. In this mystical revelation that precedes the creative process, the "being of Being" rises up before the artist in the undulating, reverberating lines, shapes, and colors of the motif.[5] The artist's ability to bring the correspondences to life through his own mystical, revelatory, creative power is the essence of genius.

Pain and suffering, *la douleur*, were considered essential for the development of such an artistic sensibility. It was believed that the true artist must endure suffering in order to reach the ecstatic heights of mystic communion with universals or ideas necessary to creativity. Accordingly, *la douleur* was considered to be a "fertilizing pain" that heightened and refined the sensibility, and thus fortified and purified the artist, preparing him for his experience of absolute truth. The suffering poet, *le poète maudit*, was an exalted Symbolist ideal represented by Rimbaud, among many others. Gauguin assumes this role in his *Christ in Gethsemane, Self Portrait* of 1889, in which he has depicted himself in the guise of Christ and, thus, as a martyr to his art.

Mental illness as the extreme exacerbation of *la douleur* became, for many, the ultimate paradigm for creativity during this period. The mad were thought to have direct access to mystical revelation. Symbolist theories of artistic genius employed terminology developed from the medical codification of mental illnesses during the period by pioneers in psychopathology such as Pierre Janet. Aurier, for example, characterized Van Gogh as a "terrible and maddened genius, often sublime, sometimes grotesque, always near the pathological," and used medical terms such as *hyperaestheticism, névrosé,* and *idée fixe* to describe the sources of his creativity.[6] One among many extreme and infamous treatises of the time that directly connected madness to genius was written by the Italian Cesare Lombroso, translated into French as *L'Homme de génie* (Man of Genius) in 1889. He treats the subject from a pseudoscientific standpoint. Such scientific justification marks a major transition from the more intuitive understanding of mad genius during the romantic period, toward a determinism based on "scientific fact" that validated not only that stereotype, but also the notion of the inferiority of women and non-Caucasian races as well, as we shall see.

Like the Symbolists, Lombroso argues that mental illness is a stimulant to genius.[7] Illness actually has the potential, he says, to change a mediocre intelligence into an extraordinary one.[8] After all, the genius does not possess "ordinary intellectual health." His profile of the genius and the madman is, therefore, one of difference, of "abnormality" as he refers to it. Both stand outside of their milieu, separate from the common populace, in a state of grace that allows them to see better and more clearly what others cannot.[9] This exalted state of exclusion and difference parallels the Symbolist ideal of the *poet-voyant,* with his superior vision, and the *isolé,* that is, the artist who necessarily isolates himself from his milieu in order to avoid its contaminating effects.[10]

The heightened value of this exclusion is most clearly revealed in its privileged relation to creativity. Both the genius and the madman have a natural creativity, "la force créatrice," defined as "the association of audacious and unexpected ideas," although only the genius is able to evaluate his own ideas.[11]

Thus, creativity is not understood by Lombroso as a reasoned, deliberate process, utilizing varying levels of intuition, but as an inspired, excessive act that allows the imagination to soar beyond the boundaries of mundane existence. Such a state echoes that of ecstatic mystical revelation and "transcendental emotivity" demanded of Symbolist artists. This model of creative madness suggests the prophetic madness of the oracle.

Women, however, were not believed to be capable of the lucid, profound, and sibylline madness necessary to creativity. Lombroso, for example, believes genius in women to be limited.[12] Since heredity and race play such an important role in his theory, it is not surprising that oppressive social constructions that constrain women are not alluded to. "In the history of genius," he claims, "women have but a small place. Women of genius are rare exceptions in the world. . . . They are, above all, conservators. Even the few who emerge have, on near examination, something virile about them. As Goncourt said, there are no women of genius; the women of genius are men." He goes on to invoke the now familiar argument, that "if there had been in women a really great ability in politics, science &c., it would have shown itself in overcoming the difficulties opposed to it; . . ."[13] In other words, if women have not been great (a questionable assumption in itself, and one based on conventional definitions of greatness), then they cannot ever be great. His is a purely deterministic, circular argument.

The very nature of women was thought to predispose them toward a more chaotic form of madness, untempered by the intellect and uncontrolled by critical faculties necessary to creativity. Such notions became "scientifically" mandated during the nineteenth century, and absolutely determined and defined the female character; they were imbued with particular authority through the discourse of medicine and the philosophy of social Darwinism.[14] The medical profession defined women by their reproductive functions, which were seen as biologically unstable.[15] For example, psychiatrists of the Victorian period generally understood women to be more prone to insanity than men "because the instability of their reproductive systems interfered with their sexual, emotional, and rational control." Such vulnerability "linked to the biological crisis of the female life cycle—puberty, pregnancy, childbirth, menopause, . . . was used as a reason to keep women out of the professions, to deny them political rights, and to keep them under male control in the family and the state," according to Elaine Showalter.[16]

This medical concept of women as biologically unstable and inferior was accompanied by evolutionary theories of female intellectual inferiority. Such ideas had consequences for the arts as well. In 1871, Darwin, in the *Descent of Man*, explained that, through natural selection, "man had become superior to woman in courage, energy, intellect, and inventive genius, and thus would inevitably excel in art, science, and philosophy." Women, on the other hand, excelled in "intuition, perception, and imitation," which Darwin defined as "signs of inferiority, characteristic of the lower races, and therefore of a past and lower state of civilization."[17] Such inferiority implies, of course, that no intellectual or creative activity is possible.

Nineteenth-century writer George Moore sums up many of these ideas.

Woman's nature is more facile and fluent than man's. Women do things more easily than men, but they do not penetrate below the surface, and if they attempt to do so the attempt is but a clumsy masquerade in unbecoming costume. . . . [I]n the higher arts, in painting, in music, and literature, their achievements are slight indeed. . . .[18]

A tendency toward physical and mental illness was believed to be a direct consequence of the frailty and weakness of the female nature. According to this model, woman is frail and passive if controlled, yet if her emotions are unchecked, she becomes incoherent and dangerous. She is the exemplar of moral purity, and yet underneath this facade lurks the potential for a frightening and even revolting impropriety.[19] Women were seen as susceptible to the overwhelming and engulfing potential of a chaotic, sensual, and earthbound nature, and too fragile to withstand the powerful ecstatic emotions such a nature aroused without succumbing to nervous disease. Bound so closely to the material world, woman was not able to transcend it, as the model for creativity demanded; her frail intellect abandoned her for the refuge of illness. Indeed, a cult of female invalidism was prevalent from the mid- to the late nineteenth century.[20] Illness was idealized as part of the mythology of the fragility of women's superior purity, which in turn made them vulnerable and necessarily dependent on men.

The ideal of the sickly woman appears in art by both men and women of the Symbolist period, such as in the Symbolist painting by Romaine Brooks, *Le Trajet* (ca. 1911). Bram Dijkstra describes this image as "a passive entity waiting to be acted upon, . . . a willing victim in a world in which aggression is the privilege of the other."[21] Such artistic models for women only further contributed to the development of the ideology of the female character outlined here, whether passive invalid or sacrificial victim as in the art of the Symbolist Paul Gauguin.

Gauguin's art illustrates the way such concepts of woman as nature, particularly representative of the irrational and the primitive, were embedded in the artistic theory and practice of the period. His images are more sympathetic, at least superficially, than the representations of women as engulfing *femme fatales* so common to the period, such as Franz von Stuck's *Sin* (1895) or the many vampire women in the work of Edvard Munch. Compared to such images, Gauguin's works appear sensual, as opposed to sexually vociferous. Nevertheless, Gauguin's opposition between the Western Eve and the Primitive Eve represents only another side of the nineteenth-century stereotype of "woman as nature."

In works such as Gauguin's bas-relief, *Soyez Amoureuses, Vous Serez Heureuses* (1889, Museum of Fine Arts, Boston), he sympathizes with the necessarily parasitic dependence of contemporary Western women on marriage as the only role available to them and even sees Western men as the corrupters and exploiters of women and of civilization. He himself plays out the role of the corrupted male in this work, the demonic temptor who represents the lascivious nature of civilized man, a monster (as he describes himself) who grabs the hand of the resisting and despairing woman and ironically tells her to "be in love and you will be happy."[22] Yet his ideal is not woman liberated from such domestic prostitution, but one who passively and even heroically submits to it. Biologically bound to the regeneration of the human race, woman inevitably becomes a willing sacrifice to that greater end.

In *The Loss of Virginity* (1890, see figure 1), Gauguin equates the fall of woman, represented through the plucked and wilting flower and the fox, with the harvested grain behind her, and with the sacrifice of Christ through her crossed feet and her prone position.[23] She embraces the fox, though with a melancholy air, as a sign of her willingness to suffer at the hands of lustful men in order to regenerate life. According to Gauguin, it is woman's nature to give herself to men in order to create life; the act of love, for women, concerns conception only. Western woman in this stereotype is denied her own sexuality, and forced into the rigid role of the standard bearer of purity who only submits to the debasement of sex for the higher purpose of procreation. Thus, female creativity belongs solely in the realm of physical reproduction.[24]

In Gauguin's depiction of the primitive Eve, this image is altered, although it is just as restrictive. His primitive Eves can be seen to represent the paradoxical duality of woman as nature: on the one hand, they are superstitious and ignorant, as in the *Spirit of the Dead Watching* (1892, Albright-Knox Art Gallery, Buffalo) or in *Barbaric Folk Tales* (1902, Folkwang Museum, Essen), where the devil comes to life as the two young women frighten themselves while telling folk stories. On the other hand, the primitive Eve also represents a new morality, "through which the artificiality of civilization could be transcended."[25] She enjoys her sensuality without shame.[26] Here the inherent value structure in the nature-culture dichotomy is reversed. For Gauguin, woman as the embodiment of ignorance and man of knowledge has an inverse value to what one might expect. In *When Will You Marry?* (1891, Kunstmuseum, Basel), for example, we see the westernized woman, recognizable

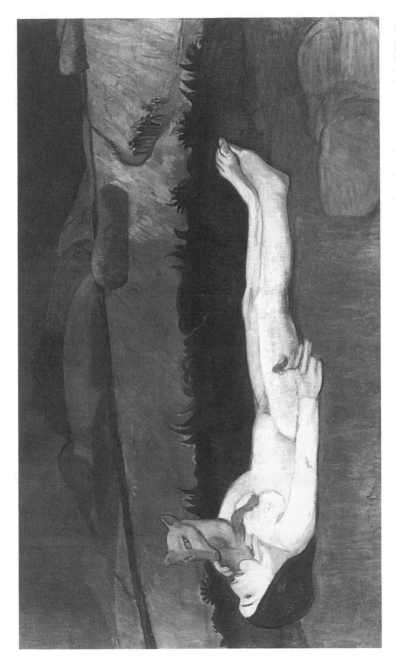

Fig. 1. Paul Gauguin, *The Loss of Virginity*, 1890. Oil on canvas, 35.5″ × 51.5″. The Chrysler Museum, Norfolk, Va. Gift of Walter P. Chrysler, Jr. (Photo: Museum.)

by her high-necked collar, Western clothes, and sly, thin face, representing the corruption of purity that comes with knowledge through
education. As Gauguin said to Strindberg, "The Eve of your civilized
imagination makes misogynists of . . . almost all of us."[27] She raises her
hand in a teaching gesture toward the wide-eyed, innocent, and voluptuous primitive Eve, still pure in her ignorance. Gauguin's dichotomy
may not be as overtly negative as that created by the medical profession
and "scientific" studies, but it is just as oppressive. Women are still signs
of the primitive as the irrational, as in Von Stuck's painting, only here
the irrational is connected with the supposed purity and superiority of
the "original," ignorant state rather than the corrupted state of depravity.

However much one may wish to renounce these stereotypes of women
and illness, madness, and irrationality, women seemingly *were* prone to
nervous disorders during this period. Principal among them was hysteria,
in which the creative potential of ecstatic emotion is rechanneled into
unproductive disease. Hysteria was seen as a stereotypically female disease; it peaked in frequency during the late nineteenth century, a particularly restrictive period for women. It is exactly during this period
that science steps in to codify women's heightened emotional states as
nervous disease. By the end of the nineteenth century, "'hysterical' had
become almost interchangeable with 'feminine' in literature, where it
stood for all extremes of emotionality," according to Showalter.[28] Indeed,
it was a disease that embodied the very nature of femininity as it was
understood by the nineteenth century and, thus, warrants the suggestion
that the disease itself may be the product of a socially constructed role
for women. Rather than a result of faulty heredity, biological determinism, or "unsatisfied sexual and maternal drives" as it was seen by much
of the medical establishment, Showalter suggests that reasons for its real
manifestations concern "women's intellectual frustration, lack of mobility," lack of "autonomy and control," and the fact that they were "unsatisfied and thwarted in other aspects of their lives."[29] Both Sigmund Freud's
and Josef Breuer's analysis of hysteria in the famous case of Anna O.
explicitly related it to the social repression of women.[30]

For a great many women, the constrained and limited social opportunities available, resulting in large part from "scientific" studies of their
nature, led to a suffering and anguish that manifested itself as physical
and mental illness, particularly as nervous diseases such as hysteria.
Many women enacted it as a form of release; for some it also represented

a form of rebellion, although hardly a productive one. According to Shoshana Felman:

> Depressed and terrified women are not about to seize the means of production and reproduction: quite the opposite of rebellion, madness is the impasse confronting those whom cultural conditioning has deprived of the very means of protest or self-affirmation.[31]

Certain traits of hysteria that often annoyed nineteenth-century doctors also suggest that the illness may have been a result of an attempt to rebel, consciously or unconsciously, against enforced social roles. Female hysterics were described by one such person as "typically energetic and passionate, 'exhibiting more than usual force and decision of character, of strong resolution, fearless of danger, bold riders, having plenty of what is termed *nerve.*'"[32] They were also said to express "'unnatural' desires for privacy and independence."[33] One doctor noted the large percentage of "unconventional women," such as artists and writers, among his hysteric patients. Indeed, hysteria was the disease "most strongly identified with the feminist movement" at the end of the century.[34] This profile of the hysteric points exactly to those women who would be most frustrated by their lack of freedom, and would seem to correspond to the Symbolist ideal of the artist-madman-genius who is different from the "common masses."[35] However, their frustration often involved the channeling of creative energies into illness, an illness that was not only an accepted form of release but one that was encouraged and even expected by the medical establishment.

Descriptions of hysteria in the late nineteenth century are not only caricatures of femininity but also resemble quite closely an ecstatic experience that has somehow short-circuited. The relation of hysteria to creativity is noted by Freud himself when he says that "a case of hysteria is a caricature of a work of art."[36] Indeed, one of the stages of hysteria, as defined by J.-M. Charcot, the doctor most influential in its definition and medical status in the late nineteenth century, included ecstasy.[37] While the hysterical woman in Charcot's model enacts the ecstatic state necessary for creativity, she, as a result of her nature, cannot sustain or control it in order to transform it into art.[38]

Women were also widely considered to be prone to a "hyperaesthesia of the senses," and hysteria was seen as the means of giving vent to it.[39]

We recall that the "maddened genius," Van Gogh, whom Aurier also characterized as a hyperaesthetic, gave vent to his excessive sensibility in "great" works of art.

Thus defined as an ideologically constructed, primarily female mental illness permeated with nineteenth-century concepts of femininity, hysteria parallels the predominantly male discourse of madness as genius among Symbolist theorists. Madness in women as nervous agitation and hysterical and overt emotionalism is related to the madness Lombroso and others describe as genius. In effect, hysteria was the physical manifestation of the representation of women as emotionally frail and thus capable of grand and indulgent emotion only in the guise of illness or madness. Its concepts and its actuality diverted women from creativity in theory and often in practice as well.

The discourse on the category of "woman" during the late nineteenth century was used to support male superiority in the realm of creativity. At the same time, the silencing of the female voice as an authority in defining the female condition veiled the contradiction inherent in this argument: women did create, despite the theoretical supposition that denied them this ability.[40]

Indeed, there is a tremendous difference between the way women were seen during the Symbolist period and their actual creative process. Despite attempts to force women artists into the male mold by their critics, either read as "male" when their art is powerful, or as "female" when their work is delicate (or less strong), a number of women forged their own model of creativity, even if unconsciously, through a negotiation of the dominant model. I will briefly discuss two such women artists: sculptor Camille Claudel and painter Suzanne Valadon.

The life of Camille Claudel (1864–1943), a very gifted sculptor, heartbreakingly parallels the model of women and madness, especially the description of the hysteric as frustrated professional, although her illness was diagnosed as paranoia rather than hysteria. In 1913, only a few days after her father's death, to whom she was very close, her mother, a bourgeois woman who had long resented her daughter's libertine lifestyle, and her brother, poet Paul Claudel, convinced by who knows what paradigm of female madness, institutionalized her as insane. She remained there for the rest of her life—thirty years—despite the fact that doctors twice recommended that she should be released; she wrote her mother pleading to allow it, even "offering to abandon her share of the inheritance."[41] After her confinement, she refused to touch clay again.

Despite the quality of her work, and its critical acceptance, she was not financially successful and fell into increasing poverty after her final breakup, in 1898, with sculptor Auguste Rodin, her lover and co-worker for fourteen years. She did not receive the public commissions needed to support the expensive medium of bronze sculpture. She lived in seclusion and increasing isolation, progressively becoming more deranged. She broke and burned many of her plaster and marble works.[42] She certainly did show signs of disintegration, at least according to her brother when he saw her after years away in 1909. Appalled, he wrote in his journal, "Camille / insane, enormous, with a soiled face, speaking incessantly in a monotonous metallic voice."[43] However, one wonders to which standards of female behavior and appearance he was comparing her.

In fact, from her letters, it appears that she was generally lucid during those thirty years,[44] during which she remained institutionalized within a system that constructed women as mentally fragile and thus to be cared for. She wrote to her brother Paul, "Madhouses are houses made on purpose to cause suffering. . . . I cannot stand any longer the screams of all these creatures." And about her mother, in 1939 at age 75:

> At this holiday season I think ever of our dear mamma. I have never seen her since the day when you took the fatal decision of sending me off to an insane asylum! I think of the beautiful portrait I did of her in the shade of our lovely garden. The large eyes in which you could read a secret pain, the spirit of resignation which reigned over her whole face, her hands folded on her knees in complete abnegation; everything spoke of modesty, a sense of duty pushed to an excess, that was our poor mother. I have never seen the portrait again (any more than I have seen her).

She then goes on to speak of Rodin, and her paranoia surfaces, although not without reason: "I do not think that the odious person of whom I speak to you so often has had the audacity to attribute it to himself, as he has done my other works, it would be just too much, the portrait of my mother!"[45] Indeed, Rodin almost certainly sold works under his name for which she was partially responsible. We know, for example, that she worked on the *Gates of Hell*, as seen in her model, *Greed and Lust* (1885). Her paranoia toward him, therefore, was not so exaggerated. His star ascended as hers fell and, as a woman of great ambition, this must have been particularly upsetting.

Her statements do not sound like the ravings of a madwoman.

She was paranoid, unconventional, but never violent. Was this enough to exile her for life? "Some of her friends claimed she was never crazy at all."[46]

To think of a woman of such talent and intellect confined to such a dreary place for thirty years arouses outrage and pity. However, even more upsetting is the way in which this circumstance is allowed to cloud the productivity of her earlier life. Unfortunately, even in the recent studies that attempt to reclaim her for the present, her art is too often linked to her fateful relationship to Rodin and her grief at their parting. Her life and her art are intermingled unconscionably, in terms of *la douleur*. Reine-Marie Paris, her grand niece, for example, says *La Valse* (1892, see figure 2)[47] and *Sakountala* (1905, marble, Musée Rodin, Paris) "reflect the precarious happiness of the couple, or their short-lived reconciliation." *La Petite châtelaine* (1893–94, bronze, private collection) "reflects the child she could not bear." *Clotho* (1893, see figure 3) "captures the unhappiness of a deserted woman."[48] Yet, at the same time that Paris is allying Claudel's creative energy directly to her affair with Rodin, she claims that there is no proof that Claudel suffered a great passion for Rodin. Her affection for him was always "reasonable and measured," she says, despite her fiery temperament, and "ambition was not absent from it."[49] Even her madness was said to be reflected in her art, although it is never explained how one creates in a state of insanity. *Perseus et la Gorgone* (1898–1902, marble, private collection), for example, "with its emphasis on crawling serpents, signals her emerging madness," according to Paris.[50] This latter statement is really insupportable, considering the rational clarity and emotional coolness of this finely carved marble work. In another part of her essay, Paris further sees the decapitated head of this sculpture as "her response to [Rodin's] torment."[51] All this denigrates Claudel's art by limiting it to the realm of her relation to a man and denying its larger meaning.

During the last years of her creative life, Camille Claudel developed an aesthetic that fit no previous or contemporary models and is almost certainly related to a female experience on some level, as in *The Gossips* (1897, see figure 4). Yet virtually nothing has been written on this aspect of her art.

Another artist who fell between the cracks of male-constructed history is French painter Suzanne Valadon (1865–1938). She, too, in her various images of women, developed her own aesthetic outside the bounds of male models of creativity, an aesthetic that reflects the contradictions of

Fig. 2. Camille Claudel, *La Valse*, 1892. Bronze, 43.2×23×34.3 cm. Musée Rodin, Paris. (Photo: B. Jarret.) © 1991 SPADEM/ARS NY.

Fig. 3. Camille Claudel, *Clotho*, 1893. Plaster. Musée Rodin, Paris.
(Photo: B. Jarret.) © 1991 SPADEM/ARS NY.

Fig. 4.   Camille Claudel, *Les Bavardes* (The Gossips), 1897. Onyx and bronze, 44.9×42.2×39 cm. Musée Rodin, Paris. (Photo: B. Jarret.) © 1991 SPADEM/ARS NY.

her own position as a relatively free, libertine woman of the people in a male society, yet bound by the ideology of femininity of her time. Despite these obvious contradictions in her work, male critics, a number of whom have written entire treatises on her art and especially her life, consistently read her work as powerful and thus masculine, reflecting the male model of creativity described previously. She is also characterized as having suffered immensely, the requisite *la douleur* that we recall is necessary to creativity. One critic, for example, describes her amazingly honest and blunt *Self Portrait with Nude Breasts* (1932, Paris, private collection) as revealing suffering and tragic destiny.[52] For me, however, her strength is more prominent in this portrait than is *la douleur.*

Rosemary Betterton, in her recent essay on the artist, redresses this reading of Valadon. She claims that, rather than reflecting any male model, her work "marks a point of resistance to dominant representations of female sexuality in early twentieth-century art."[53] However, Valadon's nudes do not always resist such representations; sometimes they participate in them. She employs a wide range of positions, from dominated seduction to total ease and relaxation. Often within the same painting, her nudes reflect both the conventional, objectified pose presented for a male gaze and the intimacy of women among women, in everyday activities such as bathing, as in the drawing *La Petite Normande* (1920s).[54] The figure is both in an attitude of relaxed complacency, with her legs planted firmly, and of objectification, with her hand on her breast in a traditional gesture of proffering the female fruit.

In *The Future Unveiled* (1912, see figure 5), this duality is also present. The beautiful, voluptuous blonde model extends her body along the couch for the viewer's delectation, and, certainly, this painting is very much about her body. It is turned toward the viewer and totally open to him or her. Her wavy hair streams down her back and tumbles over the edge of the divan. Along the back of the couch, next to her legs, is a richly colored, even "oriental," drape or robe. She thus belongs to the genre of the romantic odalisque, as painted by Ingres or Matisse. Yet she also is totally relaxed, and looks down at the dressed, darker woman at the foot of the divan reading her fortune in the cards. This second figure reflects the typical nineteenth-century construction of the woman of color as foil to the lily-white sexualized female, and another essay could be written on her role in representation, but there is also a sense of complicity or, at best, comraderie between the two women that is absent in a similar imagery with these stock types, such as Manet's *Olympia.* The reading of this painting thus vacillates between the conventionally objectified nude with exotic Other, and an intimate genre scene. Through such tension and contradictions, Valadon's images disrupt the conventional representation of the nude even while participating in it.

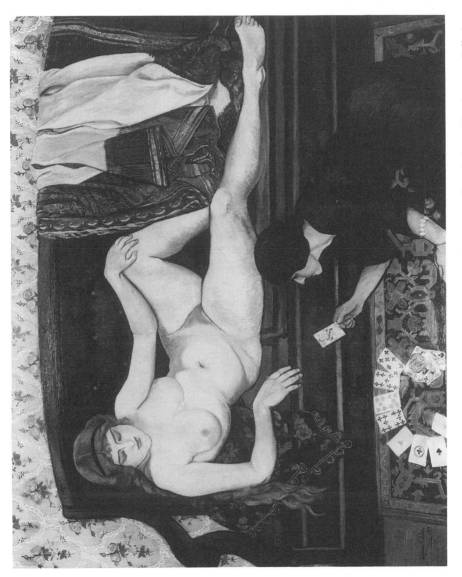

Fig. 5. Suzanne Valadon, L'Avenir dévoilé ou la tireuse (*The Future Unveiled, or The Fortune Teller*), 1912. Oil on canvas, 130×163 cm. Petit Palais, Geneva. (Photo: Museum.) © 1991 ARS NY/SPADEM/ADAGP.

Another work, *Adam and Eve* (1909, see figure 6), is also a curious combination of convention and personal freedom. This is a painting of Valadon and her young lover, André Utter, in the early years of their lifelong affair. The figures seem to have an equal sense of themselves and of themselves as equals rare in this theme, and there is little seduction taking place on either side. They are wrapped up in themselves and each other; there is no victim and no aggressor. Yet when Valadon wanted to express the joy of her new and loving and nonhierarchical relationship to Utter (she was twenty years his senior, and he admired her and her work), she turned to conventional allegory in the grand manner. However, she modifies these conventions, here by denying the viewer the voyeuristic pleasure so typical in the genre of the female nude. Another allegorical work, *La Joie de Vivre* (1911, see figure 7), contains even greater contradictions. The male to the right, also Utter, watches the nude female bathers, who reflect both states of being-looked-at-ness and unselfconsciousness. This grand composition, even in its title, recalls the typical construct of the period, "woman as nature." Artists from Renoir, Degas, and Cezanne, to Gauguin, as we have seen, rework the potent myth of woman as nature. "The nude in the landscape in particular came to signify an identification of women's bodies with the forces of nature," according to Betterton.[55] In this painting, Valadon has chosen to refer to the timeless myth of sensuality and woman as embedded in nature, yet the figures are self-absorbed as well.

Valadon's nudes pose numerous problems and raise issues related to constructed femininity and the potential role of the female gaze in slipping through that construction. The resistances to conventional interpretations, those contradictions for which no deciphering tools yet exist, are the most fruitful and obvious places to begin an investigation of models of female creativity that break through the culturally constructed incompatibility of women and creativity. This essay represents the initial phase of my research on this topic.

This study of creativity thus reveals a disjunction between artistic practice and theory, between ideas and lived experience. Unless practice has been legitimized by theory that has repercussions within a dominant ideology, it will not be recognized. In the case of women, when a model of creativity, for example, actually rejects their participation, it is highly unlikely that their creative acts will be valued as such. The persistence of theories such as those about women, madness, and creativity has

Fig. 6.   Suzanne Valadon, *Adam et Eve*, 1909. Paris Musée National d'Art
Moderne, Centre Georges Pompidou, Paris. Oil on canvas, 162×131 cm.
(Photo: Museum.) © 1991 ARS NY/SPADEM/ADAGP.

Fig. 7. Suzanne Valadon, *La Joie de Vivre*, 1911. Oil on canvas, 48⅜″ × 81″. The Metropolitan Museum of Art, New York. Bequest of Miss Adelaide Milton de Groot. (Photo: Museum.) © 1991 ARS NY/SPADEM/ADAGP.

allowed women's art to be consistently written out of history, despite the number of women artists working in various periods.[56]

NOTES

1. This essay represents a preliminary study of these issues. My research, particularly into the nature of female creativity during this period, is still ongoing. I would like to thank the *Allen Memorial Museum Art Bulletin* for permission to reprint much of the material in this essay, especially the first sections, from my article "Passionate Discontent: The Creative Process and Gender Difference in the French Symbolist Period," published there in Vol. 63, no. 1 (Summer, 1988).

2. This model permeated all levels of culture, but was at its strongest among the avant-garde.

3. Enid Starkie, *Baudelaire* (Norfolk, Conn.: New Directions, 1958), 118.

4. Since this model is particularly male, the artist it describes may also be characterized as such.

5. G.-Albert Aurier, "Le Symbolisme en peinture: Paul Gauguin," in *Oeuvres posthumes*, ed. Remy de Gourmont (Paris: Mercure de France, 1893), 217–18.

6. Aurier, "Vincent Van Gogh," in *Oeuvres posthumes*, 261–62.

7. Cesare Lombroso, *L'Homme de génie*, trans. Colonna D'Istria (Paris: F. Alcan, 1889), 2–3. Although there were other, less extreme theories of the relationship between madness and genius, this text was very influential in France.

8. Lombroso, *L'Homme*, 197.

9. Ch. Richet, "Preface," in Lombroso, *L'Homme*, v–vii.

10. See Aurier, "Essai sur une nouvelle méthode de critique," in *Oeuvres posthumes*, 186–88, for the concept of the *isolé*.

11. Richet, "Preface," xi–xiii.

12. The connection between madness and genius did not always exclude women, but it was never posited in any consistent way. Lombroso, for example, cites several women in his discussion of examples of temporary genius among the mad during bouts of madness and excitation (*L'Homme*, 270ff.).

13. Lombroso, *L'Homme*, 137–38.

14. For this brief outline of the character of women (i.e., middle-class women) as understood in the late nineteenth century, I use not only French but English sources as well. I do not mean to conflate the two, but the general profile of middle-class women, as described in the literature and particularly as it related to hysteria, is remarkably similar in both countries. In my book on this subject, greater distinctions between the two will be made.

15. Mary Poovey, "'Scenes of an Indelicate Character': The Medical 'Treatment' of Victorian Women," *Representations*, no. 14 (Spring, 1986): 146.

16. Elaine Showalter, *The Female Malady: Women, Madness, and English Culture, 1830–1980* (New York: Penguin, 1985), 55, 73.

17. Quoted in Showalter, *Female Malady*, 122.

18. George Moore, "Sex in Art," in *Modern Painting* (London: W. Scott, 1898), 226.

19. Poovey, "Scenes," 146 and passim.

20. Bram Dijkstra, *Idols of Perversity: Fantasies of Feminine Evil in Fin de Siècle Culture* (New York: Oxford University Press, 1986), 34.

21. Dijkstra, *Idols*, 51–53.

22. Gauguin to Emile Bernard, as quoted in John Rewald, *Post-Impressionism from Van Gogh to Gauguin* (New York: Museum of Modern Art, 1978), 410.

23. For similar interpretations of this painting, see Wayne Anderson, *Gauguin's Paradise Lost* (New York: Viking, 1971), 100ff.; Vojtech Jirat-Wasiutynski, "Gauguin in the Context of Symbolism" (Ph.D. diss., Princeton University, 1975), 188–268.

24. See Jirat-Wasiutynski, "Gauguin," 235.

25. L. J. Jordanova, "Natural Facts: A Historical Perspective on Science and Sexuality," in *Nature, Culture, and Gender*, ed. Carol P. MacCormack and Marilyn Strathern (Cambridge: Cambridge University Press, 1980), 43. She does not refer to Gauguin specifically, but to this stereotype generally.

26. See Gauguin's reply to Strindberg's letter in Herschel B. Chipp, *Theories of Modern Art* (Berkeley: University of California Press, 1973), 83.

27. Quoted in Chipp, *Theories of Modern Art*, 83.

28. Showalter, *Female Malady*, 129.

29. Showalter, *Female Malady*, 131–32. Others have suggested as much. Carroll Smith-Rosenberg has suggested that "hysteria might well have been the only acceptable outburst of rage, despair, or simply energy that was available to women. In the epidemic of hysteria women were conforming to the male view of their inherent sickness and finding a way to rebel against an intolerable social role" (quoted in Lorna Duffin, "The Conspicuous Consumptive: Woman as an Invalid," in *The Nineteenth-Century Woman: Her Cultural and Physical World*, ed. Sara Delamont and Lorna Duffin [London: Croom Helm, 1978], 51).

30. Showalter, *Female Malady*, 155ff.

31. Shoshana Felman, "Women and Madness: The Critical Phallacy," book review, *Diacritics* 5 (Winter, 1975): 2.

32. Showalter, *Female Malady*, 132, citing F. O. Skey from 1866.

33. Showalter, *Female Malady*, 134.

34. Showalter, *Female Malady*, 145.

35. The Symbolists often referred to "the people" as a "herd," or used other derogatory terms, unless they wished to call upon their "native," if ignorant, intuition. Then they were seen as equivalent to "noble savages."

36. Quoted in Steven Z. Levine, "Monet, Fantasy, and Freud," in *Psychoanalytic Perspectives on Art* 1 (1985): 43.

37. Steven Heath, *The Sexual Fix* (New York: Schocken, 1982), 57.

38. Charcot constructs hysteria as a series of stages and through the use of particular patients at his clinic. Ilza Veith (*Hysteria: The History of a Disease* [Chicago: University of Chicago Press, 1965], 239) notes that Charcot's assistants most likely led the patients to perform as expected. Georges Didi-Huberman (*Invention de l'hystérie: Charcot et l'iconographie photographique de la Salpêtrière* [Paris: Macula, 1982], 4–5 and passim) states outright that hysteria was invented, that is, constructed, at the Salpêtrière by Charcot.

39. Heath, *Sexual Fix*, 243.

40. Showalter (*Female Malady*, 60–61) points out that no direct accounts from the insane or their keepers are utilized in medical definitions or determinations. Poovey also

notes that "the medical representation of woman [during the Victorian period] silenced real women" ("Scenes," 156).

41. Robert Wernick, "Camille Claudel's Tempestuous Life of Art and Passion," *Smithsonian* 16 (September, 1985): 64.

42. Reine-Marie Paris, *Camille Claudel* (Washington, D.C.: National Museum of Women in the Arts, 1988), 15.

43. Quoted in Wernick, "Camille Claudel's Life," 62.

44. As Wernick put it, "It is characteristic of paranoia that it entails no impairment of the mental processes" ("Camille Claudel's Life," 64).

45. Camille Claudel, quoted in Wernick, "Camille Claudel's Life," 64.

46. Wernick, "Camille Claudel's Life," 63.

47. Many of the works cited here exist in several versions and different materials.

48. Paris, *Camille Claudel*, 14.

49. Paris, *Camille Claudel*, 52 (paraphrased from the French).

50. Paris, *Camille Claudel*, 14.

51. Paris, *Camille Claudel*, 16.

52. Nesto Jacometti (*Suzanne Valadon* [Geneva: Pierre Callier, 1947], n.p.) claims that this portrait expresses "un visage balafré par l'âge et la souffrance" and "les sillons tragiques de la destinée."

53. Rosemary Betterton, "How Do Women Look? The Female Nude in the Work of Suzanne Valadon," in *Looking On: Images of Femininity in the Visual Arts and Media*, ed. Rosemary Betterton (New York: Pandora, 1987), 222. She also suggests Valadon's negotiation with the dominant conventions, however.

54. Illustrated in Jacometti, *Suzanne Valadon*, pl. 37.

55. Betterton, "How Do Women Look?" 227.

56. Jordanova notes that "recent feminist history has shown the diversity of women's social and occupational roles" despite the inflexibility of contemporary ideas about them ("Natural Facts," 42).

Purity or Danger: Mondrian's Exclusion of the Feminine and the Gender of Abstract Painting

MARK A. CHEETHAM

In 1920, the Dutch painter Piet Mondrian published "Neo-Plasticism: The General Principle of Plastic Equivalence," an essay that amounted to a manifesto of his ideas. Since he envisioned that a new society would be realized by a "new art" created by a "new man," he dedicated this work—and by implication, both his Neoplastic art (as he called it) and worldview—"to the men of the future" (Mondrian 1986, 144). This dedication might appear to some as harmless, utopian enthusiasm for a different but fleeting style or trend in art, abstract painting. A critic as informed as W. J. T. Mitchell, for example, has recently assured us of "the obsolescence of abstraction" today, of its secure reification as "a monument to an era that is passing from living memory into history" (1989, 348), and his view fits comfortably with the widespread opinion that art is largely decorative, that it is less important and even less "real" than society writ large. But can Mondrian's ideology and material practice be neutralized so effortlessly? I will argue that they cannot, specifically because the discourse that he self-consciously fathered has established a masculinist frame for abstract painting *and* because what I see as his control over the inheritance of abstraction continues not only in painting but, as he hoped, also pervades culture generally.

Mondrian argues that abstract art is male, and Neoplasticism is indeed driven by the radical exclusion of what he deems the "feminine principle." His construction of the "feminine," however, is nothing more than an occasion for the mastery typical of dialectical reason, one whose pernicious consequences are endemic in modernism and with which we are still encumbered.[1] In attempting to put critical pressure on Mondrian's vision of abstraction and his dream of a society built on its principles

by analyzing his denigration of the feminine, I am performing what Alice
Jardine has defined as a "gynetic" reading. This reading is closely allied
to postmodernism, in opposition to the paradigmatic modernism of
Mondrian, and "has settled on the conception of 'woman' or 'the feminine'
as both a metaphor of reading and topography for writing for confronting
the breakdown of the paternal metaphor" (1985, 34). When I examine
Mondrian's abuse of the feminine and turn to contemporary Canadian
artist Allyson Clay's work as a counterexample, as I will do later in this
essay, however, I am keenly aware of just how much I am speaking as
one of Mondrian's potential addressees; that by citing Clay, discussing
her abstract painting, and arguing that she effectively intervenes to break
the pure line of inheritance Mondrian sought to establish, I am inevitably
complicit in that perniciously masculinist definition of the feminine that
I am seeking to undercut. This is one of the dangers of gynesis as it is
discussed by Jardine, and it is not a situation that I enjoy or accept
uncritically. But the main alternative that I see is to say nothing, to
accept Mondrian's exclusionary vision in the spirit of silent, mystical
reverie in which it is delivered.

Mondrian's dedication "to the men of the future" just will not go
away. It appears as the epigraph to the recent English edition of his
collected writings. More tellingly, this same phrase is also written in
huge letters (in Italian) right on the surface of an abstract painting from
1988 by German artist Gerhard Merz. Merz thus records his *homage* to
Mondrian (and that term is crucial if we remember the consequent pun
on *homme* in the French original of Mondrian's dedication). By pairing
Mondrian and Merz in this way, I hope to question the gender of contemporary abstract painting. If, as I will argue, this genre continues to
be "masculine" largely because of Mondrian's patrimony, how can women
artists work abstractly without crippling complicity? To begin to answer
this sort of question, we must first ask to what extent Mondrian did en-
gender abstract painting, to what extent the premises he established entail
a specific hierarchy of gender. These are the coordinates on which I will
focus; I am well aware, however, that in this choice I will commit sins
of exclusion not unlike those for which I condemn Mondrian. I will not,
for example, discuss that crucial generation of Canadian and U.S.
abstractionists—artists such as Guido Molinari, Claude Tousignant,
Barnett Newman, and Kenneth Noland—who continued the line of masculinist abstraction in the 1950s and after. What I sacrifice by way of a

"complete" history, however, I hope to gain by examining moments in the (necessarily) selective activities of memory as it constructs art's history. First, then, let me picture the way I see Mondrian's art and theory and the legacy they leave.

Mondrian's rhetoric and practice turn on the *purification* of the feminine principle, which, predictably, given his explicit participation in a Platonic and neo-Platonic metaphysics, is defined as material as opposed to spiritual.[2] Purity's essence is male for Mondrian, and concomitant with this identification of gender are the claims of reason. The entire fourth section of his 1917 essay, "The New Plastic in Painting," demonstrates "The Rationality of the New Plastic" (Mondrian 1986, 40), a rationality that requires the feminine as a principle to be overcome. Mondrian asserts that his stance is "clarified by *reasoning*" (40) and by "the *rationality* of art" (40). Failure to achieve the metaphysical security of this purity is thus, for him, a palpable *danger*, not only for art, but for all of society, hence my allusion to and alteration of the title of Mary Douglas's famous book *Purity and Danger*. For Mondrian, the conjunction must be changed to a disjunction: society can have purity *or* danger. To secure this purity, Mondrian effectively gave abstract painting a masculine character. In suggesting how he did this and what implications the result might have, we see that Mondrian sought to assure not only the initial gender of his progeny, but that he also attempted to guarantee the purity of the future through what amounts to nothing less than a program of aesthetic eugenics.[3]

As we have seen, Mondrian's thinking about and production of art are founded on a dialectics of reason in which the most excluded principle and individual of all is the female. He theorized about the inferiority of the feminine in some of his earliest writings and devoted the lengthy and concluding sections of his first major statement of the axioms of Neoplasticism, "The New Plastic in Painting" (1917), to a detailed defense of what he considered the intrinsic "maleness" of abstract art. He seems obsessed with the relation between male and female in the aphoristic comments of the 1912–14 *Sketchbooks*, notes that constitute the seeds of his later art theory. "Woman is against art, against abstraction . . . in her innermost being," he announces (Mondrian 1969, 19). Try as she might, a woman is "never completely an artist" (34) because her defining feminine principle, Mondrian holds, is passive, form-receiving "matter" or material, whereas the male is imbued with "force" that shapes this material according to higher principles (24). In "The New Plastic in Painting," Mondrian reveals his authority for these lamentably conventional views.[4] "Ancient wisdom," he tells us, "identified the physical, the natural, with the female, and the spiritual with the male element" (Mondrian 1986, 56 n. *g*, 57 n. *l*). As Mondrian also makes clear, the female is to be seen as individual and the male as universal. These views are, of course, Greek, specifically Aristotelian and Platonic,[5] and, in Mondrian's case, they were very likely transmitted by Theosophy.[6] But Mondrian is not content merely to follow this tradition; he dedicates himself to it with an energy sufficient to generate the novel claim that woman also embodies "tradition," both in its general cultural sense and in the visual arts specifically (Mondrian 1986, 57 n. *l*). Thus the feminine principle—which he sometimes distinguishes from the biologically female by claiming that women and men have both female and male principles in their makeup, but which, at other junctures, he conflates with the simply mundane woman—works for Mondrian as the initially negative pole within an unbalanced economy searching for equilibrium.

The feminine is the outer that opposes the male's inner values, Mondrian holds. It is material where the male is spiritual; plastically, it is horizontal (like the earth) where the male is vertical (aspiring to the Divine). These metaphysical speculations quite literally established the oppositions and purifications so common in Mondrian's signature Neoplastic compositions, with their rigorous orthogonal intersections. With a quintessentially Hegelian flare, Mondrian argues that this "negative" opposition provided by the female is actually the positive precept in the dialectic of spirit's evolution, because it stimulates the male to transcend the material altogether.

> In our time, oppression by the female, a legacy of the old mentality, still weighs so heavily on life and on art that there is little room for male-female equilibrium. As *tradition*, the female element clings to the old art and opposes anything new—precisely because each new art expression moves further away from the natural appearance of things. Consistently viewed, the female element is hostile to all art on the one hand, while on the other it not only realizes the art-idea but reaches toward art (for outwardness reaches toward inwardness). It is precisely the female element, therefore, that constructs art, and precisely its influence that creates abstract art, for it most purely brings the male to expression. (Mondrian 1986, 68–69 n. *l*)

Eve is necessary to Adam, as Mondrian notes (lending biblical authority to his views), and, like Adam, Mondrian is genuinely nostalgic for
what he envisages as the equilibrium of prelapsarian unity. As Laura
Mulvey argues with respect to Freud's gynetic vision, however, "The
feminine cannot be conceptualized as different, but rather only as *opposition* (passivity) . . ." (1989, 31).

Someone with neo-Platonic or Jungian sympathies might condone this
construction as Mondrian's acknowledgement of his own feminine side.
But with his essentialist nostalgia comes the indelicate, exclusionary
mechanism of purity, a mechanism that is decidedly patriarchal in its
subjugation or appropriation of the feminine in the name of equilibrium
and reason.[7] Mondrian's method is ruthless: "We must reject nothing of
the past but must purify everything" (Mondrian 1986, 363). His prime
target, of course, is the material, individual, female principle, for which
he harbors venomous scorn: "The feminine and material rule life and
society and shackle spiritual expression as a function of the masculine.
A Futurist manifesto proclaiming hatred of *woman* (the feminine) is
entirely justified" (137).

Mondrian's longing for the security of a unified male-female is explicitly anchored in Aristophanes's description of the creation of man and
woman in Plato's *Symposium*, the myth of the androgyne or hermaphrodite. "Besides the two sexes, male and female," Aristophanes says,
"there was a third which partook of the nature of both, and for which
we still have a name . . . 'hermaphrodite'" (Plato 1963, 189e). Zeus, however, split these ideal units into two, creating the two sexes we now
know. What he also created was a nostalgia for sexual reunification that
is analogous to the desire the soul has for the Ideas: "The work of
bisection . . . left each half with a desperate yearning for the other" (191a),
a desire that Mondrian seems to have inherited, given his praise of the
"spiritual hermaphrodite." Mondrian elaborates this dubious desire in
the extensive notes to "The New Plastic in Painting." "*Fully human* life,"
he says, "needs both outwardness and inwardness, female and male.
Life's most perfect state is *the most complete equilibrium of the two*"
(Mondrian 1986, 67). Mondrian borrows from Plato the ideal of the
supposed equality of the sexes in the hermaphrodite. In attempting to
return to this pure, equilibrated state, however, he is compelled, by his
notion of purity as the immaterial and by his conception of the feminine
as material, to purify the female principle of its sexuality in order to

realize his ideal duality. The male principle—the universal, essential, form-giving, abstract—is defined as spiritual, that is, above the materiality of physical passion and procreation, and is thus always predominant in the dialectic of equilibration. "Harmony" is achieved precisely because purification proceeds hierarchically by excluding what is held to be the female element.

Inflammatory though the term *eugenics* might sound, Mondrian's pure version of the genealogy of Neoplasticism explicitly seeks to control art's past and future history. His condemnation of the feminine does not apply only to individuals or even just to the material ingredient in society and art. Because the female is equated with tradition itself, this censure covers the entire history of art up to the advent of his abstract painting. In fact, Mondrian asserts, "representation of *any* kind, the *portrayal of any aspect of nature, whether landscape, interior, still life, etc.*, can be defined as *predominantly female*" (Mondrian 1986, 69). Thus, when he looks back at his forbears as he constructs the prehistory of abstraction, they all appear "female" in the sense that they must be purified. By constructing a genealogy of *purified females* such as Cézanne and the Cubists, he in effect controls the aesthetic breeding that evolution toward pure art must promote. The "new man" will thus be born by purifying the feminine in ways not imagined before Mondrian.

Mondrian's argument here returns us yet again to Plato, to the Plato who recommends eugenics in order to secure the stability of society,[8] and who also proclaims, in the *Phaedrus*, the need to maintain a pure, explicitly male line of inheritance through the exclusive spiritual intercourse between male master and male pupil.[9] Mondrian also ensures the male purity of abstraction's inheritance, not by censoring writing or painting as generic activities but by making sure that the female, material part of his art is conveniently transcended in his envisioned society, where art and life are one. Mondrian keeps the line pure for the men of the future.

To see how this retreat from sexual difference affects Mondrian's art, we need only look at his early, preabstract painting called *Evolution* (1911; figure 1). The triptych moves from left, to right, to center in its attempt to reproduce (not merely represent) the dawning of Theosophical knowledge in what is commonly seen as a female subject.[10] This is the now-accepted reading. What has not, to my knowledge, been underlined is the increasing "maleness" of the figure, her evolution toward the

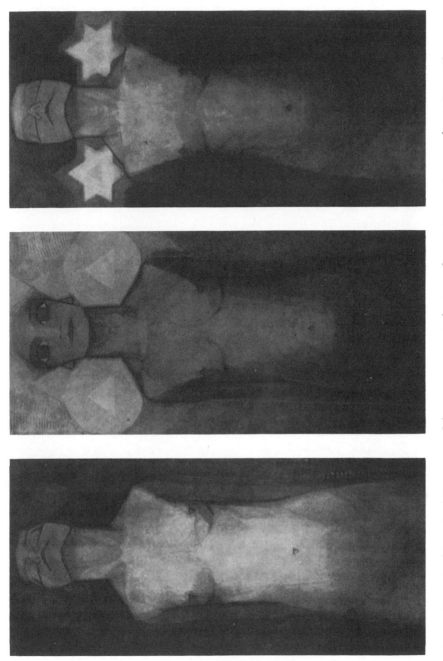

Fig. 1. Piet Mondrian, *Evolution*, 1911. Oil on canvas, triptych, 2 panels 70$^{1}/_{16}$" × 33$^{7}/_{16}$"; 1 panel 72$^{1}/_{16}$" × 34$^{1}/_{2}$". Haags Gemeentmuseum, The Hague.

purported equilibrium of the hermaphrodite. Yet this manifesto of spiritual enlightenment through art can be read as Mondrian's imaging of the spiritual hermaphrodite, of his drive to purify the feminine in order to clear the way for abstraction.[11] On the left, the figure's gender is emphasized not only by her exposed breasts but also by the way that her abundant hair (a central male erotic focus around the turn of this century) frames her face, *and*—given the notion that woman was defined as passive, receptive matter—by her apparent acquiescence to this experience. Her eyes are closed; she leans her head back, arms behind her, in a posture of ecstatic submission. This pose is unchanged on the right, but significantly, her hair seems to have been shortened. It now comes just below her jawline because the head has tilted forward slightly as she "awakens." The center panel completes this transformation. The hair has been replaced completely by a white mantle that extends from the top of the image, around the head, and into the two forms that frame the shoulders and contain large triangles. The figure faces us squarely, eyes open unnaturally wide. The female figure has been purified of her materiality. Her male, spiritual component has been strengthened so that "she" is now an equilibrated, androgynous "force." Even her jawline seems to have widened and sharpened. We focus on the upper, intellectual part of her body because of its yellow and white frame; her sexuality has become strictly relative to this purity.

As Mondrian makes clear in "The New Plastic in Painting," it is the impure female who must be improved if the male is to triumph, just as it is naturalistic art that must be purified in the name of abstraction. His reasoning here brings us to a second purpose for which the female is to be purified. The feminine embodies outwardness, he argues, while

> the male element, on the other hand, remains *inwardness* despite its exteriorization. The most purified male comes closest to *the* inward, while the most purified female shows the least outwardness. Thus, through the most purified female and the most purified male, the *inward* is brought to expression most purely. . . . True socialism signifies *equilibrium* between inward and outward culture. (Mondrian 1986, 66)

By invoking Neoplasticism's social calling in the context of his purification of gender, Mondrian has, in effect, established his ideal of hermaphroditic equilibrium as the model for society. Woman helps him to define art and art's transformation of society as the resolution of all opposition in inward, universal purity. Yet since only the male principle can achieve this state, Mondrian thus defines both the aesthetic and social realms as male, the male that subsumes a purified female. His work is, therefore, very appropriately dedicated to the men of the future, because, in his ideal world, there will be only men. For as long as artists need to reproduce through art—that is, until Mondrian's "revolution" comes and art is no longer needed—they can now do so by drawing on their inner, purified, and self-sufficient selves. For Mondrian's men of the future, reproduction "enjoys" the purity of parthenogenesis.

I now want to ask to what extent current abstract painting has been gendered by Mondrian, to what extent its practice is already speculated by his vision of the future, and whether his men of the future are claiming their right of succession. My sense is that abstraction's reference points remain masculine as defined and guaranteed by Mondrian—and also, lest I seem to be placing a reductive emphasis on his influence—by other essentialist progenitors of abstract painting such as Malevich, Kandinsky, and Kupka. I would even argue that the early abstractions of Georgia O'Keeffe, which would seem to provide a counterexample, participate in the rhetoric of purity established by these men, in a project of defining a transcendental (that is, nonmaterial and nonindividual) feminine. In our own time, Merz's *ultramariblau (ultramarine blue), 1988* celebrates this same purity. On the other hand, recent work by Vancouver painter Allyson Clay challenges this masculinist hegemony from within its own discourse, and I want to conclude with a comparison of these two directions.

Merz's painting does not look like a Mondrian, but its discourse is that of pure Neoplasticism. The painting is extremely large, 170 cm high and 475 cm long. Inside a heavy, black frame is a field of grey pigment; inside this is a field of pure blue, reminiscent of Mondrian's obsession with primary color. Most tellingly, across the top, in large black letters and numerals, runs the dedication *"Agli Uomini Del Futuro, MCMLXXXVIII,"* "to the men of the future, 1988." His homage to Mondrian turns on our recognition of both the Dutch painter's plastic and theoretical language, in this case, our recollection of the blue that was so much a part of Mondrian's purified vocabulary and of the epigraph. Again, like Mondrian before him, Merz titles his work in a supposedly neutral way, suggesting that the painting deals exclusively with pure, formal values. But we cannot possibly ignore the assertive text and its subtext of patronymic inheritance. Merz writes that "color is a memory," and even though this painting does not duplicate Mondrian's typical opposition of orthogonals and colored masses, it resonates with the feel of a Mondrian. It would be a relief to diffuse the insistence of this piece by seeing it as a parody, as an ironic—because overblown— statement about the ambitions Mondrian had for Neoplasticism. But Merz seems to want to keep Mondrian alive, to enjoy his presence. Since, in this and other recent work, he retains (as contemporary critic Ingrid Rein phrases it) a "commitment to pure, impersonal surface as the most deeply anchored of all painterly positions" (1985, 82), he is also nostalgic for the power of Mondrian's canvases, for their purity, because this purity is the shibboleth for an entire metaphysical "position." The catalog accompanying the exhibition of Merz's work at the Art Gallery of Ontario in Toronto makes this clear. Mnemosyne, we read, is Merz's muse, and his work is "an attempt to *penetrate* the past and make it contemporary; to *enter memory* itself in search of ancient wisdom" (Campbell 1988, 13; italics added). Yet two points seemingly lost to Merz's and his commentator's memory should be recalled here: first, Mnemosyne is female, the mother of the muses and thus of the arts. Second, Mondrian too searched for ancient wisdom, particularly in the writings of a great theorist of the mnemonic, Plato. Merz's recollection then, can be seen as a duplication of Mondrian's and even Plato's appropriation and violation of the feminine. And Merz seems to participate in Mondrian's pure, hermaphroditic creativity, at least if we can believe the catalog essay's stylishly but problematically Derridean claim that he "realized that memory could be used as an effective vehicle *for invaginating his work* with a language of large effects" (Campbell 1988, 22; italics added). This is the message he seems to dedicate to the men of the future with this painting.

Allyson Clay's *Lure* is an installation of four small, abstract paintings and four texts first exhibited in 1988. The paintings are hung in a horizontal line on one wall; they face the texts over a gap of about twelve feet. In the final pair, "Eye to Eye" (1988; figure 2), the painting is a simple alternation of black and white vertical bands, each of equal width. The parallel text describes, in apparently neutral terms, how to make the painting we see. The descriptive voice on the one side of the verbal-visual comparison is, we might say, echoed by its materialization on the other. But this doubleness is anything but a neat dialectic. Clay intervenes in the textual component of "Eye to Eye" with two other voices that run

I Using either cedar, hemlock, pine or fir, build a stretcher with bevelled edges I read
touch 13" square and 1 3/4" deep. Over this stretch medium weight linen read that
your and size with rabbit skin or hide glue. Prepare the glue by softening that
mouth glue crystals in water in the proportion of 1 3/8 oz of glue to one art
face of water and heat in a double boiler until dissolved. Apply two inspired
to coats to the raw linen. Prime with manufactured lead or flake white him
face thinned with turpentine. The primer coat will dry in about 48 hours, to
breath after which the surface is ready to be painted on. Make a prove
to medium out of beeswax and linseed oil by measuring 4 fluid oz of he
mind linseed oil and adding beeswax until the level of the oil reaches was
wet 4 1/2 oz. Warm this mixture in a double boiler until the wax dissolves in
to (do not allow to boil) and cool this to room temperature. On a glass charge
wet or marble surface, use a muller to grind carbon black pigment into even.
myth portions of this medium alternated with small amounts of pure if
of cold-pressed linseed oil until the consistency is thick but tractable. it
her Next make white paint by mulling titanium or zinc white pigment required
always into the linseed oil and wax mixture alternating with pure occasional
yes linseed oil as before until the the paint is thick and tractable. mutilation
look On the dry lead white surface draw two vertical lines with graphite to and
not divide the surface into thirds vertically. Divide each of these penetration
at three columns into three equal vertical columns by drawing vertical lines of
but in graphite. Paint every other column white beginning with the second the
into column from the left. While the white paint is still wet, paint the surface
me rest of the columns black. There will be five black columns including with
eye two on the left and right outer edges, and four white columns including gentle
to of equal size. Make sure all edges are clean and even. strokes

Fig. 2. Allyson Clay, "Eye to Eye," from *Lure*, 1988. Blueprint paper, 23½" × 17½". Private collection.

vertically on either side of the seemingly straightforward recipe for abstraction. On the right of the text, a passage from a contemporary painting manual reveals the discourse of dominance over a passive medium that we saw with reference to Merz's work: "I read that art inspired him to prove he was in charge even if it required occasional mutilation and penetration of the surface with gentle strokes." On the left, Clay inscribes a gently erotic evocation of what seems more like a relation between two people than between artist and canvas: "I touch your mouth / face to face / breath to mind / wet to wet myth of her always / yes / look not at but into me / eye to." In a statement accompanying the exhibition, she writes, "It is necessary to reveal some of this implicit historical hierarchy in order to be able to claim painting as a viable territory for an alternative set of values which are not primarily defined within patriarchy" (1988, n.p.). The simplicity of the images and their instructions work within a tradition of reductive *purity* by which Clay, too, has been influenced, for example by Vancouver artist Ian Wallace, whose early abstract work paid direct homage to Mondrian. But she seeks to have her "voice" heard in this often authoritarian, silent tradition, "to have an argument" with these views, as she puts it (1989).

With her spatial interventions and her small, individual, and very personal scale, Clay dismembers masculinist practices in order to re-member abstraction differently. She is inevitably implicated in this tradition even in her opposition to it and *lured* by its authority, its aura, but she can also use this point of reference to offer a critique of its hierarchical assumptions and methods. There is no retreat from the erotic as in Mondrian, no purification. One response to Clay's questioning of abstraction—one I have also too often encountered—is the objection that "Mondrian was a nice guy." While I believe that his theory of the feminine demonstrates just the opposite all too well, the very fact that such a "defense" is articulated in such specifically gendered terms is reason enough to acknowledge—and resist—the continuing potency of Mondrian's addresses to the men of the future. What Clay's abstraction offers is an impure and un-reasonable work that holds promise for those disenfranchised by the men of the past.

NOTES

1. I hope that this essay can contribute to debates on the gender politics of modernism in Europe, but this is not the context in which to address such issues directly. For an introduction to these concerns, see Dubreuil-Blondin 1983 and Pollock 1988.

2. I discuss this debt in detail in Cheetham 1991.

3. Mondrian's thinking here follows Plato's to a remarkable extent and even parallels ideas promoted by the Nazis, whom Mondrian criticized in the 1940s. Mondrian was certainly no Nazi, but his aesthetic of purity, which, like Hitler's, was constructed around artistic practice but expanded immediately into a blueprint for society, has chillingly fascist overtones. I discuss this matter fully in Cheetham 1991.

4. Mondrian could have found these and related denigrations of the feminine in innumerable sources in the late nineteenth and early twentieth centuries (see, for example, Dijkstra 1986). What I find most interesting, however, is his use of Plato as his source.

5. Plato equates matter and the feminine in the *Symposium* (190B) and *Menexenus* (238A). For a more detailed analysis of the feminine in ancient Greek culture, see Lloyd 1984, 2-9. Carolyn G. Heilbrun (1982) traces the history of androgyny. On pictorial depictions of the androgyne, see Wind 1967, 212ff.

6. See Welsh 1971 for a general discussion of Mondrian and Theosophy. Welsh does not discuss Mondrian's exclusion of the feminine.

7. Londa Schiebinger presents what I see as an analogous explanation for the historical personification of Science as female. "Scientia," she argues, "is feminine in early modern culture . . . because the scientists—the framers of the scheme—are male: the feminine scientia plays opposite the male scientist" (1988, 675).

8. "If we are to keep our flock at the highest pitch of excellence, there should be as many unions of the best of both sexes, and as few of the inferior, as possible, and . . . only the offspring of the better unions should be kept. . . . No one but the rulers must know how all this is being effected; otherwise our herd of Guardians may become rebellious" (Plato 1974, 459).

9. In the *Timaeus* (50c-d; 51e ff.), Plato also identifies the Forms as the father of all reality. On male inheritance in Plato, see Norris 1987, 30.

10. For a conventional and relentlessly formalist reading of this painting, see Champa 1985, 19.

11. Welsh has mentioned the androgynous appearance of these figures (1971, 47), and, of course, androgyny was a widespread ideal around the turn of the twentieth century (see Pierrot 1981). My aim is to take these general observations further by showing how central androgyny was to Mondrian's notion of purity.

REFERENCES

Campbell, James D. 1988. *Mnemosyne or the Art of Memory: Gerhard Merz*. Toronto: Art Gallery of Ontario.

Champa, Kermit Swiler. 1985. *Mondrian Studies*. Chicago: University of Chicago Press.

Cheetham, Mark A. 1991. *The Rhetoric of Purity: Essentialist Theory and the Advent of Abstract Painting*. New Art History and Criticism. Cambridge and New York: Cambridge University Press.

Clay, Allyson. 1988. *LURE*. Vancouver: Artspeak Gallery.

Clay, Allyson. 1989. "Lecture." University of Western Ontario.

Dijkstra, Bram. 1986. *Idols of Perversity: Fantasies of Female Evil in Fin de Siècle Culture*. Oxford: Oxford University Press.

Douglas, Mary. 1984. *Purity and Danger: An Analysis of the Concepts of Pollution and Taboo.* London: Ark.

Dubreuil-Blondin, Nicole. 1983. "Feminism and Modernism: Paradoxes." In *Modernism and Modernity: The Vancouver Conference Papers,* ed. Benjamin H. D. Buchloh, Serge Guilbaut, and David Solkin, 195–212. Halifax: NSCAD.

Heilbrun, Carolyn G. 1982. *Toward a Recognition of Androgyny.* New York: Norton.

Jardine, Alice A. 1985. *Gynesis: Configurations of Women and Modernity.* Ithaca and London: Cornell University Press.

Lloyd, Genevieve. 1984. *The Man of Reason: "Male" and "Female" in Western Philosophy.* Minneapolis: University of Minnesota Press.

Mondrian, Piet. 1969. *Two Mondrian Sketchbooks.* Ed. and trans. J. Joosten and R. Welsh. Amsterdam: Meulenhoff International.

Mondrian, Piet. 1986. *The New Art—The New Life: The Collected Writings of Piet Mondrian.* Ed. and trans. Harry Holtzman and Martin S. James. Boston: G. K. Hall.

Mitchell, W. J. T. 1989. "Ut Pictura Theoria: Abstract Painting and the Repression of Language." *Critical Inquiry* 15:348–71.

Mulvey, Laura. 1989. *Visual and Other Pleasures.* London: Macmillan.

Norris, Christopher. 1987. *Derrida.* Cambridge, Mass.: Harvard University Press.

Pierrot, Jean. 1981. *The Decadent Imagination.* Trans. Derek Coltman. Chicago: University of Chicago Press.

Plato. 1963. *The Collected Dialogues of Plato.* Ed. and trans. Edith Hamilton and Huntington Cairns. Princeton: Princeton University Press.

Plato. 1974. *Republic.* Trans. F. M. Cornford. Oxford: Oxford University Press.

Pollock, Griselda. 1988. *Vision and Difference: Femininity, Feminism, and the Histories of Art.* London: Routledge.

Rein, Ingrid. 1985. "Cliffhanging." *Artforum* 24, no. 3: 80–83.

Schiebinger, Londa. 1988. "Feminine Icons: The Face of Early Modern Science." *Critical Inquiry* 14, no. 1 (Summer): 675–91.

Welsh, Robert P. 1971. "Mondrian and Theosophy." In *Piet Mondrian: Centennial Exhibition.* New York: Guggenheim Museum.

Wind, Edgar. 1967. *Pagan Mysteries in the Renaissance.* London: Penguin.

Physiology, Phrenology, and Patriarchy: The Construction of George Eliot

KRISTIN BRADY

Somewhat to my surprise, I found her intensely feminine. Her slight figure, — it might almost be called diminutive, —her gentle, persuasive air, her constrained gesticulation, the low, sweet voice, —all were as far removed from the repulsive phenomenon, the "man-woman," as it is possible to conceive. The brow alone seemed to betray her intellectual superiority.[1]

The large canon of texts inscribed with the name George Eliot has long been a subject of literary interpretation and has recently received a wide range of responses from feminist critics. My concern here, however, is not with the woman's texts, but rather with the woman *as text*. I shall examine, in short, the discourse—extending from the nineteenth century into the twentieth—that has constructed a particular image of the character, life, and writing of Marian Evans, the woman who published under the name George Eliot. This discourse, I would like to suggest, generally perceives and interprets Evans in terms of a nineteenth-century definition of gender difference based on an equation of woman with her reproductive organs. One succinct example of this definition can be seen in the description offered in 1892 by Dr. M. L. Holbrook on the creation of the female sex: it was "as if the Almighty," he remarked, "had taken the uterus and built up a woman around it."[2] This equation of the woman with her uterus was an outgrowth of the nineteenth-century scientific definitions of gender difference, which were based, as Thomas Laqueur has pointed out, on a model "of biological divergence." By the late eighteenth century, he noted, "[A]n anatomy and physiology of incommensurability replaced a metaphysics of hierarchy in the representation of women in relation to men."[3] Such a definition, which admitted no commonality between genders, naturalized—and thus justified—the already existing social and cultural differences between the sexes. If woman was the heart (that is to say, uterus), in relation to the man's head (that is to say, brain), then the separate spheres of the man's public world and the woman's domestic world were merely social manifestations of essential, natural differences. To unsettle these binary oppositions was to tamper with nature itself.

An influential idea in this construction of incommensurable difference between the sexes (though, in fact, it contradicts the idea of incommensurability) was that of the human body as a closed system containing a limited amount of heat or energy: the woman's body, it was believed, expended this energy through her reproductive organs. Not only by the bearing and nurturing of children, but even by the periodic function of menstruation, women were seen as using up their physical heat—leaving little or no energy that could travel to the head or brain. The man, in contrast, free of the draining properties of the uterus, could expend his energy in a mental direction—could, in short, exercise his reason. In this pre-Freudian, pre-Lacanian view of gender difference, the relationship of presence to absence was in one sense a curious reversal of the current formulation: men were defined not by the presence of a penis, but by the absence of a uterus. This association of the woman with presence rather than with absence did not, however, make her the privileged term in the binary opposition. Associated with the presence of the uterus, it was believed, was the whole range of behavior labeled by nineteenth-century scientific and medical discourse as hysteria. To possess a uterus was to have an excess of nervous energy that, when given too much expression, had to be contained by such measures as the rest cure (which included systematic douching), clitoridectomy, and institutionalization—not to mention marriage. For this reason, the female body was perceived to be not merely different from the male body but also the source of a distinct pathology. The nineteenth century thus inscribed on its construction of woman a host of anxieties about the body and, more particularly, about sexuality.[4]

It was in this climate of thinking that George Eliot's character, life, and writing were first constructed by her contemporaries, who attempted, in various ways, to define her according to their own preconceived notions about gender difference. This task was a monumentally difficult one, however, for Marian Evans failed to conform to the cultural imperatives in significant ways. A woman who was considered to be unattractive to men and who openly expressed her sexuality in a relationship outside marriage while never bearing children; a woman who usurped the masculine prerogatives of learning the classical languages, of mastering current scientific and philosophical ideas, and of supporting herself as a writer; a woman who readily assumed the position of sage among her friends and associates—such a woman both invited and resisted the standard reduction to a uterus surrounded by a female body. Thus, although the extant responses to Eliot by no means represent a monolithic reaction, many of them can be classified in one of two general categories.[5] The tendency was either to insist on Eliot's essential femininity or to see her as a freak of nature, a monstrous anomaly in whom feminine and masculine traits waged a destructive conflict. In both these cases, moreover, there was a general preoccupation with Eliot's female body, the site of her potentially hysterical uterus and the sign of her problematic position in the symbolic order.

Among Eliot's contemporaries, there was often an interest in Eliot's head—the assumption being that she was born with a male head and a female trunk. These interpretations were often shaped by the influential pseudoscience of phrenology, which, though it did not concern itself explicitly with gender difference, implied a theory of female inferiority by its assumption that large brains were more intelligent than small ones.[6] For those adhering to such thinking, Eliot's appearance was perplexing, and many people commented on what they perceived to be the unusually large size of her head and features. Annie Adams Fields, for example, speculated that "her brain must be heavier than most men's,"[7] and both Alfred Tennyson and Charles Eliot Norton commented on Eliot's "masculine face."[8] Even as recently as 1955, Humphry House noted, without offering a source, that Eliot's skull "was said to be broader from brow to ear than any other recorded skull except Napoleon's."[9]

Speculations about the size of Eliot's head often led to theories about its relationship to her female body. Joseph Jacobs remarked on the "massiveness of the head as contrasted with the frailty of the body," while Kegan Paul described what he saw as a "disproportion" between Eliot's "grand and massive" head and the "little fragile" body that had to bear "this weight of brow and brain"—a phenomenon that George Willis Cooke (in his 1883 biography) took as an explanation for Eliot's weak health.[10] Predictably, observations about the size of Eliot's head led to speculations about what happened inside it. Herbert Spencer, for example, made these pronouncements about his old friend and intellectual comrade:

I can tell you of no woman save George Eliot in whom there has been this union of high philosophical capacity with extensive acquisition. . . . While I say this, however, I cannot let pass the occasion for remarking that, in her case as in other cases, mental powers so highly developed in women are in some measure abnormal and involve a physiological cost which the feminine organization will not bear without injury more or less profound.[11]

While Spencer fantasized about the harm that a powerful philosophical mind could do to a weak female body, another old friend of Eliot's turned his attention to the consequences for Eliot's writings of her being a woman. Frederic Harrison took the natural image of giving birth, often used to describe the creative work of both female and male writers, and—transforming the image from the biological to the pathological— made writing seem a grotesquely unnatural activity for a middle-aged woman:

To the last her periods of mental gestation were long, painful, and unhopeful. Parturition was a dangerous crisis, and the long-expected infant was reared with misgivings like some *enfant de miracle,* born late in the mother's life, at the cost of infinite pain, much anxiety, and amidst the wondering trepidation of expectant circles of friends.

Harrison then transformed the image of difficult birth into still another metaphor for creativity that implied the inappropriateness of Eliot's body for her mental task:

Even in her best books we never quite get over the sense of almost painful elaboration, of a powerful mind having rich gifts striving to produce some rare music with an unfamiliar and uncongenial instrument. It reminds us of Beethoven evolving his majestic sonatas on an untuned and dilapidated old piano, the defects of which he could not himself hear.[12]

Though Harrison's metaphor in this case is not explicitly gender-coded, its immediate contiguity and parallel relationship with the image of the middle-aged female body giving birth suggests a radical disjunction between, on the one hand, Eliot's "powerful" masculine mind possessing the "rich gifts" of a male artist such as Beethoven and, on the other hand, her "uncongenial" aging feminine body, which is too "dilapidated" to execute its important task. If George Eliot's mind was a burden to her body, as Spencer thought, then her body, in Harrison's view, was a grossly inadequate "instrument" for that mind. In both cases, the female metabolism is seen as a handicap for the professional thinker and writer.

Gendered readings of the sort that Spencer's and Harrison's appraisals represent are not confined to the observations of a few of Eliot's perplexed, intimate friends. From the time that she first became established as a writer, and throughout the biography and criticism about her— even in remarks that are meant to praise—there is a long tradition of dissecting Eliot's body and mind according to their presumed feminine and masculine traits. After meeting Eliot in 1873, for example, John Fiske wrote these confused sentiments to his wife:

> I never saw such a woman. There is nothing a bit masculine about her; she is thoroughly feminine and looks and acts as if she were made for nothing but to mother babies. But she has a power of *stating* an argument equal to any man.[13]

In a similar vein of admiration and bafflement, Bret Harte wrote in 1880, "She reminds you continually of a man—a bright, gentle, lovable, philosophical man—without being a bit *masculine*. Do you understand me?"[14] Both Fiske and Harte, like many others, seem to have been fearful of applying the label "masculine" to George Eliot, even though they could see attributes in her that they thought were exclusively confined to men. To do so, apparently, would be to deny her femininity and, therefore, to identify her with the stereotypical bluestocking, who, as Elaine Showalter has noted, "was seen as tough, aggressive, pedantic, vain, and ugly."[15] There was simply no acceptable place in the sexual iconography of Victorian patriarchy for the intellectual woman. A letter Henry James wrote to his father when he first met Eliot in 1869 typifies those accounts by men (and women) who had difficulty in reconciling her physical appearance and personality with their own assumptions about gender difference:

> To begin with she is magnificently ugly—deliciously hideous. . . . Now in this vast ugliness resides a most powerful beauty which, in a very few minutes steals forth and charms the mind, so that you end as I ended, in falling in love with her. Yes behold me literally in love with this great horse-faced bluestocking. I don't know in what the charm lies, but it is thoroughly potent. An admirable physiognomy—a delightful expression, a voice soft and rich as that of a counseling angel—a mingled sagacity and sweetness—a broad hint of a great underlying world of reserve, knowledge, pride and power—

a great feminine dignity and character in these massively plain features—a hundred conflicting shades of consciousness and simpleness—shyness and frankness—graciousness and remote indifference—these are some of the more definite elements of her personality. . . . Altogether, she has a larger circumference than any woman I have ever seen.[16]

James's account reads like a jumbled list of the binary oppositions that define sexual difference in patriarchal culture: references to Eliot's "beauty" and "charm," to her "delightful expression" and "soft" voice, to her "sweetness," "simpleness," and "shyness" evoke a conventional image of femininity, while allusions to "ugliness," potency, "sagacity," "knowledge, pride and power," to "consciousness," "frankness," and "remote indifference" signal stereotypical masculinity. In order to contain all these seemingly conflicting traits, James invented the idea of Eliot's "larger circumference"—a width that could encompass in one body what culture had divided between two.

What the youthful James described in such ambivalently enthusiastic terms made George Eliot for many others a uniformly troubling and forbidding presence. In the eyes of some later writers—among them, George Bernard Shaw and W. B. Yeats—this "larger circumference" often transformed her, as Showalter has suggested, into a phallic mother whose massive authority intimidated future generations.[17] A common response to the magnitude of Eliot's influence was to strip it of its power by ridiculing it. Algernon Swinburne, for example, called Eliot "an Amazon thrown sprawling over the crupper of her spavined and spur-galled Pegasus"—a mock epic image deriding not only Eliot's body and her art but, more particularly, the relationship between the two.[18] The implication is that Eliot's "Amazon" body has provoked the diseased poetic inspiration figured in her "spur-galled Pegasus"—only to find itself then mastered and ejected by the sickly animal.

A mocking strategy seems also to color the somewhat milder observations of William Barry, writing in 1904, who made these remarks about Eliot's "epic representation . . . of the living world":

> Doubtless it implies a certain affinity of her mind with the masculine, which is considered to dwell chiefly upon laws and abstractions. Goethe has often been called the Poet of Science; George Eliot perhaps deserves the name of the Epic Pythoness of Science.[19]

Here the reverent and neutrally intellectual term "Poet," applied to the

male writer Goethe, becomes, when applied to the female writer, "Pythoness"—a nineteenth-century version of the "charge of oracularity" that
Thomas M. Lennon has analyzed in a seventeenth-century context as a
gender-coded insult identifying irrational discourse with the enigmatic,
vehicular, and explicitly feminine voice of the oracle (the Delphic Pythia
or the Virgilian Sybil of Cumae) (see his essay, this volume). By asso-
ciating Eliot with the priestess whose voice served as a medium of prophecy in the temple of Apollo, Barry thus implicitly defines her writing,
not as the articulate and coherent discourse of the male poet—who, like
Apollo, speaks clearly—but as the contamination of that discourse by
the female oracle, whose voice makes Apollo's message inscrutable. As
Lennon points out, moreover, there is a link between the oracular voice
and the speech of diabolic possession, of witchcraft, and of hysteria. To
call Eliot a pythoness rather than a poet is thus not merely to acknowledge her gender; it is simultaneously a way of gendering her discourse—
and so of excluding its presumably occult qualities from the pure category
of masculine poetry. The strategy also provides a way of making Eliot
the *medium* of a discourse rather than its originator. More generally,
the pythoness reference suggests a sinister physical power and, when
compared to the term *poet*, a transformation not simply from the poetic
to the oracular and from the reverent to the sinister, but also from the
human to the bestial: the woman poet is made more animal than human,
more physical than mental—and, as such, more ridiculous than sublime.
As a "Pythoness," she is also, paradoxically, a female phallus—an icon
of feminine knowledge and potency.

A similarly mixed iconography informs the comments of Edmund
Gosse, who, in 1906, called George Eliot a "ludicrous pythoness."[20] In
this case, the charge of oracularity is made all the more insulting by its
association with the word *ludicrous*, which cancels even the occult and
dangerous dimensions in the allusion. Barbara Stephen's observation,
made in her 1927 book on Girton College, that in the nineteenth century
"a well-educated woman" was seen as "a ridiculous monster" seems
literally demonstrated by the paradoxical terms of Barry's and Gosse's
mockery.[21] A cruel and defensive humor also characterizes Gosse's
description of Eliot's physical appearance, about which he confessed to
having a "violent interest." In 1919, he reminisced about Eliot as

a large, thick-set sybil, dreamy and immobile, whose massive features, somewhat grim when seen in profile, were incongruously bordered by a hat, always

in the height of the Paris fashion, which in those days commonly included an immense ostrich feather. . . . The contrast between the solemnity of the face and the frivolity of the head-gear had something pathetic and provincial about it.[22]

Gazing at Eliot's head from the perspective of an urban male, Gosse could make her look ridiculous (and himself superior) by mocking her transgressing of two carefully guarded boundaries: class and gender. He therefore singled out Eliot's incongruous "head-gear"—her attempt to disguise her provincial roots by wearing high fashion, as well as her feminine covering for what was so often viewed as a masculine brain. The sibyl image, constituting another charge of oracularity, adds to the sense of incongruity that Gosse is attempting to create, for when visualized as wearing "an immense ostrich feather," the sybil appears absurd and her knowledge loses its potent danger: the charge of oracularity, when made in terms of the body rather than the voice, moves toward the charge of hysteria. Again the oracle—even as she achieves masculine recognition—is ridiculed for her body and thus deprived of her mysterious influence. Gosse's remarks also expose an apparently unconscious linkage between his response to Eliot's head and his feelings about her "contemporary fame," which he found to be a "solemn" and "portentous thing," a "strenuous solemnity":[23] "solemnity," which is "portentous" when associated with Eliot's literary reputation, had been "pathetic and provincial" when applied to her face and head. Gosse indirectly attacks Eliot's literary status by lampooning her body.

A similar linking of Eliot's literary reputation with her physical appearance characterizes David Cecil's reference, made in 1934, to Eliot as standing "at the gateway between the old novel and the new, a massive caryatid, heavy of countenance, uneasy of attitude"[24]—a possible imitation, incidentally, of Gosse's earlier description of George Sand as "that mighty woman, the full-bosomed caryatid of romantic literature."[25] Cecil's remarks bring together two dimensions of the caryatid image: like the priestesses in the temple of Diana at Carthage, Eliot is the guardian of secret female knowledge; and even more than the draped female figures standing as pillars in Greek architecture (more phallic mothers?), Eliot is "massive" and "heavy." Though Cecil ends his remarks by admitting that Eliot was nonetheless "noble, monumental, profoundly impressive,"[26] the literalizing of her into a large and immobile statue, a "massive" (this is Gosse's word too) and overwhelming physical presence, is common to both his censure and his praise. The emphasis on heaviness, like Gosse's on incongruity, undermines any suggestion that Eliot had any real power in her role as prophetess.

An oppressive sense of Eliot's physical control seems also to inform Cecil's comparison of Eliot to a schoolteacher,

> kindly but just, calm but censorious, with birchrod in hand to use as she thinks right, and lists of good and bad conduct marks pinned neatly to her desk. And when we see all the vivid disorderly vitality of human nature ranged before her for carefully measured approval or condemnation, we tend to feel rebellious and resentful.[27]

Here, Cecil associates himself with that "vivid disorderly vitality" suppressed by the phallic mother, her birchrod in hand. In a comically rendered reversal of the standard power relations between the sexes within patriarchy, he assaults Eliot's literary reputation by invoking an image of feminine tyranny and identifying with its victims.

The defensive humor of Gosse's and Cecil's comments—with their reduction of Eliot to a physical body and their iconography of femininity as occult, absurd, monumental, and tyrannical—appears to mask a profound fear. If a woman is appropriating the male position, they seem implicitly to be asking, how and where is the masculine to be constructed? And what is the relationship of the male reader and writer to a female figure who has upset the binary opposition that places the masculine above the feminine? As Mary Jacobus has described such a situation, "Faced with sexual differences, the man sees [femininity] as unfriendly to his own narcissistically conceived identity; femininity is dangerous because, by 'infecting' him, it might erase the distinction which buttresses his idea of masculinity." As Jacobus sees it, this sense of the feminine as a threat to masculinity is the expression of a fear, not only of gender difference, but of the *différance* that informs textuality itself:

> Women become a metaphor for the singleness that writing itself has lost, so that the woman writer comes to figure both for herself and for her readers the hysterical doubleness and incompleteness which representation must repress in order to figure as true, unified, and whole—as masculine, or bearing "the serious stamp of science."[28]

Significantly, many of the gendered criticisms of Eliot's writing ascribe to her a feminine lack of exactly those illusive characteristics of truth and wholeness that repress *différance* in the literary text. The young Henry James, who could declare himself in love with the potent beauty of Eliot's physical presence, reviewed her early novels with a profound sense of masculine superiority. Praising Eliot for having "a certain masculine comprehensiveness that [Maria Edgeworth and Jane Austen] lack," he went on to say that she remained "a delightfully feminine writer" because she had "the microscopic observation, not a myriad of whose keen notations are worth a single one of those great synthetic guesses with which a real master attacks the truth."[29] As is so often the case, praise for a presumably feminine gift simultaneously occasions an assertion of lack. By definition, feminine multiplicity is made inferior to masculine phallocentric unity: difference and *différance* must be suppressed.

The same hierarchical thinking informs George Saintsbury's remarks, made in 1895, that Eliot possessed "in no ordinary degree the female faculty of receiving, assimilating, and reproducing," but that she lacked "in any great degree the male faculties of creation and judgment."[30] Feminine writing was seen as passive and imitative, in other words, while masculine writing was regarded as active and creative. A different distinction was made by John Morley, who attributed Eliot's "ever-deepening sense of the pain of the world" to feminine weakness. "She could not, he commented, as virile natures should, reconcile herself to nature."[31] In the same vein, Leslie Stephen regretted the "want of masculine fibre in George Eliot,"[32] and Arnold Bennett summarized the feeling of many of his generation:

> Her style, though not without shrewdness, is too rank to have any enduring vitality. People call it "masculine." Quite wrong! It is downright, aggressive, sometimes rude, but genuinely masculine, never. On the contrary it is transparently feminine—feminine in its lack of restraint, its wordiness, and the utter absence of feeling for form which characterizes it. The average woman italicizes freely. George Eliot, of course, had trained herself too well to do that, at least formally; yet her constant, undue insistence springs from the same essential weakness, and amounts practically to the same expedient.[33]

Here, Bennett presents Eliot as exceptional among women writers chiefly because she could disguise herself as a man, but congratulates himself for seeing through her superior self-cultivation and shrewdness, finding underneath them her essentially feminine weakness. Again, the mental and the literary are reduced, when seen in the context of a woman, to the physical: it is the feminine *rankness* of Eliot's style, its excess of physicality, that denies her the possibility of a seemingly unphysical masculine "enduring vitality." Feminine multiplicity and *difference* are seen once more as unwelcome supplements to single and whole masculine "vitality."

The sense implied by Bennett that George Eliot's male disguise of a "rude" and "aggressive" style represented a threat to the "genuinely masculine" is a common thread running through much early Eliot criticism. While those who revered her person felt the need to praise her with the term *feminine*, those who were critical of her writing could use the same label as a means of diminishing her importance. To call Eliot's writing feminine, it seems, was a way of preserving authentic masculinity—and the professional activity of writing—for men. A review of John Cross's *Life* of Eliot, for example, took the biography as evidence of "how impressionable, how emotional, how illogical, how feminine she was. . . . The person whom superficial critics long took to be the most masculine of her sex was a very woman."[34] And Richard Simpson, in remarks that set down more explicitly than usual exactly why Eliot was a threat to conventional notions of masculinity, wrote in 1863 that Eliot, unlike other women, "grasps at direct power through reasoning and speech. Having thus taken up the male position, the male ideal becomes hers,—the ideal of power."[35]

The insistence that Eliot's writing was transparently and essentially feminine extended even to judgments of her literary characters. A common complaint was that Eliot, because she was a woman, did not have a sufficiently wide experience to portray men in her fiction (the implication being that the breadth of male experience did give men the ability to present female characters).[36] One fear that seems to underlie this charge, as Edmond Scherer's remarks illustrate, is that both masculine and feminine sexuality are somehow threatened when depicted by a woman:

> I only know one of the novelist's gifts which is wanting to George Eliot. You must not look in her pages for the troubles, the excitements, the disorders of love. . . . A woman cannot sketch a man's passions, because she cannot feel them; and as for painting those of her own sex, she would have to begin by unsexing herself to dare to take the public into confidence as to the last secrets of the feminine heart. Women may write novels—novels better than those of men, but not the same. Genius in their hands meets with, "Thus far and no farther."[37]

According to Scherer, masculine sexuality is unknowable for the woman, while feminine sexuality, like the mysteries underlying the sybil's knowledge, exists only by remaining secret, by being repressed: if a woman writes of her sexuality, she will lose it—will become, indeed, "unsexed."

Many nineteenth-century readers responded to Eliot's portrayal of male characters in language of extreme and resentful mockery, as if these characters—like Eliot herself—were attacks on the very idea of masculinity. Robert Louis Stevenson, for example, asked of a friend who had written about George Eliot,

> Did you—I forget—did you have a kick at the stern works of that melancholy puppy and humbug Daniel Deronda himself?—the Prince of Prigs; the literary abomination of desolation in the way of manhood; a type which is enough to make a man forswear the love of women, if that is how it must be gained. . . . Hats off all the same, you understand: a woman of genius.[38]

Here, Stevenson uses the epithet "woman of genius" both to intensify his attack on Eliot and to withdraw it by invoking the separate and laughable standards by which women were judged.

Close to Stevenson's point of view about Deronda was the more generalized theory that Eliot's heroes, like herself writing under a male pseudonym, were really women in disguise. In 1890, William Ernest Henley spoke of a skeptical male reader whose

> sense of sex was strong enough to make him deny the possibility in any stage of being of nearly all the governesses in revolt it pleased [Eliot] to put forward as men; for with very few exceptions he knew they were heroes of the divided skirt.

Henley's casting of Eliot's heroes as women led him to call up particularly threatening or negative images of femininity: he described Deronda as "an incarnation of woman's rights," Tito Melema of *Romola* as "an improper female in breeches," and Silas Marner as "a good, perplexed old maid." Henley clearly could not reconcile the liberality of Deronda, the evil of Tito, or the vulnerability of Marner with his own conception of masculinity—and so he transformed them into images of the feminine lying outside the realm of male sexual domination: the feminist who seeks power inappropriate for women, the "improper" woman who expresses her sexuality without submitting to the restraints of marriage, and the old maid, whose sphere remains separate from those dictated for women by patriarchy. Ironically, the only male character whom Henley assumed to have "the true male principle about him" was Tertius Lydgate of *Middlemarch*, a figure whom Eliot presents as flawed for his sexism and his resulting attraction to superficial and destructive women.[39]

A similar insistence that the unlikeable qualities in Eliot's male characters are really evidence of female transvestism appears in Leslie Stephen's famous 1902 book on Eliot for the English Men of Letters series. Stephen reported that Eliot was "too thoroughly feminine to be quite at home in the psychology of the male animal." He called Stephen Guest of *The Mill on the Floss* "a mere hairdresser's block" and Tito Melema "thoroughly and to his fingers' end a woman." Henley had not explained why he thought Tito feminine, but Stephen offered a revealing explanation for this attitude. Tito, he reported, "is not cruel out of mere badness, but from effeminacy." This presumed "effeminacy" was linked in Stephen's mind to Tito's skill in achieving power through deceptiveness rather than through physical force. He spoke of Tito as "of the material of which the Delilahs are made, the treacherous, caressing, sensuous creatures who involve strong men in their meshes." Stephen admired Tito only when he acted in a direct, physical way:

> When he is fairly driven into a corner, . . . he can show his claws and act, for once, like a man. But his general position among his more violent associates is like that of a beautiful and treacherous woman who makes delicate caressing and ingenious equivocation do the work of the rougher and more downright masculine methods.

Stephen's version of sexual difference assigns to woman not passivity but a dangerous and subversive weapon: in opposition to masculine physical force is a treacherous female sensuality that deceives and entraps. It is not surprising, therefore, that Stephen, like Henley, admired what he considered to be the manliness of Lydgate. Such a reading equates the characteristics of Rosamond Vincy with feminine sexuality and posits essential masculinity as its victim. Cecil's birchrod is, for Stephen, the female body imaged as a subtly netted trap: the phallic mother has become a seductress.[40]

In the latter years of the twentieth century, as Deirdre David has pointed out, much criticism of George Eliot—rather than mocking her— has desexed her by ignoring altogether the issue of gender.[41] The underlying assumption that Eliot's femininity was a mark of weakness has continued in significant ways to operate, however. Though the grotesque iconography of the man-woman may now be muted, in other words, a sense that Eliot's intellectual activity was somehow in conflict with her gender still governs much thinking about her. In 1947, F. E. Baily detected in Eliot both "female persistence" and female obstinacy and declared she had "an enormous capacity for taking pains and acquiring facts, most unusual in a woman."[42] In her biography of 1960, Margaret Crompton repeated the commonplace that "there was a combination in [Eliot's] make-up of masculine intellect and feminine temperament,"[43] and Walter Allen declared in 1964, "However well-disciplined and 'masculine' her mind might be, she was at the mercy of her emotions, perhaps at the mercy of her need for affection and self-sacrifice."[44] Even U. C. Knoepflmacher has contributed in a small way to a gendered mode of thinking about George Eliot. In his influential *Religious Humanism and the Victorian Novel*, he attributed to her "an almost masculine mastery of the physical sciences."[45]

Knoepflmacher's was only a passing remark, however. In contrast, a major critic whose work consistently and aggressively has presented Eliot in rigidly gendered terms is Gordon S. Haight, whose 1968 biography continues to be praised, even by one feminist, for its scholarship and its objectivity.[46] In his early book on George Eliot's relationship with John Chapman (1940), Haight announced in his Preface that Eliot's whole life, with all its "strange contradictions," could be explained by invoking the phrenological reading of Eliot's skull cast by her friend Charles Bray, which declared that Marian Evans always needed "someone to lean upon" and that she "was not fitted to stand alone."[47] Haight was not the first to take Bray's interpretation as scientific fact,[48] but he is certainly the most influential scholar to have done so. In all of his biographical writing about Eliot, Haight uses Bray's comments as a leitmotif—a collection of phrases to be invoked when seeking to explain or understand the significant moments of Eliot's life, especially those that involved her relationships with men: the death of Eliot's father left her with no one to lean upon; the troubled relationship with publisher John Chapman led Eliot to see that he was not someone to lean upon; the friendship with philosopher Herbert Spencer, suspected by some at the time to have been an engagement, led to the discovery that Spencer, too, could not be leaned upon; the fulfilling relationship with journalist and scientist George Henry Lewes was the discovery, after years of searching, of someone to lean upon; the death of Eliot's editor, John Blackwood, left her professionally with no one to lean upon; Eliot's marriage to John Cross proved that she was not fitted to stand alone.[49] Haight also works Bray's imagery of feminine dependence into the chapter headings of his biography and even into his imagined descriptions of physical action. Take, for example, his account of the scandalous trip Eliot made with Lewes to Europe in 1854, an act that effectively cut her off from most social and family contacts: "They were soon under way, gliding smoothly down the Thames. Like Maggie and Stephen Guest aboard the Dutch vessel, Marian paced up and down the deck, leaning on George's arm. . . . At last she had found someone to lean upon."[50]

Haight's perpetuation of Bray's essentialist assumptions about Eliot's feminine dependence is not confined to his habit of echoing the phrases of the phrenological reading. A more subtle and pervasive form of the same endorsement can be seen in Haight's tendency, especially when presenting Eliot's decisions having to do with men, to dramatize her thoughts by using her own fictional device of free indirect speech— something he never does when treating other aspects of her life. Consider the description of Eliot's decision to make her living as a writer in London, made soon after her father's funeral and during her first trip to Europe:

> Alone, in the romantic town of her dream, Mary Ann could now rest her frayed nerves and take stock of her life. What was she to do? . . . [Her brother] Isaac had no sympathy with Mary Ann's ideas or her feelings; if he were to help, she would have to do things his way; he was certainly not a man she could lean upon. But no other had appeared ready to take the responsibility. She would be thirty in November. She had never been good looking, had none of the superficial charms that attract young men. . . . No, she must find work to support herself. But what?[51]

In Haight's fictionalized presentation, Eliot decided to write only by default because she was too ugly to find a husband who would take "responsibility" for her. A similar dramatizing technique characterizes Haight's account of Eliot's decision to return to the *Westminster Review* after her first difficult encounter with the philandering John Chapman:

> It was all too clear that John Chapman would never be the man she could lean upon. Still, to live in London, helping him unobtrusively with the *Review* would be better than never seeing him.

But how could it be contrived?[52]

Again, Eliot's actions are seen as motivated not by professional concerns but by the need for someone to lean upon. The return to the *Review,* an association that gave Eliot contact with some of the most advanced thinkers of her day, is presented as merely a contrivance allowing her to be near Chapman.

An emphasis on dependence also characterizes Haight's depiction of Eliot's famous relationship with George Henry Lewes. Repeatedly, when Haight describes Eliot and Lewes making a trip because Eliot felt the need to travel, we are told that "Lewes [carried] her off," as if she were unable to move on her own.[53] When Lewes himself was in a bad condition, however—as he often was—Haight reports that the two "set out" together.[54] Lewes is never made by Haight the *object* of Eliot's ministrations in the way that she is made the object of his, in spite of the fact that it was Lewes who was on the brink of nervous collapse when he and Eliot first went to Europe, that he was often in such states afterwards, and that Eliot on many occasions wrote or proofread for Lewes when his mental or physical health was bad.

This is not to suggest that Eliot did not feel the need, as many of her letters reveal she did, for an intense relationship with a sexual partner. In his biography of Eliot, her husband, John Cross, recalled her "absolute need of some one person who should be all in all to her, and to whom she should be all in all"[55]—an analysis, significantly, that stresses not one-sided dependence but reciprocity. Eliot's own references to her relationship with Lewes also tended to emphasize mutual dependence rather than the asymmetry that Haight describes. Eliot wrote to Bray, for example, a description of herself and Lewes that refutes Bray's own theory of one-sided dependence:

> People who have been inseparable and found *all* their happiness in each other for five years are in a sort of Siamese-twin condition that other people are not likely to regard with tolerance or even with belief.[56]

And in a letter to Harriet Beecher Stowe, Eliot alluded to the intellectual separateness and reciprocity in her relationship with Lewes: "You know the pleasure of such interchange—husband and wife each keeping to their own work, but loving to have cognizance of the other's course."[57]

Eliot also occasionally engaged in the comic ploy of describing both Lewes and herself as reversing sexual stereotypes. In one letter she called him "as nervous as a fragile woman" and in another she referred to him as "a delicate headachy woman." She also once compared herself to Lewes by claiming to be "the stronger man" of the two.[58] Lewes as well liked to make bantering jokes about gender roles. At one of their Sunday afternoon receptions, he is reported to have announced, while presiding at the teapot, "To make tea, my friends, . . . I hold is the whole duty of man."[59] If masculine and feminine roles were played out by Lewes and Eliot in their relationship, it appears the scripts were interchangeable.

Eliot's own conception of the ideal woman, moreover—one that is reflected in many of her larger-than-life heroines—encompassed stereotypically masculine and feminine traits. She once wrote to her friend Mrs. Frederick Lehmann about her sixteen-year-old daughter's writing,

> You remember what old Ben Jonson wished for his perfect woman. Besides "each softest virtue" she was to have "a manly soul." And I hope that we shall see that grander feminine type—at once sweet, strong, large-thoughted—in your Nina.[60]

Significantly, Haight and others do not pick up on statements such as these when searching for paradigms by which to read Eliot's life. Nor do they give prominence to theories of Eliot's personality that contradict or modify Bray's reading. Eliot's friend Bessie Belloc, for example, remembered that during the early 1850s, long before Eliot had established a literary reputation, she was regularly invited to the Belloc family parties because of her impressive social and intellectual presence. Belloc remembered her 1850 meeting with Eliot in terms that sound quite different from Charles Bray's condescending diagnosis:

> Not Abelard in all his glory, not the veritable Isaac Casaubon of French Huguenot fame, not Spinosa in Holland or Porson in England, seemed to my young imagination more astonishing than this woman, herself not far removed from youth, who knew a bewildering number of learned and modern languages, and wrote articles in a first-class quarterly.[61]

Another side of Eliot ignored by Bray and downplayed by Haight is that insisted upon repeatedly by Charles Hale White, who lived in the same house with Eliot during the years she worked on the *Westminster Review*. After Cross's *Life* was published in 1885, White wrote an indignant letter to the *Athenaeum* protesting that the biography had ignored her skeptical and unconventional side: "She has been removed from the class—the great and noble church, if I may call it—of the Insurgents." And in his 1894 obituary on Chapman, White reminisced again about Eliot's unusual blend of "tenderness and defiance."[62] Bray and many of his biographical descendants, however, seem to have turned the tenderness into dependence and to have ignored the defiance. In this context, it is worth noting that the only time Eliot actually described herself as leaning on someone, she was referring not to Lewes, or even to a man, but rather to Mme. d'Albert Durade, whose maternal attentions Eliot first enjoyed when she traveled to Europe after her father died. "I call her always 'maman,'" Eliot wrote to her sister in 1850, "and she is just the creature one loves to lean on and be petted by."[63]

The effect of Haight's emphasis on the idea of Eliot's feminine dependence on men has been overwhelming. Bray's quasi-scientific diagnosis, endorsed by Haight, has been transformed into incontrovertible fact. In 1975, Neil Roberts spoke of "the George Eliot we know from biographical sources, who was 'always requiring someone to lean upon.'"[64] Two years later, Joseph Wiesenfarth alluded confidently to "the ardent woman whose biography shows that she was not fitted to stand alone."[65] As recently as 1980, Kathleen Adams entitled the last chapter of her book "Someone to Lean on, Someone to Love."[66] And, surprisingly, even Sandra Gilbert and Susan Gubar momentarily assumed Haight's tone and way of thinking when they called Eliot's marriage to John Cross "the saddest sign of her inability to stand alone."[67] Finally, in the most blatant example of the tautological thinking that has created this image of George Eliot, John Purkis recently called Bray's phrenological reading an "acute diagnosis" because it "compares quite well with some of the psychological analyses of George Eliot which are to be found in modern biographies."[68] What Haight and others assumed to be true on the authority of Charles Bray is now given credence because Bray anticipated what Haight and others would say.[69] Each diagnosis validates the other.

Because Bray's interpretation of Eliot's character has had more influence on her biographies than any other single opinion, it seems worth quoting at some length. Bray based his diagnosis, published five years after Eliot's death, on a cast allegedly taken of her skull in 1844, which, he remarked proudly, "is still in my possession":

Miss Evans's head is a very large one, 22¼ inches round; George Combe, on first seeing the cast, took it for a man's. The temperament, nervous lymphatic, that is, active without endurance, and her working hours were never more than from 9 A.M. till 1 P.M. The third volume of Strauss was very heavy work to her, and she required much encouragement to keep her up to it. In her brain-development the Intellect greatly predominates; it is very large, more in length than in its peripheral surface. In the Feelings, the Animal and Moral regions are about equal; the moral being quite sufficient to keep the animal in order and in due subservience, but would not be spontaneously active. The social feelings were very active, particularly the adhesiveness. She was of a most affectionate disposition, always requiring some one to lean upon, preferring what has hitherto been considered the stronger sex, to the other and more impressible. She was not fitted to stand alone. Her sense of character—of men and things, is a predominantly intellectual one . . . [70]

Bray's allusions to the size of Eliot's skull, to the "nervous lymphatic" temperament that is "active without endurance," to the "heavy" burden that translation became for Eliot, and to the contrast between "the stronger sex" and the "more impressible" one—all these echo the language of nineteenth-century gender theories, which also often assumed the tones and terminology of scientific discourse in order to assert their a priori notions about feminine weakness. The emphasis on Eliot's body is familiar as well: this time quite literally, her mind is reduced to a physical specimen whose mold has been laid out for scientific analysis.

Bray's language is not, however, uniformly scientific, even in a loose sense of that word. A striking feature of his description is its shifting verb tenses and its analogous sliding between impersonal and personal nouns or pronouns: the "scientific" diagnosis, allegedly based on the still present evidence of the skull cast, is written in the present tense and uses impersonal nouns or pronouns (it, [t]he temperament, the Intellect, etc.), but is continually undercut by Bray's subjective memories, described in the past tense and indicated by the use of personal pronouns (she or her). Bray's attention seems, in fact, to hover between the cast in front of him and the mental picture he has conjured up of the woman he had known decades earlier—and the two visions seem continually to modify each other. The first departure from the "scientific" discourse about the skull cast comes with the recollection that Eliot worked only four hours each morning (an assertion not consistently borne out by her own accounts) and that she found the Strauss translation a tiring task. This information—presented in the past tense of memory—is offered as an illustration of the phrenological reading of her "temperament." As the passage is written, however, it is not clear whether the supposed empirical observation or the personal memory came first.

When Bray moves on to Eliot's "brain-development," he appears to return to his presumed scientific method and to base his judgments about "the Intellect" and "the Animal and Moral regions," made in the present tense of the skull cast, on precise physical measurements. But with the analysis of "[t]he social feelings," he seems again to lose control of the scientific vocabulary and method. A reference to "the adhesiveness" slides immediately into reminiscence, and this time the memory involves more interpretation than fact: "She was of a most affectionate disposition, always requiring some one to lean upon." Finally, after Bray has embellished his past-tense observations with the judgment that "she was not fitted to stand alone," he returns to the neutral present tense of scientific discourse, but continues with the personal pronoun: "Her sense of character . . . is. . . ." The verbal and logical ambiguities of Bray's style thus anticipate the circular logic of Haight's own use of Bray's observations: just as Haight and Bray validate each other, so Bray's memories give credibility to his empirical observations—and vice versa. Even if phrenology had scientific validity, Bray's method would be seriously open to question.

It should be pointed out, moreover, that Haight's choice of Charles Bray as his authority on Eliot's character is problematic from more than a scientific point of view: in addition to the fact that Bray saw little of her after she became a novelist, it should be remembered that, by his own admission, the two often had "violent quarrels" and that she taunted him more than once both for his commitment to phrenology and for his retrograde ideas about women.[71] It is not surprising, therefore, that Bray should have used the language of phrenology as a device to express his own patriarchal judgments about George Eliot. That Haight and other Eliot scholars should have embraced this view of her, above all others, also seems a telling reflection of their own preoccupations and fears: the female novelist and sage must ultimately be reduced to feminine weakness—the common feature of Eliot iconography in all its variations. The construction of George Eliot in both the nineteenth and the twentieth centuries has thus made her female body a site of enormous tension— one stage among many on which the contradictions of patriarchal culture have been enacted.

NOTES

1. Charles Warren Stoddard, "George Eliot," *Exits and Entrances: A Book of Essays and Sketches* (Boston: Lathrop, 1903), 143–44.

2. Quoted in Mary Poovey, *Uneven Developments: The Ideological Work of Gender in Mid-Victorian England* (Chicago: University of Chicago Press, 1988), 35.

3. Thomas Laqueur, "Orgasm, Generation, and the Politics of Reproductive Biology," *Representations* 14 (1986): 3.

4. For extended analyses of the nineteenth-century construction of the female body, see Ellen J. Bassuk, "The Rest Cure: Repetition or Resolution of Victorian Women's Conflicts?" in *The Female Body in Western Culture: Contemporary Perspectives,* ed. Susan Rubin Suleiman (Cambridge: Harvard University Press, 1986), 139–51; Nancy Cott, "Passionlessness: An Interpretation of Victorian Sexual Ideology, 1790–1850," *Signs* 4 (1978): 219–36; Laqueur, "Orgasm, Generation," 1–41; Poovey, *Uneven Developments*; and Elaine Showalter, *The Female Malady: Women, Madness, and English Culture, 1830–1980* (New York: Pantheon, 1985). See also Pat Jolland and John Hooper, eds., *Women from Birth to Death: The Female Life Cycle in Britain, 1830–1914* (Atlantic Highlands: Humanities, 1986) for a collection of telling excerpts from nineteenth-century medical discourse.

5. A few critics saw Eliot as a challenge to standard gender categories. See Mathilde Blind, *George Eliot* (London: Allen, 1883), 5–6; Abba Gould Woolson, *George Eliot and Her Heroines: A Study* (New York: Harper, 1886), 43–44; Margaret Oliphant, *The Victorian Age of English Literature* (London: Percival, 1892), 2:164–65.

6. For an analysis of the ideologies associated with phrenology in the nineteenth century, see Roger Cooter, *The Cultural Meaning of Popular Science: Phrenology and the Organization of Consent in Nineteenth-Century Britain* (Cambridge: Cambridge University Press, 1984).

7. Quoted in George Willis Cooke, *George Eliot: A Critical Study of Her Life, Writings, and Philosophy* (Boston: Osgood, 1883), 84. See also John Lehmann, *Ancestors and Friends* (London: Eyre, 1962), 170.

8. Hallam Tennyson, *Alfred Lord Tennyson: A Memoir by His Son* (London: Macmillan, 1897), 107; Charles Eliot Norton, *Letters of Charles Eliot Norton with Biographical Comment,* ed. Sara Norton and M. A. DeWolfe (London: Constable, 1913), 1:318.

9. Humphry House, "Qualities of George Eliot's Unbelief," *All in Due Time: The Collected Essays and Broadcast Talks of Humphry House* (London: Hart-Davis, 1955), 109.

10. Joseph Jacobs, *George Eliot, Matthew Arnold, Browning, Newman: Essays and Reviews from the Athenaeum* (London: Nutt, 1891), xvi; Cooke, *George Eliot,* 81–82, 84.

11. Quoted in David Duncan, *The Life and Letters of Herbert Spencer* (London: Williams, 1911), 296.

12. Frederic Harrison, "George Eliot," *Studies in Early Victorian Literature,* 2d ed. (London: Arnold, 1895), 231–32.

13. Quoted in George Eliot, *The George Eliot Letters,* ed. Gordon S. Haight (New Haven: Yale University Press, 1954–78), 5:464.

14. Bret Harte, *Letters of Bret Harte,* ed. Geoffrey Bret Harte (Boston: Houghton, 1926), 163

15. Elaine Showalter, "Women Writers and the Double Standard," in *Women in Sexist Society,* ed. Vivian Gornick and Barbara K. Moran (New York: Basic, 1971), 329.

16. Henry James, *Henry James Letters,* ed. Leon Edel (Cambridge, Mass.: Harvard University Press, 1974), 1:116–17.

17. See George Bernard Shaw, *Collected Letters, 1898–1910,* ed. Dan H. Laurence (New York: Dodd, 1972), 827; W. B. Yeats, *Autobiographies* (London: Macmillan, 1955), 87–

88 and *The Collected Letters of W. B. Yeats*, ed. John Kelly, asst. ed. Eric Domville (Oxford: Clarendon, 1986), 1:7–8; Elaine Showalter, "The Greening of Sister George," *Nineteenth-Century Fiction* 35 (1980): 292–311.

18. Quoted in Edmund Gosse, *The Life of Algernon Charles Swinburne* (New York: Macmillan, 1917), 236.

19. William Barry, *Heralds of Revolt: Studies in Modern Literature and Dogma* (London: Hodder, 1904), 12.

20. Edmund Gosse, *English Literature: An Illustrated Record* (London: Heinemann, 1906), 4:314.

21. Barbara Stephen, *Emily Davies and Girton College* (London: Constable, 1927), 13.

22. Edmund Gosse, "George Eliot," *London Mercury* 1, no. 1 (November, 1919): 34.

23. Gosse, "George Eliot," 43.

24. David Cecil, "George Eliot," *Early Victorian Novelists: Essays in Revaluation* (1935); rpt. in *A Century of George Eliot Criticism*, ed. Gordon S. Haight (Boston: Houghton, 1965), 210.

25. Gosse, "George Eliot," 36.

26. Cecil, "George Eliot," 210.

27. Cecil, "George Eliot," 206.

28. Mary Jacobus, *Reading Woman: Essays in Feminist Criticism* (London: Methuen, 1986), 115, 203.

29. Henry James, "*Felix Holt, the Radical*," *The Nation* 3 (August 16, 1866), rpt. in Haight, *Century*, 42.

30. George Saintsbury, *Corrected Impressions: Essays on Victorian Writers* (1895), rpt. in Haight, *Century*, 166.

31. Quoted in Frances Wentworth Knickerbocker, *John Morley and His Friends* (Cambridge, Mass.: Harvard University Press, 1943), 204.

32. Leslie Stephen, *George Eliot* (London: Macmillan, 1902), 155.

33. Arnold Bennett, *The Journals of Arnold Bennett*, comp. Newman Flower (1932), rpt. in Haight, *Century*, 169.

34. Review of J. W. Cross, ed., *George Eliot's Life as Related in Her Letters and Journals*, *Saturday Review* 59 (February 7, 1885), rpt. in *George Eliot: The Critical Heritage*, ed. David Carroll (London: Routledge, 1971), 487.

35. [Richard Simpson], "George Eliot's Novels," *Home and Foreign Review* 3 (October, 1863), rpt. in Carroll, *Critical Heritage*, 241.

36. For a description of this cultural assumption, see Elaine Showalter, *A Literature of Their Own: British Woman Novelists from Brontë to Lessing* (Princeton: Princeton University Press, 1977), 148.

37. Edmond Scherer, "George Eliot," *Essays on English Literature*, trans. George Saintsbury (London: Sampson Low, 1891), 270.

38. Robert Louis Stevenson, *The Letters of Robert Louis Stevenson to His Family and Friends*, ed. Sidney Colvin (New York: Scribner's, 1902), 1:141.

39. William Ernest Henley, *Views and Reviews: Essays in Appreciation* (1890), rpt. in Haight, *Century*, 161. For other criticism of Eliot's masculine characters, see Carroll, *Critical Heritage*, 148, 193; Anne Fremantle, *George Eliot* (London: Duckworth, 1933), 94; Robert Laing, review of *Middlemarch*, *Quarterly Review* 134 (April, 1873): 342.

40. Stephen, *George Eliot*, 104, 139–40. It is worth noting that one of the first critics

to oppose Stephen in his judgment about Eliot's male characters was his daughter, Virginia Woolf, who suggested that the presumed weaknesses in Eliot's heroes "illustrate not so much George Eliot's inability to draw the portrait of a man, as the uncertainty, the infirmity, and the fumbling which shook her hand when she had to conceive a fit mate for a heroine" ("George Eliot," *The Common Reader*, 1st ser. [1925]; rpt. in *Discussions of George Eliot*, ed. Richard Stang [Boston: Heath, 1960], 28).

41. Deirdre David, *Intellectual Women and Victorian Patriarchy* (Ithaca: Cornell University Press, 1987), 172.

42. F. E. Baily, *Six Great Victorian Novelists* (London: MacDonald, 1947), 119, 128, 113.

43. Margaret Crompton, *George Eliot: The Woman* (London: Cassell, 1960), 179.

44. Walter Allen, *George Eliot* (New York: Macmillan, 1964), 48.

45. U. C. Knoepflmacher, *Religious Humanism and the Victorian Novel: George Eliot, Walter Pater, and Samuel Butler* (Princeton: Princeton University Press, 1965), 12.

46. Carolyn Heilbrun praises Haight for "refraining from masculine interpretation" in his biography (*Towards a Recognition of Androgyny* [New York: Knopf, 1973], 183 n. 34). See also Ira Bruce Nadel, who cites Haight's book as "the apotheosis of the scholarly, academic biography" and singles out his ability "to resist interpretation of the life and the literature" ("George Eliot and Her Biographers," in *George Eliot: A Centenary Tribute*, ed. Gordon S. Haight and Rosemary T. VanArsdel [Totowa: Barnes, 1982], 114, 111).

47. Gordon S. Haight, *George Eliot and John Chapman, with Chapman's Diaries* (New Haven: Yale University Press, 1940), vii.

48. See, for example, Oscar Browning, *The Life of George Eliot* (London: Scott, 1890), 39; Frederick Locker-Lampson, *My Confidences: An Autobiographical Sketch Addressed to My Descendants* (London: Nelson, 1896), 277; Joan Bennett, *George Eliot: Her Mind and Her Art* (Cambridge: Cambridge University Press, 1962), 26; Crompton, *George Eliot*, 28, 51, 74, 93, 98, 192.

49. See Haight, *Eliot and Chapman*, 10–11, 31, 80; and *George Eliot: A Biography* (Harmondsworth: Penguin, 1985), 90, 117, 530.

50. Haight, *Biography*, 148.

51. Haight, *Biography*, 70–71.

52. Haight, *Biography*, 90.

53. Haight, *Biography*, 338, 361, 374, 382.

54. Haight, *Biography*, 423.

55. J. W. Cross, *George Eliot's Life as Related in Her Letters and Journals* (Edinburgh: Blackwood, 1887), 8.

56. Eliot, *Letters*, 3:27.

57. Eliot, *Letters*, 6:247.

58. Eliot, *Letters*, 3:179, 4:8, 3:408.

59. Matilda Betham-Edwards, *Mid-Victorian Memories* (New York: Macmillan, 1919), 45.

60. Eliot, *Letters*, 6:360.

61. Bessie Belloc, *In a Walled Garden* (London: Ward, 1895), 17–18, 5.

62. Charles Hale White, letter to *Athenaeum* (November 28, 1885): 702; and "Dr. John Chapman," *Athenaeum* (December 8, 1894): 790.

63. Eliot, *Letters*, 1:328.

64. Neil Roberts, *George Eliot: Her Beliefs and Her Art* (London: Elek, 1975), 97.

65. Joseph Wiesenfarth, *George Eliot's Mythmaking* (Heidelberg: Winter, 1977), 29.

66. Kathleen Adams, *Those of Us Who Loved Her: The Men in George Eliot's Life* (Warwick: George Eliot Fellowship, 1980), 184.

67. Sandra Gilbert and Susan Gubar, *The Madwoman in the Attic: The Woman Writer and the Nineteenth-Century Literary Imagination* (New Haven: Yale University Press, 1979), 467.

68. John Purkis, *A Preface to George Eliot* (London: Longmans, 1985), 37.

69. Only Phyllis Rose (*Parallel Lives: Five Victorian Marriages* [New York: Knopf, 1983], 300 n. 26) and Elizabeth Ermarth (*George Eliot* [Boston: Twayne, 1985], 6) have even briefly criticized Haight's use of Bray.

70. Charles Bray, *Phases of Opinion and Experience during a Long Life: An Autobiography* (London: Longmans, [1885]), 74–75.

71. Bray, *Phases*, 73. See also T. R. Wright, "From Bumps to Morals: The Phrenological Background to George Eliot's Moral Framework," *Review of English Studies* 33 (1982): 37, for references to Eliot's "facetious" letters about phrenology. For some of Eliot's taunting letters to Bray about his views on women, see Eliot, *Letters*, 2:21–22, 396.

Reasoning about Ourselves: Feminist Methodology in the Social Sciences

ALISON WYLIE

Feminist revaluations of science are now at a critical juncture. Having exposed sexist bias in an enormous range of disciplines we face a new question: how is it possible to do better? What would a nonsexist or, indeed, a feminist science look like?

Guidelines for nonsexist research have been developed in a number of contexts, as components of funding guidelines and disciplinary codes of practice, as well as in connection with feminist critiques of science and general methodological discussions (for an example of the former, see the Social Sciences and Humanities Research Council of Canada handbook, "On the Treatment of the Sexes in Research"; Eichler and Lapointe 1985). Perhaps the most detailed is Eichler's "Practical Guide" to *Nonsexist Research Methods* (Eichler 1988): as an antidote to various "primary problems" that she identifies with extant practice, she urges that researchers guard against "gender insensitivity," that they not treat (analyze, label) otherwise identical phenomena differently because of their gender association and that they not generalize the attributes of one gender to the whole of a population or treat them as an analytic or evaluative norm (Eichler 1988, 6).

But more challenging and controversial are a range of directives that have been articulated for self-consciously *feminist* research. From the outset, those who have suspected that extant methods are part of the problem—that they replicate, perhaps even generate, sexist bias—have asked whether there might not be distinctively feminist methods for inquiry. Perhaps these would be phenomenological and qualitative methods, rather than quantitative, or some feminist transformation of historical materialism (O'Brien 1981), or a "political hermeneutics" (MacKinnon 1982). Increasingly, however, this seems the wrong question to ask. As Harding puts it, the "preoccupation with method mystifies what have been the most interesting aspects of feminist research process" (Harding 1987, 19); it is the "fetishization of method itself" (1987, 20) that feminists should resist. This is, in fact, a recurrent theme that incorporates a number of different considerations. Vickers warns that if a "uniform reconstruction of method" were to emerge (Vickers 1982, 43), it would certainly bring with it "the dangers of a new orthodoxy."[1] Numerous others have rejected the quest for a "correct" approach, a method that is proof against sexist bias, on the ground that this puts misplaced trust in technical fixes for conceptual problems; any method can be used in a sexist manner (Eichler 1987, 32). Longino observes, in this connection, that the sciences are so diverse methodologically, it is implausible that they "might be equally transformed by [a feminist] framework" (Eichler 1987, 53).

Nevertheless, Longino, and most of those who mistrust the quest for a feminist method, maintain that there is something or, perhaps, a range of things distinctive about feminist research qua feminist. Typically this is identified with a "general 'orientation'" derived from feminist political theory and practice (Stanley and Wise 1979, 273). Feminist research, on this account, should be a matter of "doing feminism in another context" (Stanley and Wise 1983a, 195) or, as Longino puts it, of "doing science as a feminist," rather than of doing "feminist science" (Longino 1987, 53). What I propose to do here is examine various proposals that have been made for "doing science as a feminist" with the aim of identifying what they share, as feminist, and of articulating, if not resolving, some problems raised by their divergence on a number of crucial issues.

Two Models for Feminist Research

Whatever else feminist research may be, it addresses a set of problems that bear at least a family resemblance to one another in being of concern to feminists. Most widely, it is conceived as research that provides a basis for critically reassessing extant ideology and theory where this leaves out women altogether or significantly distorts or devalues their activities and lives as women. In this, its encompassing aim is to empower women by recovering the details of their experience and activities, by "piecing together a way of understanding the world from the point of view of women" on this basis (Brunsdon 1978, 26), by delineating "pervasive patterns of subordination" that have "marked the fortunes of women" (Keohane and Gelpi 1982, x), and by providing an explanatory understanding of the nature and sources of the patriarchal oppression revealed in these emerging patterns. Some add the requirement that problems be addressed that are of concern to particular groups of women and that research results be presented in a form that is both accessible and useful to them (e.g., Acker, Barry, and Esseveld 1984, 425).

Often, commitment to these general aims is associated with the more specific requirement that a central feature of feminist research must be a consideration of women's "lived reality," their concrete, particular, personal experience. This is advocated not just as a necessary basis for addressing questions of concern to women—for getting at the gendered dimensions of social life that conventional categories of analysis obscure, and for "test[ing] thinking against experience, making sure that it remains rooted in the real lives of women" (Keohane and Gelpi 1982, ix)—but as a consequence of commitment to feminist principles (Eichler 1987, 33); the articulation and "validation" of women's experience is an end to be valued in itself whatever other ends it may support. It is in this connection that consciousness raising, conceived as a process of recovering and analyzing "the politics of the personal," is often invoked as a model for research practice (e.g., in MacKinnon 1982).[2] Where the "first principle" of consciousness raising, as articulated in the early 1970s (e.g., in Ms. 1972, 1), is never to challenge or question experiential accounts, sometimes the commitment to focus on women's experience is aligned with a requirement to treat it as veridical.

While most feminist researchers would subscribe to the general aim of empowering women in various of the senses I have described, differences do arise when they consider the question of what this commitment entails for practice. This is especially clear when they discuss the practical implications of making experience central and ask whose experience is at issue, how it is to ground the articulation of general explanatory accounts of women's situation, and whether the commitment to take women's experience seriously really means that they can never question experience, or "go beyond" it in pursuit of these explanatory aims. I discern two models of research practice—two distinct "general orientations"—emerging in response to these questions: a "collectivist" model of inquiry and a "self-study" model.

The Collectivist Model. The first model[3] focuses on the experience of women as research subjects and takes the requirement of fidelity to this experience to mean that women should be asked rather than told what they are experiencing and why; "as researchers, we must not impose our definitions of reality on those researched" (Acker, Barry, and Esseveld 1983, 425). At a descriptive level, this means that researchers should be particularly careful to design research so that discrepancies between their constructs and the understanding of subjects can be identified (e.g., Acker, Barry, and Esseveld 1983, 430). On the consciousness-raising model, research is to be conducted as a dialectical process in which the feminist investigator "continually test[s] the plausibility of [her] work against her own experience as well as against the experience of other women" (Vickers 1982, 36).[4] At an explanatory level, the commitment to take subjects' experience seriously requires that women be acknowledged to have a credible theoretical, explanatory grasp of what goes on in their lives. Indeed, those sympathetic to ethnomethodology argue that the explanatory constructs a researcher generates are simply another "version," an alternative with no particular claim to privilege over the accounts formulated by (other) participants in the subject context.

This attention to the experience and self-understanding of women is aligned with various ethical requirements. Minimally, research must not be exploitative; "research that aims to be liberating should not in the process become only another mode of oppression" (Acker, Barry, and Esseveld 1983, 425).[5] Beyond this it is routinely argued that subjects should not be "objectified," turned "into objects of scrutiny and manipulation" (Acker, Barry, and Esseveld 1983, 425), that the "illusion" of a sharp separation of researcher (qua "knower") from the objects of study be abandoned, and, most important, that the power differences constituting the standard hierarchical relationship between researcher and subject be eliminated as far as possible (Oakley 1981, 41). These recommendations have implications for the roles of both researcher and researched in feminist inquiry. Researchers, it is argued, must be acknowledged to enter the research relationship as concretely situated (social) individuals whose subjective experience and social engagement with the subjects of study inevitably affects what they come to understand. The virtue in this is that the processes by which knowledge is constructed, specifically, their partiality, are made "visible," a subject of the research process itself and a basis for reflexive critique.[6]

This revaluation of the status of the researcher is secondary, however, to the emphasis put on the importance of transforming the role of research subjects. Again and again it is insisted that subjects must be actively involved in the research process as coparticipants at various levels, sometimes in determining the direction of research, more often as collaborators in the description and interpretation of their experience, and sometimes in formulating and assessing explanatory, theoretical constructs. Oakley's critique of standard guidelines for interviewing that demand both detachment and rapport—the "mythology of 'hygienic' research" (Oakley 1981, 58)—represents one strategy for implementing these directives. She argues, on moral and methodological grounds, for a collaborative, nonhierarchical relationship with interviewees governed by the principle, "no intimacy without reciprocity" (Oakley 1981, 49).[7] Acker, Barry, and Esseveld push further this commitment to active involvement. They made a concerted effort not just to engage subjects at a personal level in the process of data collection, but to involve them directly in analysis and interpretation. This proved difficult in a number of respects, however. They worked with a group of women who were by no means all feminists and frequently "had to confront discrepancies between our ideas and interpretations and those of the women we interviewed" (Acker, Barry, and Esseveld 1983, 427). They were especially concerned that the results of their analysis—an identification of common themes in the experiences of their subjects as women reentering the work force—would be upsetting to at least some of those they had interviewed, and decided, in the end, "not to include them as active participants in the analysis . . ." (Acker, Barry, and Esseveld 1983, 429).

Acker, Barry, and Esseveld thus confront a dilemma. It seems that the ideal of involving subjects in research on a fully active, egalitarian basis—as coparticipants in a potentially emancipatory process of inquiry—can only be realized when dealing with subjects who are "very much like us," and yet this carries with it the threat of "eliminating most women from our view and limiting the usefulness of our projects" (Acker, Barry, and Esseveld 1983, 434). In the end, Acker, Barry, and Esseveld find this latter consequence unacceptable, more unacceptable, that is, than qualifying the commitment to fully engage (all) subjects in research. So it is the ideal of conducting research as a collective enterprise that they compromise.

A further problem arises even when it is possible to involve subjects in analysis. Acker, Barry, and Esseveld observe that, when it came to analysis, "we had to assume the role of the people with the power to define" (Acker, Barry, and Esseveld 1983, 429); it was they who determined the categories and dimensions of analysis along which commonalities and differences might be assessed. What they sought from subjects was, primarily, a critical check on the adequacy of their constructs. In

this capacity, they found they could not avoid some degree of objectification of their subjects: "If we were to fulfil the emancipatory aim for
the people we were studying [indeed, as demanded by them],[8] we had
to go beyond the faithful representation of their experience, beyond
'letting them talk for themselves' and put those experiences into the
theoretical framework with which we started the study, a framework
that links women's oppression to the structure of Western capitalist society" (Acker, Barry, and Esseveld 1983, 429–30). In fact, this sometimes
meant not just taking their subjects' experiences as an "object," in the
sense of requiring explanation in terms other than those constitutive of
the experience, but also, on occasion, treating them in terms that coun-
tered the self-understanding of the research subjects themselves. Consequently, despite a deep commitment to "understand reality from the
perspective of the people experiencing it" (1983, 431)—to "grant them
full subjectivity," to avoid "violating their reality" (429)—Acker, Barry,
and Esseveld found that they could not always take the experiential
perspective of subjects at face value if they were to pursue the further
aims of understanding how it arose, what it has in common with other
women's experiences, and how it is, in this sense, "political." They see
their main challenge as that of maintaining a "difficult balance between
granting respect to the other's interpretation of her reality, while going
beyond that interpretation to comprehend its underlying relations"
(Acker, Barry, and Esseveld 1983, 429).

This appreciation of conflict between the animating commitments of
feminist research, and the conclusion that an interest in understanding
the patriarchal conditions of experience requires sometimes that its integrity be questioned, is by no means unique to the three researchers whose
work I have been describing. In an early paper, Dorothy Smith declares
at one point that, contra the administrative impulse of sociology to
control and appropriate the experience of others, in feminist research
"their reality, their varieties of experience must be an unconditional
datum" (Smith 1987, 93). But she then goes on to insist that "no amount
of observation of face-to-face relations, no amount of analysis of
commonsense knowledge of everyday life, will take us beyond our essential ignorance of how it is put together" (94); the emancipatory potential
of feminist research requires us to "posit . . . a total socioeconomic order
'in back' of [any given experiential moment]," to seek the "determinants"
of experience outside experience (94).[9]

More recently, there has been a spate of literature directly criticizing "experientialism." In a 1987 article, Grant rejects outright the notion that direct experience is, or should be taken as, a "necessary precondition for knowledge" (Grant 1987, 105) and inveighs against the threat of relativism that she sees looming in an uncritical privileging of "unmediated experience" (Grant 1987, 110–13). Brunsdon argues, in a similar vein, that "the dependence on direct experience [and common sense] is one of the aspects of our oppression" (Brunsdon 1978, 25); it precludes "the construction of a coherent oppositional world. . . . It produces an understanding of events as episodic and random" (Brunsdon 1978, 25). The effect is often to confirm subordination as inevitable, and to limit the scope and effectiveness of political action. In the view of these critics, the feminist revaluation of women's experience should be construed as a commitment to take their subjects' experience seriously *as a point of departure*, not as immune to challenge and criticism.

The Self-study Model. However compelling these critiques of experientialism may be, there remain proponents of the feminist commitment to recover and revalue the experience of women who reject, out of hand, the balancing of compromises associated with the collectivist model of practice. Stanley and Wise, for example, hold that the essential feature of feminist practice must be its "insistence on the validity of women's experience" (Stanley and Wise 1983b, 135), and they will countenance no qualification of this commitment. In particular, they reject any form of argument for "going beyond" the personal, for treating it as a point of departure, a "resource," to be used in constructing explanatory theories that postulate structures, processes, or, indeed, a "reality" beyond women's experience (Stanley and Wise 1983b, 81). Feminist researchers who are prepared to question the integrity or veracity of experiential reports, in the course of treating them as a "springboard" to theory, risk slipping back into precisely the "'expert' analytical and theoretical approaches" that have so effectively silenced and excluded women in the past (Stanley and Wise 1983b, 56).

Where the commitment to privilege women's experience comes into conflict with a demand for broader theoretical understanding, Stanley and Wise are prepared to repudiate any mode of theorizing that might involve reassessment or displacement of the theories and perceptions of subjects, "what women and men have to tell us about their lives" (Stanley and Wise 1983b, 83–84). This includes any quest after structural explanations (Stanley and Wise 1983b, 83, 85), any attempt to "generaliz[e] from [subjective experiences]" (83), and sometimes any postulation of "'real' conditions of oppression outside experience and understanding" (81). Realities are, they argue, negotiated constructs and any theorizing that suggests otherwise just constructs a myth, usually an oppressive myth. Their constructive proposal is that feminists should adhere to the model of consciousness-raising practice that, they argue, requires that they "go back into the personal," rather than beyond it, in order to "explicate . . . to examine in detail exactly what this experience is" (84).

On some occasions they seem to argue this approach on pragmatic, methodological grounds. Feminists *need not* go beyond "the personal" because any conditions relevant for understanding women's experience and oppression can be revealed within (or, through direct analysis of) experience, contra the arguments of Dorothy Smith cited earlier. They insist, in this connection, that "power and its use can be examined within personal life" and that, in fact, "the political *must* be examined in this way" because "the system [the array of institutions that oppress women] is experienced *in* everyday life, and isn't separate from it" (Stanley and Wise 1983b, 54).[10]

On other occasions, however, their argument turns on considerations of (feminist) principle. Stanley and Wise insist that, above all else, feminists have a moral and political responsibility to resist any imposition of the reality or standpoint of one person on others or any privileging of one perspective over another (1983b, 112).[11] When they confront the possibility that the experience of diverse others may be contradictory, or reported interpretations of experience implausible or incoherent, they reiterate that, because all realities are constructed, there can never be grounds for judging a subject "wrong" in what she claims about *her* reality. In one instance they observe that "if a housebound, depressed, battered mother of six with an errant spouse says she's *not* oppressed, there's little point in us telling her she's got it wrong because of the objective reality of her situation" (Stanley and Wise 1983b, 112); her account is "*truth* for her," and there can be no justification for "attempting to impose our reality on [such subjects]" (113).[12] Thus, they seem prepared to embrace precisely the relativist implications that led others to qualify feminist proscriptions against judgement.

When they consider the implications of taking seriously the perceptions of deeply sexist men (rapists, batterers, obscene phone callers) they are prepared to conclude that, although people must not be treated as objects, it is not incumbent on the feminist researcher to involve subjects as active participants in research; "we do not want people, 'the

researched,' to have more involvement in designing questionnaires, interpreting statistical or other results" (Stanley and Wise 1983b, 170). In
particular, they see no justification for allowing the input of sexist subjects
to shape feminist findings. When they discuss "the place of the personal
within research," they turn immediately to questions about the "presence
of the researcher" (150), a presence that cannot be avoided and that they
say is, in any case, the primary source and grounding of all theoretical
understanding.[13] In fact, despite references to the experiences of subjects
as the proper object of inquiry, these "others" continually slip out of
view; it is the experience of the researcher that draws Stanley and Wise's
attention.

Two principles reinforce what I identify as a persistent tendency, in
Stanley and Wise's discussion, to shift the focus of feminist research
inward. One is epistemic: implicit in their proscriptions against imposition is a deep skepticism about whether we can ever grasp the experience
of others. Perhaps we inevitably "impose," or project, our own reality
when we purport to describe that of another; perhaps we can never do
more than describe *our* experience of their actions, descriptions, testimonials, or interactions with us. But more fundamentally, Stanley and
Wise embrace what amounts to an ethical principle to the effect that not
only should we avoid imposing our realities on others, we should avoid
speaking for them. I detect in this something of the feminist stance
recently articulated by Trebilcot when she says, "I speak only for
myself . . . in the sense that an account I give reports only my understanding of the world or, more accurately, only my *with*standing in the
world" (Trebilcot 1988, 4),[14] and adds to this a stringent "principle of
nonpersuasion" (5). Taken together, the implication of commitment to
feminist principles seems to be that the experience of the researcher
becomes not just the (only) source and ground of understanding, but
also its primary object.

This approach to doing research as a feminist is embodied, at least
in part, in the early work of the Vancouver Women's Research Center;
this is, in fact, one example of feminist research that Stanley and Wise
identify as going some distance toward realizing their ideals (Stanley
and Wise 1983b). One member of the Center describes feminist research
as a matter of "study[ing] your own community" (Jacobson 1977) that
requires, first, that you, the researcher, "locate yourself" in your community, and then that you proceed by analyzing your own "everyday
world" as a member of this community, gradually "broadening the

boundaries" of your exploration so you begin to formulate an account of this community "as you know it" (Jacobson 1977, 11–13). There is no discussion of how the perceptions of others might be incorporated; the report closes with the observation that such research is never "complete" inasmuch as there are always alternative accounts that could be given. Similarly, Stanley and Wise's work on obscene phone calls is largely an analysis of the impact of these calls on their own lives and understanding of patriarchy (Stanley and Wise 1979). They give a brief thematic analysis of the content of obscene calls that they received while running a lesbian feminist help line, but do not return to them either to develop the content analysis or to consider factors that might be responsible for the unrelenting hostility of those responsible for the calls. In short, they do not "go beyond" their own experience of the calls; they present, in general terms, the conception of hostile patriarchy that they formed as a result of suffering the harassment of these calls over an extended period.

In this second model of what it is to do research as a feminist, then, the commitment to respect the integrity of "the personal"—meaning each individual's "subjectivity" or "reality"—takes precedence over all other concerns. In the process, it displaces both the ideal of conducting research as an egalitarian, collective effort at consciousness raising, and the objective of achieving any general, explanatory understanding of women's situation. Followed through consistently as proposed by Stanley and Wise, these principles dramatically narrow the scope of feminist research—it becomes, in their hands, virtually autobiographical—hence, my reference to this approach as one of "self-study," rather than of collective study.[15]

"Back Into" Consciousness Raising

Faced with this divergence of thinking about what it is to do research (specifically, social scientific research) "as a feminist," one response might be to encourage all the various alternatives and see what they contribute. This is attractive, especially given that each may have different ranges of application and given the diversity of problems that concern feminists. Certainly it is important to feminists to understand something about rapists and obscene phone callers, as well as about women's lives (their own and those of others), and these subjects pose rather different methodological problems. But beyond complementary differences in

approach, there are some quite deep problems inherent in the way interpretations of core feminist commitments have diverged, even when the
same commitments are recognized as the source of inspiration and direction for feminist research.

The difficulty with the self-study model is, most simply, that it
endorses a relativism that compromises the emancipatory potential of
feminism and feminist research. As Acker, Barry, and Esseveld argue,
"When all accounts are equally valid, the search for 'how it actually
works' becomes meaningless" (Acker, Barry, and Esseveld 1983, 429),
and yet the search for just this sort of understanding has been a central
goal of feminism both in its critical dimension, when it means to oppose
dominant theories that deny or trivialize women's experience of oppression, and in its constructive dimension, when it seeks an understanding
of how patriarchal structures work as a necessary basis for effective
political action. Ironically, even Stanley and Wise claim, at one point,
that they do not mean to deny "the existence of an 'objective reality,'"
adding that "social facts" are "as real and constraining as tables and
chairs" (Stanley and Wise 1983b, 111). Presumably they would agree,
given this, that the emancipatory potential of feminism depends on
establishing just exactly what these real and constraining "facts" come
to. It is perhaps significant, in this connection, that Stanley and Wise
do allow, in the case where the battered woman's "objective reality"
seemed to belie her experiential testimony, that it may sometimes be
appropriate to ask "how and why people construct realities in the way
that they do" (Stanley and Wise 1983b, 112). This is the only point at
which they make this proposal, not surprisingly given that it suggests
that "reality disjunctures" may require one to "go beyond" the experience
in question and inquire into conditions that shape it of which the subject
herself is not conscious. But it is a significant break with their uncom-
promising position on the integrity of experience. It suggests a perfectly
good sense in which you can discover (or conclude) that a subject's
assessment of her own experience is "wrong," namely, when this assessment is internally incoherent or inconsistent with the experience that she
herself reports. And it suggests an appreciation that the possibility of
critically rethinking your experience is an essential part of any emancipatory program of research or action.

Where the practice of consciousness raising is cited on all sides as a
source of guidelines for research practice, it is perhaps relevant to ask
what veracity is accorded experience in these contexts. It is certainly the

case that the widely cited "Guide to Consciousness Raising" published in *Ms.* (1972), identifies as the "most important [rule]" that of "never challenging another woman's experience": "in describing personal feelings and experience, there is no right or wrong," therefore it is never appropriate to "give advice or judge a woman's testimony" (Ms. 1972, 22); "what a sister says may seem inaccurate to you but it is true for her at that moment" (23). Participants are, moreover, encouraged to "speak personally, subjectively and specifically"; generalizations and abstractions inevitably "misrepresent" precisely the details of diverse personal experience that consciousness raising means to bring into view (22). Nevertheless, the purpose of giving testimony in this way is described as that of learning "who we are," of discerning "common elements in our experience" and determining how these relate to the role and status of women "as a group" (23). To this end, it is recommended that consciousness-raising sessions conclude with a "summing up" discussion in which commonalities are noted and further questions raised, and, in this context, critical reflection seems crucial. The "Guide" suggests, for example, that questions be raised about language use as a "key," one assumes to assumptions about the subordinate status of women that are so pervasive they shape even the reflective discourse of women engaged in consciousness raising (23).

Accounts of consciousness-raising practice in succeeding years return again and again to these latter, often proscribed, critical, and generalizing dimensions of the process. A *Ms.* editor, reporting on her experiences the next year, describes her consciousness-raising group as "tough and candid" and seems to consider these attributes the crucial catalyst for changes in her self-understanding and political appreciation of the status of women (Pogrebin 1973, 104). Indeed, the process of *raising* one's consciousness is routinely described as transformative. It is a matter of coming to consciousness of things "not formerly perceive[d]" (Cassell 1977, 16), of recognizing the extent to which experiences thought to be idiosyncratic are shared by women, as women (33), of developing an awareness that this "larger group is degraded and oppressed" (50), and, finally, of coming to a critical understanding of how patriarchal institutions—the family, marriage—systematically oppress women. In short, consciousness raising is a process by which women come to see that the personal is political and thereby "reconsider . . . their political, economic, and social position in relation to that of men" (Jenkins and Kramer 1978, 72). It is a process by which they redefine themselves.[16]

In all of this, experience and personal testimony is to be respected. Often it is observed that consciousness-raising groups were, for many women, the first and perhaps the only context in which they could articulate their perceptions without being corrected, spoken for, or silenced. But it does not follow from this that such testimony must be treated as inviolate, as an "unconditional" datum. Even in the *Ms.* "Guide," the assertion that a woman's account of her own experience is to be treated as "true for her at that moment" is followed by the observation that if she is to discover it wrong, she must do this herself (*Ms.* 1972, 23). The emphasis is on *change*, on critical reassessment of experience and of the standard construals of experience that shape it and inform social action. Most important, the process of change in question is not one that can be undertaken in isolation; it is crucially a matter of recovering the *socio-political* dimension of experience—of learning in what sense you are a (gendered) social being—and this can only be accomplished collectively. Indeed, it is properly a collective accomplishment. The reason you "speak your experience" *to and with others* is precisely so that, with their critical input and their experience as a basis for comparison, you can begin to see where your "constructions of reality" are suspect, what you may have forgotten or suppressed, and where you have internalized general schemas for interpreting experience that are neither consistent with your own experience nor with that of others on whom you had projected it. Taken as a whole, the process is deeply and essentially critical—not just self-critical but mutually critical—and it is centrally one of "going beyond" your own experience. It is a process of learning to "make 'she' speak for more than 'herself'" that certainly takes as its point of departure a commitment to "first learn[ing] to speak *for and of herself*" (Brunsdon 1978, 28),[17] but by no means remains at the level of speaking experience.

The Place of Criticism

The limitations of consciousness raising that leaves experience where it finds it in direct testimony are notorious: "All the sympathy and empathy and sexual solidarity in the world cannot together substitute for a clear-headed [ideological] understanding of the causes of oppression and the psychological reflex within ourselves" (Brunsdon 1978, 73). Strikingly similar concerns have been raised by Geiger and Zita about feminist pedagogy when it is seen to encourage personal disclosure without critical analysis: "The group begins to uncritically validate each and every reaction . . . [often] leading to the vacuous belief that personal descriptive truth to which the individual allegedly has privileged epistemic access is all that needs to be said" (Geiger and Zita 1985, 112–13). The difficulty here is not just that the quality of classroom dialogue is compromised but that, in fact, this sort of practice systematically obscures the extent to which experience is itself concretely situated, and the speaking of it a socially constructed event: "Well-intentioned liberal acceptance of 'every woman's point of view' [results in] the responses [being] perceived as idiosyncrasies of the individual, as testimonials pure and simple, rather than as particular points of view that reflect specific social positions" (Geiger and Zita 1985, 144). Although they are not specifically concerned with feminist research practice, I suggest that Geiger and Zita address the same destructive paradox in feminist principles as I have found at the heart of the self-study model of feminist research. The commitment to comprehend/disclose the *political* nature of the personal is defeated by an impulse to support and validate formerly suppressed points of view at all costs. Experience is merely revalued rather than reevaluated.

I propose that it is as important in feminist research as in feminist teaching to cultivate what Geiger and Zita describe as "a willingness to practice thoughtful self-criticism and self-censorship and to accept criticism as well as support from others" (Geiger and Zita 1985, 117). Without the development of critical discourse and critical inquiry, the potential for transformative change is irretrievably lost, both for individuals and for women as a collectivity. In this spirit, I argue that feminist research should, indeed, take consciousness raising as a model but should draw inspiration specifically from the probing, political analyses women have developed together in these contexts. The most compelling reason to embrace the collectivist model of feminist research is that it builds on these (often suppressed) aspects of consciousness raising; it urges us to "go beyond experience" in a search for explanatory understanding of its conditions and genesis that requires precisely the forms of critical (collective) inquiry that have proven essential to the emancipatory potential of feminist practice in a wide range of contexts.

I would add two further considerations that tell in favor of the collectivist model. The first is that, where feminist theory has been centrally concerned to bring into view the socially constructed nature of our identities and consciousness, it is at least incongruous, if not inconsistent, to insist that feminist researchers should treat experience as an "unconditional datum." The central impetus for and paradox of feminist inquiry is awareness that,

> ... feelings are ... both access to truth ... and an artifact of politics. There is both suspicion of feelings and an affirmation of their health. They become simultaneously an inner expression of outer lies and a less contaminated resource for verification. . . . (MacKinnon 1982, 21)

> Taking situated feelings and common detail (common here meaning both ordinary and shared) as the matter of political analysis, it explores the terrain that is most damaged, most contaminated, yet therefore most women's own, most intimately known, most open to reclamation. (22)

Consequently, the integrity and efficacy of "personal" experience should stand as a primary object of critical investigation, not as a presupposition of inquiry. The second consideration is that, where a degree of objectification of ourselves—of going beyond our own experience—seems an essential condition of *self-understanding*, there is no good reason to rule it out a priori where others are concerned on grounds that it is an inappropriate way of treating intentional "subjects."

Given this, I conclude that the most pressing task for feminist research is to develop the analytic tools necessary for investigating the relationship between personal experience and the context of experience, structured as it is by factors of race, class, age, ethnicity, nationality, and sexual orientation, as well as by gender. The process of inquiry, in which these conceptual tools are hammered out, is necessarily dialectical, one of "political hermeneutics," to borrow MacKinnon's term, given that, where feminist research is concerned, we have no option but to seek an understanding of "women's condition from within the perspective of [our] experience, not outside it" (MacKinnon 1982, 22).[18] The crucial task will be to give an account of criticism that differentiates the forms necessary for feminist inquiry—forms that are constructive, respectful of and responsive to women's experience—from the oppressive and destructive forms all too common in dominant disciplinary traditions of research.

NOTES

1. Stanley and Wise object that "the idea that there is only 'one road' to the feminist revolution, only one type of 'truly feminist' research, is as limiting and as offensive as

male-biased accounts of research that have gone before" (Stanley and Wise 1983b, 26). And McCormack argues that methodology should be seen as a means, not an end, something that should be responsive to change in the content of science and that need not (indeed, probably cannot) be determined in advance of inquiry (McCormack 1987, 20).

2. From the outset feminist theorists have argued that understanding women's experience and oppression as women is a matter of coming to see that the *"personal* is political." Brunsdon insists, in this connection, that "the essence of feminism" is its "revaluation of women's experience" in just this sense (1978, 24). Likewise, Stanley and Wise maintain that the "exploration and analysis of consciousness is the key to everything else about feminism" (1983b, 149), while MacKinnon insists that "feminism is the theory of women's point of view," and that "consciousness raising," conceived as a process of recovering and articulating this point of view through the collective "speaking of experience," is its "quintessential expression" (1982, 21). It is in this spirit that Keohane and Gelpi advocate feminist research that is conceived as an extension of the "experiential thinking" they find central to consciousness raising (1982, xi).

3. The collectivist model might alternatively be described as a communalistic model of research, following Carlson's distinction between communal and agentic research (Bernard 1973; Eichler 1987; Reuben 1978).

4. Frequently it is concern with the inadequacies (specifically, the gender bias) of standard quantitative instruments and methodologies that gives rise to discussions about the ways in which researchers' presuppositions may systematically distort (or, indeed, simply exclude) the experience and perceptions of women. Those who do not want to see feminist researchers abandon quantitative methodologies altogether recommend that they be supplemented by qualitative approaches on the principle that "we need information from women, about women's lives and work, before we can adequately generate the framework [i.e., define variables, frame questions] that will allow us to carry out survey research that fully includes women" (Jacobson 1977, 6). In analysis of the limitations of Canadian census data, Armstrong and Armstrong argue that qualitative approaches can serve both as a check on the theoretical assumptions that inform quantitative research design—a way of determining whether the range of census options for reporting household organization or employment status capture the full range of women's activities and roles— and as a means of filling in the details of "the broad outline" provided by statistical data (Armstrong and Armstrong 1978, 58, 76). Oakley and Oakley (1979) make similar points about the British census.

5. In fact, this is not so "minimal" a requirement, as Stacey describes in reflection on her misgivings about ethnographic methods. Although these are widely seen as more compatible with feminist commitments than less engaged (more "remote") methodologies, she comes to the conclusion that, in fact, "the appearance of greater respect for and equality with research subjects . . . masks a deeper, more dangerous form of exploitation" (Stacey 1988, 22).

6. Smith argues that "an alternative sociology [one appropriate to feminism] must be reflexive . . . [it is] one that preserves in it the presence, concerns, and experience of the sociologist as knower and discoverer" (Smith 1987, 92). Likewise, Stanley and Wise insist that unless research analysis and reports include an account/consideration of the research process itself, "the sources of the researcher's knowledge are hidden from scrutiny" (1983a, 195).

7. See, however, Stacey's discussion of Oakley's recommendations for further thoughts on the complexities and dangers inherent in these sorts of intimate and reciprocal research relationships (Stacey 1988, 22).

8. Acker, Barry, and Esseveld note that, in fact, their research subjects would not allow them to abdicate this role: "They were hesitant about being negative but were clearly critical [of our initial efforts]. What they wanted, they said, was more of our own sociological analysis. They wanted us, the researchers, to interpret their experience to them" (1983, 429–30).

9. Smith adds that "it is not possible to account for one's directly experienced world or how it is related to the worlds which others directly experience who are differently placed by remaining within the boundaries of the former" (1987, 94).

10. Stanley and Wise conclude, on the basis of the discussion elaborating these points, that all the institutions through which women are oppressed "can best be examined and understood through an exploration of relationships and experiences within everyday life" (1983b, 54, 58).

11. An earlier statement of this principle is particularly clear: "Feminism directly confronts the idea that one person or set of people have the right to impose definitions of reality on others" (Stanley and Wise 1979, 373).

12. Stanley and Wise conclude this statement with the intriguing qualification that interference or imposition is unjustifiable "when they [the subjects] don't want us to" (1983b, 113), suggesting that one might be justified in imposing their "reality" on another if given some indication that this other did want them to do this. What would this amount to in the case of an individual whose oppression so undermines her sense of self she is inclined to accept or invite the imposition of any strong will and associated definition of reality?

13. They reject "positivist" methodologies that require disengagement (Stanley and Wise 1983b, 157), and insist that "there is no way we can avoid deriving theoretical constructs from experience," in the sense that the process of research is centrally one in which the researchers' theoretical perceptions are changed as their experiences in research contexts unfold (1983b, 161). They go on to say that it is the "presence of the personal *within research experience*" that must be reclaimed on feminist principles, and the associated discussion suggests that it is specifically the experiences of the researcher that are at issue (1983b, 158).

14. Trebilcot elaborates: "I use 'withstanding' to mean both that I am standing with wimmin and that I am withstanding patriarchy" (1988, 4).

15. In a sense, this introspective focus may also broaden the scope of feminist research. Where the researcher is under no compunction to involve subjects in the research process, it is possible to consider any group of people, activities, or context, as they impinge on the researcher and her experience, without compromising the feminist character of the research (as in the case of Stanley and Wise's study of obscene telephone calls). Stanley and Wise are, in fact, explicit on the point that the reason they consider the researcher under no constraint to involve subjects in the design, direction, or interpretation of her research is because they "reject a feminist research which is concerned with women" (1983b, 170).

16. In a retrospective assessment, MacKinnon argues that the slogan "the personal is political" should not be treated as a metaphor or analogy; it is a literal, descriptive claim

that to know the politics of women's situation is "to know their personal lives" and that the "authentic politics of women's personal lives" as revealed to themselves and others in the process of giving testimony, is "powerlessness to men" (1982, 21).

17. In this quotation, Brunsdon is alluding to Rowbotham's observation that "the present inability of 'she' to speak for more than herself is a representation of reality," which she cited a few pages earlier (Brunsdon 1978, 26).

18. MacKinnon's full statement is: "Through consciousness raising, women grasp the collective reality of women's condition from within the perspective of that experience, not outside it" (1982, 22). She goes on to say that this is a process that aims at "the collective reconstitution of the meaning of women's social experience as women live through it. . . . Its method stands inside its own determinations to uncover them, just as it criticizes them in order to value them in its own terms, in order to have its own terms at all" (29).

REFERENCES

Acker, Joan, and Kate Barry. 1984. "Comments on MacKinnon's 'Feminism, Marxism, Method, and the State.'" *Signs* 10, no. 1: 175–79.

Acker, Joan, Kate Barry, and Joke Esseveld. 1983. "Objectivity and Truth: Problems in Doing Feminist Research." *Women's Studies International Forum* 6, no. 4: 423–35.

Armstrong, Pat, and Hugh Armstrong. 1987. "Beyond Numbers: Problems with Quantitative Data." In *Women and Men: Interdisciplinary Readings on Gender*, ed. Greta Hofmann Nemiroff, 54–79. Montreal: Fitzhenry and Whiteside.

Bernard, Jessie. 1973. "My Four Revolutions: An Autobiographical History of the ASA." In *Changing Women in a Changing Society*, ed. Joan Huber, 11–39. Chicago: University of Chicago Press.

Brunsdon, Charlotte. 1978. "'It Is Well Known that by Nature Women are Inclined to be Rather Personal.'" In *Women Take Issue: Aspects of Women's Subordination*, ed. Women's Studies Group, Center for Cultural Studies, University of Birmingham, 18–34. London: Hutchinson.

Carlson, Rae. 1972. "Understanding Women: Implications for Personality Theory and Research." *Journal of Social Issues* 28, no. 2: 17–32.

Cassell, Joan. 1977. *A Group Called Women: Sisterhood and Symbolism in the Feminist Movement*. New York: David McKay.

Eichler, Margrit. 1987. "The Relationship between Sexist, Nonsexist, Woman-centered and Feminist Research in the Social Sciences." In *Women and Men: Interdisciplinary Readings on Gender*, ed. G. Hofmann Nemiroff, 21–53. Montreal: Fitzhenry and Whiteside.

Eichler, Margrit. 1988. *Nonsexist Research Methods: A Practical Guide*. Boston: Allen and Unwin.

Eichler, Margrit, and Jeanne Lapointe. 1985. *On the Treatment of the Sexes in Research*. Ottawa: Social Sciences and Humanities Research Council of Canada.

Geiger, Susan, and Jacqueline N. Zita. 1985. "White Traders: The Caveat Emptor of Women's Studies." *Journal of Thought* 20:106–21.

Grady, Kathleen E. 1981. "Sex Bias in Research Design." *Psychology of Women Quarterly* 5, no. 4: 628–36.

Grant, Judith. 1987. "I Feel Therefore I Am: A Critique of Female Experience as the Basis for a Feminist Epistemology." *Women and Politics* 7, no. 3: 99–114.

Harding, Sandra. 1986. *The Science Question in Feminism.* Ithaca, N.Y.: Cornell University Press.

Harding, Sandra. 1987. "The Method Question." *Hypatia* 2, 3: 19–36.

Jacobson, Helga E. 1977. *How to Study Your Own Community: Research from the Perspective of Women.* Vancouver: Vancouver Women's Research Center.

Jenkins, Lee, and Cheris Kramer. 1978. "Small Group Process: Learning from Women." *Women's Studies International Quarterly* 1:67–84.

Kelly, Alison. 1978. "Feminism and Research." *Women's Studies International Quarterly* 1:225–32.

Keohane, Nannerl O., and Barbara C. Gelpi. 1982. "Foreword." In *Feminist Theory: A Critique of Ideology,* ed. N. O. Keohane, M. Rosaldo, and B. C. Gelpi, vii–xii. Chicago: University of Chicago Press.

Longino, Helen. 1987. "Can There Be a Feminist Science?" *Hypatia* 2, no. 3: 51–64.

McCormack, Thelma. 1987. "Feminism and the New Crisis in Methodology." Paper presented at the conference "The Effects of Feminist Approaches on Research Methodologies," University of Calgary.

MacKinnon, Catharine A. 1982. "Feminism, Marxism, Method, and the State: An Agenda for Theory." In *Feminist Theory: A Critique of Ideology,* ed. N. O. Keohane, M. Rosaldo, and B. C. Gelpi, 1–30. Chicago: University of Chicago Press.

Ms. 1972. Editorial. "Women's Body, Women's Mind: A Guide to Consciousness Raising." *Ms.* 1 (July): 18–23.

The Nebraska Feminist Collective. 1983. "A Feminist Ethic for Social Science Research." *Women's Studies International Forum* 6, no. 5: 535–43.

Oakley, Ann. 1981. "Interviewing Women: A Contradiction in Terms." In *Doing Feminist Research,* ed. Helen Roberts, 30–61. London: Routledge and Kegan Paul.

Oakley, Ann, and Robin Oakley. 1979. "Sexism in Official Statistics." In *Demystifying Social Statistics,* ed. John Irvine, Ian Miles, and Jeff Evans, 172–89. London: Pluto Press.

O'Brien, Mary. 1981. *The Politics of Reproduction.* Boston: Routledge and Kegan Paul.

Pogrebin, Letty Cotlin. 1973. "Rap Groups: The Feminist Connection." *Ms.* 1 (March): 80–83, 98–100.

Reuben, Elaine. 1978. "In Defiance of the Evidence: Notes on Feminist Scholarship." *Women's Studies International Quarterly* 1:215–18.

Smith, Dorothy E. 1987. "A Women's Perspective as a Radical Critique of Sociology." In *Feminism and Methodology: Social Science Issues,* ed. Sandra Harding, 84–96. Bloomington: Indiana University Press.

Stacey, Judith. 1988. "Can There Be a Feminist Ethnography?" *Women's Studies International Forum* 11:21–27.

Stanley, L., and S. Wise. 1979. "Feminist Research, Feminist Consciousness, and Experiences of Sexism." *Women's Studies International Quarterly* 2:359–74.

Stanley, L., and S. Wise. 1983a. "'Back into the Personal' or: Our Attempt to Construct 'Feminist Research.'" In *Theories of Women's Studies,* ed. Gloria Bowles and Renate Duelli Klein, 192–209. London: Routledge and Kegan Paul.

Stanley, L., and S. Wise. 1983b. *Breaking Out: Feminist Consciousness and Feminist Research.* London: Routledge and Kegan Paul.

Trebilcot, Joyce. 1988. "Dyke Methods." *Hypatia* 3, no. 2: 1–14.

Vickers, Jill McCalla. 1982. "Memoirs of an Ontological Exile: The Methodological Rebellions of Feminist Research." In *Feminism in Canada,* ed. A. Miles and G. Finn, 27–46. Montreal: Blackrose Books.

Women's Place in Communicative Reason

MARIE FLEMING

The notion of a communicative reason is closely associated with the German philosopher Jürgen Habermas. For over a decade and in numerous publications he has contrasted his view of reason, which is marked by dialogism and community, with the monologic and autonomous concept of the Kantian tradition. Habermas believes that his philosophy calls for a major shift in our understanding of reason. Whatever one makes of this claim, the attention that his work is currently attracting in the humanities and social sciences surely reflects contemporary concerns about the value and status of Western science and rationality. It is of some interest, moreover, that Habermas's conception of a communicative reason, which is an explicit response to philosophical difficulties resulting from an older tradition of German philosophy, bears striking resemblances to important features of recent Anglo-American feminist theorizing on the problems of Western reason.

Feminists, too, have resisted strong claims to autonomous reason, and have also suggested counterproposals for a historical and dialogic reason. Some of this theorizing is self-consciously worked out within—and to various degrees against—German philosophy. Seyla Benhabib, for example, has argued for a dialogic reason and has drawn heavily on Habermas, despite her reservations about his continued links to Kantianism.[1] Nancy Fraser and Iris Marion Young, though more critical of Habermas, are nonetheless impressed with the dialogical elements of his theories.[2] This predisposition toward a historical and dialogic reason is also shared by feminists who do not take up the challenges of contemporary German philosophy. In fact, Anglo-American feminists are more apt to connect their discussions to Carol Gilligan's empirical research in cognitive and moral psychology.[3] This reference to a non-German source raises further questions, however, since Gilligan, too, echoes recent "German" themes when she stresses the narrative and contextual nature of women's moral reasoning. In view of this aspect of her work, it is not so surprising that Benhabib, whose credentials in German philosophy are beyond dispute, should see in Habermas's concept of communicative reason some basis for a constructive response to Gilligan.[4]

How can we explain these apparent connections between Anglo-American feminist theory and important strains in contemporary German philosophy? Certainly, they do not appear to be motivated by the same considerations—the one inspired by practical questions about sex-gender oppression and the other concerned with epistemological and ethical issues in Kantian philosophy. Moreover, questions of gender are virtually absent from Habermas's works. What is it then that is being said in this convergence of themes? Is reason *autonomous* or is it *communicative?* And what difference, if any, does the answer make to feminists?

I want to elucidate the problems that these questions pose for feminism by examining the place of women in Habermas's model of communicative reason. That he rarely refers to questions of gender is no evidence that women have no place in his analysis; a text that does not explicitly authorize a view of gender may, nonetheless, be deeply committed to one. Though my concern is with Habermas's version of communicative reason, the analysis should have wider implications, because he is not the only contemporary German philosopher who advocates such a position.[5] Before addressing the question of women's place in communicative reason, I shall suggest how, initially, we might understand the distinction between autonomous and communicative reason.

Autonomous reason is marked by strong claims to impartiality and is readily apparent in the rationality practices that constitute Western science. Here, autonomy is sought through the provision that scientists strive to divest themselves of desires, passions, and other bodily associated diversions, in order to achieve a position sufficiently disinterested to allow legitimate claims to impartiality, neutrality, and objectivity. While Habermas has gone to great lengths to identify the instrumental (means-end) rationality that is privileged in Western science,[6] he has been less critical of aspects of scientific reasoning noted by feminists, especially those related to its inherent compulsion to transcend bodies and other historical contingencies and to reduce the objects of thought to universal laws.[7] Claims to autonomy are also central to modern ethical and political theory, both the deontological tradition stemming from Kant and the utilitarian one that reaches back to Jeremy Bentham and John Stuart Mill. In an important sense, deontological and utilitarian ethics are distinctive and competing tendencies within modern ethical and political theory, because the former asserts the priority of the right over the good and the latter the priority of the good. However, both traditions share a common ground in their commitment to impartiality and autonomy. Whereas deontological ethics makes this commitment explicit within the context of a reason that it stipulates as specifically normative, utilitarian ethics—which rejects the strong concept of a normative reason—implicitly appeals to the ideal of impartiality through its advocacy of instrumental reason in the operationalization of its "greatest happiness" principle.[8]

There is growing conviction among feminists that Western reason privileges masculine experiences, especially in its emphasis on abstract thinking and the value of autonomy.[9] Not only have the major treatises been written by Western men—which is sufficient cause to ask questions, but there are good grounds for believing that the ethics of justice and rights, which is an integral part of the tradition of autonomy, is, in fact, a moral orientation specific to males, defined as a group, in modern Western societies. This debate—on which I shall draw below—indicates a fundamental restructuring of the rationality problem. As Fraser sees it, "The feminist interrogation of autonomy is the theoretical edge of a movement that is literally remaking the social identities and historical self-interpretations of large numbers of women and of some men."[10]

An event of importance for the debate in feminist philosophy was the publication of Carol Gilligan's research in cognitive and moral psychology. Working along the lines of Lawrence Kohlberg's developmental model, Gilligan located a female voice previously unheard in moral and political theory. According to Gilligan, women's moral judgement is contextual and narrative, reflective of human beings who see themselves as fundamentally connected with others. This contextual reasoning could only appear as confusion in Kohlberg's male-centered, autonomous model that stipulated impartiality and universal reason to be constitutive of moral judgement as such.[11] For feminists, Kohlberg's thesis is one further manifestation of what Genevieve Lloyd has called the traditional "maleness of Reason."[12]

In view of these developments, we have had to confront the question

of how to respond to a hegemonic, male-centered tradition of autonomous reason that relegates women's experiences to the sphere of the
irrational. However, just as feminists begin to grapple with the prejudices
of *autonomous* reason, this model appears on the verge of becoming
obsolete and about to be replaced by an elaborate model of *communicative* reason. Even more perplexing is the fact that the new model,
which also says nothing about women, nonetheless contains elements
that also seem to have found their way into feminist analyses.

On first sight, there appear to be valid grounds for finding communicative reason an attractive alternative. According to Habermas, it is
dialogic rather than monologic. The subject or agent is no longer the
solitary figure implicit in autonomous reason, but a collectivity of
socially rooted individuals that produces intersubjectively derived judgements on issues of generalizable interest for the community. Thus, while
claims to universality and impartiality continue to be made, communicative reason is also historically situated and self-reflexively responsive
to human interests. Moreover, it is supposedly grounded in human
speech; in principle, anyone who speaks is entitled to participate.
Granted, there are residual elements of autonomous reason, notably in
the retention of claims to universality and impartiality.[13] Still, we cannot
simply dismiss a concept of reason that privileges the dialogical and
promises to accommodate the historical, because, on the whole, feminists
have argued for a dialogic and historical reason.

For the moment I shall put to one side the suspicion of feminists that
the value of autonomy is inherently masculine and discuss communicative reason from the perspective of the opportunities it allows for
women's participation. If the basic premise of the communicative model
is that anyone who speaks should be able to participate, it is certainly
worth inquiring whether women can have a place in communicative
reason. In addressing the question of women's *presence*, however, I have
no recourse but to take up the striking fact of their virtual *absence* from
the many volumes by Habermas. That is not to say that absence, in and
of itself, is a mark against communicative reason, since men are also
not explicitly referred to by gender. More important is the question of
the nature of women's absence. Not only are Habermas's references to
women fleeting and not meant to address sexual differences, but an
occasional appearance also suggests the curious possibility that women
can be both visible and invisible. What *kind* of absence is this?

I shall now introduce and explore three possible interpretations: (1)

Habermas means to include women as full participants in communicative reason; (2) communicative reason, as elaborated by Habermas, is flawed, but contains within it a potential for women's inclusion that can be theorized in a gender-sensitive analysis; and (3) the absence of women is constitutive of communicative reason.

Interpretation One

The question of whether Habermas means to include women is no mere quibble. Communicative reason represents an updated social contract and is a sophisticated version of rights theory. It is, thus, indebted to concepts of dialogue and community that developed in early modern Europe and gained their philosophical expression in the works of the social contract theorists (Hobbes, Locke, and Rousseau). As a variant of social contract theory, Habermas's philosophy must, therefore, be assessed against the background of a feminist literature that unmasks the concept of a social contract and its accompanying notion of rights as historically and culturally designed to secure civil rights for males.

Susan Moller Okin maintains that Rousseau—the philosopher who bequeathed the concept of the general will—not only saw no need to provide for women's participation in public life, but went to some lengths, in defiance of the logic of his own theories, to ensure our exclusion. There can be little doubt, as she argues, that the individuals in the various versions of the social contract were male heads of households.[14] This position is also supported by Benhabib and Cornell, who write that liberal political theory has always situated the family in the sphere of the "precontractual" or the "state of nature."[15] Such reflections point in the direction of a corrective that would adjust for traditional inequalities by bringing women into the sphere of civil society. Both Benhabib, as discussed below, and Okin have made attempts to broaden the parties to the contract.[16] However, the matter may be far more complex, as Carole Pateman's recent work suggests.

Pateman's analysis would appear to be a challenge to the view that women have been simply left behind in the state of nature. According to her argument, women, too, are bound by a contract, though one that has been repressed. She insists that the *social* contract has historically and logically presupposed a *sexual* contract that secures men's sex-right (or political right) to women's bodies. In an impressive analysis, she demonstrates that the coexistence of public *equality* and private *inequality* is not a contradiction of the modern "fraternal" patriarchy, but represents the logic of a "coherent social structure." One might, in view of such arguments, wonder whether the public space, as identified by social contract theory, can logically tolerate the inclusion of women.[17]

In response, it might be argued that, while such charges have historical interest, this tradition of community no longer reflects the reality of the West in the late twentieth century. One might also contend that both women and men are entitled to share in communicative reason, because anyone who speaks is entitled to participate. Such a position, however, would have to deal with Fraser's objections that suggest that ominous consequences flow from Habermas's failure to theorize the gender subtext underlying his theory of communicative action.[18] Her remarks are pertinent here, since Habermas's theory of communicative action, to which Fraser directs her attention, has its source in his conception of communicative reason.

Fraser argues convincingly that Habermas has not been able to see how certain roles that are crucial for his analysis are gendered. For example, the roles of citizen and worker are, socially and historically, unquestionably masculine and those of child rearer and consumer are feminine. But in Habermas's theory, citizens have no gender and there is no mention of the child rearer role. But if the citizen-speaker role is traditionally masculine, as Pateman also insists,[19] then to leave the gender of citizens unthematized is to leave it masculine, and implicitly to support the traditional view that the public sphere is proper to men. Similarly, not to mention the feminine role of child rearing is to fail to challenge the widespread assumption that women will continue to fill it.[20]

Despite the fundamental tenet of communicative reason that anyone who speaks participates in the speech community, it is at least open to question whether there will be female voices. To put the case against Habermas more strongly, it is difficult to see how an analysis that draws uncritically on categories that have traditionally privileged male experiences can produce liberating results for either sex. A minimal requirement would have to be an attempt to understand how those categories have operated in the production of women's oppression. From this perspective, of course, any "liberating" theory is necessarily feminist—which is to say no more than that it has to be against sexism and patriarchy.[21] Not only does Habermas's model of communicative reason leave much to be desired, but it is implicitly conservative—of male privileges.

Interpretation Two

The potential for women's inclusion in communicative reason is a position that is argued forcefully by Seyla Benhabib.[22] Before examining her proposal, I want to give a brief overview of the sort of understanding of modernity that is implied in this and similar proposals.

Perhaps the first point to make is that any call for women's *inclusion* in a community of equals is also an acknowledgement of their cultural and historical *exclusion*. In the realm of political and moral theory, the argument for women's inclusion begins with the recognition that notions of a social contract and rights were initially designed to respond to male needs in the public realm historically populated by men. According to the traditional understanding of this contract model of community, human subjects gather by right to negotiate about objects. We know now that this model is gendered; culturally and historically, subjects are men and the objects about which they negotiate are women and non-human nature. Not only can the model not account for women's experiences; it can no longer respond to the concerns of large numbers of men, as they adjust to the demands of changing relationships between women and men—not to mention changing perspectives on nonhuman nature. It would seem to follow that, as we dismantle historical and cultural barriers to women's participation in public life, so, too, must we challenge male patterns of reasoning once believed to be universally valid. The premises underlying this position are sound. It is much more difficult to determine which directions to take in our challenges to male reasoning.

Benhabib is convinced that communicative reason can be adjusted to allow for women's inclusion and, specifically, those needs of both women and men that were left untheorized in the tradition of autonomous reason. Linking her discussion to questions about sex-gender differences raised by Gilligan, she argues that communicative reason has the potential to synthesize justice and autonomy—the masculine values—with care and connectedness—the feminine values. I have elsewhere and in some detail examined Benhabib's proposal, and I cannot deal with it at any length here.[23] Briefly, her concern is to find a way to dislodge the privilege of justice and rights questions in moral and political theory and to make room for the historical and contingent, including needs related to family and friendship matters.

The difficulty for Benhabib's efforts is that Habermas places discussion of needs in the public as well as the private spheres, but restricts the sphere of public discussion by weeding out all matters that have to do with personal or private interests. That is, his communicative model attempts to preclude public discussion of private matters. Benhabib needs to challenge this aspect of the model, since she identifies the problem of women's inclusion in communicative reason with the question of making room for public discussion of the traditionally private. She tries to solve this problem as follows. She maintains that communicative reason vacillates between two models of public life and two models of community— on the one hand a legalistic-juridical public life with notions of justice and rights and, on the other, a participatory-democratic public life based on needs and solidarity. By a series of complex and technical steps, Benhabib (not unproblematically) eliminates this vacillation. In short, she reestablishes communicative reason in the form of a participatory-democratic public life and a community of needs and solidarity. She claims that women can have a place in this revised model.

One thing to note is that, very soon after her analysis begins, references to sexual differences disappear from her text, and genderless individuals reappear. Second, the problem *and* the solution are phrased in terms of the hierarchical binary opposition of public and private. Third, the public or traditionally privileged pole of the opposition retains its supremacy. In the end, everything that is private, that heretofore had been dismissed, becomes potentially a public matter, to be evaluated publicly, dialogically, and rationally. Fourth, this drive for transparency *fails* to obliterate the private, since Benhabib's communicative reason would identify as epistemically *false needs* those experiences that resist verbalization. That which cannot be articulated is false. The private realm, like its counterpart in the tradition of autonomous reason, remains dark, incomprehensible, and irrational. But whereas the private once held some truth, it now returns as the false.

What is wrong here? Benhabib's premise is that legalistic-juridical public life contains a masculine bias and represses the feminine. However, she assumes that a participatory-democratic public life, which incorporates the discussion of needs, is not legalistic-juridical—or at least not in the same sense, or to the same degree, as required by the Kantian tradition. Because she decides to work within the closure of the public-private dichotomy, she is pulled from the beginning to the public pole, the masculine sphere. In an effort to accommodate women's experiences, she enlarges the domain of objects susceptible to legal-juridical intervention. She also reinstates a private that is not only unknowable but false, and her public is populated by genderless individuals.

For some years now, we have been aware that the operation of Western dialectics requires the neutralization of differences; we should not be surprised that, as energetic as Benhabib is in her effort to make room for the "other" sex in communicative reason, this system would continue to produce genderless individuals. But how can these individuals be genderless? Human beings are not spirits, as Benhabib herself reminds us, and everyone has to be *one* of *two* genders. As several French feminists insist, a patriarchal dualistic logic *requires* that one sex efface the other; the victory always goes to the masculine one.[24] Can women have a place in communicative reason? Not as women, if it is true that the sex of the participants must remain masculine.[25]

Interpretation Three

Is women's absence somehow necessary? Communicative reason is grounded in human speech, but what are we to make of this, in view of the previously mentioned difficulties?

According to Habermas's account, the linguistic-social bond is necessarily and fundamentally rational. His argument traces a historical and developmental logic and may be summarized as follows. Premodern societies had recourse to fate or the name of God to settle contentious issues. However, the secularization of society, combined with the recent dislodging of theories of representation, have left us with no way to establish normative rightness or propositional truth except through the medium of rational argumentation. According to this developmental logic, "normatively secured" agreements are replaced by ones that are "communicatively achieved"; in any event, only the latter can be considered socially acceptable or legitimate. In short, as the older sources of legitimacy (fate or God) have lost their authority, social actors have been increasingly thrown back upon their own resources. They have had to learn to produce agreements through rational argumentation, and they have also had to admit into the discussion ever more spheres of experience once believed to be beyond question.[26]

This intersubjective discursive activity is, for Habermas, essentially liberating. Not only does the rationalization of the communicative process develop in the direction of agreements that are communicatively achieved and thus "free" in the sense that interacting humans assume ever more responsibility for their utterances—and for their actions—but there is a logic of equality inherent in the unavoidable and idealizing presuppositions that accompany rational argumentation. For example, participants in a speech situation must suppose that the conditions for an unlimited and unconstrained discourse obtain and that they, as participants, are sufficiently free from external and internal constraints, so as to be able to come to a genuine (unforced) consensus on the basis of the force of the better argument. It also must be supposed that participants each have an effective equality of chances to present their views and that they each assume responsibility for their claims to validity. According to this view, the reciprocity that characterizes the relationship between participants in dialogue is *in principle* egalitarian (*in fact*, the relation may be, and usually is, unequal) and it is from this "idealized" relationship that we derive the notion of the universalization of normative validity claims and the ideas of freedom and equality.[27] The account also requires that individuals be genderless. Since we have learned to be suspicious about such a result, we shall have to pursue the matter further.

A central tenet of Habermas's thesis is that we are not at liberty to decide on the value of rationality. According to the "inner logics" of communicative rationality, he argues, validity claims are raised and, if challenged, redeemed through providing grounds or reasons. Speakers must be prepared to deal with three possible kinds of challenges to the validity of an utterance: (1) its truth, that is, whether it corresponds to anything in the world; (2) its rightness or legitimacy, that is, whether it is socially acceptable or morally responsible; and (3) the speaker's truthfulness or authenticity. Since these validity claims are always already "there" in a speech situation—whether we like it or not—Habermas concludes that rationality cannot be a value. In fact, he is adamant that participants in discourse do not—and cannot—make a decision "for the rationality inherent in linguistic understanding." We are "always already orientated," he says, toward the validity claims of truth, rightness, and truthfulness, and these must be reciprocally recognized if we want to reach a consensus.[28] In Habermas's defense, one might suggest that we can change our minds about the value we place on education or private property, for example, whereas we are *not free in the same way* to become irrational. His position is clearer, if we understand it in terms of a distinction between law and morality. Whereas substantive norms—or values—are determined within the structures of speech, rationality is the law that governs what can be said. No one can stand outside the law and remain rational. I would like to explore some of the implications of this important point.

According to Habermas, every validity claim requires a yes/no response not merely as a feature of the sociohistorical practice that is Western rationality, but also, and more importantly, as a component of the implicit knowledge or communicative competence of interacting adult humans. It follows from this argument that (non-Western) social practice in which there is a higher tolerance for contradiction is sociohistorically less evolved, though not essentially different.[29] There are important aspects of this account, especially as it concerns non-Western societies, that I want to resist. For the purposes of the present discussion, however, I shall bracket Habermas's claim of a *universal* communicative competence and restrict the applicability of the theory to Western experience. This strategy involves suspending judgement on the question of the validity of the larger claim—which seems virtually unresolvable—while permitting examination of the more manageable claims, as these reflect on the nature of Western rationality.

I want especially to underline the importance of Habermas's finding that, given the structures of (Western) rationality, everything has to be valued or weighed—declared valid or invalid. Not only do validity claims logically require redemption. The value of valuing is itself reinforced with every utterance, since in each case the utterance must *count as*— be reckoned or valued as—true and right and truthful. Establishing agreement is thus interlaced with determining what is to be regarded as true and right, as well as with legislating the value of valuing. Even if rationality is not a "value"—as Habermas insists—the practices of rationality, nonetheless, constitute the site of the act of valuing. It is a strength of Habermas's model of communicative reason that it helps us understand important dimensions of how this valuing takes place. No one else, including Jacques Derrida, has come close to Habermas in showing how dialogue—even ordinary conversation—is saturated with the act of valuing.

Unfortunately, the strength of Habermas's analysis is also its weakness. Having uncovered the operation of the law of valuing, he seeks to hypostatize it. Of note is his failure to take up a question posed a century ago by Friedrich Nietzsche, a question that is crucial for feminism: What is the value of the values themselves?[30] What is the value of the values good/bad, true/false, mind/body, rational/irrational, man/woman? This is a system of *valuing* that identifies women with everything that is devalued. Showing that rationality is not a value, to be embraced or rejected at will, does not put an end to the question of the value of valuing. We cannot allow the name of the law to become a modern substitute for fate or God.

An urgent question is just where women's "legislated" inferiority takes place. If the decree is enacted only at the level of the redemption of validity claims, *the level of morality*, we could introduce different legislation and, hence, come to value women as equals and full members of community. However, since the legislated inferiority of women inheres (as well) in dualistic logic, *the level of the law*, women as embodiments of negativity are a structural necessity of the ratio, so that with each utterance we reenact the law that there shall be "women." The system of valuing that requires yes/no responses must continue to produce women. Moreover, according to this logic, we women can only be "emancipated" if we are no longer "women." This requirement places us women in an impossible situation because our sex is decreed from birth, whereas the public realm is necessarily masculine. That there is something incongruous about women who inhabit the "wrong" sphere can be sensed in the strong tendency to think in terms of *women* doctors, *women* writers, *women* supervisors, and so on.[31]

An important argument in favor of the communicative model—made by Habermas himself and generally acknowledged—is its explicit dialogism over against Kantian monologism. This communicative aspect can lead to the belief that Habermas's theory, with adjustments, can provide a basis for feminist critiques. Benhabib's proposal, for example, rests on the hope that the dialogic model allows for the inclusion of women as equals. The question that must be addressed is how this inclusion is possible within a system of valuing in which women are structurally and necessarily devalued. The participants in communicative reason may be equal, but they are also masculine.

A telling sign of the gender of Critical Theory is an argument made by Albrecht Wellmer, himself a proponent of a discourse ethic. According to Wellmer, the monologism of the Kantian position has been overdrawn. He maintains that Kant's vision of the legislating individual requires an acknowledgement of the interests of others and a sense of community.

The monologue associated with this tradition is more plausibly understood, he suggests, as an imaginary dialogue with affected others. Thus,
even though Kant himself left many questions unanswered, his Kingdom
of Ends and his categorical imperative presuppose a community and
logically require an actual dialogue.[32] Though Wellmer is inclined to
think that a discourse ethic can be responsive to women's concerns, the
position that he develops is vulnerable to the preceding criticisms. His
case is also weakened by a missed opportunity—opened up by his own
analysis—to explore the significance of the gendered community at the
center of Kantian philosophy. There is little doubt that Kant's community
is a community of men.

Despite these limitations—and to some extent because of them—
Wellmer's analysis of dialogue and ethics in Kant's philosophy can provide additional perspectives on the discourse of modernity. We can draw
on this reading of Kant, for example, to show that Habermas's model
of communicative reason is constituted largely through elements left
unthematized, but operative, in the male-centered, autonomous tradition. Instead of delivering the radical shift in our self-understanding of
reason that he promises, Habermas has concretized the Kantian vision
and reconceptualized it as a community of speakers in which validity
claims are reciprocally recognized and explicitly subject to yes/no
responses. If *autonomous* reason is already an implicitly *communicative*
reason, they belong to the same episteme and cannot be justifiably viewed
as fundamentally different and competing traditions. In other words, the
communicative reason that Habermas offers cannot be a genuine alternative if it is already an integral part of that discourse that produces
autonomous reason in the first place.[33] The question I asked at the
beginning, whether reason is autonomous or communicative, is thus
displaced by the more pressing question of whether communicative reason, as formulated by Habermas, is but another expression of the same
philosophy of the subject that legislates women as Other and irrational.

For some decades and until recently, Anglo-American analytic philosophers believed that they had escaped Kant, but, as Richard Rorty
has convincingly argued, the perceived split between analytic and Continental philosophy has been exaggerated. From this perspective, Kantian
philosophy is not self-enclosed but, rather, builds on and subsumes Lock-
ean and Cartesian notions of mental processes and mental substance.
As the "master" philosophy, it thus sets the stage for its further development in both its Continental and analytic variants.[34] As both

"traditions" respond to poststructuralist challenges, it is increasingly evident that they share a Kantian heritage. The difficulty in escaping this heritage is something that feminists have also sometimes underestimated. It is perhaps not simply a coincidence that contemporary German philosophy and Anglo-American feminism have expressed similar aspirations.

Some Concluding Remarks

How is it that someone like Habermas, who is so influential in contemporary philosophy, is either unaware of feminist critiques of modernity or, even worse, unconcerned about them? Martin Jay noted the absence of sex-gender questions in Habermas's recent book on the philosophical discourse of modernity from Kant and Hegel to Michel Foucault and Derrida.[35] Habermas, he writes in a long review of the book, "provides us with a brilliant reading of the master thinkers of the tradition (all of whom turn out to be men, which may account for the unfortunate absence of any gender dimension in his story)."[36] It is not clear from Jay's formulation whether the "masters" selected by Habermas for examination simply happened to be men or whether Habermas was compelled to select men since all the "masters" have been men. In any case, it is a mystery how the sex of these masters explains the absence of sex-gender questions in Habermas's examination of their views. It is also disturbing that Jay introduces and disposes of the gender question in a parenthetical remark. After this aside, he continues to discuss Habermas's thesis on modernity without further mention of feminist perspectives.

A charitable explanation of Habermas's failure to engage feminist critiques might relate it to his fear of mysticism. Throughout his discussion of the philosophical discourse of modernity, for example, there is the recurring theme that mysticism and assorted political evils will result from a defiance of the principle of noncontradiction. This anxiety is particularly acute in his discussion of the philosophical connections between Derrida and Martin Heidegger.[37] It is also historically understandable; Habermas's deep concern about Germany's Nazi past and his determined defense of the liberating features of modernity as the best guarantee against a resurgence of rightist thinking are well known. But whatever the source of Habermas's worries, his intention has been conservative from the start. While he sets himself the task of *reconstructing* the pragmatic features of human communication, his object domain has been a male-dominated, Western sociopolitical practice. Under the circumstances, he could not help but reproduce the self-understanding of a male-centered tradition of Western reason.

Paradoxically, there are also considerable advantages for feminism in such an account. Though Habermas fails to address the important question of the value of valuing, he provides important insights into the (male) self-understanding of Western reason that have been obscured in less systematic and more self-consciously critical analyses. His "success" in charting this self-understanding is inadvertently suggested in a remark by Richard Bernstein, who reports that he experienced a "shock of recognition" when he began to read Habermas's work in the 1960s.[38] An adequate account of the tradition of reason that contributes to sex-gender oppression is clearly important. As Gayatri Spivak advises in another context: "We must use and attend to 'the patriarchy's' own self-critique, even as we recognize that it is irreducibly determined to disable us."[39] Spivak was urging feminists to be wary of the "discourse of man" that inheres in the deconstructive practices of Derrida. We need to be at least as vigilant in the face of philosophical self-critiques that do not acknowledge their sex-gender biases.

But there is more to be gained than simply a "better" understanding of the androcentric tradition of Western reason. This comes into view once we begin to note that the position Habermas defends places him in an odd situation. On one level, his adoption of a naturalistic stance toward logic ensures that his account will reproduce dualistic categories that are repressive for women. On another level, however, his analysis contains an internal dynamic that is destructive of the rational argumentation he wants to promote. Since his account of reason is blind— and deaf—to the various claims to validity inherent in Western logic, he risks falling into the mysticism he rejects. This difficulty arises because there is a strong tendency throughout Habermas's writings to identify *all* philosophical challenges to dualism with mysticism and irrationality. But such an identification cannot be maintained and is itself evidence of a conflation of rationality and Western logic. In fact, there does not seem to be any legitimate basis on which one can exclude challenges to dualism from the arena of rational argumentation. Admittedly, a demand for the redemption of the validity claims inherent in dualistic categories would have a transformative effect on Habermas's account of communicative reason. That is to say, we may end up with a radically different communicative reason than the one that informs his theory of communicative action. The crucial point is that a challenge to dualism is already a logical possibility of Habermas's theory. Wellmer provides unwitting support for this argument when he writes that "the notion of communicative rationality is . . . meant to indicate a conception (and self-conception) of symbolic communication which does not allow for *any* validity claims to be exempt in principle from possible critical examination" (italics in original).[40]

The stand I am defending is neither pessimistic nor optimistic—or, rather, it is both. It is difficult not to conclude that, at this historical juncture, feminists, too, must speak through an economy that privileges the masculine pole of the masculine/feminine dichotomy. That is to say, we cannot simply uncouple dualistic logic and reason, since it is through the medium of this logic that our historical and cultural practices have been—and continue to be—intelligible and meaningful. Nonetheless, as we chart the dislocations in our "normal" understandings of what seems reasonable, we are surely experiencing historical changes of some moment. The fact that dualistic logic is somehow *unreasonable* is already an indication that the traditionally close connection between reason and a *particular* logic is open to serious questioning. Whether reason is necessarily or only contingently male centered is an issue that remains unresolved.

NOTES

1. Seyla Benhabib, "The Generalized and the Concrete Other: The Kohlberg-Gilligan Controversy and Feminist Theory," *Praxis International* 5, no. 4 (January, 1986): 402–24; also published in Seyla Benhabib and Drucilla Cornell, eds., *Feminism as Critique: On the Politics of Gender* (Minneapolis: University of Minnesota Press, 1987), 77–95. Cf. Seyla Benhabib, *Critique, Norm, and Utopia: A Study of the Foundations of Critical Theory* (New York: Columbia University Press, 1986), 279ff.

2. Nancy Fraser, "What's Critical About Critical Theory? The Case of Habermas and Gender," in Benhabib and Cornell, *Feminism as Critique*, 31–56; Iris Marion Young, "Impartiality and the Civic Public: Some Implications of Feminist Critiques of Moral and Political Theory," in Benhabib and Cornell, *Feminism as Critique*, 57–76. See also Nancy Fraser, "Toward a Discourse Ethic of Solidarity," *Praxis International* 5, no. 4 (January, 1986): 425–29.

3. Carol Gilligan, *In a Different Voice: Psychological Theory and Women's Development* (Cambridge, Mass.: Harvard University Press, 1982). Cf. the essays in Lorraine Code, Sheila Mullet, and Christine Overall, eds., *Feminist Perspectives: Philosophical Essays on Method and Morals* (Toronto: University of Toronto Press, 1988).

4. Benhabib, "Generalized and Concrete Other."

5. In the German literature, Habermas and Karl-Otto Apel are the key proponents

of a communicative or discourse ethic. See Albrecht Wellmer's discussion in his *Ethik und Dialog: Elemente des moralischen Urteils bei Kant und in der Diskursethik* (Frankfurt: Suhrkamp Verlag, 1986), 51ff. Cf. Karl-Otto Apel, "Sprechakttheorie und transzendentale Sprachpragmatik zur Frage ethischer Normen," 10–173; and Jürgen Habermas, "Was heisst Universalpragmatik?" 174–272; both in *Sprachpragmatik und Philosophie*, ed. Karl-Otto Apel (Frankfurt: Suhrkamp Verlag, 1976). Cf. also Jürgen Habermas, *Moralbewußtsein und kommunikatives Handeln* (Frankfurt: Suhrkamp Verlag, 1983).

6. Jürgen Habermas, *The Theory of Communicative Action*, 2 vols., trans. Thomas McCarthy (Boston: Beacon Press, 1984 and 1987).

7. See esp. Sandra Harding, *The Science Question in Feminism* (Ithaca, N.Y.: Cornell University Press, 1986).

8. For a critical assessment of contemporary "deontological liberalism" that has attracted attention in philosophical and feminist circles, see Michael J. Sandel, *Liberalism and the Limits of Justice* (Cambridge: Cambridge University Press, 1982). Cf. Benhabib, "Generalized and Concrete Other" and Young, "Impartiality."

9. Cf. remarks in Alison Jaggar, *Feminist Politics and Human Nature* (Totowa, N.J.: Rowman and Allanheld, 1983), esp. 27ff.; Benhabib, "Generalized and Concrete Other."

10. Nancy Fraser, "Michel Foucault: A 'Young Conservative?'" *Ethics* 96 (October, 1985): 182.

11. Carol Gilligan, *Different Voice*. A landmark analysis for the debate on autonomy in feminist psychoanalytic theory was Nancy Chodorow's *The Reproduction of Mothering: Psychoanalysis and the Sociology of Gender* (Berkeley: University of California Press, 1978).

12. Genevieve Lloyd, *The Man of Reason: "Male" and "Female" in Western Philosophy* (Minneapolis: University of Minnesota Press, 1984).

13. For Habermas's position, see esp. his *Theory of Communicative Action*.

14. Susan Moller Okin, *Women in Western Political Thought* (Princeton, N.J.: Princeton University Press, 1979), 99ff. Cf. Jean Bethke Elshtain, *Public Man, Private Woman: Women in Social and Political Thought* (Princeton, N.J.: Princeton University Press, 1981).

15. Benhabib and Cornell, *Feminism as Critique*, 10.

16. See Susan Moller Okin, "Justice and Gender," *Philosophy and Public Affairs* 16, no. 1 (Winter, 1987): 42–72.

17. Carole Pateman, *The Sexual Contract* (Stanford: Stanford University Press, 1988).

18. Fraser, "What's Critical?"

19. Fraser, "What's Critical?" 169, n. 26, expresses strong agreement with the analysis in Carole Pateman, "The Personal and the Political: Can Citizenship Be Democratic?" lecture at the University of California, Berkeley, February, 1985.

20. Fraser, "What's Critical?"

21. I agree with the strategy of Toril Moi who, while noting the varieties of feminisms, characterizes as feminist any theory that attempts to transcend sexism and patriarchy. See her *Sexual/Textual Politics: Feminist Literary Theory* (London: Methuen, 1985).

22. Seyla Benhabib, "Generalized and Concrete Other" and *Critique*.

23. This section draws on a detailed examination of Benhabib's position. See Marie Fleming, "The Gender of Critical Theory," *Cultural Critique* 13 (Fall, 1989): 119–41.

24. Cf. Luce Irigaray, *Speculum of the Other Woman* (Ithaca, N.Y.: Cornell University Press, 1985); Hélène Cixous, "The Laugh of the Medusa," *Signs* 1, no. 4 (Summer, 1976):

875–93; Hélène Cixous and Catherine Clément, *The Newly Born Woman* (Minneapolis: University of Minnesota Press, 1986). See also Jacques Derrida and Christie V. McDonald, "Choreographies," *Diacritics* 12 (1982): esp. 72.

25. My analysis does not endorse the distinction between sex and gender. I agree with Monique Wittig that sex and gender is an anachronistic distinction. See Monique Wittig, "One is Not Born a Woman," *Feminist Issues* 1, no. 2 (Winter, 1981): 47–54; and "The Category of Sex," *Feminist Issues* 2, no. 2 (Fall, 1982): 63–68. We are used to thinking of sex as a biological given and gender as culturally imposed. There are good reasons for feminists not to acknowledge the distinction between nature and culture, which underlies the sex or gender distinction. But sex—male or female—is not something that preexists language and culture. Rather, as Wittig argues, it is an evaluative term that categorizes and classifies humans on the basis of their reproductive capacities.

26. See Jürgen Habermas, *Communication and the Evolution of Society*, trans. Thomas McCarthy (Boston: Beacon Press, 1979) and *Theory of Communicative Action*.

27. Cf. Jürgen Habermas, "Wahrheitstheorien," in *Wirklichkeit und Reflexion* (Pfullingen: Verlag Günther Neske, 1973), 211–65; and *Moralbewußtsein*.

28. Jürgen Habermas, "A Reply to My Critics," in *Habermas: Critical Debates*, ed. John B. Thompson and David Held (Cambridge, Mass.: MIT Press, 1982), 227. Cf. his "What Is Universal Pragmatics?" in *Communication*, 1–68. See Benhabib (*Critique*, 317ff.), who argues for a weaker version of Habermas's thesis.

29. Cf. Habermas's discussion of the rationality debates in *Theory of Communicative Action*, 1:43ff.

30. Friedrich Nietzsche, *On the Genealogy of Morals* (New York: Vintage Books, 1969). For Habermas's response to Nietzsche, see his *The Philosophical Discourse of Modernity: Twelve Lectures* (Cambridge, Mass.: MIT Press, 1987), esp. 83ff.

31. Cf. Wittig, "Category of Sex."

32. Wellmer, *Ethik und Dialog*, 14ff.

33. Michel Foucault and Jacques Derrida have made us aware of this aspect of the logic of Western discourse. See esp. Michel Foucault, *The Order of Things: An Archaeology of the Human Sciences* (New York: Vintage Books, 1973) and his *The Archaeology of Knowledge* (London: Tavistock Publications, 1974).

34. See esp. Richard Rorty, *Philosophy and the Mirror of Nature* (Princeton: Princeton University Press, 1979).

35. Habermas, *Philosophical Discourse*.

36. Martin Jay, Review of Habermas, *The Philosophical Discourse of Modernity*, *History and Theory* 28, no. 1 (1989): 96.

37. Habermas, *Philosophical Discourse*, 131ff. Cf. his "Work and Weltanschauung: The Heidegger Controversy from a German Perspective," *Critical Inquiry* 15, no. 2 (Winter, 1989): 431–56.

38. Richard J. Bernstein, *Beyond Relativism and Objectivism: Science, Hermeneutics, and Praxis* (Philadelphia: University of Pennsylvania Press, 1985), xv.

39. Gayatri Chakravorty Spivak, "Displacement and the Discourse of Woman," in *Displacement: Derrida and After*, ed. Mark Krupnick (Bloomington: Indiana University Press, 1987), 191.

40. Albrecht Wellmer, "Reason, Utopia, and the *Dialectic of Enlightenment*," in *Habermas and Modernity*, ed. Richard J. Bernstein (Cambridge, Mass.: MIT Press, 1985), 53.

The Unicorn in the Garden

LORRAINE CODE

Expertise and Authority

The conceptions of knowledge that inform mainstream epistemology rely upon a set of implicit beliefs about subjectivity and cognitive agency. The subject is neutral, purely rational, and detached in his disengaged observation of the object; the object remains inert in and unaffected by the knowing process. Paradigmatic examples of knowledge tend to be drawn from observations of medium-sized physical objects, with the consequence that a distanced, and often controlling and manipulative relation of subject to object has come to be the accepted relation. All of these beliefs pivot around the assumption that cognitive activity, including inquiry in the human sciences, should be conducted on the model of natural scientific inquiry, especially as it is practiced in physics. In this essay, I shall examine some implications of this ongoing commitment to the ideal of a unified scientific methodology, applicable alike in the physical and the human sciences. With special reference to women's psychic well-being, I shall claim that the discursive construction of femininity that is legitimated by "expert" scientific findings exercises a subtle and constant control over women in their everyday lives, often literally "driving them crazy."

With its emphasis on the passivity and manipulability of the objects of knowledge, mainstream epistemology endorses a research methodology that has a generalized distorting and immobilizing effect upon human subjects when they occupy the place of the "objects" studied. The methodology renders them as personally invisible, as faceless, and as interchangeable as the placeholders on either side of the "S knows that P" formula in which "standard" knowledge claims are ordinarily presented. Debates in the human sciences about the merits of quantitative versus qualitative research methods come out so often in favor of the former that it is tempting to conclude that the persistent appeal of quantitative methodology derives, at least in part, from the entrenched belief, central to the empiricist project and its latter-day variants, that human beings are knowable in just the same way as physical objects are. That is to say, anything that is *knowable about them*, in the proper philosophical sense of 'know,' is knowable just as objects are known: by the received, and idealized, methodology of the natural sciences. In such assimilations, human subjectivity vanishes in the knowledge that purports to explain people's "nature" and their experiences.

Mainstream epistemology is principally preoccupied with formal questions and, hence, with the formal adequacy of social scientific knowledge. I want to suggest that questions of content need equally to be addressed, and that the applicability and significance of formal principles varies according to the content of the knowledge under consideration. In this essay, then, I am interested in institutionalized, "public" knowledge about women as it derives out of an (often implicit) endorsement of some version of the unity of science/unity of knowledge projects. More specifically, my concern is with the content of institutionalized knowledge of or about women as it is manifested in the conceptualization and treatment of women's "madness." I want to locate this "knowledge" in relation to a more general pattern of expert, authoritarian constructions of femininity, as they are embedded in the common sense of Western capitalist societies.[1] Complex institutional patterns of knowledge about women legitimate networks of authority and expertise to sustain oppressive power structures that are held in place by the veneration of all things scientific in late twentieth century societies.

My discussion will focus on features of the content of knowledge of or about women: on how women are represented both in everyday, "man in the street" knowledge and in the structures and institutions of various branches of knowledge *about* people. A peculiar range of representations of woman's "nature" informs media depictions of women's lives, medical judgements about women's health, educational claims about women's intelligence, historical analyses of women's experiences, philosophical conceptions of female personhood, and psychological prescriptions for normal womanhood. It is evident in all of these domains—as in analogous ones I have not named—that "knowledge" of what a woman is and can do derives at least as much from ideology, folklore, prejudice, and intractable misconceptions as it does from endeavors to see women clearly. It is not enough to discount this "knowledge" as mere error, for it is so deeply entrenched that more than a denial is required to dislodge it. It is, frequently, endorsed by women themselves, as well as by men.

Women often have difficulty claiming the authority they require to take responsibility for their lives, in the face of the intransigence of institutionalized structures of power-knowledge, which define their subjectivity for them, and are stubbornly deaf to criticism.[2] Enmeshed in such structures in innumerable aspects of their lives, women are commonly thwarted in their efforts to achieve the cognitive and moral autonomy that is crucial to the development of effective agency. In consequence, women too often live as self-fulfilling prophecies, adhering to the restricted options constructed for them by experts who claim to know them better than they could hope to know themselves. Indeed, it is nothing short of ironic that everyone can be an expert about women—about what they are and what they can be or do—except women themselves, whose self-presentation is constantly discredited by institutionalized claims of a higher expertise.

To illustrate these points, I shall draw first upon *For Her Own Good*, Barbara Ehrenreich and Deirdre English's now-classic study of "the scientific answer to the Woman Question, as elaborated over the last hundred years by a new class of experts—physicians, psychologists, domestic scientists, child-raising experts."[3] Subsequently, I shall consider two of the many studies of women and madness where epistemological claims are most clearly visible: Elaine Showalter's *The Female Malady* and Jill Matthews's *Good and Mad Women*.[4] In their demonstrations of the role of empirical investigation in perpetuating stereotypes of women, in terms of what "science has proved . . ." about women's natural inferiority and proper place in relation to men, and about the best ways to deal with women's unhappiness, anxiety, and depression, these studies provide good reasons for discounting the putative disinterestedness of scientific inquiry.

I shall examine these works for their epistemological implications; but my purpose is not to derive traditional epistemological conclusions about the nature, justification, and warrantability of knowledge claims. I am interested, rather, in what they reveal about the role of ideology in the production of knowledge, and the relations of power and knowledge in the establishment of expertise and authority.

The Unicorn in the Garden

James Thurber's fable "The Unicorn in the Garden" is an instructive tale, though for reasons that no doubt differ from his own reasons for telling it.[5] A man looks up from his breakfast to see a unicorn in the garden. He is both excited and delighted; but when he tells his wife, who is still in bed, she comments coldly: "The unicorn is a mythical beast." The man insists; she is convinced that he must be crazy. Yet when the police and a psychiatrist arrive, in response to her summons, and challenge the man to confirm his report of seeing a unicorn in the garden, he denies that he reported any such thing: "The unicorn is a mythical beast." So his wife is pronounced "crazy as a jay bird" and taken away cursing and screaming to be shut up in an institution, while the husband lives happily ever after.

Now Thurber draws from this story the moral "Don't count your boobies until they are hatched"; and Martin Hollis, who cites it in support of his critique of "strong program" relativism, maintains:

> It seems patent that the truth of the various beliefs makes all the difference. If there actually was a unicorn in the garden, his belief is not certifiable. If he actually said there was, her belief that he did needs no psychiatrist to explain it. The psychiatrist intervenes only when beliefs are false or irrational.[6]

His point is to argue that there are facts of the matter that determine the credibility of his—the man's—position against the obvious irrationality of hers, the wife's; to show that it is by no means "a matter of indifference whether to send for a zookeeper or a psychiatrist."[7]

Hollis's is one possible reading of the Thurber story. But another, equally plausible one bears upon the issues of authority, expertise, and power that are at work in this incident. Can it be just a coincidence that it is the man who is believed and the woman who is pronounced crazy? Perhaps, but it is unlikely. It would be a better world—certainly it would be one where gender politics were more equitable than they are now, and objectivist theories of knowledge might more straightforwardly apply—if it were reasonable to conclude with confidence that a psychiatrist intervenes only when beliefs and actions are consistently false, erratic, or irrational by some external and apolitical standard. But the politics of madness evidently contribute to the outcome here, as they do in too many analogous instances for one to be sanguine about concurring readily with Hollis's faith in the epistemic warrantability of psychiatric judgment.

Hollis's faith is, plainly, sustained by a belief that expert judgment is informed by objective knowledge of *the facts.* Such knowledge is achieved through observation, and by reason, whose autonomous exercise leads to an ever-increasing accumulation of the kind of knowledge that establishes experts—such as psychiatrists—in their positions of authority. The cluster of received assumptions about knowledge and reason that I have cited in the previous section offers implicit support to conclusions such as the one Hollis draws.

Central among these assumptions as they bear upon this issue are the beliefs that knowers can be self-sufficient in their knowing, and that objects of knowledge are independent and separate from them. Hence, knowledge can be studied and evaluated simply as a *product* of inquiry. Details of the processes of its production are irrelevant to its shape, content, and/or evaluation; knowledge judged worthy of that name will be timelessly and placelessly true. Particularly in empiricist theories, perception and memory are regarded as the principal sources of knowledge. Testimony, narrowly construed as little more than opinion or hearsay, is accorded minimal significance and dependability. Yet "testimony" includes the entire range of knowledge that other people communicate, from simple information, to media reportage, to the content of the textbooks on which most "experts" rely. It incorporates the first-person experiential reports upon which psychiatrists, for the most part, must base their judgments.

According to the "autonomy-of-knowledge" argument,[8] knowledge properly so-called, will, in fact, *transcend* experience, whose particularity can only muddle its purity and clarity. Hence, a rift is assumed between practice and theory that privileges theory over practice. This rift is particularly apparent in the method of abstracting simplified (and hence clarified) sample knowledge claims to serve as exemplars for discerning the necessary and sufficient conditions for the existence of knowledge. It is not so important that the samples should show how people know in their everyday lives, as that, through its exemplary nature, a sample should reveal conditions of justification or falsification. Indeed, it might even be a mistake to locate a sample claim in the world, to contextualize it, because mixing it in with the muddled and contingent aspects of real situations leads to a loss of clarity and, hence, to theoretical inadequacy.

Although *individual*, autonomous knowers are often represented as the producers of such knowledge claims, these clearly are the abstract individuals of post-Enlightenment thought. Their specificity, and their cognitive "locations"—cultural, racial, historical, class- or gender-derived—are irrelevant to their cognitive agency. Hence, again, first-person experiential accounts are accorded minimal value.

In the Thurber fable, however, action is taken on the basis of a judgment according to which *one* first-person experiential account is granted greater credibility than the other. It is by no means clear how standard epistemology, with its distrust of experiential evidence and its commitment to impartiality, can evaluate such situations. Hollis, in common with the objectivists to whom he declares his allegiance, believes that the rationally informed expertise of the psychiatrist equips him to judge, reliably, *which* accounts are true. Indeed, established claims to authoritative expertise, in present-day Western societies, are commonly articulated against the background of just that regulative ideal of a neutral, detached, perfectly impartial scientific knowledge, in whose acquisition political and other "subjective" factors are scrupulously eliminated. Hollis plainly believes that the judgment that dispatches the woman to the booby hatch is neutrally derived, and factually based, in just these senses.

Thurber's story is only a fable, written to amuse. But his wit gains in pungency and bite from its resonance with events in the real world. In just one week the press reports Soviet acknowledgements of the political misuse of psychiatric committal, just as it is depicted in Solzhenitsyn's *The First Circle*; and tells of an eighty-two-year-old U.S. woman released after nearly six decades in a mental hospital, with an official claim that she "never belonged in an institution." It is true that this woman had been having "nervous spells" when she was interviewed for admission; but the interview—at least as it is reported—scarcely seems to justify committal. When the psychiatrist asked her the difference between a cow and a horse, she replied, "You milk a cow, but you can't milk a horse"—adding "You're not making as big a fool of me as you think." The diagnosis was "psychosis, equivalent of epilepsy."[9]

Now the juxtaposition of these two examples shows that it would be facile to conclude that the politics of madness derive simply from a masculine conspiracy to suppress "irrational" female behavior. At least as many male Soviet dissidents as female ones have been held in psychiatric institutions. In Western societies, one often reads of men's unjustifiable committals. Yet in most cases, committal is linked with under-class social status and unequal relations of power and authority. Indeed, in the broader social context, Hollis's faith in the translucency and detached neutrality of psychiatric judgment seems to be misplaced.

Plainly, there are gender-specific forces at work in psychiatric practice, manifested in consistently more frequent psychiatric and therapeutic interventions in women's lives than in men's lives. Some of these interventions, it is true, are sought by women themselves; hence, they are often described as freely chosen. But such descriptions fail to take into account the sense in which choices, too, are discursively, ideologically constituted. Whether such choices can be called "free" is a matter of considerable debate. The fact that there *are* gender-specific assumptions at work here— as there are in the concentration of "expert" control over femininity in all of its permissible social manifestations, contrasted with lesser control over the construction of masculinity—is not open to dispute. Women, as they are positioned in Western, science-venerating cultures, are widely and unduly dependent upon expert (masculine) intervention in all aspects of their lives. That dependence is apparent even in their childbearing and child-rearing practices, which the same ideological constructions of femininity designate as their own essential functions.

Barbara Ehrenreich and Deirdre English note striking similarities in relationships between women and experts and traditional relationships between women and men. They claim that, in the middle of the nineteenth century, women began to respond with dependency and trust to a group of experts whose authority "rested on the denial or destruction of women's autonomous sources of knowledge."[10] Ehrenreich and English connect the rise of specialized, professionalized forms of expertise with the growth of the market economy in post-industrial revolution societies, and consequent redrawings of the boundaries between the public and private spheres of human life. They link women's loss of control over the productive processes that passed into the factory system with the "commodification" of women's traditional arts and skills and the end of their authoritative social roles.

The epistemological moves by which expert authority established itself appear to have been curious ones. They attest to a growing veneration of science, which produced concerted endeavors to place human skills, arts, and wisdom on a scientific footing. Women's healing arts, their midwifery skills, their household management and child-raising techniques, all became subjects of scientific study. Yet—and this is the curious aspect—if English and Ehrenreich are right, "the new scientific expert . . . became an authority . . . [whose] business was not to seek out what is *true*, but to pronounce on what is *appropriate*."[11] Clearly they are postulating a closer connection between knowledge and human interests than an objectivist philosophy of science would claim. The point is that, when one asks "Appropriate for whom? by what criteria? and to what end?" the answers appear to center around the desirability of maintaining relationships of female dependence upon masculine authority. Such relationships are instituted, allegedly, for women's own good. But it is difficult to believe that the good referred to is really "their own good" as authoritative women would articulate it.

Ehrenreich and English document the intervention, in every dimension of women's lives, of "the ideology of a masculinist society, dressed up as objective truth,"[12] and drawing sustenance from entrenched stereotypes of women. They claim a correlation between the increase of such interventions and the end of a "unique dignity" that, they believe, women had been able to realize in the practice of their healing arts, midwifery, and domestic productivity.[13] Susceptible to the rhetoric of the new scientific era that promised so much, and rendered increasingly passive by a growing mystification of expertise, women learned to look to the experts for guidance. Hence, English and Ehrenreich maintain that women abdicated habits of thinking for themselves and acting with confidence in their own wisdom: habits that those who exercised them appear to have developed with scant regard for any ideology that proclaimed their incapacity to do so. Their engagement in such thought and action became increasingly invisible as they signed over the responsibility for their well-being to a new generation of scientific experts.

It is to a complex reciprocal influence of the upper-class *and* masculine superiority of the majority of its practitioners that Ehrenreich and English attribute the fact that *medicine* increasingly became an authority in women's lives. The doctor was endowed with a mystified prestige derived, above all, from his training in esoteric scientific domains to which women had little or no access. Knowledge, increasingly, became a commodity of privilege. Indeed, the prestige of science extended rapidly into the domains of housework and child-rearing: housekeeping was reconceptualized as a full-time profession, and women began to draw "prodigiously on the advice of male experts in an attempt to lay the basis for

a *science* of child-raising and a *science* of housework."[14] The point seems
to be that when science is so highly venerated throughout society, then
anyone who ignores it in favor of reliance upon her own experiences,
intuitions, and skills violates a fundamental epistemic imperative. If
being judged responsible depended upon relinquishing trust in their own
skills in favor of a more distinguished expertise, it is scarcely surprising
that women would do what was expected of them.[15] The experts decreed
that a woman's power had to be channeled *away* from any temptation
to participate knowledgeably in esoteric, public knowledge, and channeled toward concentration in the private domain, upon her child.[16]
There, too, her power had to be carefully controlled and all of her
decisions managed—from the kind of relationship she should establish
with her child to the kind of detergent she should buy. Lurking beneath
these complex and interwoven prescriptions is a conception of women
as unbalanced, fundamentally hostile, and out of control, and of motherhood—and femaleness—as pathology. Ehrenreich and English cite Dr.
Joseph Reingold of the Harvard Medical School, who maintained that
"maternal destructiveness was built into the female psyche . . . it arose
from a fundamental horror at being female, which was the 'basic conflict
of the woman's personality.'"[17]

The conflation of femininity with pathology is a constant thread
running through expert endeavors to control women: to channel their
sexuality to conform with masculine expectations, to direct their practical
endeavors even in the areas of their lives designated essentially theirs,
and to shape their psyches according to male-defined conceptions of
what it is to be a good woman. All of these endeavors rest upon a highly
contestable knowledge base, constructed as much out of stereotypes and
ideology as from observation, clear judgment, and fact. Its effects are
most strikingly visible in conceptions of female madness; this is no
surprise in view of the fact that women have often been declared, simply
as women—as potential hysterics—to exist constantly on the verge of
madness. For this reason I shall focus, in the remainder of this section,
on madness as at once a symptom and a metaphor of women's oppression.

In the late 1860s, Seymour Haden, in a speech to the British Obstet-
rical Society, declared that, as practitioners among women, obstetricians

have constituted ourselves . . . the guardians of their honour. . . . We are, in
fact, the stronger, and they the weaker. They are not in a position to dispute
anything we say to them, and we, therefore, may be said to have them at
our mercy. . . . [18]

Quoting Haden's remarks in her study of women, madness, and English culture from 1830 to 1980, Elaine Showalter observes that although the management of women's minds was carried out more subtly in the lunatic asylums of the time, "it too expressed the power of male psychiatrists over definitions of femininity and insanity. . . . Women's training to revere such authority in the family often made them devoted and grateful patients of fatherly asylum superintendents."[19] Such were the sexual power relationships in Victorian medicine.

The central theme of Showalter's book is the "equation between femininity and insanity that goes far beyond statistical evidence or the social conditions of women"—the notion of madness as "the essential feminine nature unveiling itself before scientific male rationality."[20] In a similar vein, Jill Matthews, whose book, *Good and Mad Women,* is subtitled "The historical construction of femininity in twentieth-century Australia," claims that the gender order of every society creates an ideology of femininity through which it establishes what it means to be a good woman and requires women to approximate that ideal in their lives. The ideology is bizarre, and ultimately crazy making, for it has no definite or constant content. Like the stereotypes at work within it, there is no evidence to show that the ideal is derived from empirical, objective investigations of "female nature." Wild fluctuations in prescriptions for being a good woman map more readily onto perceived (patriarchal) necessities to curb and control women's understandings of their possibilities than onto women's own self-perceptions and aspirations. Femininity as a concept is an empty shell. It purports to capture the essence, the absolute meaning of being a woman, yet it is open to infusion with content by whomever conjures it into use. Hence, Matthews maintains, "Every woman's body and life, everything she does . . . become the objects of a struggle for control by competing forces, each force proclaiming itself the upholder of the true ideal of femininity."[21]

In the case notes of female psychiatric patients and in manifestations of the ideal of femininity in conceptions of women's sexuality, work, and mothering in twentieth-century Australia, Matthews, like Ehrenreich and English, discerns a pattern in which professionals and experts become the overseers of the gender order, and madness or goodness become categories for controlling women and maintaining that order. A diagnosis of madness usually incorporates—if, indeed, it does not focus solely upon—ways in which a woman's behavior deviates from a social norm. Thus, for example, one nineteenth-century writer on *The Functions and*

Disorders of the Reproductive Organs contends that women are not *normally* "troubled" with sexual feeling, though he acknowledges "the existence of sexual excitement terminating even in nymphomania, a form of insanity which those accustomed to visit lunatic asylums must be fully conversant with." His contention prompts Lynda Nead to observe that "desires which are defined as commonplace in men are treated as a form of madness in women."[22]

Analogously, Showalter records the Darwinian belief that mental breakdown occurs when women attempt to defy their essential nature, to seek alternatives to their maternal function, and to resist the idea that they exist to help and serve men.[23] Like the experts whose ascendency Ehrenreich and English document, Darwinian psychiatrists extended their authority

> to the courtroom, where they made pronouncements on the family and the education of youth; . . . the bedroom, where they defined acceptable sexual behaviour; and . . . the state, where they proposed mental hygiene as the model of social discipline.[24]

In all of these areas, women's vulnerability increased with their rhetorically induced willingness to believe in the authority of scientific expertise.

Epistemologically, the most striking conclusion that emerges from these studies is that female "madness" is a largely undefined experience or state. New definitions are constructed and old ones abandoned or modified with each new scientific development and every major shift in the sociopolitical-economic climate. It is difficult either to discern objective criteria by which women are, consistently, judged mad (or sometimes sane), or to pinpoint objective social norms whose transgression inevitably invites the diagnosis. These studies show how difficult it is for a woman to *know* how she should be in order not to be declared mad; and to *know* the criteria by which she is ultimately diagnosed. They illustrate problems women tend to experience in making other people realize that they do *know* something of what is going on in their own lives and in believing that the authorities and experts they encounter really *know* enough to legitimate their positions of authority.

First-person experiential evidence is consistently undervalued and paternalistically reinterpreted in these diagnoses. Charlotte Perkins Gilman's *The Yellow Wallpaper*, which I have discussed elsewhere, is a classic illustration of this point.[25] When Gilman drew up as "objective" as possible an account of her own mental suffering in preparation for her consultation with Dr. S. Weir Mitchell, who was to supervise her rest cure, Mitchell indicated his complete lack of interest. From his patients he did not require information—based even on their own experiences. He wanted complete obedience, based on his interpretation of what their experiences must be. The story of Camille Claudel, whose remarkable sculptures were overshadowed by those of her teacher and lover, Auguste Rodin, is equally poignant. In consequence of having "placed herself beyond the pale of sanctioned femininity," Claudel suffered humiliation and retribution from her family and society, which caused her to withdraw "into an increasingly alienated state." Her committal to a mental hospital for thirty years on the basis of a medical certificate obtained, against her will, by her brother, leaves open the question "whether or to what extent Claudel was insane."[26] Her own pleas for freedom were dismissed. In these situations, as in countless others like them, control is exercised over patients rendered doubly vulnerable and passive: both by the immobilizing nature of their suffering, whose genuineness persists throughout diverse endeavors to define it, and by the authoritarian nature of an expertise with little discernibly objective basis.

Madness emerges, then, as "the impasse confronting those whom cultural conditioning has deprived of the very means of protest or self-affirmation."[27] Showalter observes that photographs of mad women in nineteenth-century medical texts reveal that "doctors imposed cultural stereotypes of femininity and female insanity on women who defied their gender roles."[28] And Matthews writes of a psychiatric patient who "attempted throughout her life to be a good woman as was demanded by various people important to her, but she was confronted by a series of incongruous meanings which she could not reconcile."[29] Women's efforts to be *good* women, according to fluctuating ideological requirements, are often doomed to failure. Inconsistent and contradictory demands built into the ideological construction of femininity contribute to the sense of failure, desperation, and utter confusion that often appears in women's diagnoses as mad, both historically and today. On the basis of such diagnoses, women are admitted and readmitted to (institutional) psychiatric care, where they must learn to be good (according to yet another standard) to secure their release.

Now one might wonder why women would not reclaim their divergent experiences as evidence of superiority or heightened sensitivity, rather than acquiescing in diagnoses of mental instability and madness. But the answer is distressingly simple: the structures of madness are already in place to account for those experiences. Michel Foucault's (admittedly gender-blind) tracing of linkages between madness and animality, where passion is the declared basis of madness, indicate that it is no wonder that women would constantly doubt their own sanity.[30] Features by which madness is commonly represented in the grayer areas this side of psychosis and features of stereotypical representations of woman's nature in hegemonic discourse are remarkably congruent.

A set of dichotomies—mind/body, culture/nature, reason/passion, among others—informs the construction of rationality as a regulative ideal in the history of Western thought.[31] Those dichotomies parallel the male/female dichotomy both descriptively and evaluatively. In each pair of concepts, the second term (body, nature, passion, and female) is consistently accorded lesser value and stands for the less controllable attribute. Women's greater closeness to nature, it is believed, causes their "animal" (passionate) natures consistently to overrule their reason. Hence it is perhaps not surprising that Foucault's description of madness could be read, equivalently, as a description of femaleness.

> The animality that rages in madness dispossesses man of what is specifically human in him; not in order to deliver him over to other powers, but simply to establish him at the zero degree of his own nature. For classicism, madness in its ultimate form is man in immediate relation to his animality, without other reference, without any recourse.[32]

As Foucault points out, "Unchained animality could be mastered only by *discipline* and *brutalizing*."[33] The same is clearly true of deviant, defiant, or passionate femininity.

Foucault writes of "the savage danger of madness" and its relation to "the danger of the passions and their fatal concatenation."[34] He maintains that passion creates the very possibility of madness, and that "moralists of the Greco-Latin tradition . . . chose to define passion as a temporary and attenuated madness."[35] Given that it has been women's lot to be aligned essentially and naturally with passions and animality, it is small wonder that madness, too, should seem to be their lot. Conceptions of knowledge that derive from the assumption that knowers are perfectly rational cannot, by definition, cope with *unreason*. They are unable to accommodate the unruly aspects of human nature (animality, passion) which, in Foucault's account, slide so readily into madness. The achievement of rationality depends, in short, upon the suppression of passions and animality. They must be relegated to another realm, attributed to lesser beings, and confined to inferior modes of knowledge and action. Perhaps, then, it is no coincidence that women, who are believed to be at the mercy of their animal natures, should become the lepers, the scapegoats of scientific societies. By such a move, rational man is able to deny the aspects of his being that threaten his rational autonomy.

These revelations about the social and scientific construction of madness are nothing short of bizarre, however, in a science such as medicine, with its claim to have a solid basis in empirical observation. They are particularly odd by the standards of the empiricist theory of knowledge taken for granted in medical science. Empiricists, avowedly, put great store in first-person perceptual and observational reports, maintaining that a "privileged access" to one's own experience confers upon such reports a special claim to credibility. For an empiricist such as Bertrand Russell, in fact, "knowledge by acquaintance" of one's own sensory input is accorded *foundational* status in a system of knowledge.[36] Although it would be an exaggeration to describe most people as empiricists in their everyday lives in just the sense Russell intends, there is considerable folk wisdom embedded in the contention that I can know what I am feeling and experiencing better than anyone else can. Hence it is not difficult to imagine the damage that is done by a systematic denial of these claims on the part of established and powerful experts whom a person has been trained to respect and trust. Epistemologically, these problems demonstrate the inadequacy—indeed, the absurdity—of a (scientistic) epistemological picture that claims a basis in experience, yet denies validity to the experience-based stories women tell.

The Cat Is on the Mat

Wittgenstein's observation that "knowledge is in the end based on acknowledgment" encapsulates the problem with which I have been engaged.[37] Yet the capacity to gain acknowledgment is gender related in a way Wittgenstein himself would not have envisioned; and its gender specificity is multidimensional. Like any cognitive agent, a female would-be knower has to claim acknowledgment from her fellow participants in a form of life. But advancing such claims is as much a political matter as it is a straightforwardly epistemological one. Before she can so much as seek acknowledgment, a woman must free herself from stereotyped conceptions of her under-class epistemic status, her cognitive incapacity, and her ever-threatening irrationality. She has to achieve this freedom both in the eyes of other people, who too often deny her capacity by refusing to listen or give credence, and from her own standpoint, shaped as it also may be by a stereotype-informed belief that neither her experiences nor her deliberative capacities are trustworthy sources of knowledge.

A simple perceptual example will demonstrate what is at issue. Consider one of the most common "S knows that P" examples: say, Sara knows that the cat is on the mat.[38] Now suppose that Sara's claim "the cat is on the mat" is contradicted by everyone around her: by people she knows and loves, who live in the house where the mat is located, by passing strangers, and by "vision experts" summoned to check her perceptual powers. All of these people consistently insist that there is no cat on the mat. How long would Sara be able to defend the veridicality of her perception if *everyone* else, both now and over time, attested to the mat's emptiness? My sense is that she would soon begin to suspect she was hallucinating and would be disturbed about it, even if her visual observations checked out positively with her other senses: she can touch the cat, hear it purr. Even the simplest of observational knowledge claims depend, more than people ordinarily realize, upon corroboration, acknowledgment, either in word or in deed. When someone is in doubt about what she thinks she hears or sees, she is as likely to call upon someone else to confirm her impression as she is to check it by any other means—and to call someone else again, if agreement is still not possible. If everyone consistently walked around the mat, Sara might never even have wondered; if everyone walked across the cat, she would have been perturbed much earlier.

Now suppose Sara's cat on the mat experience is generalized throughout her perceptual life: there are innumerable instances in which she has strong and persistent perceptions that no one else has. These experiences are vivid, and in every respect indistinguishable from those of her perceptions that seem to be quite normal, in the sense that the question of requiring acknowledgment for them does not so much as arise. It is hard to imagine how a person could live with a generalized conviction of her perceptual idiosyncrasy without becoming wholly bewildered, distraught, and confused; nor how she could allude in any way to those experiences without being judged at worst peculiar, at best, quite mad. Sara would rapidly lose the capacity to trust her own observations (or, if these peculiarities were hers from birth, she would never acquire that capacity). It is unlikely that her friends or associates would take her observational claims seriously—*either* her idiosyncratic ones, *or* her "normal" ones.[39]

It is instructive to engage seriously with this seemingly fanciful scenario: to think one's way into it and try to imagine how it would be, minute by minute, to live it. For my point is that it is not so fanciful. It generalizes readily to women's epistemic lives per se: ironically, perhaps not so readily to their everyday perceptual experiences as to their more complex endeavors to know—but to those even slightly more complex. The irony is that because it is quite easy to support an argument to the effect that both women and men see cats on mats pretty much indistinguishably in similar circumstances, it appears to be nonsensical to suggest that women's knowledge claims frequently are suppressed for want of acknowledgment. Yet women are often, both metaphorically and literally, driven crazy by their incapacity to gain any greater acknowledgment for their knowledge claims (which, on one level, they *know* must be valid) than Sara can for her claim that the cat is on the mat. These are not isolated, hallucinatory experiences for women. They are sufficiently pervasive for women, finally, to suspect that they must be wrong after all, that clearly they have missed the important point, and that the experts—who determine the norm from which women's perceptions diverge so radically—*must* be right.

In my discussion of women and madness, I drew attention to the ease with which self-doubt is created and feeds into women's special vulnerability, born of excessive dependence. There is a noteworthy connection between the production of that dependence and vulnerability and the *cognitive posture* experts assume in relation to their clients/patients. Showalter, for example, describes the reluctance of Victorian asylum superintendents to listen to their patients "to find out how they felt and why";[40] she records Charcot's manner of looking carefully at hysterical patients yet paying "very little attention to what they were saying."[41] She writes of Freud's excessive haste in imposing "his own language on [Dora's] mute communications."[42] Instructively, she contrasts these three postures with the approach of Josef Breuer, who "respected the intelligence of his hysterical female patient, encouraged her to speak, and then listened carefully to what she said."[43] The crucial difference, as I see it, turns upon acknowledgment. There is no more effective means of creating epistemic dependence than systematically withholding acknowledgment from a person's cognitive utterances; no more effective way of maintaining structures of epistemic privilege and vulnerability than evincing a persistent distrust in a person's efforts to claim cognitive authority; no surer way of demonstrating a refusal to know a person *as* a person than observing her "objectively" without taking seriously what her experiences mean to her.

The crucial epistemic-political challenge for women, then, is to devise strategies for claiming their cognitive competence and authority, their knowledgability, and their right to know. The first step toward the development of such strategies is to take responsibility for oneself and to refuse epistemic oppression. But the means of so doing cannot be those of the autonomous, self-sufficient knower, for acknowledgment persistently withheld obliterates such self-affirmation, sooner rather than later. Such strategies can be mounted in *collective* social critique and active constructions of meaning. They can derive from critical analyses of the workings of power in conferring the status of knowledge upon conclusions more accurately characterized as conjectural, hypothetical, working theories. They gain force from an understanding of the intrications of knowledge and power in the perpetuation of social structures and institutions. Women's successes in forming health collectives and in seeking access to feminist therapy and legal advice are but a few examples of feminist demonstrations that such power can also be made accessible to the oppressed, who need no longer assume the stance of victim and suppliant, in thrall to expert mystification. Although victory is by no means total, women's achievements in refusing to occupy the oppressed position are noteworthy.

Foucault observes that he has

> a sense of the increasing vulnerability to criticism of things, institutions, practices, and discourses. A certain fragility has been discovered in the very bedrock of existence—even, and perhaps above all, in those aspects of it that are most familiar, most solid and most intimately related to our bodies and to our everyday behaviour.[44]

Women have been able to exploit this vulnerability in breaking the hegemony of authoritarian expertise. Their projects acquire increased momentum from the fact that feminists, increasingly, are in a position to "fight science with science." They are well advanced in the project of reevaluating the function of science in Western societies, and of revealing reasons for suspicion of scientific pretensions to discover the "nature of human beings," or to act as a "neutral arbiter" in social debates.[45] It is a matter of achieving a proper balance between an informed skepticism and credulity. Too stringent a skepticism can impede possibilities of obtaining the help one may need; yet excessive credulity generates a powerless vulnerability. Women can learn, collectively, to give and withhold acknowledgment and, hence, to claim power for their own knowledge. Michèle le Doeuff's wry observation that "knowledge about women has always been masculine property" begins to read like an observation that *belongs* in the past tense.[46] When it makes sense to be confident that it no longer holds, it will perhaps be possible to assert, with Hollis, that a psychiatrist intervenes "only when beliefs are false or irrational." Until then, it is difficult to be sure whether the man saw a unicorn in the garden, or not.

NOTES

This essay is an earlier version of chapter 5 of Lorraine Coder *What Can She Know? Feminist Theory and the Construction of Knowledge.* Copyright © 1991 by Cornell University. Used by permission of the publisher, Cornell University Press. Work on the book, and hence on this project, was made possible by a Canada Research Fellowship from the Social Sciences and Humanities Research Council of Canada.

1. I am using the term *common sense* in Gramsci's sense, to refer to the embedded ideologies and prejudices that implicitly shape social attitudes, virtually invisibly. See Antonio Gramsci, *Selections from the Prison Notebooks,* trans. and ed. Quintin Hoare and Geoffrey Nowell-Smith (New York: International Publishers, 1971).

2. The power-knowledge connection comes from the writings of Michel Foucault. See, especially, his *Power/Knowledge: Selected Interviews and Other Writings, 1972–1977,* ed. Colin Gordon, trans. Colin Gordon, Leo Marshall, John Mepham, and Kate Soper (New York: Pantheon Books, 1980). The power in the power-knowledge complex is not the hegemonic, sovereign power of a political tyrant. It manifests itself, rather, in the ways in which modes of discourse become established and take on "totalizing" effects such that, in the practices they legitimate, other ways of thinking are suppressed and rendered invisible. There is neither a single locus nor an identifiable agent of power, yet power is constitutive of human subjectivity and of possibilities of action and understanding.

3. Barbara Ehrenreich and Deirdre English, *For Her Own Good: 150 years of the Experts' Advice to Women* (New York: Doubleday, 1978), 4.

4. Elaine Showalter, *The Female Malady: Women, Madness, and English Culture, 1830–1980* (New York: Penguin, 1987); Jill Julius Matthews, *Good and Mad Women: The Historical Construction of Femininity in Twentieth-Century Australia* (Sydney: Allen and Unwin, 1984).

5. James Thurber, *Fables for our Time* (New York: Harper and Row, 1939), 65.

6. Martin Hollis, "The Social Destruction of Reality," in *Rationality and Relativism*, ed. Martin Hollis and Steven Lukes (Cambridge, Mass.: MIT Press, 1982), 76.

7. Hollis, "Social Destruction," 77.

8. The phrase is Sandra Harding's, in her "Why Has the Sex-Gender System Become Visible Only Now?", in *Discovering Reality*, ed. Sandra Harding and Merrill Hintikka (Dordrecht, Reidel, 1983), 311–24.

9. *Globe and Mail* (Toronto), November 24, 1987.

10. Ehrenreich and English, *Her Own Good*, 4.

11. Ehrenreich and English, *Her Own Good*, 28.

12. Ehrenreich and English, *Her Own Good*, 5.

13. Ehrenreich and English, *Her Own Good*, 14. Ehrenreich and English do not take issue with the essential femaleness of this lost "dignity," or of the skills that they claim as women's own. Their book was written before difference and specificity became the crucial issues for feminist theory that they have become in the late 1980s and early 1990s.

14. Ehrenreich and English, *Her Own Good*, 142.

15. For an extended analysis of the kind of responsibility that is at issue here, see Lorraine Code, *Epistemic Responsibility* (Hanover, N.H.: University Press of New England, 1987).

16. See Ehrenreich and English, *For Her Own Good*, 190.

17. Ehrenreich and English, *For Her Own Good*.

18. Showalter, *Female Malady*, 78.

19. Showalter, *Female Malady*, 78.

20. Showalter, *Female Malady*, 3.

21. Matthews, *Good and Mad Women*, 8.

22. Lynda Nead, *Myths of Sexuality* (Oxford: Basil Blackwell, 1988), 50. The book quoted is by William Acton, published in London in 1857.

23. Showalter, *Female Malady*, 123.

24. Showalter, *Female Malady*, 105.

25. See Lorraine Code, "Credibility: A Double Standard," in *Feminist Perspectives: Philosophcal Essays on Methods and Morals*, ed. Lorraine Code, Sheila Mullett, and Christine Overall (Toronto: University of Toronto Press, 1988), 64–88.

26. The quotations about Claudel are from Anne Higonnet's review, "A Woman Turned to Stone," *Women's Review of Books* 5, no. 12 (September, 1988): 6.

27. Showalter, *Female Malady*, 5.

28. Showalter, *Female Malday*, 86.

29. Matthews, *Good and Mad Women*, 7.

30. See Michel Foucault, *Madness and Civilization*, trans. Richard Howard (London, Tavistock, 1967).

31. See Genevieve Lloyd, *The Man of Reason: "Male" and "Female" in Western Philosophy* (Minneapolis: University of Minnesota Press, 1984), for an extended discussion of the construction and effects of these dichotomies in the history of Western philosophy.

32. Foucault, *Madness*, 74.

33. Foucault, *Madness*, 75.

34. Foucault, *Madness*, 85.

35. Foucault, *Madness*, 89.

36. See, for example, Bertrand Russell, *The Problems of Philosophy* (Oxford: Oxford

University Press, 1912), chap. 5; and his "Knowledge by Acquaintance and Knowledge by Description," in *Mysticism and Logic* (London: Allen and Unwin, 1963), 152–67.

37. Ludwig Wittgenstein, *On Certainty*, ed. G. E. M. Anscombe and G. H. von Wright, trans. Denis Paul and G. E. M. Anscombe (New York: Harper Torchbooks, 1972), § 378.

38. The example is frequently used in Richard Foley, *The Theory of Epistemic Rationality* (Cambridge, Mass.: Harvard University Press, 1987), which is representative of state-of-the-art epistemology.

39. As Wittgenstein remarks, "If I were contradicted on all sides and told that this person's name was not what I had always known it was (and I use "know" here intentionally), then in that case the foundation of all judging would be taken away from me" (*On Certainty*, § 613).

40. Showalter, *Female Malady*, 61.

41. Showalter, *Female Malady*, 154.

42. Showalter, *Female Malady*, 160.

43. Showalter, *Female Malady*, 157.

44. Foucault, *Power/Knowledge*, 80.

45. The phrases are from Londa Schiebinger, "Women and Science," *Signs* 12, no. 2 (Winter, 1987): 328.

46. Michèle le Doeuff, "Women and Philosophy," *Radical Philosophy* 17 (Summer, 1977): 7.

Contributors

Susan Bordo holds the Joseph C. Georg Professorship in philosophy at Le Moyne College. She is the author of *The Flight to Objectivity: Essays on Cartesianism and Culture* (1987) and the coeditor of *Gender/Body/ Knowledge: Feminist Reconstructions of Being and Knowing* (1989). Her most recent book is *Unbearable Weight: Essays on Feminism, Western Culture, and the Body* (forthcoming).

Kristin Brady is the author of *George Eliot* (forthcoming) and *The Short Stories of Thomas Hardy* (1982), as well as articles and reviews on Hawthorne, Eliot, Hardy, and feminist theory. She is an associate professor at the University of Western Ontario, where she teaches courses in nineteenth-century literature and feminist theory.

Mark A. Cheetham is the author of *The Rhetoric of Purity: Essentialist Theory and the Advent of Abstract Painting* (1991) and *Remembering Postmodernism: Trends in Recent Canadian Art* (1991), as well as the coeditor of *Theory between the Disciplines: Authority/Vision/Politics* (1990). He is associate professor in the Department of Visual Arts and the Centre for the Study of Theory and Criticism at the University of Western Ontario.

Lorraine Code is professor of philosophy at York University. In addition to numerous articles in theory of knowledge and feminist theory, she is the author of *Epistemic Responsibility* (1987) and coeditor of *Changing Patterns: Women in Canada* (1988) and of *Feminist Perspectives: Philosophical Essays on Method and Morals* (1988). Her most recent book is *What Can She Know? Feminist Theory and the Construction of Knowledge* (1991).

Marie Fleming is associate professor of political science at the University of Western Ontario. She is the author of *The Geography of Freedom: The Odyssey of Elisée Reclus* (1988) and is now completing a book on rationality, discourse, and gender in Habermas's philosophy and social theory.

Elizabeth D. Harvey is the coeditor of *Soliciting Interpretation: Literary Theory and Seventeenth-Century English Poetry* (1990) and the author of *Ventriloquized Voices: Gender and Transvestism in the English Renaissance* (forthcoming). She teaches in the English Department, the Centre for Women's Studies and Feminist Research, and the Centre for the Study of Theory and Criticism at the University of Western Ontario.

Alison M. Jaggar is professor of philosophy and women's studies at the University of Colorado at Boulder. She has also taught at the University of Illinois at Chicago, the University of California at Los Angeles, and Rutgers University, where she held the Laurie New Jersey Chair in Women's Studies. Her books include *Feminist Frameworks*, coedited with Paula Rothenberg (1984), *Feminist Politics and Human Nature* (1983), and *Gender/Body/Knowledge: Feminist Reconstructions of Being and Knowing*, coedited with Susan R. Bordo (1989). Currently she is working on *Feminism and Moral Theory*, supported by a fellowship from the Rockefeller Foundation.

Thomas M. Lennon is dean of the Faculty of Arts and professor of philosophy at the University of Western Ontario. Almost all his research and publications are in the history of seventeenth-century philosophy.

Patricia Mathews teaches art history at Oberlin College. She specializes in art theory and feminist art history; she has written *Aurier: Symbolist Art Criticism and Theory* (1986) and is now coediting an anthology of feminist art history and criticism and finishing a book on gender and creativity in late nineteenth-century France.

Kathleen Okruhlik works chiefly in history and philosophy of science. She is an associate professor of philosophy and was founding director of the Centre for Women's Studies and Feminist Research at the University of Western Ontario. Her published work includes a coedited volume on Leibniz as well as several articles on Leibniz, Newton, and Kant. Most recently, she has been involved in a research project on feminist critiques of science that was funded by the Social Sciences and Humanities Research Council of Canada.

Hilda L. Smith is the director of the Center for Women's Studies and associate professor of history at the University of Cincinnati. Author of *Reason's Disciples: Seventeenth-Century English Feminists* (1982) and, with Susan Cardinale, *Women and Literature of the Seventeenth Century: An Annotated Bibliography Based on Wing's Short Title Catalogue* (1990), she is preparing a monograph focusing on the conflation of the modern individual and the adult male, "All Men and Both Sexes: False Universals of Human Experience."

Julie Robin Solomon teaches English at American University in Washington, D. C. She has published articles on Virginia Woolf, Thomas Harriot, Francis Bacon, and Shakespeare. With the help of a National Endowment for the Humanities Newberry Library Fellowship, she is currently working on a book entitled *Francis Bacon and the Obscure Objectivity of Desire.*

Alison Wylie works in philosophy of the social sciences and has a long-standing interest in archaeological research practice; she is coeditor of *Critical Traditions in Contemporary Archaeology* (1989) and is currently involved in a study of feminist research initiatives in North American archaeology. She teaches philosophy at the University of Western Ontario, where she was recently codirector, with Kathleen Okruhlik, of the research project "Philosophical Feminism: Challenges to Science."

Index

Acker, Joan, 227–30, 235, 241n
Adams, Kathleen, 218, 224n
Adams, Mary, 58n
Agricola, George, 64
Ainsworth, Henry, 89, 108n, 111n
Allen, Walter, 214, 223n
Anderson, Fulton, 109n, 111n
Anderson, Wayne, 184n
Angers, Julien Eymard d', 56n
Apel, Karl Otto, 260n, 261n
Aquinas, Thomas, 3, 22, 54n, 82, 105n
Aristotle, 3, 27, 41, 63, 66, 67, 138n, 146, 190
Armstrong, Hugh, 240n
Armstrong, Pat, 240n
Arnauld, A, 39, 40, 44, 46, 47, 54n, 57n, 58n
Arnault, Lynne, 161n
Astell, Mary, 7, 28, 30, 31, 33, 34, 37n, 52, 59n
Aubrey, John, 97, 112n
Augustine, Saint, 22, 81, 82, 105n, 107n, 149
Augustus, 49
Aurier, G.-Albert, 164, 172, 183n
Austen, Jane, 210
Averell, James, 122, 123, 139n, 141

Babington, Gervase, 108n, 111n
Bacon, Ann, 90, 97, 109n
Bacon, Anthony, 112n
Bacon, Francis, 8, 9, 64–66, 74, 75, 76, 77,
    79–81, 88, 90–93, 96–103, 104n, 109n–13n

Bacon, Roger, 92, 110n
Baily, F, E, 214, 223n
Baker, Thomas, 54n
Barnham, Alice, 96
Barry, Kate, 227–30, 235, 241n
Barry, William, 206, 207, 222n
Bassuk, Ellen J., 221n
Baudelaire, Charles, 163, 164, 183n
Bauer, Robert J., 104n
Bayle, François, 44, 54n, 60
Bayle, Pierre, 44, 56n, 60
Beauvoir, Simone de, 3, 149
Beethoven, Ludwig van, 204
Behn, Aphra, 59n
Belloc, Bessie, 223n
Benhabib, Seyla, 16, 245, 246, 249, 251–53, 256, 260n, 261n
Bennet, Arnold, 210, 211, 222n
Bennet, Joan, 223n
Bentham, Jeremy, 247
Bentley, Richard, 42, 55n, 60
Berg, Christine, 8, 18n, 50, 51, 52, 58n, 60
Berkeley, George, 54n
Bernard, Emile, 184n
Bernard, Jessie, 240n
Bernheimer, Richard, 106n
Bernstein, Richard, 259, 262n
Berry, Philippa, 8, 18n, 50, 51, 52, 58n, 60
Betham-Edwards, Matilda, 223n
Betterton, Rosemary, 178, 180, 185n
Blackwood, John, 215
Blind, Mathilde, 221n
Bochner, Joan, 51
Bolkin, Elly, 162n

Bonnevant, Mme. de, 53
Bordo, Susan, 6, 65, 76, 127, 137n, 138n, 141, 160n, 161n, 162n
Bourdelot, Abbé, 54n
Bourdieu, Pierre, 151
Bouwsma, William, 88, 106n, 107n, 108n, 11n
Bovet, Richard, 49, 58n
Boyle, Robert, 54n
Bracken, Harry M., 59n, 60
Brathwait, Richard, 24, 36n
Bray, Alan, 112n
Bray, Charles, 14, 215–20, 224n
Breuer, Josef, 170, 278
Brinvilliers, Marie-Marguerite, 56n
Brontë, Charlotte, 104n
Brooks, Romaine, 167
Browne, Peter, 42, 54n, 55n
Browning, Oscar, 223n
Brunsdon, Charlotte, 226, 231, 237, 240n, 242n
Burthogge, Peter, 54n

Cady, Joseph, 112n
Calhoun, Cheshire, 139n
Calvin, John, 9, 50, 77, 80–91, 93–96, 98, 102, 103, 105n–11n
Campbell, James D, 199
Carlson, Rae, 240n
Carré, J.-R, 55n, 56n, 57n
Cary, Mary, 50
Casaubon, Meric, 40, 41, 45
Cassell, Joan, 236
Cavendish, Margaret (Duchess of Newcastle), 28, 37n
Cecil, David, 208, 209, 222n
Cedrenus, Georgius, 55n
Cézanne, Paul, 180, 192
Champa, Kermit Swiler, 199n
Chapman, John, 214–16, 218, 223n
Charcot, Jean-Martin, 18, 171, 184n, 278
Châtelet, Gabrielle-Emilie du, 32, 33
Cheetham, Mark, 199n
Chipp, Herschel B, 184n

Chodorow, Nancy, 144–46, 150, 151, 161n, 261n
Christina of Sweden, 53
Chrysippus, 55n
Chrysostom, John, 46, 107n
Cixous, Hélène, 149, 161n, 261n, 262n
Clapham, Henoch, 89, 108n
Claudel, Camille, 13, 172, 174, 185n, 274, 281n
Claudel, Paul, 172
Clay, Allyson, 13, 188, 195, 196, 198
Clément, Catherine, 161n, 262n
Code, Lorraine, 260n, 280n, 281n
Cohen, I. B., 63, 76
Collins, Anthony, 41, 42, 55n
Combahee River Collective, 159
Condé, The Great, 54n
Conway, Anne, 53
Cooke, George Willis, 203, 221n
Cooter, Roger, 221n
Cordemoy, Gerauld, 53
Cornell, Drucilla, 249, 261n
Cott, Nancy, 221n
Cranmer, Thomas, 51
Crompton, Margaret, 214, 223n
Cross, John, 211, 215, 216, 218, 223n
Cusa, Nicholas of, 107n

Danto, Arthur, 162n
Darwin, Charles, 166
David, Deirdre, 213, 223n
Davies, Eleanor, 50
Davies, Kathleen M., 36n
Da Vinci, Leonardo, 107n
Deason, Bruce, 109n
Dee, John, 110n
Dégàs, Edgar, 180
De Grignan, Mme., 53
Delamont, Sara, 184n
Derrida, Jacques, 149, 150, 161n, 196, 255, 258, 259, 262n
Descartes, René, 6, 9, 22, 30, 34, 39, 40, 41, 45, 47, 52, 53, 54, 138n, 149, 155; cartesian, 7, 35n, 54,

59n, 60n, 65, 152, 153, 156, 159, 257
D'Ewes, Simonds, 97, 112n
Dewey, John, 138n, 150, 154, 159
DeWolfe, M. A., 221n
Diderot, Denis, 26, 27, 36n
Didi-Huberman, Georges, 184n
Dijkstra, Bram, 167, 184n, 199n, 199
Dinnerstein, Dorothy, 144–46, 150, 161n
Diodati, Giovanni, 106n
Diotima, 137
Doeuff, Michéle le, 280, 282n
Donne, John, 107n
Douglas, Mary, 189, 200
Dowey, Edward A., 87, 108n
Dreyfus, Hubert, 162n
Dubartas, Guillaume, 106n
Dubreuil-Blondin, Nicole, 198n, 200
Duffin, Lorna, 184n
Du Maurier, Daphne, 112n
Duncan, David, 221n
Dupré, Marie, 53
Durade, Mme d'Albert, 218
Du Roure, Jacques, 41, 45, 55n
Du Serre, M., 51

Eagleton, Terry, 88, 108n
Easlea, Brian, 161n
Eccles, Audrey, 36n
Edgeworth, Maria, 210
Egerton, Sara Fyge, 21, 28, 35n
Ehrenreich, Barbara, 265, 269–73, 280n, 281n
Ehrman, Esther, 37n, 38n
Eichler, Margrit, 225–27, 240n
Eliot, George, 14, 17, 201–20, 220n–24n
Elshtain, Jean Bethke, 261n
English, Deirde, 265, 269–73, 280n, 281n
Epicurus, 41
Ermarth, Elizabeth, 224n
Esseveld, Joke, 228–30, 235, 241n
Eusebius, 43, 49, 55n
Evans, Katherine, 59n

Farrington, Benjamin, 65, 76, 104n
Fee, Elizabeth, 71, 72, 76
Felman, Shoshana, 171, 184n
Fields, Annie Adams, 203
Filmer, Robert, 60n
Fisher, Berenice, 141n
Fiske, John, 205
Flax, Jane, 127
Fleming, Marie, 261n
Foley, Richard, 282n
Fontenelle, B., 43, 44, 46, 54, 55n, 56n, 57n, 58n, 59n, 60
Fontenrose, Joseph, 57n, 58n, 60
Forstman, H., Jackson, 86, 105n, 107n, 108n
Foucault, Michel, 147, 148, 151, 157, 161n, 162n, 258, 261n, 262n, 275, 279, 280n–82n
Fox, George, 51
Fox, Margaret Fell, 59n
Fraser, Antonia, 19, 35n
Fraser, Nancy, 245, 247, 250, 260n, 261n
Fremantle, Anne, 222n
Freud, Sigmund, 12, 18, 170, 171, 278

Gassendi, Pierre, 39, 41, 60n
Gauguin, Paul, 164, 167, 168, 170, 180, 183n, 184n
Geiger, Susan, 237, 238
Gelpi, Barbara C., 226, 227, 240n, 243
Gendreville, Mme. de, 53
George, Margaret, 35n
Gibbens, Nicholas, 111n
Gilbert, Sandra, 218, 224n
Gilligan, Carol, 3, 4, 16, 18n, 22, 146, 161n, 245–47, 251, 260n, 261n
Gilman, Charlotte Perkins, 273
Goethe, Johann, 207
Goodall, Jane, 134
Gosse, Edmund, 207–9, 222n
Gouge, William, 24, 36n
Gramsci, Antonio, 280n
Grandier, Urbain, 47
Grant, Judith, 231

Graves, Robert, 104n
Griffin, Susan, 132
Grimshaw, Jean, 144, 146–48, 150–53, 155, 156, 161n
Grosseteste, Robert, 92
Gubar, Susan, 218, 224n
Guibourg, Abbé, 56n
Guild, William, 90, 109n

Habermas, Jürgen, 16, 17, 245, 246, 248–51, 253–60, 260n–62n
Haden, Seymour, 271, 280
Haight, Gordon S., 214–18, 220, 223n, 224n
Harding, Sandra, 4, 5, 18n, 59n, 161n, 225, 226, 261n, 281n
Harrison, Frederic, 204, 205, 221n
Harte, Bret, 205, 221n
Haydn, Hiram, 109n
Heath, Steven, 184n
Hegel, Georg Wilhelm Friedrich, 5, 22, 154, 258
Heidegger, Martin, 258
Heilbrun, Carolyn G., 199n, 223n
Henley, William Ernest, 212, 213, 222n
Herold, Christopher, 33, 37n, 38n
Heywood, Thomas, 49, 58n
Higonnet, Anne, 281n
Hill, Christopher, 36n
Hill, Thomas, 110n
Hillman, James, 161n
Hitler, Adolph, 199n
Hobbes, Thomas, 27, 37n, 60n, 249
Hofman, Melchior, 51
Holbrook, M. L., 201
Hollis, Martin, 266–69, 280, 281n
Hommecour, Mme. d', 53
Hooper, John, 221n
House, Humphrey, 203, 221n
Hume, David, 138n
Hunter, Michael, 59n

Iamblicus, 49
Ingres, Jean-Auguste-Dominique, 178
Irigaray, Luce, 149, 161n, 261n

Jacobs, Joseph, 203, 221n
Jacobson, Helga, 233, 234, 240n
Jacobus, Mary, 209, 222n
Jacometti, Nesto, 185n
Jaggar, Alison M., 133, 137n, 261n
James, Henry, 205, 206, 210, 221n, 222n
James, William, 138, 162n
James I., 99
Janet, Pierre, 164
Jardine, Alice, 188, 200
Jay, Martin, 258, 262n
Jehlen, Myra, 104n
Jenkins, Lee, 236
Jirat-Wasiutynski, Vojtech, 184n
Jolland, Pat, 221n
Jonson, Ben, 217
Jordanova, L. J., 184n, 185n
Jung, Carl, 148
Justin Martyr, St., 55n

Kamm, Josephine, 35n
Kandinsky, Wassily, 195
Kant, Immanuel, 16, 22, 70, 71, 138n, 245–47, 252, 256–58, 261n
Keller, Evelyn Fox, 6, 18n, 65, 76, 104n, 113n, 134
Keohane, Nannerl O., 226, 227, 240n
Kilpatrick, Franklin P., 139n
Kindi, Abu-Yusef Al-, 92
Kinnock, Neil, 140n
Kitcher, Philip, 70, 76
Knickerbocker, Frances W., 222n
Knoepflmacher, U. C., 214, 223n
Knox, R. A., 58n, 59n
Kohlberg, Lawrence, 3, 4, 247, 260n
Kovecses, Zoltan, 121
Kramer, Cheris, 236
Kramer, Heinrich, 49, 58n
Kristeva, Julia, 145, 146, 150, 155, 161n
Kupka, Frantisek, 195

LaForge, Louis de, 53
La Grange, Jean-Baptiste de, 41, 45, 54n

Lakoff, George, 121
La Mothe Le Vayer, 44, 56n
Lapointe, Jeanne, 225
Laqueur, Thomas, 201, 221n
La Voisin, Catherine, 56n
Leclerc, Jean, 44
Le Guin, Ursula, 77–79, 88, 104n
Lehmann, John, 221n
Leibniz, Gottfried Wilhelm, 33, 138n
Lennon, Thomas M., 54n, 207
Levine, Steven Z., 184n
Lévy-Bruhl, Lucien, 43, 55n
Lewes, George, 214, 216, 217
Lewontin, R. C., 117
Leyden, Jack of, 51
Lindberg, David, 110n
Lloyd, Genevieve, 2, 3, 6, 7, 18n, 22,
    23, 35n, 76, 99, 113n, 138n, 161n,
    199n, 200, 247, 261n, 281n
Locke, John, 40, 42, 54n, 55n, 59n,
    60n, 162n, 249, 257
Locker-Lampson, Frederick, 223n
Lombroso, Cesare, 165, 183n
Longino, Helen, 226
Lucan, 46
Luther, Martin, 50, 51, 82, 105n
Lutz, Catherine, 118

Macaulay, Catherine, 32
McClintock, Barbara, 134
MacCormack, Carol P., 184n
McCormack, Thelma, 240n
McDonald, Christie, 262n
Mack, Phillis, 36n
MacKinnon, Catherine A., 104n, 225,
    227, 239, 240n–42n
Mackintosh, H. R., 87
McLaughlin, Andrew, 125, 139n
Makin, Bathsua, 28, 29, 37n
Malebranche, Nicholas, 39, 40, 44,
    46, 47, 53, 54, 54n, 57n, 58n, 59n
Malevich, Kasimir, 195
Malueq, Sara Ellen Procious, 36n
Mandeville, Bernard de, 33
Manet, Edouard, 178
Marsak, Leonard, 55n, 56n, 57n

Marx, Karl, 10, 156
Masham, Dumaris Cudworth, 53
Matisse, Henri, 178
Matthews, Jill, 265, 272, 274, 280n,
    281n
Melancthon, Philipp, 58n
Merchant, Carolyn, 5, 18n, 63–65,
    69, 75, 76, 101, 104n, 113n, 127
Merton, Robert, 107n
Merz, Gerhard, 13, 188, 195, 196, 198
Mill, John S., 124, 247
Miller, Perry, 108n
Milton, John, 26, 36n, 57n, 89, 105n,
    109n, 111n
Mitchell, W. J. T., 187
Moebius, George, 44, 56n
Moi, Toril, 261n
Molinari, Guido, 188
Molyneux, William, 54n
Mondrian, Piet, 13, 187–92, 194–96,
    198, 199n
Moore, George, 166, 183n
Moravcsik, Julius, 138n
More, Thomas, 100
Moréri, Louis, 56n, 57n
Morgan, John, 107n
Morley, John, 210
Mullet, Sheila, 260
Mulvey, Laura, 191
Munch, Edvard, 167
Munzer, Thomas, 51

Nadel, Ira Bruce, 223n
Nagel, E., 126
Nagel, Thomas, 156, 162n
Nead, Lynda, 281n
Nettesheim, Agrippa von, 27, 36n,
    37n
Newman, Barnett, 188
Newton, Isaac, 33, 63
Nicholson, Linda, 160n
Nietzsche, Friedrich, 138n, 150, 156,
    157, 159, 162n, 255, 262n
Noland, Kenneth, 188
Norris, Christopher, 199n
Norris, John, 59n

Norton, Charles Eliot, 203, 221n
Norton, Sara, 221n
Nyquist, Mary, 79, 104n, 105n, 109n

Oakley, Ann, 228, 229, 240n, 241n
Oakley, Robin, 240n
O'Brien, Mary, 225
O'Keeffe, Georgia, 195
Okin, Susan Moller, 249, 261n
Okruhlik, Kathleen, 71, 72, 76
Oliphant, Margaret, 221n
Origen, 107n
Outlaw, Lucius, 153, 154
Outresale, Mme. d', 53
Overall, Christine, 260n

Paris, Reine-Marie, 174, 185n
Parker, Patricia, 79, 104n, 105n
Partee, Charles, 106n
Patai, Raphael, 104n
Pateman, Carole, 249, 250, 261n
Patricius, 45
Paul, Kegan, 203
Percy, Henry, 97
Perry, Ruth, 37n
Petchesky, Rosalind, 147, 161n
Peters, R. S., 140n
Phaedrus, 115
Phillips, J. A., 104n
Philo of Alexandria, 81, 105n, 107n
Pico della Mirandola, Giovanni, 82,
    91, 92, 105n, 110n
Pierrot, Jean, 199n
Plato, 2, 22, 27, 41, 43, 46, 55n, 60n,
    115, 137, 146–49, 189–91, 199n,
    200; neoplatonic, 64, 66, 92, 107n
Pletho, Giorgius Gemistus, 45
Plutarch, 56n, 58n
Pogrebin, Letty Cotlin, 236
Pollock, Griselda, 198n
Poovey, Mary, 183n, 184n, 185n,
    221n
Popkin, Richard, 56n, 58n, 61
Popper, Karl, 59n, 61
Porphyry, 55n
Poullain de la Barre, F. G., 53, 59n

Pratt, Minnie Bruce, 157, 158, 162n
Psellus, 45
Purkis, John, 218, 224n

Quinby, Lee, 127
Quine, W. V. O., 162n

Rabinow, Paul, 162n
Rainolds, John, 57n
Raphael, D., 162n
Rawley, William, 98, 113n
Reingold, Joseph, 271
Renoir, Jean, 180
Reuben, Elaine, 240n
Rewald, John, 184n
Reynier, Gustave, 59n, 61
Rimbaud, Arthur, 164
Roberts, Neil, 218, 224n
Rodin, Auguste, 173, 174, 274
Rohault, Jacques, 53, 54n
Rorty, Richard, 117, 150, 257, 262n
Rosaldo, Michelle, 121
Rose, Hilary, 59n, 134
Rose, Phyllis, 224n
Rossi, Paolo, 104n, 113n
Rousseau, Jean-Jacques, 22, 32, 249
Rowbotham, Sheila, 242n
Russell, Bertrand, 276, 281n

Sablé, Mme. de, 53
Saintsbury, George, 210, 222n
Sand, George, 208
Sandel, Michael, 261
Sartre, Jean-Paul, 22
Scarry, Elaine, 107n, 111n
Schacter, Stanley, 119
Scheman, Naomi, 127
Scherer, Edmond, 211, 212, 222n
Schiebinger, Londa, 199n, 200, 282n
Schott, Robin, 87, 88, 108n, 127
Schuggar, Thomas, 51
Schumaker, Wayne, 110n
Scot, Reginald, 48, 49, 58n, 61
Selinger, Suzanne, 87, 88, 108n
Sergeant, John, 54n
Sevigné, Mme. de, 53

Shakespeare, William, 128
Shaw, George Bernard, 206, 221n
Showalter, Elaine, 166, 170, 183n,
    184n, 185n, 205, 206, 221n, 222n,
    265, 272-74, 278, 280n-82n
Simpson, Richard, 211
Singer, Jerome, 119
Smith, Barbara, 162n
Smith, Dorothy, 230, 231, 240n, 241n
Smith, Hilda L., 7, 35n, 36n, 37n,
    52, 53, 59n, 60n
Smith-Rosenberg, Carrol, 184n
Socrates, 137
Solzhenitsyn, A., 268
Spedding, James, 96, 97, 111n
Spelman, E. V., 119, 138n, 140n
Spencer, Herbert, 203-05, 214
Spiller, Michael, 54n
Spivak, Gayatri, 259, 262n
Sprenger, James, 49, 58n
Stacey, Judith, 240n, 241n
Staël, Germaine de, 32, 33, 37n
Stanley, L., 226, 231-35, 239n-41n
Stanley, Thomas, 45, 57n
Starkie, Enid, 183n
Stephen, Barbara, 207, 222n
Stephen, Leslie, 210, 213, 222n
Stevenson, Robert Louis, 212, 222n
Stoddard, Charles Warren, 220n
Stone, Lawrence, 111n
Storch, Nicholas, 51
Stowe, Harriet Beecher, 216
Strabo, 58n
Strathern, Marilyn, 184n
Strindberg, August, 170, 184n
Suleiman, Susan Rubin, 221n
Swedenborg, Emmanuel, 163
Swift, Jonathan, 54n
Swinburne, Algernon, 206

Tate, Nahum, 37n
Tennyson, Alfred, 203
Tennyson, Hallam, 221n
Teresa of Avila, 40
Tertullian, Quintus Septimius
    Florens, 55n

Thalberg, Irving, 130
Thatcher, Margaret, 140n
Theognis, 57n
Thomas, Keith, 36n, 57n
Thomassin, Louis, 44, 57n
Thurber, James, 266, 268, 280n
Touchet, Mervyn, 112n-13n
Tousignant, Claude, 188
Trapnel, Anna, 50
Trebilcot, Joyce, 233, 241n
Trible, Phyllis, 104n

Utter, André, 180

Valadon, Suzanne, 13, 172, 174, 178,
    180, 185n
Van Dale, Antonius, 44, 54, 55n, 56n
Van Gogh, Vincent, 12, 164, 172,
    183n, 184n
Vatier, Antoine, 53
Veith, Ilza, 184n
Vickers, Jill McCalla, 226, 228
Vigne, Mlle. de la, 53
Virgil, 46
Vives, Juan, 24, 36n
Voltaire, François-Marie Arouet de,
    33, 37n
Von Stuck, Franz, 167, 170

Walker, Williston, 110n, 111n
Wallace, Ian, 198
Walsh, William, 37n
Wase, Christopher, 36n
Webster, Charles, 36n
Wedgewood, C. V., 19, 20, 35n
Weinberger, J., 113n
Wellmer, Albrecht, 256, 257, 261n,
    262n
Welsh, Robert P., 199n
Wernick, Robert, 185n
Weyer, Johan, 49
Whately, William, 111n
White, Charles Hale, 223n
Wierzbicka, Anna, 121
Wiesenfarth, Joseph, 218, 224n
Willet, Andrew, 90, 109n

Winchilsea, Anne, 21, 28
Wind, Edgar, 199n
Winegarten, Renee, 37n, 38n
Wise, S., 226, 231–35, 239n–41n
Wittgenstein, Ludwig, 17, 276, 281n
Wittig, Monique, 262n
Wolley, Hannah, 28, 29, 37n
Wollstonecraft, Mary, 32, 33, 37n
Woodward, Hezekiah, 36n
Woolf, Virginia, 104n, 223n
Woolson, Abba Gould, 221n

Wright, T. R., 224n

Yeats, W. B., 206, 221n
Yolton, John, 55n
Young, Iris, 152, 161n, 245, 260n, 261n
Young, R., M., 127

Zilsel, Edgar, 113n
Zita, Jacqueline N., 237, 238
Zwingli, Ulrich, 50